3 1205 00314 4845

Kawasaki
Vulcan 700/750 and 800
Service and Repair Manual

by Alan Ahlstrand

Models covered
Vulcan 700. 699cc. 1985
Vulcan 750. 749cc. 1985 thru 2001
Vulcan 800. 805cc. 1995 thru 2001
Vulcan 800 Classic. 805cc. 1996 thru 2001
Vulcan 800 Drifter. 805cc.1999 thru 2001

ABCDE
FGHIJ
KLMNO
PQRST

in any form or by any means, electronic or mechanical, including photocopying, recording or by any information storage or retrieval system, without permission in writing from the copyright holder.

ISBN **1 56392 457 9**

British Library Cataloguing in Publication Data
A catalogue record for this book is available from the British Library.

Library of Congress Control Number 2002104471
Printed in the USA

Haynes Publishing
Sparkford, Nr Yeovil, Somerset BA22 7JJ, England

Haynes North America, Inc
861 Lawrence Drive, Newbury Park, California 91320, USA

02-256

© Haynes North America, Inc. 2002
With permission from J.H. Haynes & Co. Ltd.

A book in the **Haynes Service and Repair Manual Series**

Contents

LIVING WITH YOUR KAWASAKI VULCAN

Introduction

Daily (pre-ride) checks

MAINTENANCE

Routine maintenance and servicing

Contents

REPAIRS AND OVERHAUL

Engine, transmission and associated systems

Chassis and bodywork components

Electrical system

Wiring diagrams

REFERENCE

Index

Kawasaki
The Green Meanies

by Julian Ryder

Kawasaki Heavy Industries

Kawasaki is a company of contradictions. It is the smallest of the big four Japanese manufacturers but the biggest company, it was the last of the four to make and market motorcycles yet it owns the oldest name in the Japanese industry, and it was the first to set up a factory in the USA. Kawasaki Heavy Industries, of which the motorcycle operation is but a small component, is a massive company with its heritage firmly in the old heavy industries like shipbuilding and railways; nowadays it is as much involved in aerospace as in motorcycles.

In fact it may be because of this that Kawasaki's motorcycles have always been quirky, you get the impression that they are designed by a small group of enthusiasts who are given an admirably free hand. More realistically, it may be that Kawasaki's designers have experience with techniques and materials from other engineering disciplines. Either way, Kawasaki have managed to be the factory who surprise us more than the rest. Quite often, they do this by totally ignoring a market segment the others are scrabbling over, but more often they hit us with pure, undiluted performance.

The origins of the company, and its name, go back to 1878 when Shozo Kawasaki set up a dockyard in Tokyo. By the late 1930s, the company was making its own steel in massive steelworks and manufacturing railway locos and rolling stock. In the run up to war, the Kawasaki Aircraft Company was set up in 1937 and it was this arm of the now giant operation that would look to motorcycle engine manufacture in post-war Japan.

They bought their high-technology experience to bear first on engines which were sold on to a number of manufacturers as original equipment. Both two- and four-stroke units were made, a 58 cc and 148 cc OHC unit. One of the customer companies was Meihatsu Heavy Industries, another company within the Kawasaki group, which in 1961 was shaken up and renamed Kawasaki Auto Sales. At the same time, the Akashi factory which was to be Kawasaki's main production facility until the Kobe earthquake of 1995, was opened. Shortly afterwards, Kawasaki took over the ailing Meguro company, Japan's oldest motorcycle maker, thus instantly obtaining a range of bigger bikes which were marketed as Kawasaki-Meguros. The following year, the first bike to be made and sold as a Kawasaki was produced, a 125cc single called the B8 and in 1963 a motocross version, the B8M appeared.

The three cylinder two-stroke 750 H2

Model development

Kawasaki's first appearance on a road-race circuit came in 1965 with a batch of disc-valve 125 twins. They were no match for the opposition from Japan in the shape of Suzuki and Yamaha or for the fading force of the factory MZs from East Germany. Only after the other Japanese factories had pulled out of the class did Kawasaki win, with British rider Dave Simmonds becoming World 125 GP Champion in 1969 on a bike that looked astonishingly similar to the original racer. That same year Kawasaki reorganized once again, this time merging three companies to form Kawasaki Heavy Industries. One of the new organization's objectives was to take motorcycle production forward and exploit markets outside Japan.

KHI achieved that target immediately and set out their stall for the future with the astonishing and frightening H1. This three-cylinder air-cooled 500 cc two-stroke was arguably the first modern pure performance bike to hit the market. It hypnotized a whole generation of motorcyclists who'd never before encountered such a ferocious, wheelie inducing power band or such shattering straight-line speed allied to questionable handling. And as for the 750 cc version ...

The triples perfectly suited the late '60s, fitting in well with the student demonstrations of 1968 and the anti-establishment ethos of the Summer of Love. Unfortunately, the oil crisis would put an end to the thirsty strokers but Kawasaki had another high-performance ace up their corporate sleeve. Or rather they thought they did.

The 1968 Tokyo Show saw probably the single most significant new motorcycle ever made unveiled: the Honda CB750. At Kawasaki it caused a major shock, for they also had a 750 cc four, code-named New York Steak, almost ready to roll and it was a double, rather than single, overhead cam motor. Bravely, they took the decision to go ahead – but with the motor taken out to 900 cc. The result was the Z1, unveiled at the 1972 Cologne Show. It was a bike straight out of the same mould as the H1, scare stories spread about unmanageable power, dubious straight-line stability and frightening handling, none of which stopped the sales graph rocketing upwards and led to the coining of the term 'superbike'. While rising fuel prices cut short development of the big two-strokes, the Z1 went on to found a dynasty, indeed its genes can still be detected in Kawasaki's latest products like the ZZ-R1100 (Ninja ZX-11).

This is another characteristic of the way Kawasaki operates. Models quite often have very long lives, or gradually evolve. There is no major difference between that first Z1 and the air-cooled GPz range. Add water-cooling and you have the GPZ900, which in turn metamorphosed into the GPZ1000RX and then the ZX-10 and the ZZ-R1100. Indeed, the last three models share the same 58mm

The first Superbike, Kawasaki's 900 cc Z1

One of the two-stroke engined KH and KE range - the KE100B

stroke. The bikes are obviously very different but it's difficult to put your finger on exactly why.

Other models have remained effectively untouched for over a decade: the KH and KE single-cylinder air-cooled two-stroke learner bikes, the GT550 and 750 shaft-drive hacks favored by big city despatch riders and the GPz305 being prime examples. It's only when they step outside the performance field that Kawasakis seems less sure. Their first factory customs were dire, you simply got the impression that the team that designed them didn't have their heart in the job. Only when the Classic range appeared in 1995 did they get it right.

Racing success

Kawasaki also have a more focused approach to racing than the other factories. The policy has always been to race the road bikes and with just a couple of exceptions that's what they've done. Even Simmonds' championship winner bore a strong resemblance to the twins they were selling in the late '60s and racing versions of the 500 and 750 cc triples were also sold as over-the-counter racers, the H1R and H2R. The 500 was in the forefront of the two-stroke assault on MV Agusta but wasn't a Grand Prix winner. It was the 750 that made the impact and carried the factory's image in F750 racing against the Suzuki triples and Yamaha fours.

The factory's decision to use green, usually regarded as an unlucky color in sport, meant its bikes and personnel stood out and the phrase 'Green Meanies' fitted them perfectly. The Z1 motor soon became a full 1000 cc and powered Kawasaki's assault in F1 racing, notably in endurance which Kawasaki saw as being most closely related to its road bikes.

That didn't stop them dominating 250 and 350 cc GPs with a tandem twin two-stroke in the late '70s and early '80s, but their path-

The GT750 - a favorite hack for despatch riders

breaking monocoque 500 while a race winner never won a world title. When Superbike arrived, Kawasaki's road 750s weren't as track-friendly as the opposition's out-and-out race replicas. This makes Scott Russell's World title on the ZXR750 in 1993 even more praiseworthy, for the homologation bike, the ZXR750RR, was much heavier and much more of a road bike than the Italian and Japanese competition. The fact that Russell's title remains the only Superbike world crown

won by an across-the-frame four is testament to both bike and rider.

After the ZXR came the ZX-7R and the ZX-9R, a new generation of supersportsters that managed to be useable on the road as well as the track. The 750 version stuck with carburetors while the rest of the Superbike pack went on to fuel injection, something which still gives Kawasaki's racers a few more problems to deal with than their opposition. Getting a ZX-7RR Superbike to work perfectly means getting knife-edge set-up precisely right. A fraction either way and the bike goes from competitive to unrideable.

The first ZX-9R was greeted with less than overwhelming reviews mainly due to its bulk, but when the C1 model arrived for '98 after a serious weight-loss program the big Kawasaki was truly a match for the then king of the hill, the FireBlade. Sales figures reflected the revised opinions of the road-testers, but a year later the Yamaha R1 arrived to re-arrange the parameters by which cutting edge sportsters are judged. But if you don't spend all your biking time at track days, the big Kawasaki is at least as good a road bike as the competition., especially if you're big, tall, or in the habit of carrying a passenger from time to time.

The company's Supersport 600 contenders have, like the bigger bikes, been more sports-tourers than race-replicas, yet they too have been competitive on the track. Indeed, the flagship bike, the ZZ-R1100, is most definitely

The high-performance ZXR750

a sports tourer capable of carrying two people and their luggage at high speed in comfort all day and then doing it again the next day. Try that on one of the race replicas and you'll be in need of a course of treatment from a chiropractor.

Through doing it their way Kawasaki developed a brand loyalty for their performance bikes that kept the Z1's derivatives in production until the mid-'80s and turned the bike into a classic in its model life. You could even argue that the Z1 lives on in the shape of the 1100 Zephyr's GPz1100-derived motor. And that's another Kawasaki invention, the retro bike. But when you look at what many commentators refer to as the retro boom, especially in Japan, you find that it is no such thing. It is the Zephyr boom. Just another example of Japan's most surprising motorcycle manufacturer getting it right again.

The Ninja ZX-7R ZX750P model

The Kawasaki Vulcan 700/750 and 800

Kawasaki's first entry into the growing cruiser market was the Vulcan 750 in 1985. The bike's chopper styling, with a long front fork, high handlebars and minimal fenders, was similar to its Harley-Davidson competitors, but the Vulcan offered more technical sophistication, with dual overhead cams, dual carburetors, liquid cooling and shaft drive. Ironically, Kawasaki went to considerable effort to disguise these advantages. The timing chain arrangement included a separate upper and lower chain for each cylinder, joined by a dual idler sprocket. This allowed the DOHC engine to have both a narrower angle between the cylinders and narrower cylinder heads, for a closer resemblance to Harley's narrow-angle pushrod engines. The heavily finned cylinders and cylinder heads disguised the liquid cooling (Harleys, of course, being air cooled). Finally, the driveshaft was partially hidden by running an exhaust pipe alongside it.

The Vulcan 700, which was produced for the US market in 1985, was a smaller-bore

version of the 750. Its displacement of 699 cc allowed it to escape the big-bike tariff of 1984-1987, which was imposed by the US government to assist Harley-Davidson, at that time in dire financial straits.

The Vulcan 800, first appearing in 1995, was less of a muscle bike and more of a cruiser than the 750. The standard version of the 800 resembled the Vulcan 750's chopper styling. However, the dual overhead cams had been replaced by single cams and the shaft drive had been replaced by a chain. The twin rear shocks gave way to a simulated rigid-frame rear suspension. A couple of other styling changes added to the cruiser image: Both exhaust pipes were now on the right side of the bike, instead of one on each side, and a single round air cleaner on the right side of the bike replaced the 750's dual, oval-shaped air cleaners.

Changes to the engine complemented the new styling. With the increase in displacement came a lower compression ratio, single overhead cams and a single carburetor, bringing the power band lower in the rpm range. While the strongest version of the

Vulcan 750 reached peak horsepower at 7500 rpm, the 800's horsepower peak occurred at 7000 rpm. More importantly for a cruiser, peak torque, reached at 6000 rpm in the 750, was achieved at only 3300 rpm in the 800.

Styling changes continued with the 1996 introduction of the Vulcan 800 Classic, with two-tone paint, full-size fenders and chrome outer tubes for the upper fork tubes.

The most recent addition to the mid-size Vulcan tribe is the 800 Drifter, which appeared in non-US markets in 1999 and in the US for 2001. Its very distinctive styling is aimed at the retro market, with pull-back handlebars, floorboards, fore-and-aft shift pedals, dual pipes blending into a single fishtail muffler, full-coverage fenders and a long headlight nacelle reminiscent of the 1940s. Because the rear fender moves up and down with the suspension, Drifter models have either a single saddle or a dual seat with its pillion raised high enough to allow clearance for suspension movement.

Both the Vulcan 750 and the Vulcan 800 continue in production.

Acknowledgements

Our thanks are due to Kawasaki Motors (UK) Ltd for permission to reproduce certain illustrations used in this manual. We would also like to thank Grand Prix Sports of Santa Clara, California, for supplying the motor-cycles used in the photographs throughout this manual; Anthony Morter, service manager, for arranging the facilities and fitting the project into his shop's busy schedule; and Craig Wardner, service technician, for doing the mechanical work and providing valuable technical information. The introduction "Kawasaki - The Green Meanies" was written by Julian Ryder, with additional information on the Vulcan 750 and 800 models by Alan Ahlstrand.

About this manual

The aim of this manual is to help you get the best value from your motorcycle. It can do so in several ways. It can help you decide what work must be done, even if you choose to have it done by a dealer; it provides information and procedures for routine maintenance and servicing; and it offers diagnostic and repair procedures to follow when trouble occurs.

We hope you use the manual to tackle the work yourself. For many simpler jobs, doing it yourself may be quicker than arranging an appointment to get the motorcycle into a dealer and making the trips to leave it and pick it up. More importantly, a lot of money can be saved by avoiding the expense the

shop must pass on to you to cover its labor and overhead costs. An added benefit is the sense of satisfaction and accomplishment that you feel after doing the job yourself.

References to the left or right side of the motorcycle assume you are sitting on the seat, facing forward.

We take great pride in the accuracy of information given in this manual, but motorcycle manufacturers make alterations and design changes during the production run of a particular motorcycle of which they do not inform us. No liability can be accepted by the authors or publishers for loss, damage or injury caused by any errors in, or omissions from, the information given.

Engine and frame numbers

The frame serial number is stamped into the right side of the steering head. The engine number is stamped into the right side of the crankcase and is visible from the right side of the machine. Both of these numbers should be recorded and kept in a safe place so they can be given to law enforcement officials in the event of a theft.

The frame serial number and engine serial number should also be kept in a handy place (such as with your driver's license) so they are always available when purchasing or ordering parts for your machine.

The model code (e.g. VN800-B1) can be determined from the frame serial numbers in the accompanying table.

Vulcan 700/750

Model	Year	Initial frame number
VN700-A1 (US)	1985	JKAVN6A1*FA000001
VN750-A1 (Canada)	1985	JKAVNDA1*FA000001
VN750-A2 (US, Canada)	1986	JKAVNDA1*GA002501
VN750-A2 (US)	1986	JKAVNDA1*GB500001
VN750-A2 (Europe, general)	1986	VN750A-002501
VN750-A3 (US, Canada)	1987	JKAVNDA1*HA005501
VN750-A3 (US)	1987	JKAVNDA1*HB508301
VN750-A3 (Europe, general)	1987	VN750A-005501
VN750-A4 (US, Canada)	1988	JKAVNDA1*JA006701
VN750-A4 (US)	1988	JKAVNDA1*JB509501
VN750-A4 (Europe, general)	1988	VN750A-006701
VN750-A5 (US, Canada)	1989	JKAVNDA1*KA007901
VN750-A5 (US)	1989	JKAVNDA1*KB510701
VN750-A5 (Europe, general)	1989	VN750A-007901
VN750-A6 (US, Canada)	1990	JKAVNDA1*LA009001
VN750-A6 (US)	1990	JKAVNDA1*LB512901
VN750-A7 (US, Canada)	1991	JKAVNDA1*MB515101
VN750-A8 (US, Canada)	1992	JKAVNDA1*NB517301
VN750-A9 (US, Canada)	1993	JKAVNDA1*PB520601
VN750-A9 (Europe, general)	1993	VN750A-600001
VN750-A10 (US, Canada)	1994	JKAVNDA1*RB524801
VN750-A10 (Europe, general)	1994	VN750A-602001
VN750-A11 (US)	1995	JKAVNDA1*SB529701
VN750-A12 (US)	1996	JKAVNDA1*TB534900
VN750-A13 (US)	1997	JKAVNDA1*VB536701
VN750-A14	1998	JKAVNDA1*WB538501
VN750-A15	1999	JKAVNDA1*XB539401
VN750-A16	2000	JKAVNDA1*YB541601
VN750-A17	2001	JKAVNDA1*IB543401

Vulcan 800

Model	Year	Initial frame number
VN800-A1 (US)	1995	JKBVNCA1*SA000001
VN800-A1 (except US)	1995	VN800A-000001
VN800-A2 (US)	1996	JKBVNCA1*TA030001
VN800-A2 (except US)	1996	VN800A-030001
VN800-A3 (US)	1997	JKBVNCB1*VA050001
VN800-A3 (except US)	1997	VN800A-050001
VN800-A4 (US)	1998	JKBVNCA1*WA06301
VN800-A4 (US)	1998	JKBVNCA1*WB500001
VN800-A4 (except US)	1998	VN800A-050001
VN800-A5/A5L (US)	1999	JKBVNCA1*XA07501
VN800-A5/A5L (US)	1999	JKBVNCA1*XB501401
VN800-A5/A5L (except US)	1999	JKBVN800AAA-075001
VN800-A6	2000	JKBVNCA1*YB503301
VN800-A7	2001	JKBVNCA1*IB5001

Vulcan 800 Classic

Model	Year	Initial frame number
VN800-B1	1996	JKBVNCB1*TA030001
VN800-B1	1996	VN800A-030001
VN800-B1 (Germany)	1996	VN800B-000001
VN800-B2	1997	JKBVNCB1*VA050001
VN800-B2	1997	VN800A-050001
VN800-B2 (Germany)	1997	VN800B-005001
VN800-B3	1998	JKBVNCB1*WA050001
VN800-B3	1998	VN800A-063001
VN800-B3 (Germany)	1998	VN800B-008001
VN800-B4	1999	JKBVNCB1*XA750001
VN800-B4	1999	JKBVNCB1*XB502701
VN800-B4	1999	JKBVN800ABA075001
VN800-B5	2000	JKBVNCB1*YA083001
VN800-B5	2000	JKBVNCB1*YB506101
VN800-B5	2000	JKBVN800ABA083001
VN800-B6	2001	JKBVNCB1*IA089001
VN800-B6	2001	JKBVNCB1*IB089001
VN800-B6	2001	JKBVN800ABA089001

Vulcan 800 Drifter

Model	Year	Initial frame number
VN800-C1	1999	JKBVNCC1*XA000001
VN800-C1	1999	JKBVN800CCA00000
VN800-C2	2000	Not available
VN800-E1	2001	JKBVNCE1*1A000001
VN800-E1	2001	JKBVN800CEA012001

Buying spare parts

Once you have found all the identification numbers, record them for reference when buying parts. Since the manufacturers change specifications, parts and vendors (companies that manufacture various components on the machine), providing the ID numbers is the only way to be reasonably sure that you are buying the correct parts.

Whenever possible, take the worn part to the dealer so direct comparison with the new component can be made. Along the trail from the manufacturer to the parts shelf, there are numerous places that the part can end up with the wrong number or be listed incorrectly.

The two places to purchase new parts for your motorcycle – the accessory store and the franchised dealer – differ in the type of parts they carry. While dealers can obtain virtually every part for your motorcycle, the accessory dealer is usually limited to normal high wear items such as shock absorbers, tune-up parts, various engine gaskets, cables, chains, brake parts, etc. Rarely will an accessory outlet have major suspension components, cylinders, transmission gears, or cases.

Used parts can be obtained for considerably less than new ones, but you can't always be sure of what you're getting. Once again, take your worn part to the salvage yard for direct comparison.

Whether buying new, used or rebuilt parts, the best course is to deal directly with someone who specializes in parts for your particular make.

The engine number is stamped in the top of the crankcase on the right-hand side of the engine

The frame number is stamped in the right-hand side of the steering head

Professional mechanics are trained in safe working procedures. However enthusiastic you may be about getting on with the job at hand, take the time to ensure that your safety is not put at risk. A moment's lack of attention can result in an accident, as can failure to observe simple precautions.

There will always be new ways of having accidents, and the following is not a comprehensive list of all dangers; it is intended rather to make you aware of the risks and to encourage a safe approach to all work you carry out on your bike.

Asbestos

● Certain friction, insulating, sealing and other products - such as brake pads, clutch linings, gaskets, etc. - contain asbestos. Extreme care must be taken to avoid inhalation of dust from such products since it is hazardous to health. If in doubt, assume that they do contain asbestos.

Fire

● Remember at all times that gasoline is highly flammable. Never smoke or have any kind of naked flame around, when working on the vehicle. But the risk does not end there - a spark caused by an electrical short-circuit, by two metal surfaces contacting each other, by careless use of tools, or even by static electricity built up in your body under certain conditions, can ignite gasoline vapor, which in a confined space is highly explosive. Never use gasoline as a cleaning solvent. Use an approved safety solvent.

● Always disconnect the battery ground terminal before working on any part of the fuel or electrical system, and never risk spilling fuel on to a hot engine or exhaust.

● It is recommended that a fire extinguisher of a type suitable for fuel and electrical fires is kept handy in the garage or workplace at all times. Never try to extinguish a fuel or electrical fire with water.

Fumes

● Certain fumes are highly toxic and can quickly cause unconsciousness and even death if inhaled to any extent. Gasoline vapor comes into this category, as do the vapors from certain solvents such as trichloro-ethylene. Any draining or pouring of such volatile fluids should be done in a well ventilated area.

● When using cleaning fluids and solvents, read the instructions carefully. Never use materials from unmarked containers - they may give off poisonous vapors.

● Never run the engine of a motor vehicle in an enclosed space such as a garage. Exhaust fumes contain carbon monoxide which is extremely poisonous; if you need to run the engine, always do so in the open air or at least have the rear of the vehicle outside the workplace.

The battery

● Never cause a spark, or allow a naked light near the vehicle's battery. It will normally be giving off a certain amount of hydrogen gas, which is highly explosive.

● Always disconnect the battery ground terminal before working on the fuel or electrical systems (except where noted).

● If possible, loosen the filler plugs or cover when charging the battery from an external source. Do not charge at an excessive rate or the battery may burst.

● Take care when topping up, cleaning or carrying the battery. The acid electrolyte, even when diluted, is very corrosive and should not be allowed to contact the eyes or skin. Always wear rubber gloves and goggles or a face shield. If you ever need to prepare electrolyte yourself, always add the acid slowly to the water; never add the water to the acid.

Electricity

● When using an electric power tool, inspection light etc., always ensure that the appliance is correctly connected to its plug and that, where necessary, it is properly grounded. Do not use such appliances in damp conditions and, again, beware of creating a spark or applying excessive heat in the vicinity of fuel or fuel vapor. Also ensure that the appliances meet national safety standards.

● A severe electric shock can result from touching certain parts of the electrical system, such as the spark plug wires (HT leads), when the engine is running or being cranked, particularly if components are damp or the insulation is defective. Where an electronic ignition system is used, the secondary (HT) voltage is much higher and could prove fatal.

Remember...

✗ **Don't** start the engine without first ascertaining that the transmission is in neutral.

✗ **Don't** suddenly remove the pressure cap from a hot cooling system - cover it with a cloth and release the pressure gradually first, or you may get scalded by escaping coolant.

✗ **Don't** attempt to drain oil until you are sure it has cooled sufficiently to avoid scalding you.

✗ **Don't** grasp any part of the engine or exhaust system without first ascertaining that it is cool enough not to burn you.

✗ **Don't** allow brake fluid or antifreeze to contact the machine's paintwork or plastic components.

✗ **Don't** siphon toxic liquids such as fuel, hydraulic fluid or antifreeze by mouth, or allow them to remain on your skin.

✗ **Don't** inhale dust - it may be injurious to health (see Asbestos heading).

✗ **Don't** allow any spilled oil or grease to remain on the floor - wipe it up right away, before someone slips on it.

✗ **Don't** use ill-fitting wrenches or other tools which may slip and cause injury.

✗ **Don't** lift a heavy component which may be beyond your capability - get assistance.

✗ **Don't** rush to finish a job or take unverified short cuts.

✗ **Don't** allow children or animals in or around an unattended vehicle.

✗ **Don't** inflate a tire above the recommended pressure. Apart from overstressing the carcass, in extreme cases the tire may blow off forcibly.

✔ **Do** ensure that the machine is supported securely at all times. This is especially important when the machine is blocked up to aid wheel or fork removal.

✔ **Do** take care when attempting to loosen a stubborn nut or bolt. It is generally better to pull on a wrench, rather than push, so that if you slip, you fall away from the machine rather than onto it.

✔ **Do** wear eye protection when using power tools such as drill, sander, bench grinder etc.

✔ **Do** use a barrier cream on your hands prior to undertaking dirty jobs - it will protect your skin from infection as well as making the dirt easier to remove afterwards; but make sure your hands aren't left slippery. Note that long-term contact with used engine oil can be a health hazard.

✔ **Do** keep loose clothing (cuffs, ties etc. and long hair) well out of the way of moving mechanical parts.

✔ **Do** remove rings, wristwatch etc., before working on the vehicle - especially the electrical system.

✔ **Do** keep your work area tidy - it is only too easy to fall over articles left lying around.

✔ **Do** exercise caution when compressing springs for removal or installation. Ensure that the tension is applied and released in a controlled manner, using suitable tools which preclude the possibility of the spring escaping violently.

✔ **Do** ensure that any lifting tackle used has a safe working load rating adequate for the job.

✔ **Do** get someone to check periodically that all is well, when working alone on the vehicle.

✔ **Do** carry out work in a logical sequence and check that everything is correctly assembled and tightened afterwards.

✔ **Do** remember that your vehicle's safety affects that of yourself and others. If in doubt on any point, get professional advice.

● If in spite of following these precautions, you are unfortunate enough to injure yourself, seek medical attention as soon as possible.

1 Engine/transmission oil level check

Before you start:

✔ Start the engine and allow it to reach normal operating temperature.

Caution: Do not run the engine in an enclosed space such as a garage or workshop.

✔ Stop the engine and support the motorcycle on its sidestand. Allow it to stand undisturbed for a few minutes to allow the oil level to stabilize. Make sure the motorcycle is on level ground.

✔ The oil level is viewed through the window in the clutch cover on the right-hand side of the engine. Wipe the glass clean before inspection to make the check easier.

Bike care:

● If you have to add oil frequently, you should check whether you have any oil leaks. If there is no sign of oil leakage from the joints and gaskets the engine could be burning oil (see *Troubleshooting*).

The correct oil

● Modern, high-revving engines place great demands on their oil. It is very important that the correct oil for your bike is used.

● Always top up with a good quality oil of the specified type and viscosity and do not overfill the engine.

Oil type	
Through 2000	API grade SE, SF or SG
2001 and later	API grade SE, SF or SG or API grade SH or SJ with JASO MA
Oil viscosity	
In cold climates	SAE 10W-40 or 10W-50
In warm climates	SAE 20W-40 or 20W-50

1 With the motorcycle held vertical, check the oil level in the inspection window at the bottom of the clutch cover. The level should lie between the upper and lower level marks (arrowed).

2 The Vulcan 750 oil filler cap is located at the top of the right crankcase cover. Unscrew the cap to add oil.

3 The Vulcan 800 oil filler cap is in the same location; place a large coin in the slot and turn it with pliers to unscrew the cap. Add the specified oil to bring the level to the upper mark on the inspection window, but don't overfill.

2 Coolant level check

> ⚠️ **Warning: DO NOT remove the filler neck pressure cap to add coolant. Topping up is done via the coolant reservoir tank filler. DO NOT leave open containers of coolant about, as it is poisonous.**

Before you start:

✔ Make sure you have a supply of coolant available (a mixture of 50% distilled water and 50% corrosion inhibited ethylene glycol anti-freeze is needed).

✔ Always check the coolant level when the engine is cold.

Caution: Do not run the engine in an enclosed space such as a garage or workshop.

✔ Ensure the motorcycle is held vertical while checking the coolant level. Make sure the motorcycle is on level ground.

Bike care:

● Use only the specified coolant mixture. It is important that anti-freeze is used in the system all year round, and not just in the winter. Do not top the system up using only water, as the system will become too diluted.

● Do not overfill the reservoir tank. If the coolant is significantly above the F (full) level line at any time, the surplus should be siphoned or drained off to prevent the possibility of it being expelled out of the overflow hose.

● If the coolant level falls steadily, check the system for leaks (see Chapter 1). If no leaks are found and the level continues to fall, it is recommended that the machine is taken to a Kawasaki dealer for a pressure test.

1 The Vulcan 750 coolant reservoir is located on the right side of the bike. The coolant level lines are visible on the side of the reservoir. Unscrew the cap (arrow), add coolant to bring the level to the upper line, then tighten the cap securely.

2 The Vulcan 800 coolant reservoir is hidden behind the engine, which has been removed for clarity in this photo. Coolant level in the transparent hose (visible on the right side of the bike) should be between the F and L marks on the reservoir.

3 Unscrew the cap (arrow), add coolant to bring the level to the upper line, then tighten the cap securely. Be sure not to mistake the coolant reservoir cap for the oil filler cap, which is located in the right crankcase cover.

3 Brake fluid level check

The rear brake fluid level check only applies to Vulcan 800 Drifter models.

 Warning: Hydraulic fluid can harm your eyes and damage painted surfaces, so use extreme caution when handling and pouring it and cover surrounding surfaces with rag. Do not use fluid that has been standing open for some time, as it absorbs moisture from the air which can cause a dangerous loss of braking effectiveness.

Before you start:

✔ Ensure the motorcycle is held vertical while checking the levels. Make sure the motorcycle is on level ground.

✔ Make sure you have the correct hydraulic fluid. DOT 4 is recommended. Never reuse old fluid.

✔ Wrap a rag around the reservoir being worked on to ensure that any spillage does not come into contact with painted surfaces.

Bike care:

● The fluid in the front and rear brake master cylinder reservoirs will drop slightly as the brake pads wear down.

● If any fluid reservoir requires repeated topping-up this is an indication of a hydraulic leak somewhere in the system, which should be investigated immediately.

● Check for signs of fluid leakage from the hydraulic hoses and components – if found, rectify immediately.

● Check the operation of both brakes before taking the machine on the road; if there is evidence of air in the system (spongy feel to lever or pedal), it must be bled as described in Chapter 7.

1 With the front brake fluid reservoir as level as possible, check that the fluid level is above the LOWER level line on the inspection window (early 700/750 models use a rectangular reservoir, but the inspection window is the same). The UPPER level line is visible on the outside of rectangular reservoirs, and cast on the inside of round reservoirs.

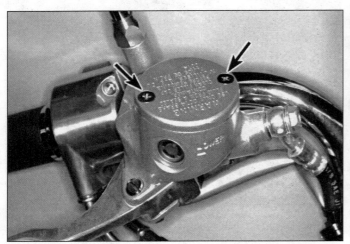

2 If the level is below the LOWER level line, remove the cover screws (arrows) and lift off the cover and diaphragm. Top up fluid to the upper level line; don't overfill the reservoir, and take care to avoid spills (see WARNING above). Compress the diaphragm, reinstall the diaphragm and cover and tighten the screws securely.

3 The rear brake fluid reservoir on Vulcan 800 Drifter models is visible through the cutout in the protective cover. The fluid level must be between the UPPER and LOWER level lines.

4 Remove the protective cover, unscrew the cap and remove the diaphragm. Top up fluid to just below the UPPER line, then compress the diaphragm and install the diaphragm and cap.

5 If the motorcycle has rear drum brakes (all models except Vulcan 800 Drifter), check lining wear. Press the brake pedal and note the position of the wear indicator pointer. If it's past the USABLE RANGE area cast on the brake drum, it's time for new brake shoes (see Chapter 7).

4 Suspension, steering and final drive checks

Suspension and Steering:
● Check that the front and rear suspension operate smoothly without binding.
● Check that the suspension is adjusted as required.
● Check that the steering moves smoothly from lock-to-lock.

Final drive:
● On chain drive models, check the drive chain slack isn't excessive and adjust it if necessary (see Chapter 1).
● On chain drive models, lubricate the chain if it looks dry (see Chapter 1).

● On shaft drive models, inspect the differential for oil leakage and check the oil level if leaks can be seen (see Chapter 1).

5 Legal and safety checks

Lighting and signalling:
● Take a minute to check that the headlight, tail light, brake light, instrument lights and turn signals all work correctly.
● Check that the horn sounds when the switch is operated.
● A working speedometer graduated in mph is a statutory requirement in the UK.

Safety:
● Check that the throttle grip rotates smoothly and snaps shut when released, in all steering positions. Also check for the correct amount of freeplay (see Chapter 1).
● Check that the engine shuts off when the kill switch is operated.
● Check that sidestand return spring holds the stand securely up when retracted.

Fuel:
● This may seem obvious, but check that you have enough fuel to complete your journey. If you notice signs of fuel leakage – rectify the cause immediately.
● Ensure you use the correct grade unleaded fuel – see Chapter 4 Specifications.

4 Tire checks

The correct pressures:

● The tires must be checked when **cold**, not immediately after riding. Note that low tire pressures may cause the tire to slip on the rim or come off. High tire pressures will cause abnormal tread wear and unsafe handling.
● Use an accurate pressure gauge.
● Proper air pressure will increase tire life and provide maximum stability and ride comfort.

Tire care:

● Check the tires carefully for cuts, tears, embedded nails or other sharp objects and excessive wear. Operation of the motorcycle with excessively worn tires is extremely hazardous, as traction and handling are directly affected.
● Check the condition of the tire valve and ensure the dust cap is in place.
● Pick out any stones or nails which may have become embedded in the tire tread. If left, they will eventually penetrate through the casing and cause a puncture.

● If tire damage is apparent, or unexplained loss of pressure is experienced, seek the advice of a tire fitting specialist without delay.

Tire tread depth:

● Kawasaki recommends a minimum of 1 mm on the front tire. The minimum on the rear tire is 2 mm, or 3 mm if the motorcycle is ridden at speeds over 80 mph.
● Many tires now incorporate wear indicators in the tread. Identify the triangular pointer or 'TWI' mark on the tire sidewall to locate the indicator bar and replace the tire if the tread has worn down to the bar.

Tire pressures

Front (Vulcan 700/750 models)	28 psi (1.93 Bar)
Front (Vulcan 800 models) and rear (all models)	
Up to 97.5 kg (215 lbs) load	28 psi (1.93 Bar)
Over 97.5 kg (215 lbs) load	32 psi (2.2 Bar)

1 Check the tire pressures when the tires are **cold** and keep them properly inflated.

2 Measure tread depth at the center of the tire using a tread depth gauge.

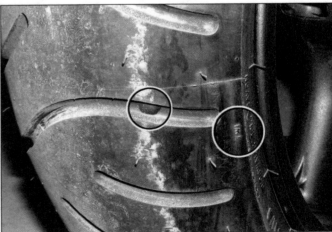

3 Tire tread wear indicator bar and its location marking (usually either an arrow, a triangle or the letters TWI) on the sidewall (arrowed).

Chapter 1
Tune-up and routine maintenance

Contents

1

Specifications

Engine

Spark plugs (Vulcan 700/750 models)

Standard type

1985 through 1999

US, Canadian, Australian, Italian models ... NGK DP7EA-9 or ND X22EP-U9

All other models ... NGK DPR7EA-9 or ND X22EPR-U9

2000 and later ... NGK DP7EA-9 or ND X22EP-U9

Optional type

1985 through 1999

US, Canadian, Australian, Italian models ... NGK DP8EA-9 or ND X24EP-U9

All other models ... NGK DPR8EA-9 or ND X24EPR-U9

2000 and later ... NGK DP8EA-9 or ND X24EP-U9

Gap ... 0.8 to 0.9 mm (0.031 to 0.035 inch)

Spark plugs (Vulcan 800 models)

Type ... NGK CR7E or ND U22ESR-N

Gap ... 0.7 to 0.8 mm (0.024 to 0.031 inch)

Engine idle speed

Vulcan 700/750
    1988 and 1989 Swiss models .... 1300 +/- 50 rpm
    All others .... 1000+/-50 rpm
Vulcan 800
    California and Swiss models .... 1300 +/- 50 rpm
    All others .... 1000+/-50 rpm

Valve clearances (COLD engine)

Vulcan 700/750.. Hydraulic; not adjustable
Vulcan 800
    Intake.. 0.10 to 0.15 mm (0.004 to 0.006 inch)
    Exhaust
        2001 Vulcan 800-E1 (Drifter)... 0.20 to 0.25 mm (0.008 to 0.010 inch)
        All other Vulcan 800 models .... 0.25 to 0.30 mm (0.010 to 0.012 inch)

Cylinder compression pressure

Vulcan 700/750 models.. 890 to 1370 kPa (119 to 185 psi)
Vulcan 800 models .... 855 to 1315 kPa (124 to 191 psi)

Carburetor synchronization (Vulcan 700/750 models)

Vacuum difference between cylinders.. Less than 2 cm Hg (0.391 inch Hg)

Cylinder numbering

From front to rear of bike... 1-2

Chassis

Brake pad minimum thickness .... 1.0 mm (0.040 inch)
Brake pedal position
    Vulcan 700/750 models... 55 to 65 mm (2-3/16 to 2-5/16 inches) above top of footpeg
    Vulcan 800 models
        2001 Vulcan 800-E1 (Drifter)... Approximately 97 mm (3-51/64 inch) above top of floorboard
        All other Vulcan 800 models .... Approximately 65 mm 2-9/16-inch) above top of footpeg
Freeplay adjustments
    Throttle grip .... 2 to 3 mm (0.08 to 0.12 inch)
    Clutch lever (gap between lever and lever bracket
        When freeplay is taken up) .... 2 to 3 mm (0.08 to 0.12 inch)
    Brake pedal
        Vulcan 700/750 models .... 20 to 30 mm (0.8 to 1.2 inch)
        Vulcan 800 models
            With rear drum brake... 20 to 30 mm (0.8 to 1.2 inch)
            With rear disc brake.. Not adjustable
    Choke lever (Vulcan 700/750 only).. 2 to 3 mm (0.08 to 0.12 inch)
Drive chain slack (Vulcan 800 models)
    Standard... 25 to 30 mm (1 to 1-3/16 inch)
    Limit... 25 to 35 mm (1 to 1-13/32 inch)
Battery electrolyte specific gravity (Vulcan 700/750 only)..................... 1.280 at 68 degrees F (20 degrees C)
Minimum tire tread depth
    Front .... 1.0 mm (0.04 inch)
    Rear (Vulcan 700/750) .... 2.0 mm (0.08 inch)
    Rear (Vulcan 800)
        Below 130 kph (80 mph) .... 2.0 mm (0.08 inch)
        Above 130 kph (80 mph) .... 3.0 mm (0.12 inch)
Tire pressures (cold)
    Front
        Vulcan 700/750 and Vulcan 800 2001 (E1) Drifter .... 28 psi (1.9 Bar)
        Vulcan 800 (except 2001 E1 Drifter)
            Up to 215 lbs (97.5 kg) .... 28 psi (1.9 Bar)
            Over 215 lbs (97.5 kg) .... 32 psi (2.5 Bar)
    Rear
        Up to 215 lbs (97.5 kg).. 28 psi (1.9 Bar)
        Over 215 lbs (97.5 kg).. 32 psi (2.5 Bar)

Torque specifications

Oil drain plug .... 20 Nm (174 inch-lbs)
Oil filter... 18 Nm (159 inch-lbs)
Oil screen cap bolt .... 18 Nm (159 inch-lbs)
Coolant drain bolt
    Vulcan 700/750 models... 8.8 Nm (78 inch-lbs)
    Vulcan 800 models .... 11 Nm (95 inch-lbs)

Cylinder drain bolts (Vulcan 700/750 models) .... 8.8 Nm (78 inch-lbs)
Spark plugs .... 18 Nm (159 inch-lbs)
Valve cover bolts .... See Chapter 2

Recommended lubricants and fluids

Engine/transmission oil
Type
  Through 2000 .... API grade SE, SF or SG
  2001 and later .... API grade SE, SF or SG or API grade SH or SJ with JASO MA
Viscosity
  In cold climates .... SAE 10W40 or 10W50
  In warm climates .... SAE 20W40 or 20W50
Capacity (Vulcan 700/750 models)
  With filter change .... 4.0 liters (4.2 US qt, 7.0 Imp pt)
  Oil change only .... 2.8 liters (2.9 US qt, 4.9 Imp pt)
Capacity (Vulcan 800 models
  With filter change .... 2.9 liters (3.0 US qt, 5.26 Imp pt)
  Oil change only .... 2.7 liters (2.8 US qt, 4.9 Imp pt)
Coolant
  Type .... 50/50 mixture of ethylene glycol based antifreeze and soft water
  Capacity (including reserve tank)
    Vulcan 700/750 models .... 1.5 liters (1.58 US qt, 2.72 Imp pt)
    Vulcan 800 models .... 2.4 liters (2.5 US qt, 4.35 Imp pt)
Brake fluid .... DOT 4

Fork oil
Type
  Vulcan 700/750 models .... SAE 10W20 - fork oil
  Vulcan 800 models .... SAE 10W fork oil
Amount
  Vulcan 700/750 models
    Dry fill
      US, Canada .... 362 +/- 2.5 cc (12.2 +/- 0.08 US fl oz, 10.2 +/- .07 Imp fl oz)
      All except US, Canada .... 373 +/- 2.5 cc (12.6 +/- 0.08 US fl oz, 10.5 Imp fl oz)
    At oil change
      US, Canada .... 310 cc (10.5 US fl oz, 8.73 Imp fl oz)
      All except US, Canada .... 320 cc (10.8 US fl oz, 9.0 Imp fl oz)
  Vulcan 800
    VN800-A models
      Dry fill .... 340 +/- 4 cc (11.5 +/- 0.13 US fl oz, 9.75 +/- 0.11 Imp fl oz)
      At oil change .... Approximately 290 cc (9.8 US fl oz, 8.16 Imp fl oz)
    VN800-B models (Classic)
      Dry fill .... 310 +/- 4 cc (10.5 US fl oz, 8.73 Imp fl oz)
      At oil change .... Approximately 265 cc (8.95 US fl oz, 7.46 Imp fl oz)
    VN800-C models (1999-2000 Drifter)
      Dry fill .... 385 cc (13.0 US fl oz, 10.84 Imp fl oz)
      At oil change .... Not specified
    VN800-E models (2001 Drifter)
      Dry fill .... 320 +/- 4 cc (10.8 US fl oz, 9.0 Imp fl oz)
      At oil change .... Approximately 270 cc (9.12 US fl oz, 7.6 Imp fl oz)
Oil level (spring removed and fork fully compressed)
  Vulcan 700/750 models
    US and Canadian models .... 215 +/- 10 mm (8.46 +/- 0.39 inches)
    All except US and Canadian models .... 230 +/- 10 mm (9.05 +/- 0.39 inches)
  Vulcan 800 models
    VN800-A models .... 292 +/- 2 mm (11.5 +/- 0.008 inches)
    VN800-B models (Classic) .... 286 +/-2 mm (11.25 +/- 0/008 inches)
    VN800-C models (1999 and 2000 Drifter) .... 213 mm (8.38 inches)
    VN800-E models (2001 Drifter) .... 280 +/- 2 mm (11.0 +/- 0.008 inches)
Miscellaneous
  Wheel bearings .... Medium weight, lithium-based multi-purpose grease
  Swingarm pivot bearings .... Medium weight, lithium-based multi-purpose grease
  Cables and lever pivots .... Chain and cable lubricant or 10W30 motor oil
  Sidestand/centerstand pivots .... Medium-weight, lithium-based multi-purpose grease
  Brake pedal/shift lever pivots .... Chain and cable lubricant or 10W30 motor oil
  Throttle grip .... Multi-purpose grease or dry film lubricant

1

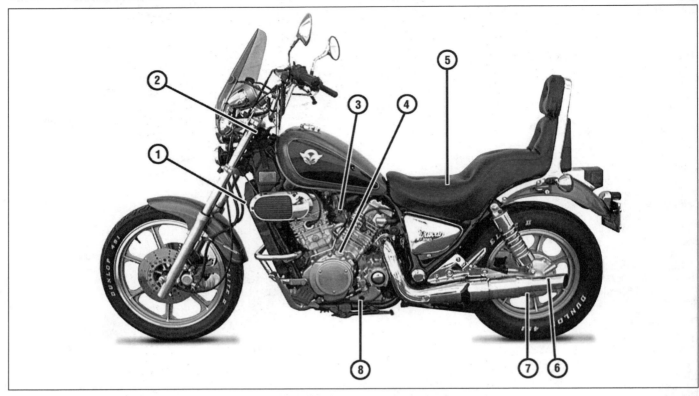

Component locations – Vulcan 700/750 models

1	Left air filter	5	Battery
2	Steering head bearing adjuster	6	Differential filler plug
3	Idle speed adjuster	7	Differential drain bolt
4	Engine oil filler plug	8	Engine oil level window
		9	Front brake fluid reservoir

10	Cooling system pressure cap
11	Right air filter
12	Cooling system drain bolt

13	Engine oil drain plug
14	Coolant reservoir
15	Rear brake wear indicator
16	Rear brake adjuster

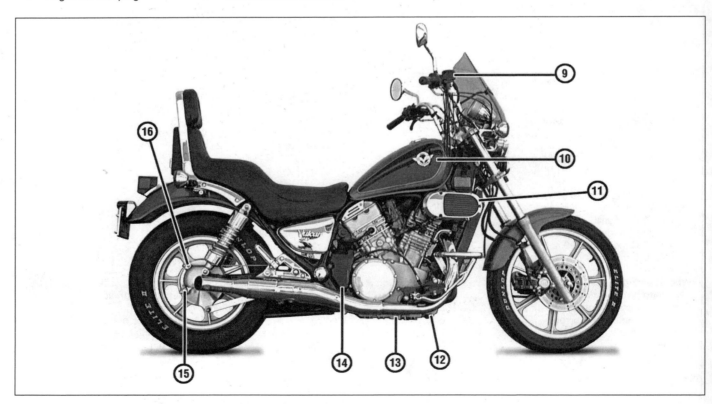

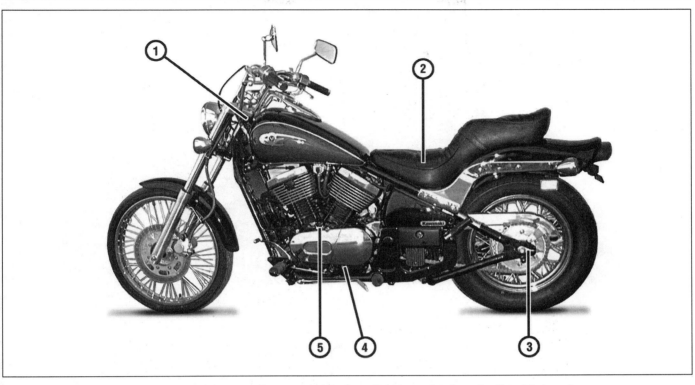

Component locations – Vulcan 800 standard and Classic models (standard model shown)

1	Steering head bearing adjuster	6	Front brake fluid reservoir	11	Coolant reservoir
2	Battery	7	Cooling system drain bolt	12	Right chain adjuster
3	Left chain adjuster	8	Idle speed adjuster	13	Rear brake wear indicator
4	Engine oil level window	9	Engine oil drain bolt	14	Rear brake adjuster
5	Engine oil filler plug	10	Air filter		

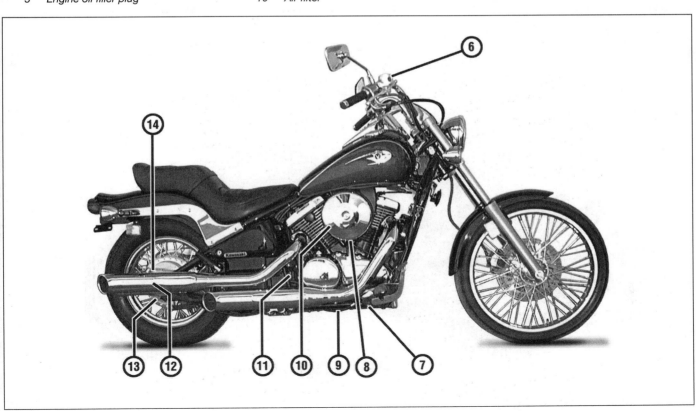

1

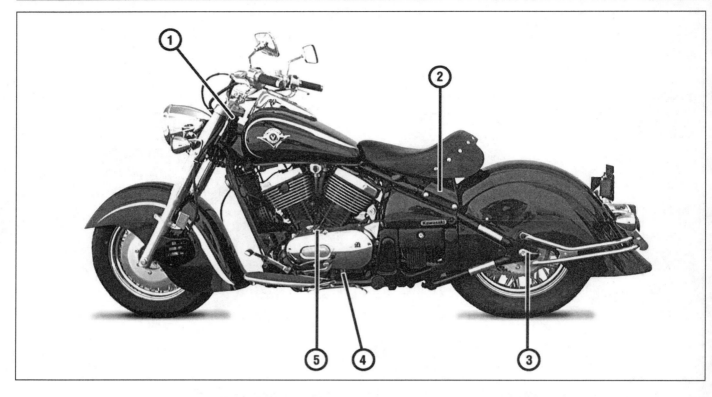

Component locations – Vulcan 800 Drifter

1	Steering head bearing adjuster	4	Engine oil level window	8 Air filter
2	Battery	5	Engine oil filler plug	9 Idle speed adjuster
3	Left chain adjuster	6	Front brake fluid reservoir	10 Cooling system drain bolt
		7	Rear brake fluid reservoir	

1 Steering head bearing
    adjuster
2 Battery
3 Left chain adjuster

4 Engine oil level window
5 Engine oil filler plug
6 Front brake fluid reservoir
7 Rear brake fluid reservoir

8 Air filter
9 Idle speed adjuster
10 Cooling system drain bolt

11 Engine oil drain bolt
12 Coolant reservoir
13 Right chain adjuster

1 Kawasaki Vulcan Routine maintenance intervals

Note: *The pre-ride inspection outlined in the owner's manual covers checks and maintenance that should be carried out on a daily basis. It's condensed and included here to remind you of its importance. Always perform the pre-ride inspection at every maintenance interval (in addition to the procedures listed). The intervals listed below are the shortest intervals recommended by the manufacturer for each particular operation during the model years covered in this manual. Your owner's manual may have different intervals for your model.*

Daily or before riding

Check the engine oil level
Check the fuel level and inspect for leaks
Check the engine coolant level and look for leaks
Check the operation of both brakes - also check the fluid level and look for leakage (disc brakes)
Check the tires for damage, the presence of foreign objects and correct air pressure
Check the throttle for smooth operation and correct freeplay
Check the operation of the clutch - make sure the freeplay is correct
Make sure the steering operates smoothly, without looseness and without binding
Check for proper operation of the headlight, taillight, brake light, turn signals, indicator lights, speedometer and horn
Make sure the sidestand and centerstand (if equipped) return to their fully up positions and stay there under spring pressure
Make sure the engine STOP switch works properly

After the initial 500 miles (800 km)

This service is usually performed by a dealer service department, since the bike is still under warranty. It consists of all of the daily checks plus:
All of the 3000 mile checks
Engine oil and filter change
Air filter element cleaning
Idle speed adjustment
Drive chain slack adjustment (chain drive models)
Final drive oil change (shaft drive models)

Every 200 miles (300 km)

Lubricate the drive chain and check play (chain drive models) (Section 3)

Every 3000 miles (5000 km)

Check the drive chain and sprockets for wear (chain drive models) (Section 3)
Check the brake fluid level (Section 4)
Check the brake disc(s), pads, drum and shoes (if equipped) (Section 5)
Check/adjust the brake pedal position (Section 6)
Check the operation of the brake light (Section 7)
Check the tires and wheels (Section 8)
Lubricate all cables (Section 9)
Lubricate the clutch and brake lever pivots (Section 9)
Lubricate the shift/brake lever pivots and the sidestand/centerstand pivots (Section 9)
Adjust the clutch freeplay (Section 10)
Check the steering (Section 11)

Check the battery electrolyte level (Section 12)
Clean and gap the spark plugs (Section 13)
Check the operation of the air suction valves (if equipped) (Section 14)
Check the evaporative emission control system (California models) (Section 15)
Check/adjust the throttle and choke operation and freeplay (Section 16)
Check/adjust the idle speed (Section 17)
Check/adjust the carburetor synchronization (Section 18)

Every 6000 miles (10,000 km)

All of the items above plus:
Adjust the valve clearances (Section 19)
Replace the spark plugs (Section 13)
Clean the air filter element (Section 20)
Check the exhaust system for leaks and check the tightness of the fasteners (Section 21)
Check the cleanliness of the fuel system and the condition of the fuel and vacuum hoses (Section 22)
Lubricate the swingarm needle bearings (and rear suspension linkage needle bearings on Vulcan 800 models) (Chapter 6)
Check the tightness of all fasteners on the motorcycle (Section 23)
Check the suspension (Section 24)
Check the differential oil (shaft drive models) (Section 4)
Change the engine oil and oil filter (Section 25)

Every 12,000 miles (20,000 km) or two years

Lubricate the steering head bearings (Chapter 6)
Change the brake fluid (Chapter 7)
Lubricate the drum brake cam (Vulcan 700/750 models) (Chapter 7)
Replace the air filter element (also replace after every five cleanings) (Section 20)

Every 18,000 miles (30,000 km) or two years

Check the cooling system and replace the coolant (Sections 26 and 27)

Every 18,000 miles (30,000 km)

Change the fork oil (Section 28)

Every 24,000 miles (36,000 km)

Change the differential oil (shaft drive models) (Section 29)

Every two years

Overhaul the brake caliper(s) and master cylinder(s) (Chapter 7)
Check and lubricate the wheel bearings (Chapter 7)
Lubricate the speedometer gear (Chapter 9)

Every four years

Replace the fuel hoses (Chapter 4)
Replace the brake hose(s) (Chapter 7)

2.3 Decals in various locations include safety, emissions and maintenance information

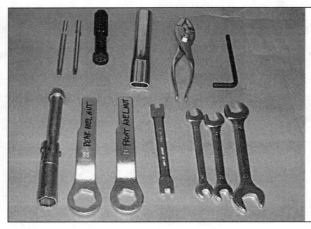

2.7 A tool kit is included with the motorcycle (Vulcan 800 tool kit shown)

2 Introduction to tune-up and routine maintenance

Refer to illustrations 2.3 and 2.7

1   This Chapter covers in detail the checks and procedures necessary for the tune-up and routine maintenance of your motorcycle. Section 1 includes the routine maintenance schedule, which is designed to keep the machine in proper running condition and prevent possible problems. The remaining Sections contain detailed procedures for carrying out the items listed on the maintenance schedule, as well as additional maintenance information designed to increase reliability.

2   Since routine maintenance plays such an important role in the safe and efficient operation of your motorcycle, it is presented here as a comprehensive check list. For the rider who does all of the bike's maintenance, these lists outline the procedures and checks that should be done on a routine basis.

3   Maintenance information is printed on decals in various locations on the motorcycle **(see illustration)**. If the information on the decals differs from that included here, use the information on the decal.

4   Deciding where to start or plug into the routine maintenance schedule depends on several factors. If you have a motorcycle whose warranty has recently expired, and if it has been maintained according to the warranty standards, you may want to pick up routine maintenance as it coincides with the next mileage or calendar interval. If you have owned the machine for some time but have never performed any maintenance on it, then you may want to start at the nearest interval and include some additional procedures to ensure that nothing important is overlooked. If you have just had a major engine overhaul, then you may want to start the maintenance routine from the beginning. If you have a used machine and have no knowledge of its

history or maintenance record, you may desire to combine all the checks into one large service initially and then settle into the maintenance schedule prescribed.

5   The Sections which outline the inspection and maintenance procedures are written as step-by-step comprehensive guides to the performance of the work. They explain in detail each of the routine inspections and maintenance procedures on the check list. References to additional information in applicable Chapters are also included and should not be overlooked.

6   Before beginning any maintenance or repair, the machine should be cleaned thoroughly, especially around the oil filter, spark plugs, cylinder head covers, side covers, carburetor(s), etc. Cleaning will help ensure that dirt does not contaminate the engine and will allow you to detect wear and damage that could otherwise easily go unnoticed.

7   The motorcycle comes from the factory with a tool kit that's useful for some of the maintenance procedures, as well as for emergency repairs **(see illustration)**. If the factory tool kit is missing or incomplete, you can put together your own or order the factory tool kit from a Kawasaki dealer.

3 Drive chain and sprockets (Vulcan 800 models) - check, adjustment and lubrication

Check

Refer to illustrations 3.3 and 3.6

1   A neglected drive chain won't last long and can quickly damage the sprockets. Routine chain adjustment and inspection isn't difficult and will ensure maximum chain and sprocket life.

2   To check the chain, place the bike on its stand and shift the transmission into Neutral. Make sure the ignition switch is off.

3   Push up on the bottom run of the chain and measure the slack midway between the two sprockets **(see illustration)**, then compare your measurements to the value listed

3.3 Check drive chain play halfway along the bottom run of the chain

in this Chapter's Specifications. As the chain stretches with wear, adjustment will periodically be necessary. Since the chain will rarely wear evenly, rotate the rear wheel so that another section of chain can be checked; do this several times to check the entire chain.

4   In some cases where lubrication has been neglected, corrosion and galling may cause the links to bind and kink, which effectively shortens the chain's length. Such links should be thoroughly cleaned and worked free. If the chain is tight between the sprockets, rusty or kinked, it's time to replace it with a new one. If you find a tight area, mark it with felt pen or paint, and repeat the measurement after the bike has been ridden. If the chain's still tight in the same area, it may be damaged or worn. Because a tight or kinked chain can damage the transmission bearings, it's a good idea to replace it with a new one.

5   Remove the chain guard. Check the entire length of the chain for damaged rollers, loose links and pins, and missing O-rings and replace it if damage is found. **Note:** *Never install a new chain on old sprockets, and never install a used chain on new sprockets - replace the chain and sprockets as a set.*

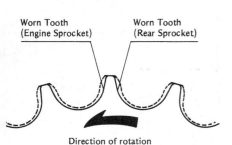

3.6 Check the sprockets in the areas indicated to see if they're worn excessively

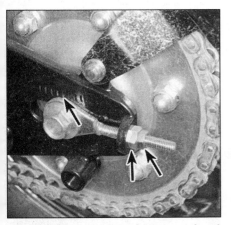

3.11 Loosen the locknut (right arrow) and turn the adjusting nut (center arrow); align the adjuster with the same mark on each side of the bike (left arrow)

6   Remove the front sprocket cover (see Chapter 6). Check the teeth on the front sprocket and the rear sprocket for wear **(see illustration)**.

Adjustment

Refer to illustrations 3.10a, 3.10b and 3.11

7   Remove the rear muffler for access to the chain adjuster on the right side of the bike (see Chapter 4).
8   Support the bike with the rear wheel off the ground and rotate the rear wheel until the chain is positioned with the tightest point at the center of its bottom run.
9   Loosen the rear brake adjusting nut (see Section 7).
10   Remove the cotter pin from the rear axle nut, then loosen the axle nut with the 22 mm wrench in the bike's tool kit or a 22 mm open-end wrench **(see illustrations)**.
11   Loosen the locknuts on the adjuster bolts **(see illustration)**.
12   Turn the chain adjusting bolts on both sides of the swingarm until the proper chain tension is obtained (get the adjuster on the chain side close, then set the adjuster on the opposite side). Be sure to turn the adjusting bolts evenly to keep the rear wheel in align-

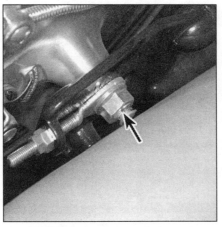

3.10a Remove the cotter pin (arrow) . . .

ment. If the adjusting bolts reach the end of their travel, the chain is excessively worn and should be replaced with a new one (see Chapter 6).
13   When the chain has the correct amount of slack, make sure the marks on the adjusters correspond to the same relative marks on each side of the swingarm **(see illustration 3.11)**.
14   Tighten the axle nut snugly, then apply the rear brake firmly to center the shoes. Recheck drive chain slack and readjust if necessary, then tighten the axle nut to the torque listed in the Chapter 7 Specifications and install a new cotter pin. If necessary, turn the nut an additional amount to line up the cotter pin hole with the castellations in the nut - don't loosen the nut to do this.
15   Tighten the adjuster locknuts and adjust the rear brake (see Section 7).

---

4   Fluid levels - check

Engine oil

1   Engine oil level should be checked before every ride as described in *Daily (pre-ride) checks* at the beginning of this manual, as well as at the specified maintenance intervals.

Brake fluid

2   Fluid level in the front brake master cylinder (and the rear brake master cylinder on Vulcan 800 models) should be checked before every ride as described in *Daily (pre-ride) checks* at the beginning of this manual, as well as at the specified maintenance intervals.

Coolant

3   Coolant level in the reservoir tank should be checked before every ride as described in *Daily (pre-ride) checks* at the beginning of this manual, as well as at the specified maintenance intervals.

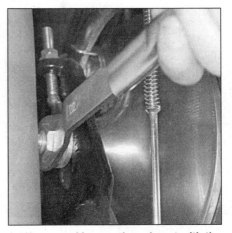

3.10b . . . and loosen the axle nut with the wrench from the bike's tool kit or an open-end wrench

Final drive oil (shaft drive models)

Refer to illustration 4.6

4   Final drive oil in Vulcan 700/750 models should be checked at the specified maintenance interval; before every ride, take a quick look for signs of leakage around the differential housing.
5   Support the bike securely in a level position. **Warning:** *When the bike is operated, the final drive unit gets hot enough to cause burns. If the machine has been ridden recently, make sure the final drive unit is cool to the touch before checking the level.*
6   Remove the filler plug from the final drive housing **(see illustration)**.
7   Look inside the hole and check the oil level. It should be even with the bottom of the hole. If it's low, add oil of the type listed in this Chapter's Specifications with a funnel or hose, then reinstall the filler plug and tighten to the torque listed in this Chapter's Specifications.

4.6 Here are the Vulcan 750 differential filler plug (right arrow) and drain plug (left arrow)

1

5.2 Look into the front of the caliper to check the brake pads for wear (arrows)

5.4 If the pointer (lower arrow) goes past the Usable Range indicator, the linings are worn and must be replaced; the adjuster (upper arrow) is used to set brake pedal freeplay

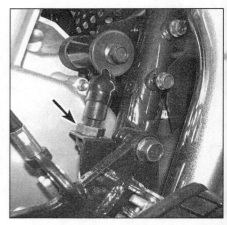

6.6 To adjust the rear brake light switch, hold the switch body and turn the locknut (arrow)

5 Brake pads and linings - wear check

Refer to illustrations 5.2 and 5.4

1 Disc brake pads and drum brake linings should be checked at the recommended intervals and replaced with new ones when worn beyond the limit listed in this Chapter's Specifications (disc brakes) or Chapter 7 (drum brakes).

2 To check disc brake pads, remove the caliper (without disconnecting the brake hose) so you can see clearly into the front of the brake caliper (see Chapter 7). The brake pads should have at least the specified minimum amount of lining material remaining on the metal backing plate **(see illustration).**

3 If the pads are worn excessively, they must be replaced with new ones (see Chapter 7).

4 To check drum brake linings, press the brake pedal firmly and look at the indicator on the brake drum **(see illustration).** If the pointer is beyond the Usable Range scale, replace the brake shoes (see Chapter 7).

6 Brake system - general check

Refer to illustration 6.6

1 A routine general check of the brakes will ensure that any problems are discovered and remedied before the rider's safety is jeopardized.

2 Check the brake lever and pedal for loose connections, excessive play, bends, and other damage. Replace any damaged parts with new ones (see Chapter 7).

3 Make sure all brake fasteners are tight. Check the brake pads and linings for wear (see Section 5) and make sure the fluid level in the reservoir is correct (see *Daily (pre-ride) checks* at the beginning of this manual). Look for leaks at the hose connections and check for cracks in the hoses. If the lever is spongy, bleed the brakes as described in Chapter 7.

4 Make sure the brake light operates when the brake lever is depressed.

5 Make sure the brake light is activated when the rear brake pedal is depressed approximately 15 mm (0.6 inch).

6 If adjustment is necessary, hold the switch and turn the adjusting nut on the switch body **(see illustration)** until the brake light is activated when required. Turning the nut out will cause the brake light to come on sooner, while turning it in will cause it to come on later. If the switch doesn't operate the brake lights, check it as described in Chapter 9.

7 The front brake light switch is not adjustable. If it fails to operate properly, replace it with a new one (see Chapter 9).

7 Brake pedal position and play - check and adjustment

1 Rear brake pedal position is largely a matter of personal preference. Locate the pedal so that the rear brake can be engaged quickly and easily without excessive foot movement. The recommended factory setting is listed in this Chapter's Specifications.

Rear drum brake models

Refer to illustration 7.2

2 To adjust the position of the pedal, loosen the locknut on the adjusting bolt, turn the bolt to set the pedal position and tighten the locknut **(see illustration).**

3 If necessary, adjust the brake light switch (see Section 6).

4 With the pedal position adjusted correctly, check freeplay. Apply the rear brake and compare the pedal travel with that listed in this Chapter's Specifications.

5 To adjust the freeplay, turn the adjuster at the rear end of the brake rod **(see illustration 5.4).**

7.2 To adjust the brake pedal position, loosen the locknut (upper arrow) and turn the adjusting bolt (lower arrow) (Vulcan 800 standard model shown)

Rear disc brake models

6 Pedal position is adjusted by changing the length of the master cylinder pushrod (see Chapter 6).

8 Tires/wheels - general check

Refer to illustration 8.4

1 Routine tire and wheel checks should be made with the realization that your safety depends to a great extent on their condition.

2 Check the tires carefully for cuts, tears, embedded nails or other sharp objects and excessive wear. Operation of the motorcycle with excessively worn tires is extremely hazardous, as traction and handling are directly affected. Measure the tread depth at the center of the tire and replace worn tires with new ones when the tread depth is less than specified.

3 Repair or replace punctured tires as

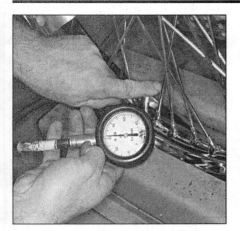

8.4 Use an accurate gauge to check the air pressure in the tires

8.7 Check the tension of the spokes periodically, but don't over-tighten them

soon as damage is noted. Do not try to patch a torn tire, as wheel balance and tire reliability may be impaired.

4   Check the tire pressures when the tires are cold and keep them properly inflated **(see illustration)**. Proper air pressure will increase tire life and provide maximum stability and ride comfort. Keep in mind that low tire pressures may cause the tire to slip on the rim or come off, while high tire pressures will cause abnormal tread wear and unsafe handling.

Cast wheels

5   The cast wheels used on some models are virtually maintenance free, but they should be kept clean and checked periodically for cracks and other damage. Never attempt to repair damaged cast wheels; they must be replaced with new ones.

6   Check the valve stem locknuts to make sure they are tight. Also, make sure the valve stem cap is in place and tight. If it is missing, install a new one made of metal or hard plastic.

Wire wheels

Refer to illustration 8.7

7   The wire wheels used on some models should be checked periodically for cracks, bending, loose spokes and corrosion. Never attempt to repair damaged wheels; they must be replaced with new ones. Loose spokes can be tightened with a spoke wrench **(see illustration)**, but be careful not to overtighten and distort the wheel rim.

9   Lubrication - general

Refer to illustrations 9.3a, 9.3b and 9.3c

1   Since the controls, cables and various other components of a motorcycle are exposed to the elements, they should be lubricated periodically to ensure safe and trouble-free operation.

2   The footpegs, clutch and brake lever, brake pedal, shift lever and side and centerstand (if equipped) pivots should be lubricated frequently. In order for the lubricant to be applied where it will do the most good,

the component should be disassembled. However, if chain and cable lubricant is being used, it can be applied to the pivot joint gaps and will usually work its way into the areas where friction occurs. If motor oil or light grease is being used, apply it sparingly as it may attract dirt (which could cause the controls to bind or wear at an accelerated rate). **Note:** *One of the best lubricants for the control lever pivots is a dry-film lubricant (available from many sources by different names).*

3   The clutch cable should be separated from the handlebar lever and bracket before it is lubricated **(see illustration)**. This is a convenient time to inspect the Teflon bushing at the end of the cable. The cable should be treated with motor oil or a commercially available cable lubricant which is specially formulated for use on motorcycle control cables. Small adapters for pressure lubricating the cables with spray can lubricants are available and ensure that the cable is lubricated along its entire length **(see illustration)**. If motor oil is being used, tape a funnel-shaped piece of heavy paper or plastic to the end of the cable, then pour oil into the funnel and suspend the end of the cable upright **(see illustration)**. Leave it until the oil runs down into the cable and out the other end. When attaching the cable to the lever, be sure to lubricate the barrel-shaped fitting at the end with high-temperature grease. **Note:** *While you're lubricating, check the barrel end of the cable for fraying. Replace frayed cables.*

4   To lubricate the throttle cables (and choke cable on Vulcan 700/750 models), disconnect the cable(s) at the lower end, then lubricate the cable with a pressure lube adapter **(see illustration 9.3b)**. See Chapter 4 for the choke cable removal procedure.

5   The speedometer cable should be removed from its housing and lubricated with motor oil or cable lubricant.

6   Refer to Chapter 6 for the swingarm needle bearing lubrication procedure.

1

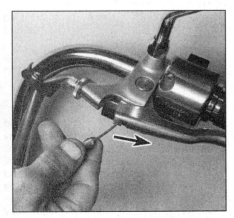

9.3a Line up the slots in the bracket, locknut and adjuster, then rotate the cable in the direction of the arrow, slide it through the slots and lower it out of the lever

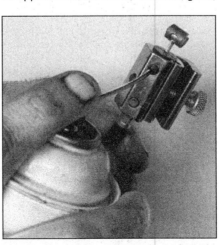

9.3b Lubricating a cable with a pressure lube adapter (make sure the tool seats around the inner cable)

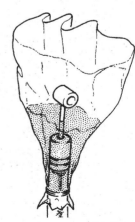

9.3c Lubricating a control cable with a makeshift funnel and motor oil

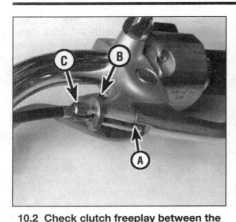

10.2 Check clutch freeplay between the lever and bracket

   A   Check freeplay here
   B   Locknut
   C   Adjuster

10 Clutch - check and adjustment

Refer to illustration 10.2

1   Correct clutch freeplay is necessary to ensure proper clutch operation and reasonable clutch service life. Freeplay normally changes because of cable stretch and clutch wear, so it should be checked and adjusted periodically.

2   Clutch cable freeplay is checked at the lever on the handlebar. Slowly pull in on the lever until resistance is felt, then note how far the lever has moved away from its bracket at the pivot end **(see illustration)**. Compare this distance with the value listed in this Chapter's Specifications. Too little freeplay may result in the clutch not engaging completely. If there is too much freeplay, the clutch might not release fully.

Vulcan 700/750 models

Refer to illustrations 10.3 and 10.4

3   Loosen the mid-line cable adjuster as far as possible, so there is slack in the clutch cable **(see illustration)**.

4   Turn the release lever by hand until the clutch starts to disengage. At this point, the lever will become hard to turn. The gap in the release lever should align with the cast rib on the front bevel gear case **(see illustration)**. If it doesn't, remove the release lever pinch bolt, take off the lever and reinstall it on the shaft in the correct position (with the gap and rib aligned, and the cable at an angle of 70 to 80-degrees to the lever), then install and tighten the pinch bolt.

5   Adjust freeplay at the clutch lever by loosening the locknut and turning the adjuster until the desired freeplay is obtained **(see illustration 10.2)**. Always retighten the locknut once the adjustment is complete.

6   Once the release lever alignment and clutch lever freeplay have been correctly adjusted (Steps 4 and 5), use the mid-line adjuster to take up all slack in the cable **(see illustration 10.3)**.

10.3 Loosen the locknut (lower arrow) and turn the midline cable adjuster (upper arrow) to create slack in the cable (Vulcan 750 models)

10.9 Loosen the clutch cable locknuts (arrows) completely, then make the adjustment at the handlebar (Vulcan 800 models)

Vulcan 800 models

Refer to illustration 10.9

7   If freeplay at the lever is incorrect, adjust it by loosening the locknut and turning the adjuster until the desired freeplay is obtained **(see illustration 10.2)**. Always retighten the locknut once the adjustment is complete.

8   If you can't obtain the correct adjustment with the adjuster at the handlebar, remove the front muffler for access to the lower cable adjuster (see Chapter 4).

9   Slide the rubber cover back from the lower cable adjuster. Loosen the adjusting nuts at the lower end of the cable completely **(see illustration)**.

10   Loosen the knurled locknut at the clutch handlebar lever and turn the adjuster in or out to expose approximately 5 or 6 mm of threads between the adjuster and the locknut.

11   Pull the clutch cable tight to remove all slack, then tighten the adjusting nuts against the bracket at the lower end of the cable.

12   Turn the adjuster at the clutch lever until the correct freeplay is obtained, then tighten

10.4 The release lever gap (lower arrow) should align with the cast rib (upper arrow) just as the clutch starts to disengage (Vulcan 750 models)

the locknut.

13   If the proper amount of freeplay still can't be obtained, the cable must be replaced (see Chapter 2).

11 Steering head bearings - check and adjustment

1   These motorcycles are equipped with tapered roller steering head bearings which can become dented, rough or loose during normal use of the machine. In extreme cases, worn or loose steering head bearings can cause steering wobble that is potentially dangerous.

Check

2   To check the bearings, place the motorcycle on the centerstand (if equipped). If not, prop it securely upright. Block the machine so the front wheel is raised off the ground.

3   Point the wheel straight ahead and slowly move the handlebars from side-to-side. Dents or roughness in the bearing races will be felt and the bars will not move smoothly.

4   Next, grasp the fork legs and try to move the wheel forward and backward. Any looseness in the steering head bearings will be felt. If play is felt in the bearings, adjust the steering head as follows:

Adjustment

Refer to illustrations 11.6, 11.7 and 11.8

5   Remove the fuel tank (see Chapter 4). If you're working on a Vulcan 700/750 model, remove the handlebar (see Chapter 6).

6   Loosen the fork lower pinch bolts **(see illustration)**. This allows the necessary vertical movement of the steering stem in relation to the fork tubes.

7   Loosen (DO NOT remove) the steering stem bolt **(see illustration)**.

8   Use a spanner wrench (C-spanner) to adjust the steering stem locknuts as a pair

11.6 Loosen the lower pinch bolt on each fork (arrow)

11.7 Loosen the steering stem bolt (arrow) but don't remove it or the stem will slip down

11.8 Use a spanner wrench like this one to loosen or tighten the steering stem locknut (upper triple clamp removed for clarity)

(see illustration).

9   If play is excessive, tighten the steering by turning the upper locknut clockwise until the steering head is tight but does not bind when the forks are turned from side-to-side. If the steering is too tight, turn the lower locknut to loosen it. In each case, keep both locknuts together.

10   Retighten the steering stem bolt and the fork pinch bolts, in that order, to the torque values listed in the Chapter 6 Specifications.

11   Recheck the steering head bearings for play as described above. If necessary, repeat the adjustment procedure. Reinstall all parts previously removed.

12   Refer to Chapter 6 for steering head bearing lubrication and replacement procedures.

12   Battery electrolyte level/specific gravity - check

Refer to illustrations 12.2a, 12.2b and 12.6
Warning: *Be extremely careful when han-*

dling or working around the battery. The electrolyte is very caustic and an explosive gas (hydrogen) is given off when the battery is charging.
Note 1: *Parts of this procedure apply to fillable batteries, installed as original equipment on Vulcan 700/750 models. The maintenance-free batteries used on Vulcan 800 models do not require periodic checks of the electrolyte level.*
Note 2: *The first Steps describe battery removal. If the electrolyte level is known to be sufficient it won't be necessary to remove the battery.*

1   Remove the seat (see Chapter 8).

2   Unbolt and move aside any electrical components mounted near the battery that obstruct battery removal, then unbolt the battery retainer and lift it off **(see illustrations)**. Note the position of the carburetor vent tube and battery vent tube.

3   Remove the bolts securing the battery cables to the battery terminals (remove the negative cable first, positive cable last) **(see illustration 12.2a or 12.2b)**. Pull the battery

straight up to remove it. The electrolyte level will now be visible through the translucent battery case - it should be between the Upper and Lower level marks.

4   If it is low, remove the cell caps and fill each cell to the upper level mark with distilled water. Do not use tap water (except in an emergency), and do not overfill. The cell holes are quite small, so it may help to use a plastic squeeze bottle with a small spout to add the water. If the level is within the marks on the case, additional water is not necessary.

5   Next, check the specific gravity of the electrolyte in each cell with a small hydrometer made especially for motorcycle batteries. These are available from most dealer parts departments or motorcycle accessory stores.

6   Remove the caps, draw some electrolyte from the first cell into the hydrometer **(see illustration)** and note the specific gravity. Compare the reading to the Specifications listed in this Chapter. **Note:** *Add 0.004*

12.2a On Vulcan 750 models, remove the battery retainer screw, pivot the retainer rearward off the battery, disconnect the negative cable and then the positive cable

12.2b On Vulcan 800 models, remove two or three retainer screws, depending on model (arrows), lift the retainer off, disconnect the negative cable and then the positive cable

12.6 On Vulcan 750 models, check the specific gravity with a hydrometer

1

13.2a On Vulcan 750 models, disconnect the plug wires from the front and rear cylinders (arrows), then do the same thing on the other side of the engine (there are two plugs per cylinder)

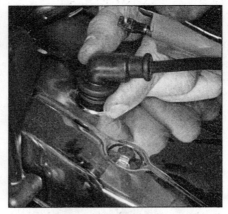

13.2b On Vulcan 800 models, work the single plug boot loose from each cylinder

13.2c Unscrew the plug with the correct size spark plug socket and an extension where necessary

points to the reading for every 10-degrees F above 68-degrees F (20-degrees C) - subtract 0.004 points from the reading for every 10-degrees below 68-degrees F (20-degrees C). Return the electrolyte to the appropriate cell and repeat the check for the remaining cells. When the check is complete, rinse the hydrometer thoroughly with clean water.

7   If the specific gravity of the electrolyte in each cell is as specified, the battery is in good condition and is apparently being charged by the machine's charging system.

8   If the specific gravity is low, the battery is not fully charged. This may be due to corroded battery terminals, a dirty battery case, a malfunctioning charging system, or loose or corroded wiring connections. On the other hand, it may be that the battery is worn out, especially if the machine is old, or that infrequent use of the motorcycle prevents normal charging from taking place.

9   Be sure to correct any problems and charge the battery if necessary. Refer to Chapter 9 for additional battery maintenance

and charging procedures.

10   Install the battery cell caps, tightening them securely. Reconnect the cables to the battery, attaching the positive cable first and the negative cable last. Make sure to install the plastic cap over the positive terminal. Be very careful not to pinch or otherwise restrict the battery vent tube (fillable batteries), as the battery may build up enough internal pressure during normal charging system operation to explode.

13 Spark plugs - replacement

Refer to illustrations 13.2a, 13.2b, 13.2c, 13.6a, 13.6b and 13.7

1   This motorcycle is equipped with spark plugs that have 12 mm threads and an 18 mm wrench hex. Make sure your spark plug socket is the correct size before attempting to remove the plugs.

2   Disconnect the spark plug caps from the spark plugs **(see illustrations)**. If available, use compressed air to blow any accumulated debris from around the spark plugs. Remove the plugs **(see illustration)**.

3   Inspect the electrodes for wear. Both the center and side electrodes should have square edges and the side electrode should be of uniform thickness. Look for excessive deposits and evidence of a cracked or chipped insulator around the center electrode. Compare your spark plugs to the color spark plug reading chart. Check the threads, the washer and the ceramic insulator body for cracks and other damage.

4   If the electrodes are not excessively worn, and if the deposits can be easily removed with a wire brush, the plugs can be regapped and reused (if no cracks or chips are visible in the insulator). If in doubt concerning the condition of the plugs, replace them with new ones, as the expense is minimal.

5   Cleaning spark plugs by sandblasting is permitted, provided you clean the plugs with a high flash-point solvent afterwards.

6   Before installing new plugs, make sure they are the correct type and heat range. Check the gap between the electrodes, as they are not preset. For best results, use a wire-type gauge rather than a flat gauge to check the gap **(see illustration)**. If the gap must be adjusted, bend the side electrode only and be very careful not to chip or crack

13.6a Spark plug manufacturers recommend using a wire type gauge when checking the gap - if the wire doesn't slide between the electrodes with a slight drag, adjustment is required

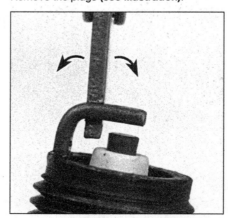

13.6b To change the gap, bend the side electrode only, as indicated by the arrows, and be very careful not to crack or chip the ceramic insulator surrounding the center electrode

13.7 A length of rubber hose will save time and prevent damaged threads when installing the spark plugs

14.2 On Vulcan 750 models, remove the bolts (arrows) and take off the air suction valve cover

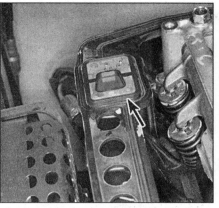

14.3a On Vulcan 800 models, remove the valve covers for access to the air suction valves (arrow)

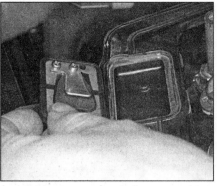

14.3b Lift the valve out of the cylinder head for inspection

the insulator nose (see illustration). Make sure the washer is in place before installing each plug.

7   Since the cylinder heads are made of aluminum, which is soft and easily damaged, thread the plugs into the heads by hand. Since the plugs are quite recessed, slip a short length of hose over the end of the plug to use as a tool to thread it into place (see illustration). The hose will grip the plug well enough to turn it, but will start to slip if the plug begins to cross-thread in the hole - this will prevent damaged threads and the accompanying repair costs.

8   Once the plugs are finger tight, the job can be finished with a socket. If a torque wrench is available, tighten the spark plugs to the torque listed in this Chapter's Specifications. If you do not have a torque wrench, tighten the plugs finger tight (until the washers bottom on the cylinder head) then use a wrench to tighten them an additional 1/4 turn. Regardless of the method used, do not over-tighten them.

9   Reconnect the spark plug caps.

14 Air suction valves - check

Refer to illustrations 14.2, 14.3a and 14.3b

1   The air suction valves, installed on US and Swiss models only, are one-way check valves that allow fresh air to flow into the exhaust ports. The suction developed by the exhaust pulses pulls the air from the air filter, through a hose to the air switching valve, through a pair of hoses and a pair of reed valves, and finally into the exhaust ports. The introduction of fresh air helps ignite any fuel that may not have been burned by the normal combustion process.

2   If you're working on a Vulcan 700/750 model, disconnect the hoses from the air suction valves (one on each cylinder) (see illustration). Remove the bolts and lift off the covers.

3   If you're working on a Vulcan 800 model, remove the valve covers (see Chapter 2). Note how each air suction valve is

installed in its seat, then lift it out (see illustrations).

4   Check the valves for cracks, warping, burning or other damage. Check the area where the reeds contact the valve holder for scratches, separation and grooves. If any of these conditions are found, replace the valve.

5   Wash the valves with solvent if carbon has accumulated between the reed and the valve holder.

6   Installation of the valves is the reverse of removal. Be sure to use a new gasket.

15 Evaporative emission control system (California models only) - check

1   This system, installed on California models to conform to stringent emission control standards, routes fuel vapors from the fuel system into the engine to be burned, instead of letting them evaporate into the atmosphere. When the engine isn't running, vapors are stored in a carbon canister.

Hoses

2   To begin the inspection of the system, remove the seat, fuel tank and side covers (see Chapters 4 and 8 if necessary). Inspect the hoses from the fuel tank, carburetors and liquid/vapor separator to the canister for cracking, kinks or other signs of deterioration.

Component inspection

3   Label and disconnect the hoses, then remove the separator and canister from the machine (see Chapter 4).

4   Check the separator closely for cracks or other signs of damage. If these are found, replace it.

5   Inspect the canister for cracks or other signs of damage. Tip the canister so the nozzles point down. If fuel runs out of the canister, the liquid/vapor separator is probably bad. The fuel inside the canister has probably caused damage, so it would be a good idea to replace it also.

16 Throttle and choke operation/grip freeplay - check and adjustment

Throttle check

1   With the engine stopped, make sure the throttle grip rotates easily from fully closed to fully open with the front wheel turned at various angles. The grip should return automatically from fully open to fully closed when released. If the throttle sticks, check the throttle cables for cracks or kinks in the housings. Also, make sure the inner cables are clean and well-lubricated.

2   Check for a small amount of freeplay at the grip and compare the freeplay to the value listed in this Chapter's Specifications.

Throttle adjustment

Refer to illustrations 16.3, 16.5a and 16.5b

Note: *These motorcycles use two throttle cables - an accelerator cable and a decelerator cable.*

3   Freeplay adjustments can be made at the throttle end of the cable. Loosen the locknut on the cable where it leaves the handlebar (see illustration). Turn the adjuster until the desired freeplay is obtained, then

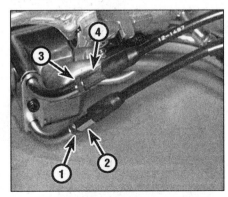

16.3 Throttle cable adjuster details

1   *Decelerator cable locknut*
2   *Decelerator cable adjusting nut*
3   *Accelerator cable locknut*
4   *Accelerator cable adjusting nut*

1

16.5a On Vulcan 750 models, loosen the locknuts (arrows) to create slack in both throttle cables at the carburetors

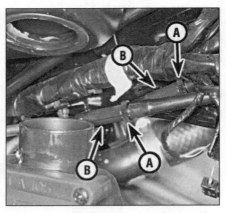

16.5b On Vulcan 800 models, loosen the locknuts (A) and turn the adjusters (B) to create slack in both throttle cables at the midline cable adjusters

16.10 On Vulcan 750 models, check freeplay at the choke lever . . .

retighten the locknut.

4   If the cables can't be adjusted at the grip end, adjust them at the lower ends (Vulcan 700/750) or at the mid-cable adjusters (Vulcan 800). To do this, first remove the fuel tank (see Chapter 4).

5   Loosen the locknuts on both throttle cables **(see illustrations)**, then turn both adjusting nuts in completely. This will create a large amount of freeplay at the throttle grip.

6   Make sure the throttle grip is in the fully closed position.

7   Turn out the adjusting nut of the decelerator cable until the inner cable just becomes tight, then tighten the locknut.

8   Turn the accelerator cable adjusting nut until the desired freeplay is obtained at the throttle grip, then tighten the locknut.

9   Make sure the throttle linkage lever contacts the idle adjusting screw when the throttle grip is in the closed throttle position.

Warning: *Turn the handlebars all the way through their travel with the engine idling. Idle speed should not change. If it does, the cables may be routed incorrectly. Correct this condition before riding the bike.*

Choke check

Vulcan 700/750 models

Refer to illustrations 16.10 and 16.11

10   Check the freeplay at the choke lever **(see illustration)**. Compare with the value listed in this Chapter's Specifications.

11   If freeplay is incorrect, loosen the locknut on the cable adjuster **(see illustration)**. Turn the adjusting nut to set freeplay, then tighten the locknut.

Vulcan 800 models

Refer to illustration 16.12

12   Inspect the choke knob and cable **(see illustration)**. The choke should pull out easily and stay out by itself. If it doesn't, adjust the knob's tension with the plastic nut behind the knob. If this doesn't help, check the plunger bushing for wear or damage and replace as necessary.

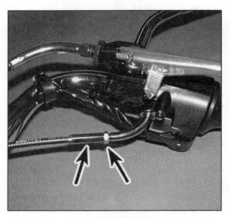

16.11 . . . and if necessary, loosen the locknut (right) and turn the adjuster (left) to change it

17   Idle speed - check and adjustment

Refer to illustrations 17.3a and 17.3b

1   The idle speed should be checked and adjusted at the specified maintenance intervals and when it is obviously too high or too low. On Vulcan 700/750 models, the carbu-

17.3a The Vulcan 750 idle speed knob is mounted on the carburetors (arrow)

16.12 Tension of the Vulcan 800 choke knob is adjusted with this nut (arrow)

retors should be synchronized as described in Section 18 as part of the procedure. Before adjusting the idle speed, make sure the valve clearances and spark plug gaps are correct. Also, turn the handlebars back-and-forth and see if the idle speed changes as this is done. If it does, the accelerator cable may not be adjusted correctly, or it may be worn out. Be sure to correct this problem before proceeding.

17.3b The Vulcan 800 idle speed knob is at the end of this stalk

18.12 Synchronize Vulcan 750 carburetors by turning the hex-headed screw beneath the carbs (arrow)

2   The engine should be at normal operating temperature, which is usually reached after 10 to 15 minutes of stop and go riding. Place the motorcycle on the centerstand (if equipped). If not, prop it securely upright. Make sure the transmission is in Neutral.
3   Turn the adjusting knob **(see illustrations)**, until the idle speed listed in this Chapter's Specifications is obtained.
4   Snap the throttle open and shut a few times, then recheck the idle speed. If necessary, repeat the adjustment procedure.
5   If a smooth, steady idle can't be achieved, the fuel/air mixture may be incorrect. Refer to Chapter 4 for additional carburetor information.

18   Carburetor synchronization (Vulcan 700/750 models) - check and adjustment

Refer to illustration 18.12
Warning: *Gasoline is extremely flammable, so take extra precautions when you work on any part of the fuel system. Don't smoke or allow open flames or bare light bulbs near the work area, and don't work in a garage where*

a natural gas-type appliance (such as a water heater or clothes dryer) is present. If you spill any fuel on your skin, rinse it off immediately with soap and water. When you perform any kind of work on the fuel system, wear safety glasses and have a fire extinguisher suitable for a class B type fire (flammable liquids) on hand.
1   Carburetor synchronization is simply the process of adjusting the carburetors so they pass the same amount of fuel/air mixture to each cylinder. This is done by measuring the vacuum produced in each cylinder. Carburetors that are out of synchronization will result in decreased fuel mileage, increased engine temperature, less than ideal throttle response and higher vibration levels.
2   To properly synchronize the carburetors, you will need some sort of vacuum gauge setup, preferably with a gauge for each cylinder, or a mercury manometer, which is a calibrated tube arrangement that utilizes columns of mercury to indicate engine vacuum.
3   A manometer can be purchased from a motorcycle dealer or accessory shop and should have the necessary rubber hoses supplied with it for hooking into the vacuum hose fittings on the carburetors.
4   A vacuum gauge setup can also be purchased from a dealer or fabricated from commonly available hardware and automotive vacuum gauges.
5   The manometer is the more reliable and accurate instrument, and for that reason is preferred over the vacuum gauge setup; however, since the mercury used in the manometer is a liquid, and extremely toxic, extra precautions must be taken during use and storage of the instrument.
6   Because of the nature of the synchronization procedure and the need for special instruments, most owners leave the task to a dealer service department or a reputable motorcycle repair shop.
7   Start the engine and let it run until it reaches normal operating temperature, then shut it off.
8   Detach the vacuum hoses from the fittings on the carburetors.

9   Hook up the vacuum gauge set or the manometer according to the manufacturer's instructions. Make sure there are no leaks in the setup, as false readings will result.
10   Start the engine and make sure the idle speed is correct.
11   The vacuum readings for both of the cylinders should be the same, or at least within the tolerance listed in this Chapter's Specifications. If the vacuum readings vary, adjust as necessary.
12   To perform the adjustment, synchronize the carburetors by turning the butterfly valve adjusting bolt as needed, using a 7mm wrench, until the vacuum is identical or nearly identical for both cylinders **(see illustration)**. Turn the bolt inward to increase vacuum at the rear carburetor; turn it outward to decrease vacuum at the rear carburetor.
13   When the adjustment is complete, recheck the vacuum readings and idle speed, then stop the engine. Remove the vacuum gauge or manometer and attach the hoses to the fittings on the carburetors.

19   Valve clearances (Vulcan 800 models) - check and adjustment

Refer to illustrations 19.5, 19.6a, 19.6b, 19.6c, 19.8, 19.14, 19.16a and 19.16b
1   The engine must be completely cool for this maintenance procedure, so let the machine sit overnight before beginning.
2   Disconnect the cable from the negative terminal of the battery.
3   Refer to Chapter 4 and remove the fuel tank.
4   Remove the valve covers (see Chapter 2).
5   Remove the cover from the crankshaft rotation bolt and timing window **(see illustration)**.
6   Position the front cylinder's piston at Top Dead Center (TDC) on the compression stroke. Do this by turning the crankshaft, with a socket placed on the crankshaft bolt,

1

19.5 Remove the screw and take the cover off the crankshaft bolt hole and timing window

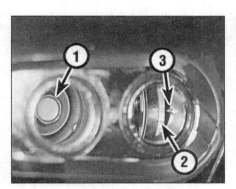

19.6a Crankshaft bolt and timing marks

1   Crankshaft bolt
2   Timing marks (on edge of flywheel)
3   Timing pointer

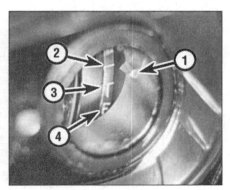

19.6b Timing mark details

1   Timing pointer
2   Top Dead Center mark
3   Letter T (indicating Top Dead Center)
4   Cylinder letter (F for front; R for rear)

19.6c The line on the camshaft sprocket should be parallel with the valve cover mating surface on the cylinder head

19.8 Measure clearance between each valve and its adjusting shim with a feeler gauge

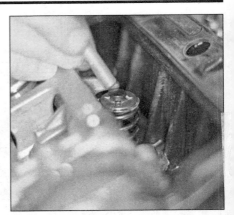

19.14 Slide the rocker arm aside and lift out the shim with a magnet

until the line next to the TF mark on the rotor is aligned with the timing mark in the timing window **(see illustrations)**. Now, check the position of the no. 1 cylinder cam sprocket - its line should be parallel to the valve cover mating surface **(see illustration)**. Piston no. 1 is now at TDC compression. **Note:** *If the cam sprocket line is not visible, the no. 1 cylinder is at TDC on its exhaust stroke. Rotate the crankshaft one full turn, so the line next to the T mark aligns with the timing pointer again*

7   With the engine in this position, all of the valves for cylinder no. 1 can be checked.

8   Start with the clearance on one of the intake valves. Insert a feeler gauge of the thickness listed in this Chapter's Specifications between each rocker arm and shim **(see illustration)**. Pull the feeler gauge out slowly - you should feel a slight drag. If there's no drag, the clearance is too loose. If there's a heavy drag, the clearance is too tight.

9   If the clearance is incorrect, write it down.

10   Repeat the clearance measurement for the other valves on the front cylinder, writing the measurements down.

11   Position the rear cylinder's piston at TDC compression. To do this, rotate the crankshaft 305-degrees counterclockwise (viewed from the left side of the bike) to align the line next to the TR mark on the rotor with the timing mark on the crankcase **(see illustration 19.5b)**. The line on the rear cylinder's cam sprocket should be parallel to the valve cover gasket mating surface **(see illustration 19.6b)**.

12   Repeat Steps 8 through 10 to measure the clearances of the rear cylinder's valves and write them down.

13   Compare the clearances to the values listed in this Chapter's Specifications. If any of the clearances need to be adjusted, go to Step 14. If all the clearances are within the specified range, go to Step 19.

14   Slide the rocker arm for the valve to be adjusted along the shaft to expose the valve adjusting shim. Pull the shim out with a mag-

EXHAUST VALVE

PART No. (92025 -)	1870	1871	1872	1873	1874	1875	1876	1877	1878	1879	1880	1881	1882	1883	1884	1885	1886	1887	1888	1889	1890
MARK	0	5	10	15	20	25	30	35	40	45	50	55	60	65	70	75	80	85	90	95	00
THICKNESS (mm)	2.00	2.05	2.10	2.15	2.20	2.25	2.30	2.35	2.40	2.45	2.50	2.55	2.60	2.65	2.70	2.75	2.80	2.85	2.90	2.95	3.00

PRESENT SHIM — Example

VALVE CLEARANCE MEASUREMENT

0.00 ~ 0.04	1.75	1.80	1.85	1.90	1.95	2.00	2.05	2.10	2.15	2.20	2.25	2.30	2.35	2.40	2.45	2.50	2.55	2.60	2.65	2.70	2.75
0.05 ~ 0.09	1.80	1.85	1.90	1.95	2.00	2.05	2.10	2.15	2.20	2.25	2.30	2.35	2.40	2.45	2.50	2.55	2.60	2.65	2.70	2.75	2.80
0.10 ~ 0.14	1.85	1.90	1.95	2.00	2.05	2.10	2.15	2.20	2.25	2.30	2.35	2.40	2.45	2.50	2.55	2.60	2.65	2.70	2.75	2.80	2.85
0.15 ~ 0.19	1.90	1.95	2.00	2.05	2.10	2.15	2.20	2.25	2.30	2.35	2.40	2.45	2.50	2.55	2.60	2.65	2.70	2.75	2.80	2.85	2.90
0.20 ~ 0.24	1.95	2.00	2.05	2.10	2.15	2.20	2.25	2.30	2.35	2.40	2.45	2.50	2.55	2.60	2.65	2.70	2.75	2.80	2.85	2.90	2.95
0.25 ~ 0.30	SPECIFIED CLEARANCE/NO CHANGE REQUIRED																				
0.31 ~ 0.35	2.05	2.10	2.15	2.20	2.25	2.30	2.35	2.40	2.45	2.50	2.55	2.60	2.65	2.70	2.75	2.80	2.85	2.90	2.95	3.00	
0.36 ~ 0.40	2.10	2.15	2.20	2.25	2.30	2.35	2.40	2.45	2.50	2.55	2.60	2.65	2.70	2.75	2.80	2.85	2.90	2.95	3.00		
0.41 ~ 0.45	2.15	2.20	2.25	2.30	2.35	2.40	2.45	2.50	2.55	2.60	2.65	2.70	2.75	2.80	2.85	2.90	2.95	3.00			
0.46 ~ 0.50	2.20	2.25	2.30	2.35	2.40	2.45	2.50	2.55	2.60	2.65	2.70	2.75	2.80	2.85	2.90	2.95	3.00				
0.51 ~ 0.55	2.25	2.30	2.35	2.40	2.45	2.50	2.55	2.60	2.65	2.70	2.75	2.80	2.85	2.90	2.95	3.00					
0.56 ~ 0.60	2.30	2.35	2.40	2.45	2.50	2.55	2.60	2.65	2.70	2.75	2.80	2.85	2.90	2.95	3.00						
0.61 ~ 0.65	2.35	2.40	2.45	2.50	2.55	2.60	2.65	2.70	2.75	2.80	2.85	2.90	2.95	3.00							
0.66 ~ 0.70	2.40	2.45	2.50	2.55	2.60	2.65	2.70	2.75	2.80	2.85	2.90	2.95	3.00								
0.71 ~ 0.75	2.45	2.50	2.55	2.60	2.65	2.70	2.75	2.80	2.85	2.90	2.95	3.00									
0.76 ~ 0.80	2.50	2.55	2.60	2.65	2.70	2.75	2.80	2.85	2.90	2.95	3.00										
0.81 ~ 0.85	2.55	2.60	2.65	2.70	2.75	2.80	2.85	2.90	2.95	3.00											
0.86 ~ 0.90	2.60	2.65	2.70	2.75	2.80	2.85	2.90	2.95	3.00												
0.91 ~ 0.95	2.65	2.70	2.75	2.80	2.85	2.90	2.95	3.00													
0.96 ~ 1.00	2.70	2.75	2.80	2.85	2.90	2.95	3.00														
1.01 ~ 1.05	2.75	2.80	2.85	2.90	2.95	3.00															
1.06 ~ 1.10	2.80	2.85	2.90	2.95	3.00																
1.11 ~ 1.15	2.85	2.90	2.95	3.00																	
1.16 ~ 1.20	2.90	2.95	3.00																		
1.21 ~ 1.25	2.95	3.00																			
1.26 ~ 1.30	3.00																				

Parts No.	Thickness
92180-1208	1.95 mm
92180-1209	1.90 mm
92180-1210	1.85 mm
92180-1211	1.80 mm
92180-1212	1.75 mm
92180-1213	1.70 mm

The shim from 1.70 to 1.95 mm thick are also available.

INSTALL THE SHIM OF THIS THICKNESS (mm)

19.16a Valve clearance adjustment chart - Vulcan 800 exhaust valves

INLET VALVE

PRESENT SHIM																				
PART No. (92025 -) 1870	1871	1872	1873	1874	1875	1876	1877	1878	1879	1880	1881	1882	1883	1884	1885	1886	1887	1888	1889	1890
MARK 0	5	10	15	20	25	30	35	40	45	50	55	60	65	70	75	80	85	90	95	00
THICKNESS (mm) 2.00	2.05	2.10	2.15	2.20	2.25	2.30	2.35	2.40	2.45	2.50	2.55	2.60	2.65	2.70	2.75	2.80	2.85	2.90	2.95	3.00

Example →

VALVE CLEARANCE MEASUREMENT

Measurement	Install the shim of this thickness (mm)
0.00 ~ 0.04	1.90 1.95 2.00 2.05 2.10 2.15 2.20 2.25 2.30 2.35 2.40 2.45 2.50 2.55 2.60 2.65 2.70 2.75 2.80 2.85 2.90
0.05 ~ 0.09	1.95 2.00 2.05 2.10 2.15 2.20 2.25 2.30 2.35 2.40 2.45 2.50 2.55 2.60 2.65 2.70 2.75 2.80 2.85 2.90 2.95
0.10 ~ 0.15	SPECIFIED CLEARANCE/NO CHANGE REQUIRED
0.16 ~ 0.20	2.05 2.10 2.15 2.20 2.25 2.30 2.35 2.40 2.45 2.50 2.55 2.60 2.65 2.70 2.75 2.80 2.85 2.90 2.95 3.00
0.21 ~ 0.25	2.10 2.15 2.20 2.25 2.30 2.35 2.40 2.45 2.50 2.55 2.60 2.65 2.70 2.75 2.80 2.85 2.90 2.95 3.00
0.26 ~ 0.30	2.15 2.20 2.25 2.30 2.35 2.40 2.45 2.50 2.55 2.60 2.65 2.70 2.75 2.80 2.85 2.90 2.95 3.00
0.31 ~ 0.35	2.20 2.25 2.30 2.35 2.40 2.45 2.50 2.55 2.60 2.65 2.70 2.75 2.80 2.85 2.90 2.95 3.00
0.36 ~ 0.40	2.25 2.30 2.35 2.40 2.45 2.50 2.55 2.60 2.65 2.70 2.75 2.80 2.85 2.90 2.95 3.00
0.41 ~ 0.45	2.30 2.35 2.40 2.45 2.50 2.55 2.60 2.65 2.70 2.75 2.80 2.85 2.90 2.95 3.00
0.46 ~ 0.50	2.35 2.40 2.45 2.50 2.55 2.60 2.65 2.70 2.75 2.80 2.85 2.90 2.95 3.00
0.51 ~ 0.55	2.40 2.45 2.50 2.55 2.60 2.65 2.70 2.75 2.80 2.85 2.90 2.95 3.00
0.56 ~ 0.60	2.45 2.50 2.55 2.60 2.65 2.70 2.75 2.80 2.85 2.90 2.95 3.00
0.61 ~ 0.65	2.50 2.55 2.60 2.65 2.70 2.75 2.80 2.85 2.90 2.95 3.00
0.66 ~ 0.70	2.55 2.60 2.65 2.70 2.75 2.80 2.85 2.90 2.95 3.00
0.71 ~ 0.75	2.60 2.65 2.70 2.75 2.80 2.85 2.90 2.95 3.00
0.76 ~ 0.80	2.65 2.70 2.75 2.80 2.85 2.90 2.95 3.00
0.81 ~ 0.85	2.70 2.75 2.80 2.85 2.90 2.95 3.00
0.86 ~ 0.90	2.75 2.80 2.85 2.90 2.95 3.00
0.91 ~ 0.95	2.80 2.85 2.90 2.95 3.00
0.96 ~ 1.00	2.85 2.90 2.95 3.00
1.01 ~ 1.05	2.90 2.95 3.00
1.06 ~ 1.10	2.95 3.00
1.11 ~ 1.15	3.00

Parts No.	Thickness
92180-1208	1.95 mm
92180-1209	1.90 mm
92180-1210	1.85 mm
92180-1211	1.80 mm
92180-1212	1.75 mm
92180-1213	1.70 mm

The shim from 1.70 to 1.95 mm thick are also available.

19.16b Valve clearance adjustment chart - Vulcan 800 intake valves

net (see illustration).

15   Determine the thickness of the shim you removed. It should be marked on the bottom of the shim, but the ideal way is to measure it with a micrometer.

16   If the clearance was too large, you need a thicker shim. If the clearance was too small, you need a thinner shim. Calculate the thickness of the replacement shim by referring to the accompanying charts (see illustrations). Caution: *Don't grind the shim thinner or it may crack while the engine is running. Don't place shim stock under a shim or it may pop out while the engine is running. Either of these will cause severe engine damage.*

17   Install the new shim and recheck the clearance. If it's within the Specifications, the valve is correctly adjusted.

18   Repeat Steps 14 through 17 to adjust any other valves that need it.

19   Once all of the valves are correctly adjusted, install the valve cover and all of the components that had to be removed to get it off. Install the cover over the crankshaft rotation bolt and timing window.

20   Air filter element - servicing

Vulcan 700/750 models

Refer to illustrations 20.1, 20.2a and 20.2b

1   Remove both air cleaner covers, one from each side of the bike (see illustration).

2   Remove the element mounting bolts and take out the filter element on one side of the bike (see illustrations).

3   Repeat Step 2 on the other side of the bike.

4   Wipe out the housing with a clean rag, then stuff a rag into each opening to keep out foreign material.

5   Check the element and its foam gasket for tears or other damage. Replace the element if it's damaged.

6   Clean the element with solvent. If compressed air is available, use it to clean the element by blowing from the inside out (from the mesh side toward the foam side). If the foam is extremely dirty or torn, replace the

1

20.1 On Vulcan 750 models, remove the screws (arrows) and take off the cover and O-ring

20.2a Remove the bolts (arrows) and take off the air cleaner element . . .

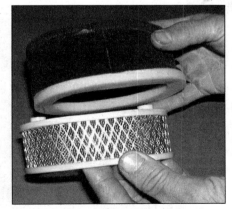

20.2b . . . and separate the element from the core

element with a new one.

7   Soak the element in clean SAE 30 engine oil. Squeeze as much oil as possible out of the element, then squeeze the element inside a clean rag to remove more oil.

Vulcan 800 models

Refer to illustrations 20.8a and 20.8b

8   Remove the cover nut and washer, lift off the air filter cover and remove the air filter element **(see illustrations)**.

9   Wipe out the housing with a clean rag, then place a clean rag in the carburetor opening to keep out dirt.

10 Tap the element on a hard surface to remove the dirt. Finish cleaning by blowing compressed air from the inside of the element to the outside.

All models

11   Reinstall the filter by reversing the removal procedure. Make sure the element is seated properly in the filter housing before installing the cover.

21   Exhaust system - check

1   Periodically check all of the exhaust system joints for leaks and loose fasteners. If tightening the clamp bolts fails to stop any leaks, replace the gaskets with new ones (a procedure which requires disassembly of the system).

2   The exhaust pipe flange nuts at the cylinder heads are especially prone to loosening, which could cause damage to the head. Check them frequently and keep them tight.

22   Fuel system - check and filter cleaning

Refer to illustrations 22.8 and 22.9

Warning: *Gasoline is extremely flammable, so take extra precautions when you work on any part of the fuel system. Don't smoke or allow open flames or bare light bulbs near the work area, and don't work in a garage where a natural gas-type appliance (such as a water heater or clothes dryer) is present. If you spill any fuel on your skin, rinse it off immediately with soap and water. When you perform any kind of work on the fuel system, wear safety glasses and have a fire extinguisher suitable for a class B type fire (flammable liquids) on hand.*

1   Check the fuel tank, the fuel tap, the lines and the carburetor(s) for leaks and evidence of damage.

2   If carburetor gaskets are leaking, the carburetor(s) should be disassembled and rebuilt by referring to Chapter 4.

3   If the fuel tap is leaking, tightening the screws may help. If leakage persists, the tap should be disassembled and repaired or replaced with a new one.

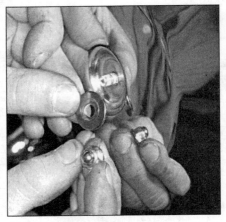

20.8a On Vulcan 800 models, remove the nut and washer . . .

22.8 Disconnect the hoses and remove the screws (arrows), then take the fuel tap out of the tank

4   If the fuel lines are cracked or otherwise deteriorated, replace them with new ones.

5   Check the vacuum hose connected to the fuel tap. If it is cracked or otherwise damaged, replace it with a new one.

6   The fuel filter, which is attached to the fuel tap, may become clogged and should be removed and cleaned periodically. In order to clean the filter, the fuel tank must be drained and the fuel tap removed.

7   Remove the fuel tank (see Chapter 4). Drain the fuel into an approved fuel container.

8   Once the tank is emptied, loosen and remove the screws that attach the fuel tap to the tank **(see illustration)**. Remove the tap and filter.

9   Clean the filter **(see illustration)** with solvent and blow it dry with compressed air. If the filter is torn or otherwise damaged, replace the entire fuel tap with a new one. Check the mounting flange O-ring and the gaskets on the screws. If they are damaged, replace them with new ones.

10   Install the O-ring, filter and fuel tap on the tank, then install the tank. Refill the tank and check carefully for leaks around the mounting flange and screws.

20.8b . . . then take off the cover and remove the element

22.9 Typical fuel tap and filter details

23   Fasteners - check

1   Since vibration of the machine tends to loosen fasteners, all nuts, bolts, screws, etc. should be periodically checked for proper tightness.

2   Pay particular attention to the following:

Spark plugs
Engine oil drain plug
Oil filter
Oil screen cover bolt
Gearshift lever
Footpegs and sidestand/centerstand
Engine mount bolts
Shock absorber mount bolts
Front axle and clamp bolt
Rear axle nut

3   If a torque wrench is available, use it along with the torque specifications at the beginning of this, or other, Chapters.

24   Suspension - check

Refer to illustration 24.3

1   The suspension components must be maintained in top operating condition to ensure rider safety. Loose, worn or damaged suspension parts decrease the vehicle's stability and control.

2   While standing alongside the motorcycle, lock the front brake and push on the handlebars to compress the forks several times. See if they move up-and-down

24.3 Check above and below the fork seals (arrows) for signs of oil leakage

25.4 Unscrew the drain plug (arrow) from the bottom of the crankcase

25.5a Unscrew the oil screen cap (arrow) . . .

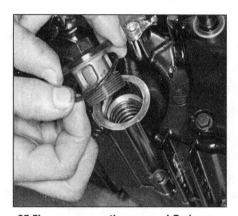

25.5b . . . remove the cap and O-ring . . .

25.5c . . . the spring and washer . . .

smoothly without binding. If binding is felt, the forks should be disassembled and inspected as described in Chapter 6.

3   Carefully inspect the area around the fork seals for any signs of fork oil leakage **(see illustration)**. If leakage is evident, the seals must be replaced as described in Chapter 6.

4   Check the tightness of all suspension nuts and bolts to be sure none have worked loose.

5   Inspect the rear shock absorber(s) for fluid leakage and tightness of the mounting nuts. If leakage is found, the shock(s) should be replaced. Replace both shocks as a pair on twin-shock models.

6   Set the bike on its centerstand (if equipped). If not, prop it securely upright. Grab the swingarm on each side, just ahead of the axle. Rock the swingarm from side to side - there should be no discernible movement at the rear. If there's a little movement or a slight clicking can be heard, make sure the pivot shaft nuts are tight. If the pivot nuts are tight but movement is still noticeable, the swingarm will have to be removed and the bearings replaced as described in Chapter 6.

25 Engine oil, filter and screen - change

Refer to illustrations 25.4, 25.5a, 25.5b, 25.5c, 25.5d and 25.6

1   Consistent routine oil and filter changes are the single most important maintenance procedure you can perform on a motorcycle. The oil not only lubricates the internal parts of the engine, transmission and clutch, but it also acts as a coolant, a cleaner, a sealant, and a protectant. Because of these demands, the oil takes a terrific amount of abuse and should be replaced often with new oil of the recommended grade and type. Saving a little money on the difference in cost between a good oil and a cheap oil won't pay off if the engine is damaged.

2   Before changing the oil and filter, warm

up the engine so the oil will drain easily. Be careful when draining the oil, as the exhaust pipes, the engine, and the oil itself can cause severe burns.

3   Prop the motorcycle upright over a clean drain pan. Remove the oil filler cap to vent the crankcase and act as a reminder that there is no oil in the engine.

4   Remove the drain plug from the bottom of the crankcase **(see illustration)** and allow the oil to drain into the pan. Discard the sealing washer on the drain plug; it should be

replaced whenever the plug is removed.

5   Unscrew the oil screen cap **(see illustration)**. Remove the cap and its O-ring, then pull the spring and oil screen out of the engine **(see illustrations)**. Clean the screen in solvent and inspect it for damage, then reinstall it in the engine. Install the washer, spring and cap, using a new O-ring if the old one is damaged.

6   As the oil is draining, remove the oil filter **(see illustration)**. If additional maintenance is planned for this time period, check

1

25.5d . . . and the screen; note carefully which end goes in first

25.6 Use an oil filter wrench like this one or a strap wrench to unscrew the filter

or service another component while the oil is allowed to drain completely.

7   Wipe any remaining oil off the filter sealing area of the crankcase.

8   Check the condition of the drain plug threads.

9   Coat the gasket on a new filter with clean engine oil. Install the filter and tighten it to the amount listed in this Chapter's Specifications.

10   Slip a new sealing washer over the drain plug, then install and tighten the plug. Tighten the drain plug to the torque listed in this Chapter's Specifications. Avoid overtightening, as damage to the engine case will result.

11   Before refilling the engine, check the old oil carefully. If the oil was drained into a clean pan, small pieces of metal or other material can be easily detected. If the oil is very metallic colored, then the engine is experiencing wear from break-in (new engine) or from insufficient lubrication. If there are flakes or chips of metal in the oil, then something is drastically wrong internally and the engine will have to be disassembled for inspection and repair.

12   If there are pieces of fiber-like material in the oil, the clutch is experiencing excessive wear and should be checked.

13   If the inspection of the oil turns up nothing unusual, refill the crankcase to the proper level with the recommended oil and install the filler cap. Start the engine and let it run for two or three minutes. Shut it off, wait a few minutes, then check the oil level. If necessary, add more oil to bring the level up to the Maximum mark. Check around the drain plug and filter housing for leaks.

14   The old oil drained from the engine cannot be reused in its present state and should be disposed of. Check with your local refuse disposal company, disposal facility or environmental agency to see whether they will accept the oil for recycling. Don't pour used oil into drains or onto the ground. After the oil has cooled, it can be drained into a suitable container (capped plastic jugs, topped bottles, milk cartons, etc.) for transport to one of these disposal sites.

26   Cooling system - check

Refer to illustrations 26.6 and 26.7

Warning: *The engine must be cool before beginning this procedure.*

Note: *Refer to Daily (preride) checks at the beginning of this manual and check the coolant level before performing this check.*

1   The entire cooling system should be checked carefully at the recommended intervals. Look for evidence of leaks, check the condition of the coolant, check the radiator for clogged fins and damage and make sure the fan operates when required.

2   Examine each of the rubber coolant hoses along its entire length. Look for cracks, abrasions and other damage. Squeeze each

26.6   DO NOT unscrew the cooling system pressure cap while the engine is hot!

hose at various points. They should feel firm, yet pliable, and return to their original shape when released. If they are dried out or hard, replace them with new ones.

3   Check for evidence of leaks at each cooling system joint. Tighten the hose clamps carefully to prevent future leaks.

4   Check the radiator for evidence of leaks and other damage. Leaks in the radiator leave telltale scale deposits or coolant stains on the outside of the core below the leak. If leaks are noted, remove the radiator (refer to Chapter 3) and have it repaired at a radiator shop or replace it with a new one. **Caution:** *Do not use a liquid leak stopping compound to try to repair leaks.*

5   Check the radiator fins for mud, dirt and insects, which may impede the flow of air through the radiator. If the fins are dirty, force water or low pressure compressed air through the fins from the backside. If the fins are bent or distorted, straighten them carefully with a screwdriver.

6   For access to the cooling system pressure cap on Vulcan 700/750 models, remove the fuel tank side covers (see Chapter 8). On Vulcan 800 models, remove the instrument cluster (see Chapter 9). Remove the pressure cap by turning it counterclockwise until it reaches a stop. If you hear a hissing sound (indicating there is still pressure in the system), wait until it stops. Now, press down on the cap with the palm of your hand and continue turning the cap counterclockwise until it can be removed **(see illustration)**. Check the condition of the coolant in the system. If it is rust colored or if accumulations of scale are visible, drain, flush and refill the system with new coolant. Check the cap gaskets for cracks and other damage. Have the cap tested by a dealer service department or replace it with a new one. Install the cap by turning it clockwise until it reaches the first stop, then push down on the cap and continue turning until it can turn no further.

7   Check the antifreeze content of the coolant with an antifreeze hydrometer **(see illustration)**. Sometimes coolant may look like it's in good condition, but might be too

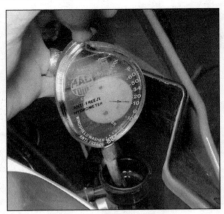

26.7   An antifreeze hydrometer is helpful in determining the condition of the coolant

weak to offer adequate protection. If the hydrometer indicates a weak mixture, drain, flush and refill the cooling system (see Section 27).

8   Start the engine and let it reach normal operating temperature, then check for leaks again. As the coolant temperature increases, the fan should come on automatically and the temperature should begin to drop. If it does not, refer to Chapter 3 and check the fan and fan circuit carefully.

9   If the coolant level is consistently low, and no evidence of leaks can be found, have the entire system pressure checked by a Kawasaki dealer service department, motorcycle repair shop or service station.

27   Cooling system - draining, flushing and refilling

Warning: *Allow the engine to cool completely before performing this maintenance operation. Also, don't allow antifreeze to come into contact with your skin or painted surfaces of the motorcycle. Rinse off spills immediately with plenty of water. Antifreeze is highly toxic if ingested. Never leave antifreeze lying around in an open container or in puddles on the floor; children and pets are attracted by its sweet smell and may drink it. Check with local authorities about disposing of used antifreeze. Many communities have collection centers which will see that antifreeze is disposed of safely. Antifreeze is also combustible, so don't store or use it near open flames.*

Draining

Refer to illustrations 27.2 and 27.3

1   Loosen the pressure cap **(see illustration 26.6).** Place a large, clean drain pan under the right side of the engine.

2   Remove the drain bolt from the bottom of the right crankcase half **(see illustration)** and allow the coolant to drain into the pan. **Note 1:** *The coolant will rush out with considerable force, so position the drain pan accord-*

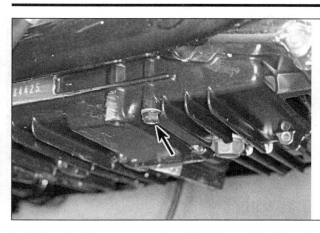

27.2 The coolant drain bolt is on the bottom of the crankcase (arrow)

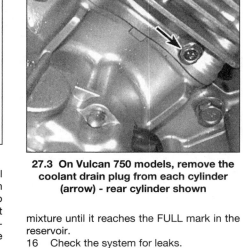

27.3 On Vulcan 750 models, remove the coolant drain plug from each cylinder (arrow) - rear cylinder shown

ingly. Remove the pressure cap completely to ensure that all of the coolant can drain.

Note 2: *Don't mistake the coolant drain plug for the engine oil drain plug, which is in the bottom center of the crankcase.*

3   If you're working on a Vulcan 700/750, remove the coolant drain plug from each cylinder **(see illustration)**.

4   Drain the coolant reservoir. Refer to Chapter 3 for the reservoir removal procedure. Wash the reservoir out with water.

Flushing

5   Flush the system with clean tap water by inserting a garden hose in the radiator filler neck. Allow the water to run through the system until it is clear when it exits the drain bolt hole. If the radiator is extremely corroded, remove it by referring to Chapter 3 and have it cleaned at a radiator shop.

6   Check the drain bolt gasket. Replace it with a new one if necessary.

7   Clean the hole, then install the drain bolt and tighten it to the torque listed in this Chapter's Specifications.

8   Fill the cooling system with clean water mixed with a flushing compound. Make sure the flushing compound is compatible with aluminum components, and follow the manufacturer's instructions carefully.

9   Start the engine and allow it to reach normal operating temperature. Let it run for

about ten minutes.

10   Stop the engine. Let the machine cool for a while, then cover the pressure cap with a heavy rag and turn it counterclockwise to the first stop, releasing any pressure that may be present in the system. Once the hissing stops, push down on the cap and remove it completely.

11   Drain the system once again.

12   Fill the system with clean water, then repeat Steps 8, 9 and 10.

Refilling

13   Fill the system with the proper coolant mixture (see this Chapter's Specifications). When the system is full (all the way up to the top of the radiator cap filler neck), install the cap and start the engine. Allow the engine to reach normal operating temperature, then shut it off.

14   Let the engine cool off for awhile, cover the radiator cap with a heavy rag and loosen it to the first stop to allow any pressure in the system to bleed off before the cap is removed completely. Recheck the coolant level in the radiator filler neck. If it's low, add more coolant until it reaches the top of the filler neck. Reinstall the cap.

15   Allow the engine to cool, then check the coolant level in the reservoir (see *Daily (pre-ride) checks* at the beginning of this manual. If the coolant level is low, add the specified

mixture until it reaches the FULL mark in the reservoir.

16   Check the system for leaks.

17   Do not dispose of the old coolant by pouring it down a drain. Instead, pour it into a heavy plastic container, cap it tightly and take it to an authorized disposal site or a service station.

28   Fork oil - replacement

Refer to illustrations 28.2, 28.3a and 28.3b

1   Place the motorcycle on the centerstand (if equipped). If not, prop it securely upright. Position a jack with a block of wood on the jack head under the engine to support the motorcycle when the fork caps are removed.

2   Pull off the fork cap **(see illustration)**. If you're working on a 1985 through 1988 Vulcan 700/750 model, bleed off the air pressure through the air valve at the top of the fork.

3   Push the top plug downward against spring pressure with a Phillips screwdriver or similar tool, remove the retaining ring and release the spring pressure **(see illustrations)**.

1

28.2 Pull off the fork cap

28.3a Push down on the fork cap plug and remove the retaining ring

28.3b Once the retaining ring is removed, release the spring pressure

28.5 Vulcan 750 models have a drain plug on each fork (arrow)

28.9 Use a funnel to pour oil into the fork

4   Lift out the cap plug with its O-ring and the spacer. Withdraw the spring seat and fork spring.

Vulcan 700/750 models

Refer to illustration 28.5

5   If you're working on a Vulcan 700/750 model, place a drain pan under the fork leg and remove the drain screw **(see illustration)**. **Warning:** *Do not allow the fork oil to contact the brake disc, pads or tire. If it does, clean the disc with brake system cleaner, wipe off the tire, and replace the pads with new ones before riding the motorcycle.*

6   After most of the oil has drained, slowly compress and release the forks to pump out the remaining oil. An assistant will most likely be required to do this procedure.

7   Check the drain screw gasket for damage and replace it if necessary. Clean the threads of the drain screw with solvent and let it dry, then install the screw and gasket, tightening it securely.

Vulcan 800 models

8   Remove the fork leg from the motorcycle (see Chapter 6). Invert it over a drain pan and pour out the oil, then reinstall the fork leg.

All models

Refer to illustrations 28.9 and 28.10

9   Pour the type and amount of fork oil, listed in this Chapter's Specifications, into the fork tube through the opening at the top **(see illustration)**. Remove the jack from under the engine and slowly pump the forks a few times to purge the air from the upper and lower chambers.

10   Fully compress the front forks (you may need an assistant to do this). Insert a stiff

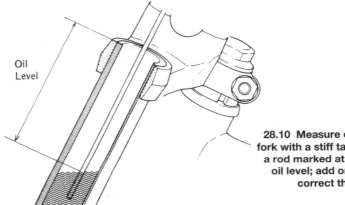

28.10 Measure oil level in the fork with a stiff tape measure or a rod marked at the specified oil level; add or drain oil to correct the level

tape measure or a marked rod into the fork tube and measure the distance from the oil to the top of the fork tube **(see illustration)**. Compare your measurement to the value listed in this Chapter's Specifications. Drain or add oil, as necessary, until the level is correct.

11   Check the O-ring on the cap plug, then coat it with a thin layer of multi-purpose grease. Install the fork spring, its seat and the spacer. **Note:** *Install the spring's small-diameter end downwards.* Install the cap plug, push it down against the spring pressure, install the retaining ring and release the cap plug.

12   Tighten the fork tube pinch bolts to the torque listed in the Chapter 6 Specifications.

13   Repeat the procedure on the other fork. Note that it is essential that the oil quantity and level is identical in each fork.

14   If you're working on a 1985 through 1988 Vulcan 700/750 model, adjust the air pressure in the front forks (see Chapter 6).

29   Final drive oil (Vulcan 700/750 models) - change

1   Ride the bike to warm the oil so it will drain completely, then prop it securely upright. **Warning:** *Be careful not to touch hot components (including the oil); they may be hot enough to cause burns.*

2   Remove the filler plug **(see illustration 4.6)**.

3   Remove the drain plug **(see illustration 4.6)**. and let the oil drain for 10 to 15 minutes.

4   Clean the drain plug, reinstall it and tighten the plug to the torque listed in this Chapter's Specifications.

5   Fill the final drive unit to the correct level with the type of oil listed in this Chapter's Specifications.

6   Install the filler plug and tighten it to the torque listed in this Chapter's Specifications.

Chapter 2
Engine, clutch and transmission

Contents

2

Specifications

General

Bore
- Vulcan 700 models ... 82.0 mm (3.228 inches)
- Vulcan 750 models ... 84.9 mm (3.342 inches)
- Vulcan 800 models ... 88.0 mm (3.464 inches)

Stroke (all models) ... 66.2 mm (2.606 inches)

Displacement
- Vulcan 700 models ... 699 cc
- Vulcan 750 models ... 749 cc
- Vulcan 800 models ... 805 cc

Compression ratio
- Vulcan 700/750 models ... 10.3 : 1
- Vulcan 800 models ... 9.5 : 1

Compression pressure
- Vulcan 700/750 models ... 890 to 1370 kPa (129 to 199 psi)
- Vulcan 800 models ... 855 to 1315 kPa (124 to 191 psi)

Camshaft and lifters (Vulcan 700/750 models)

Lobe height (intake)
    Standard... 33.450 to 33.558 mm (1.317 to 1.321 inch)
    Minimum... 33.350 mm (1.313 inch)
Lobe height (exhaust)
    Standard... 33.139 to 33.247 mm (1.304 to 1.309 inch)
    Minimum... 33.039 mm (1.300 inch)
Bearing inside diameter
    Standard... 27.000 to 27.021 mm (1.062 to 1.064 inch)
    Maximum.. 27.08 mm (1.066 inch)
Journal diameter
    Standard... 26.959 to 26.980 mm (1.061 to 1.062 inch)
    Minimum... 26.93 mm (1.060 inch)
Bearing clearance
    Standard... 0.020 to 0.062 mm (0.0008 to 0.0024 inch)
    Limit .... 0.15 mm (0.006 inch)
Camshaft runout .... Not specified
Camshaft chain 20-link length (upper and lower chains)
    Standard .... 127.0 to 127.4 mm (5.0 to 5.015 inches)
    Limit .... 128.9 mm (5.074 inches)
Lifter leakdown limit... 2.0 mm (0.087 inch)

Camshaft and rocker arms (Vulcan 800 models)

Lobe height (intake)
    Standard... 35.305 to 35.413 mm (1.389 to 1.394 inch)
    Minimum... 35.21 mm (1.386 inch)
Lobe height (exhaust)
    Standard... 35.033 to 35.141 mm (1.379 to 1.383 inch)
    Minimum... 34.93 mm (1.375 inch)
Bearing inside diameter
    Standard... 27.000 to 27.021 mm (1.062 to 1.064 inch)
    Maximum.. 27.08 mm (1.066 inch)
Journal diameter
    Standard... 26.959 to 26.980 mm (1.061 to 1.062 inch)
    Minimum... 26.93 mm (1.060 inch)
Bearing clearance
    Standard... 0.028 to 0.071 mm (0.001 to 0.003 inch)
    Limit .... 0.15 mm (0.006 inch)
Camshaft runout limit (total indicator reading) .... 0.1 mm (0.004 inch)
Camshaft chain 20-link length
    Standard... 127.0 to 127.4 mm (5.0 to 5.015 inches)
    Limit .... 128.9 mm (5.074 inches)
Rocker arm inside diameter
    Standard... 16.0 to 16.018 mm (0.630 to 0.631 inch)
    Maximum.. 16.05 mm (0.632 inch)
Rocker shaft diameter
    Standard... 15.965 to 15.984 mm (0.628 to 0.629 inch)
    Minimum... 15.94 mm (0.627 inch)

Cylinder head, valves and valve springs (Vulcan 700/750 models)

Cylinder head warpage limit .... 0.05 mm (0.002 inch)
Valve stem bend limit (total indicator reading) .... 0.05 mm (0.002 inch)
Valve stem diameter
    Standard
        Intake .... 5.475 to 5.490 mm (0.2155 to 0.216 inch)
        Exhaust .... 5.455 to 5.470 mm (0.2147 to 0.215 inch)
    Minimum
        Intake .... 5.46 mm (0.2149 inch)
        Exhaust .... 5.44 mm (0.2141 inch)
Valve head thickness
    Standard
        Intake .... 0.8 mm (0.031 inch)
        Exhaust .... 1.0 mm (0.039 inch)
    Minimum
        Intake .... 0.4 mm (0.015 inch)
        Exhaust .... 0.5 mm (0.020 inch)
Valve guide inside diameter (intake and exhaust)
    Standard... 5.50 to 5.512 mm (0.2165 to 0.2170 inch)
    Maximum.. 5.58 mm (0.2196 inch)

Valve seat width (intake and exhaust) .... 0.5 to 1.0 mm (0.020 to 0.040 in)
Valve spring free length
    Standard
        Inner .... 35.9 mm (1.413 inch)
        Outer .... 41.5 mm (1.634 inch)
    Minimum
        Inner .... 33.8 mm (1.331 inch)
        Outer .... 39.4 mm (1.552 inch)

Cylinder head, valves and valve springs (Vulcan 800 models)

Cylinder head warpage limit .... 0.05 mm (0.002 inch)
Valve stem bend limit (total indicator reading) .... 0.05 mm (0.002 inch)
Valve stem diameter
    Standard
        Intake .... 4.975 to 4.990 mm (0.1958 to 0.1956 inch)
        Exhaust .... 4.955 to 4.970 mm (0.1950 to 0.1956 inch)
    Minimum
        Intake .... 4.96 mm (0.1952 inch)
        Exhaust .... 4.94 mm (0.1944 inch)
Valve head thickness
    Standard
        Intake .... 0.5 mm (0.020 inch)
        Exhaust .... 0.8 mm (0.031 inch)
    Minimum
        Intake .... 0.3 mm (0.012 inch)
        Exhaust .... 0.8 mm (0.031 inch)
Valve guide inside diameter (intake and exhaust)
    Standard .... 5.0 to 5.012 mm (0.1968 to 0.1973 inch)
    Maximum .... 5.070 mm (0.1996 inch)
Valve seat width (intake and exhaust) .... 0.5 to 1.0 mm (0.020 to 0.040 in)
Valve spring free length
    Standard .... 40.5 mm (1.594 inch)
    Limit .... 38.6 mm (1.519 inch)

Cylinders

Bore diameter
    Vulcan 700 models
        Standard .... 82.000 to 82.012 mm (3.228 to 3.232 inches)
        Limit .... 82.1 mm (3.233 inches)
    Vulcan 750 models
        Standard .... 84.900 to 84.912 mm (0.350 to 3.342 inches)
        Limit .... 85.0 mm (3.346 inches)
    Vulcan 800 models
        Standard .... 88.000 to 88.012 mm (3.464 to 3.465 inches)
        Limit .... 88.11 mm (3.469 inches)
Taper limit .... 0.05 mm (0.002 inch)
Out-of-round limit .... 0.05 mm (0.002 inch)

Pistons

Piston diameter
    Vulcan 700 models
        Standard .... 81.942 to 81.957 mm (3.226 to 3.226 inches)
        Limit .... 81.8 mm (3.220 inches)
    Vulcan 750 models
        Standard .... 84.842 to 84.857 mm (3.222 to 3.341 inches)
        Limit .... 84.7 mm (3.334 inches)
    Vulcan 800 models
        Standard .... 87.975 to 87.990 mm (3.463 to 3.464 inches)
        Limit .... 87.83 mm (3.457 inches)
Piston-to-cylinder clearance
    Vulcan 700/750 models .... 0.043 to 0.070 mm (0.0016 to 0.0027 inch)
    Vulcan 800 models .... 0.010 to 0.037 mm (0.0004 to 0.0014 inch)
Oversize pistons and rings
    Vulcan 700/750 models .... +0.5 mm (0.020 inch) and +1.0 mm (0.039 inch)
    Vulcan 800 models .... + 0.5 mm (+0.020 inch) (one oversize only)
Ring side clearance
    Standard
        Top .... 0.03 to 0.07 mm (0.0017 to 0.0027 inch)
        Second .... 0.02 to 0.06 mm (0.0007 to 0.0023 inch)

Pistons (continued)

Ring side clearance
    Maximum
        Top.. 0.17 mm (0.0066 inch)
        Second... 0.16 mm (0.0062 inch)
Ring groove width
    Standard
        Top.. 0.102 to 0.104 mm (0.0040 to 0.0041 inch)
        Second... 1.01 to 1.03 mm (0.039 to 0.040 inch)
        Oil .... Not specified
    Maximum
        Top.. 1.12 mm (0.044 inch)
        Second... 1.11 mm (0.043 inch)
Ring thickness (top and second)
    Standard... 0.97 to 0.99 mm (0.038 to 0.039 inch)
    Minimum... 0.90 mm (0.035 inch)
Ring end gap
    Vulcan 700/750 models (top and second)
        Standard .... 0.25 to 0.45 mm (0.010 to 0.018 inch)
        Limit .... 0.75 mm (0.028 inch)
    Vulcan 800 models (top)
        Standard .... 0.25 to 0.40 mm (0.010 to 0.016 inch)
        Limit .... 0.7 mm (0.027 inch)
    Vulcan 800 models (second)
        Standard .... 0.40 to 0.55 mm (0.010 to 0.021 inch)
        Limit .... 0.9 mm (0.035 inch)

Crankshaft and bearings

Main bearing journal diameter
    Standard... 42.984 to 43.000 mm (1.692 to 1.693 inch)
    Limit .... 42.96 mm (1.691 inch)
Main bearing bore diameter
    Standard... 43.014 to 43.025 mm (1.693 to 1.694 inch)
    Limit .... 43.09 mm (1.696 inch)
Crankshaft runout limit .... 0.05 mm (0.002 inch)
Crankshaft side clearance
    Standard... 0.05 to 0.55 mm (0.002 to 0.021 inch)
    Limit .... 0.75 mm (0.029 inch)
Connecting rod side clearance
    Standard... 0.16 to 0.46 mm (0.007 to 0.018 inch)
    Maximum... 0.7 mm (0.027 inch)
Connecting rod bearing oil clearance
    Standard... 0.026 to 0.054 mm (0.001 to 0.002 inch)
    Maximum... 0.09 mm (0.003 inch)
Connecting rod big-end bore diameter
    No circle around rod weight mark.............................. 46.000 to 46.010 mm (1.8110 to 1.8114 inch)
    Circle around rod weight mark.................................. 46.011 to 46.020 mm (1.8114 to 1.8118 inch)
Connecting rod journal (crank pin) diameter
    No mark on crank throw.. 42.984 to 42.992 mm (1.6922 to 1.6925 inch)
    "1" mark on crank throw.. 42.993 to 43.000 mm (1.6926 to 1.6929 inch)
Connecting rod bend and twist limit .... 0.2 mm (0.008 inch) per 100 mm (3.94 inches)

Oil pump

Oil pump clearances (Vulcan 700/750 models)
    Outer rotor to body
        Standard .... 0.15 to 0.21 mm (0.006 to 0.009 inch)
        Wear limit .... 0.3 mm (0.012 inch)
    Inner rotor to outer rotor.. Less than 0.2 mm (0.008 inch)
    Rotor side clearance limit... 0.12 mm (0.005 inch)
Drive chain slack
    Standard... 8 to 10 mm (0.315 to 0.394 inch)
    Limit .... 13 mm (0.512 inch)

Clutch

Spring free length
    Vulcan 700/750 models
        Standard .... 33.0 to 34.2 mm (1.299 to 1.346 inch)
        Limit .... 32.6 mm (1.283 inch)

Vulcan 800 models
    Standard .... 34.2 mm (1.346 inch)
    Minimum .... 33.1 mm (1.303 inch)
Friction plate thickness
    Standard .... 2.9 to 3.1 mm (0.114 to 0.122 inch)
    Minimum .... 2.8 mm (0.110 inch)
Friction and steel plate warpage
    Standard .... 0.2 mm (0.008 inch) or less
    Limit .... 0.3 mm (0.012 inch)

Transmission

Shift fork groove width
    Standard .... 5.05 to 5.15 mm (0.199 to 0.202 inch)
    Maximum
        Vulcan 700/750 models .... 5.3 mm (0.208 inch)
        Vulcan 800 models .... 5.2 mm (0.205 inch)
Shift fork ear thickness
    Standard .... 4.9 to 5.0 mm (0.193 to 0.197 inch)
    Minimum .... 4.8 mm (0.189 inch)
Shift fork guide pin diameter
    Standard .... 5.9 to 6.0 mm (0.232 to 0.236 inch)
    Minimum .... 5.8 mm (0.228 inch)
Shift drum groove width
    Standard .... 6.05 to 6.20 mm (0.238 to 0.244 inch)
    Maximum .... 6.3 mm (0.248 inch)

Torque specifications

Engine mount through-bolt nuts .... 44 Nm (33 ft-lbs)
Right frame member bolts .... 44 Nm (33 ft-lbs)
Mount bracket to frame bolts
    Vulcan 700/750 models .... 24 Nm (17.5 ft-lbs)
    Vulcan 800 models .... 23 Nm (16.5 ft-lbs)
Valve cover bolts
    Vulcan 700/750 models .... 9.8 Nm (87 inch-lbs)
    Vulcan 800 models .... 12 Nm (104 inch-lbs)
Valve cover damper bolts (Vulcan 800 model) .... 12 Nm (104 inch-lbs)
Camshaft sprocket bolts (Vulcan 800 models) .... 49 Nm (36 ft-lbs)
Camshaft bearing cap bolts
    Vulcan 700/750 models .... 12 Nm (104 inch-lbs)
    Vulcan 800 models .... 25 Nm (18 ft-lbs)
Upper camshaft chain tensioner plug
    Vulcan 700/750 models .... 15 Nm (132 inch-lbs)
    Vulcan 800 models .... 20 Nm (174 inch-lbs)
Camshaft chain tensioner nuts and cap bolt (Vulcan 700/750 models) .. Not specified
Upper camshaft chain guide bolts (Vulcan 700/750 models) .... 24 Nm (17.5 ft-lbs)
Lower camshaft chain guide bolts (Vulcan 700/750 models) .... Not specified*
Camshaft chain guide bolts (Vulcan 800 models) .... 11 Nm (95 inch-lbs) (*)
Cylinder head bolts/nuts (Vulcan 700/750 models)
    Small nuts .... 15 Nm (132 inch-lbs)
    Large nuts .... 39 Nm (29 ft-lbs)
    Bolts .... 12 Nm (104 inch-lbs)
Cylinder head bolts/nuts (Vulcan 800 models)
    Small nuts .... 25 Nm (18 ft-lbs)
    Large nuts .... 39 Nm (29 ft-lbs)
    Bolt .... 12 Nm (104 inch-lbs)
Cylinder nuts .... 25 Nm (18 ft-lbs)
External oil line union bolts (Vulcan 700/750 models) .... 12 Nm (104 inch-lbs)
Oil line union bolt/oil pressure switch fitting .... 20 Nm (174 inch-lbs)
External shift linkage cover bolts .... 11 Nm (95 inch-lbs)
Primary drive gear bolt
    Vulcan 700/750 models .... 120 Nm (87 ft-lbs)
    Vulcan 800 models .... 155 Nm (115 ft-lbs)
Balancer bolts (left and right) .... 69 Nm (51 ft-lbs)*
Starter clutch bolts .... 34 Nm (25 ft-lbs)*
Crankcase bolts
    6 mm bolts .... 11 Nm (95 inch-lbs)
    10 mm bolts .... 39 Nm (29 ft-lbs)
Connecting rod nuts .... 46 Nm (34 ft-lbs)
Right crankcase cover (clutch cover) bolts .... 9.8 Nm (87 inch-lbs)

2

Torque specifications (continued)

Clutch spring bolts	8.8 Nm (78 inch-lbs)
Clutch center nut	130 Nm (98 ft-lbs)
Oil pump screws/bolts	11 Nm (95 inch-lbs)*
Oil pump chain guide bolt	12 Nm (104 inch-lbs)*
Oil pipe-to-crankcase bolts (left side external)...........................	5.4 Nm (48 inch-lbs)*
Oil pipe-to-crankcase bolts (internal)	11 Nm (95 inch-lbs)
Oil filter base plate bolts	7.8 Nm (69 inch-lbs)
Oil pressure relief valve..	15 Nm (11 ft-lbs)*
Oil passage screws (left side external)	5.4 Nm (48 inch-lbs) (*)
Shift pedal pivot bolt nut (Vulcan 800 models except Drifter)	29 Nm (22 ft-lbs)
Shift pedal pivot bolt (Vulcan 800 models except Drifter)	29 Nm (22 ft-lbs)
Linkage lever pinch bolt (Vulcan 800 models except Drifter)	12 Nm (104 inch-lbs)
Linkage lever pinch bolt (Vulcan 800 Drifter models)	12 Nm (104 inch-lbs)
Shift drum cam screw...	Not specified*
Shift drum bearing retainer screws...	11 Nm (95 inch-lbs)*
Return spring post	29 Nm (22 ft-lbs)*
Positioning lever bolt	11 Nm (95 inch-lbs)
Output shaft bearing retainer screws	12 Nm (104 inch-lbs)
Balancer bearing retainer screws	11 Nm (95 inch-lbs)*
Output shaft coupling nut (Vulcan 700/750 models)	120 Nm (87 ft-lbs)**

Apply non-hardening thread locking agent to the threads.

**Stake the nut after tightening.*

1   General information

The engine/transmission unit on all models is a water-cooled V-twin. The valves are operated by double overhead camshafts (Vulcan 700/750 models) or single overhead camshafts (Vulcan 800 models) which are chain driven off the crankshaft. The engine/transmission assembly is constructed from aluminum alloy. The crankcase is divided horizontally.

The crankcase incorporates a wet sump, pressure-fed lubrication system which uses a chain-driven oil pump, oil filter, mesh oil screen, a relief valve and an oil pressure switch. The transmission gears are contained in the crankcase. The balancer weights are on the outside of the crankcase, one on each side, and are connected by the balancer shaft, which passes through the crankcase.

Power from the crankshaft is routed to the transmission via the clutch, which is of the wet, multi-plate type and is chain-driven off the crankshaft. The transmission is a five-speed, constant-mesh unit.

2   Cylinder compression - check

Refer to illustration 2.5

1   Among other things, poor engine performance may be caused by leaking valves, incorrect valve clearances, a leaking head gasket, or worn pistons, rings and/or cylinder walls. A cylinder compression check will help pinpoint these conditions and can also indicate the presence of excessive carbon deposits in the cylinder heads.

2   The only tools required are a compression gauge and a spark plug wrench. Depending on the outcome of the initial test,

2.5 A compression gauge with a threaded fitting for the spark plug hole is preferred over the type that requires hand pressure to retain the seal

a squirt-type oil can may also be needed.

3   Run the engine until it reaches normal operating temperature. Place the motorcycle on the centerstand (if equipped). If not, prop it securely upright. Remove the spark plugs (see Chapter 1, if necessary). Work carefully - don't strip the spark plug hole threads and don't burn your hands. **Note:** *Vulcan 700/750 models use two spark plugs per cylinder. Remove only one plug from each cylinder for this test.*

4   Disable the ignition by unplugging the primary wires from the coils (see Chapter 5). Be sure to mark the locations of the wires before detaching them.

5   Install the compression gauge in one of the spark plug holes **(see illustration)**. Hold or block the throttle wide open.

6   Crank the engine over a minimum of four or five revolutions (or until the gauge reading stops increasing) and observe the initial movement of the compression gauge needle as well as the final total gauge reading. Repeat the procedure for the other cylinder and compare the results to the value listed in this Chapter's Specifications.

7   If the compression in both cylinders

built up quickly and evenly to the specified amount, you can assume the engine upper end is in reasonably good mechanical condition. Worn or sticking piston rings and worn cylinders will produce very little initial movement of the gauge needle, but compression will tend to build up gradually as the engine spins over. Valve and valve seat leakage, or head gasket leakage, is indicated by low initial compression which does not tend to build up.

8   To further confirm your findings, add a small amount of engine oil to each cylinder by inserting the nozzle of a squirt-type oil can through the spark plug holes. The oil will tend to seal the piston rings if they are leaking. Repeat the test for the other cylinder.

9   If the compression increases significantly after the addition of the oil, the piston rings and/or cylinders are definitely worn. If the compression does not increase, the pressure is leaking past the valves or the head gasket. Leakage past the valves may be due to insufficient valve clearances, burned, warped or cracked valves or valve seats, or valves that are hanging up in the guides.

10 If compression readings are considerably higher than specified, the combustion chambers are probably coated with excessive carbon deposits. It is possible (but not very likely) for carbon deposits to raise the compression enough to compensate for the effects of leakage past rings or valves. Remove the cylinder heads and carefully decarbonize the combustion chambers (see Chapter 2).

3 Operations possible with the engine in the frame

The components and assemblies listed below can be removed without having to remove the engine from the frame. If, however, a number of areas require attention at the same time, removal of the engine is recommended. **Note:** *The Vulcan 700/750 engine is a tight fit in the frame, so the engine must be removed for most procedures.*

Vulcan 700/750 models

Gearshift mechanism external components
Water pump
Starter motor
Clutch plates and discs
Front cylinder valve cover, camshafts and rocker arms
Cam chain tensioners

Vulcan 800 models

Gearshift mechanism external components
Water pump
Starter motor and alternator
Clutch assembly
Valve covers, camshafts and rocker arms
Cam chain tensioners
Cylinder heads
Cylinders and pistons

4 Operations requiring engine removal

1   On Vulcan 700/750 models, it is necessary to remove the engine from the motorcycle to gain access to the following components:

Rear cylinder valve cover, camshafts and rocker arms
Cylinders and pistons
Clutch housing
Alternator

2   On all models, it is necessary to remove the engine/transmission assembly from the frame and separate the crankcase halves to gain access to the following components:
Crankshaft, connecting rods and bearings
Transmission shafts
Shift drum and forks
Balancer shaft
Camshaft chain
Oil pump

5 Major engine repair - general note

1   It is not always easy to determine when or if an engine should be completely overhauled, as a number of factors must be considered.
2   High mileage is not necessarily an indication that an overhaul is needed, while low mileage, on the other hand, does not preclude the need for an overhaul. Frequency of servicing is probably the single most important consideration. An engine that has regular and frequent oil and filter changes, as well as other required maintenance, will most likely give many miles of reliable service. Conversely, a neglected engine, or one which has not been broken in properly, may require an overhaul very early in its life.
3   Exhaust smoke and excessive oil consumption are both indications that piston rings and/or valve guides are in need of attention. Make sure oil leaks are not responsible before deciding that the rings and guides are bad. Refer to Section 2 and perform a cylinder compression check to determine for certain the nature and extent of the work required.
4   If the engine is making obvious knocking or rumbling noises, the connecting rod and/or main bearings are probably at fault.
5   Loss of power, rough running, excessive valve train noise and high fuel consumption rates may also point to the need for an overhaul, especially if they are all present at the same time. If a complete tune-up does not remedy the situation, major mechanical work is the only solution.
6   An engine overhaul generally involves restoring the internal parts to the specifications of a new engine. During an overhaul the piston rings are replaced and the cylinder walls are bored and/or honed. If a rebore is done, then new pistons are also required. The main and connecting rod bearings are generally replaced with new ones and, if necessary, the crankshaft is also replaced. Generally the valves are serviced as well, since they are usually in less than perfect condition at this point. While the engine is being overhauled, other components such as the carburetors and the starter motor can be rebuilt also. The end result should be a like-new engine that will give as many trouble free miles as the original.
7   Before beginning the engine overhaul, read through all of the related procedures to familiarize yourself with the scope and requirements of the job. Overhauling an engine is not all that difficult, but it is time consuming. Plan on the motorcycle being tied up for a minimum of two weeks. Check on the availability of parts and make sure that any necessary special tools, equipment and supplies are obtained in advance.
8   Most work can be done with typical shop hand tools, although a number of precision measuring tools are required for inspecting parts to determine if they must be replaced. Often a dealer service department or motorcycle repair shop will handle the inspection of parts and offer advice concerning reconditioning and replacement. As a general rule, time is the primary cost of an overhaul so it doesn't pay to install worn or substandard parts.
9   As a final note, to ensure maximum life and minimum trouble from a rebuilt engine, everything must be assembled with care in a spotlessly clean environment.

6 Engine - removal and installation

Note: *Engine removal and installation should be done with the aid of an assistant to avoid damage or injury that could occur if the engine is dropped. A hydraulic floor jack should be used to support and lower the engine if possible (they can be rented at low cost).*

Removal

Refer to illustrations 6.15a, 6.15b, 6.16a, 6.16b and 6.18
1   Set the bike on its centerstand (if equipped) and disconnect the battery (negative cable first). If the bike doesn't have a centerstand, prop it securely upright.
2   Remove the seat (see Chapter 8) and the fuel tank (see Chapter 4).
3   Remove the side covers (see Chapter 8).
4   Drain the coolant and the engine oil (see Chapter 1).
5   Remove the air filter housing (see Chapter 4).
6   Remove the vacuum switching valve (if equipped) (see Chapter 4). If you're working on a Vulcan 700/750 model, remove the left air suction valve and its hose.
7   Remove the carburetor(s) (see Chapter 4) and plug the intake openings with rags.
8   Remove the radiator, radiator hoses and coolant tubes (see Chapter 3). If you're working on a Vulcan 700/750 model, remove the coolant reservoir tank. If you're working on a Vulcan 800 model, remove the thermostat housing and unbolt the coolant hose fittings from the cylinder heads.
9   Remove the ignition coils and brackets (see Chapter 5).
10   Remove the exhaust system (see Chapter 4).
11   Remove the shift pedal (see Section 21).
12   If you're working on a Vulcan 700/750 model, detach the front bevel gear case from the engine (see Chapter 6).
13   If you're working on a Vulcan 800 model, remove the engine sprocket cover, unbolt the engine sprocket and detach the sprocket and drive chain from the engine (see Chapter 6).
14   Disconnect the lower end of the clutch cable from the lever and remove the cable from the lower bracket (see Chapter 1).

2

6.15a Engine ground cable (Vulcan 700/750 models)

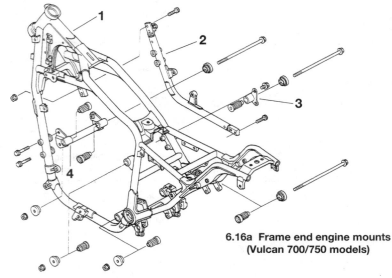

6.16a Frame end engine mounts (Vulcan 700/750 models)

6.15b Engine ground cable (Vulcan 800 models)

| 1 | Frame | 3 | Rear mount bracket |
| 2 | Right frame member | 4 | Front mount bracket |

15 Mark and disconnect the wires from the oil pressure switch, neutral switch and the starter motor. Unplug the brake light switch, alternator, sidestand and pick-up coil electrical connectors (see Chapters 5 and 9). Disconnect the engine ground cable (see illustrations).
16 Remove the frame downtube from the right side of the frame (see illustrations).
17 Support the engine with a floor jack and a wood block.
18 With the engine supported, remove the mounting bolts, starting with the upper ones and working down to the lower ones (see illustrations 6.16a, 6.16b and the accom-

panying illustration).
19 Make sure no wires or hoses are still attached to the engine.
20 With the help of at least one assistant, slowly and carefully guide the engine out the right side, away from the bike.

Installation

21 Installation is the reverse of removal. Note the following points:
a) Don't tighten any of the engine mounting bolts until they all have been installed.
b) Use new gaskets at all exhaust pipe connections.
c) Tighten the engine mounting bolts and frame downtube bolts securely.
d) Adjust the drive chain (Vulcan 800 models), rear brake, throttle cables, choke cable (Vulcan 700/750 models) and clutch cable following the procedures in Chapter 1.

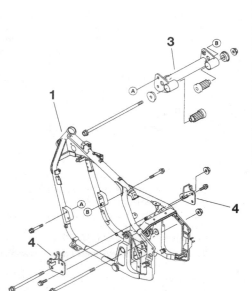

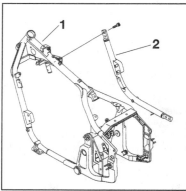

6.16b Frame and engine mounts (Vulcan 800 models)

1 Frame
2 Right frame member
3 Front mount bracket
4 Rear mount bracket

6.18 Typical engine mount and bracket (Vulcan 700/750 left front shown)

7.2a A selection of brushes is required for cleaning holes and passages in the engine components

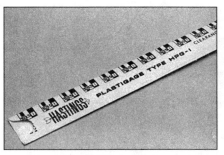

7.2b Type HPG-1 Plastigage is needed to check the crankshaft, connecting rod and camshaft oil clearances

7.3 An engine stand can be made from short lengths of 2 x 4 lumber and lag bolts or nails

7 Engine disassembly and reassembly - general information

Refer to illustrations 7.2a, 7.2b and 7.3

1 Before disassembling the engine, clean the exterior with a degreaser and rinse it with water. A clean engine will make the job easier and prevent the possibility of getting dirt into the internal areas of the engine.

2 In addition to the precision measuring tools mentioned earlier, you will need a torque wrench, a valve spring compressor, oil gallery brushes, a piston ring removal and installation tool, a piston ring compressor, a pin-type spanner wrench and a clutch holder tool (which is described in Section 20). Some new, clean engine oil of the correct grade and type, some engine assembly lube (or moly-based grease), a tube of Kawasaki Bond liquid gasket (part no. 92104-1003) or equivalent, and a tube of RTV (silicone) sealant will also be required. Although it may not be considered a tool, some Plastigage (type HPG-1) should also be obtained to use for checking bearing oil clearances **(see illustrations)**.

3 An engine support stand made from short lengths of 2 x 4's bolted together will facilitate the disassembly and reassembly procedures **(see illustration)**. The perimeter of the mount should be just big enough to accommodate the engine oil pan. If you have an automotive-type engine stand, an adapter plate can be made from a piece of plate, some angle iron and some nuts and bolts.

4 When disassembling the engine, keep "mated" parts together (including gears, cylinders, pistons, etc. that have been in contact with each other during engine operation). These "mated" parts must be reused or replaced as an assembly.

5 Engine/transmission disassembly should be done in the following general order with reference to the appropriate Sections.

Remove the cylinder heads
Remove the cylinders
Remove the pistons
Remove the clutch
Remove the external shift mechanism

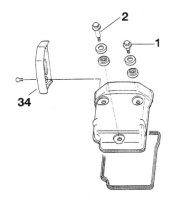

8.5 Valve cover, camshaft and timing chain details (Vulcan 700/750 models)

1 Short valve cover bolt
2 Long valve cover bolt
3 Washer
4 Grommet
5 Valve cover
6 Gasket
7 Camshafts
8 Upper front camshaft chain guide
9 Long bolt
10 O-ring
11 Upper camshaft chain
12 Idler shaft plastic plug
13 O-ring
14 Idler shaft
15 Lower front camshaft chain guide bolt (front cylinder only)
16 Washer

17 Lower front camshaft chain guide
18 Lower camshaft chain
19 Idler sprocket
20 Upper rear timing chain guide
21 Spring
22 O-ring
23 Tensioner spring plug
24 Tensioner body nut

25 Tensioner body
26 O-ring
27 Tensioner cap
28 O-ring
29 O-ring
30 Short bolt
31 Lower rear camshaft chain guide
32 Spring
33 Tensioner body
34 Heat shield

Remove the alternator rotor/stator coils and starter clutch (see Chapter 9)
Separate the crankcase halves
Remove the crankshaft and connecting rods
Remove the balancer shaft and gears
Remove the transmission shafts/gears
Remove the shift drum/forks

6 Reassembly is accomplished by reversing the general disassembly sequence.

8 Valve covers - removal and installation

Vulcan 700/750 models

Note: *The front valve cover can be removed with the engine in the frame (removal of the rear valve cover requires engine removal). If the engine has been removed, ignore the steps which don't apply.*

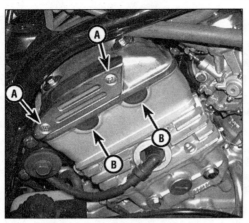

8.9 Loosen the screws (A) to remove the rear valve cover heat shield; apply silicone sealant to the edges of the seals (B)

8.23a Unbolt the valve cover and lift it off

8.23b Valve cover and cylinder head details (Vulcan 800 models)

1   Valve cover bolt
2   Washer/grommet
3   Valve cover
4   Air suction valve
5   Gasket
6   Damper
7   Damper plate
8   Camshaft bearing cap bolt
9   Camshaft bearing cap
10 Cylinder head nuts
11 Bearing cap dowel
12 Oil tube-rings
13 Oil tube
14 Valve cover gasket locating pin
15 Cylinder head nut
16 Plug
17 O-ring
18 Cylinder head
19 Cylinder head dowels
20 Gasket
21 Intake manifold O-rings
22 Intake manifold

Removal

Front valve cover

Refer to illustration 8.5

1   Set the bike on its centerstand (if equipped).
2   Remove the fuel tank, both air cleaner housings, the air cleaner ducts and the surge tank ducts (see Chapter 4).
3   Drain the engine coolant and remove the coolant hose that runs across the top of the air cleaner surge tank (see Chapters 1 and 3).
4   Disconnect the wiring harness as necessary to provide clearance to lift the surge tank up when the valve cover is removed.
5   Remove the valve cover bolts **(see illustration)**.
6   Lift the cover off the cylinder head **(see illustration 8.5)**. If it's stuck, don't attempt to pry it off - tap around the sides with a plastic hammer to dislodge it. You'll need to lift up firmly against the surge tank to make enough room to remove the valve cover.
7   If the gasket and semicircular seals didn't come off with the valve cover, remove them from the engine.

Rear valve cover

Refer to illustration 8.9

8   Remove the engine from the motorcycle (see Section 6).
9   If you're planning to remove the heat shield from the valve cover, loosen the screws now while the valve cover is still attached to the engine **(see illustration)**. Use an impact driver if necessary.
10 Remove the valve cover bolts **(see illustration 8.5)**.
11 Lift the cover off the cylinder head. If it's stuck, don't attempt to pry it off - tap around the sides with a plastic hammer to dislodge it.
12 If the gasket and semicircular seals didn't come off with the valve cover, remove them from the engine.

Installation

13 Peel the rubber gasket from the cover if it's stuck there. If it's cracked, hardened, has soft spots or shows signs of general deterioration, replace it with a new one.
14 Clean the mating surfaces of the cylinder head and the valve cover with lacquer thinner, acetone or brake system cleaner.

Apply a thin film of RTV sealant to the half-circle cutouts on the timing chain side of the head; run the sealant slightly up onto the gasket surface of the head at each corner of the semicircular seals.
15 Install the gasket to the cover. Make sure it fits completely into the cover groove.
16 Position the cover on the cylinder head, making sure the gasket doesn't slip out of place.
17 Check the rubber seals on the valve cover bolts, replacing them if necessary. Install the bolts, tightening them evenly to the torque listed in this Chapter's Specifications. If you're working on the rear cylinder head, install the valve cover heat shield and tighten the bolts securely.
18 The remainder of installation is the reverse of removal. Fill the cooling system with the recommended type and amount of coolant (see Chapter 1).

Vulcan 800 models

Removal

Refer to illustrations 8.23a, 8.23b and 8.24
19 Remove the seat (see Chapter 8).

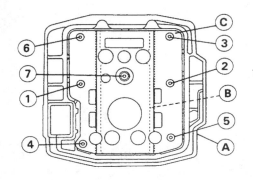

8.27 Valve cover damper plate details (Vulcan 800 models)

1-7 Bolt tightening sequence
A Valve cover
B Damper
C Damper plate

8.24 Make sure the gasket locating pin (arrow) is in position

20 Drain the cooling system (see Chapter 1). Remove the upper radiator hose, thermostat housing assembly, and any coolant hoses that will obstruct valve cover removal (see Chapter 3).
21 Remove the fuel tank, air cleaner housing, carburetor, vacuum switching valves and hoses (see Chapter 4). If you're working on the rear cylinder, remove the mufflers.
22 If you're working on the front cylinder, remove the ignition coil (see Chapter 5).
23 Unbolt the valve cover from the engine **(see illustrations)**. Lift it off and remove the gasket. Remove the air suction valve from its recess in the gasket mating surface.
24 Make sure the gasket locating pin is in the cylinder head **(see illustration)**. Wiggle it with your fingers; if it's at all loose, pull it out so it doesn't fall into the engine.
25 If necessary, unbolt the damper from inside the valve cover **(see illustration 8.23b)**. **Note:** *The bolts are secured with thread locking agent.*
26 Check the gasket for wear or deterioration and replace it if necessary.

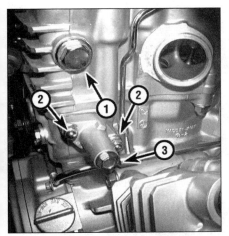

9.1 Cam chain tensioner details (Vulcan 700/750 models)

1 Tensioner cap
2 Tensioner mounting nuts
3 Tension spring cap bolt

Installation

Refer to illustration 8.27

27 If the damper was removed from inside the valve cover, install it. Apply non-permanent thread locking agent to the threads of the damper bolts, then tighten them to the torque listed in this Chapter's Specifications in the correct sequence **(see illustration)**.
28 Place the air suction valve in its recess in the cylinder head (see Chapter 1).
29 Make sure the gasket locating pin is in position **(see illustration 8.24)**. Install the gasket over the pin and position it on the mating surface.
30 Make sure the spark plug tube is in position (see Chapter 1). Install the valve cover on the cylinder head. Install the washers with their metal sides upward, then install the bolts and tighten them to the torque listed in this Chapter's Specifications.
31 The remainder of installation is the reverse of the removal steps.

9 Camshaft chain tensioner and tension spring (Vulcan 700/750 models) - removal and installation

Tensioner removal

Refer to illustration 9.1
Caution: *Once you start to remove the tensioner bolts, you must remove the tensioner all the way and reset it before tightening the bolts. The tensioner extends and locks in place, so if you loosen the bolts part way and then retighten them, the tensioner or cam chain will be damaged.*
1 Loosen the tensioner cap while the tensioner is still installed **(see illustration)**.
2 Remove the tensioner mounting nuts and take it off the engine.
3 Remove the tensioner cap and O-ring.

Tensioner installation

Refer to illustration 9.9
4 Check the O-ring on the tensioner body for cracks or hardening. It's a good idea to

replace this O-ring whenever the tensioner cap is removed.

Original tensioner

5 Place the tensioner mounting nuts where you can reach them with one hand while the other hand holds the tensioner in position in Step 7.
6 Press the end of the rod that contacts the chain into the tensioner body. At the same time, turn the other end of the rod clockwise with a screwdriver until the rod stops moving. Keep the screwdriver in this position. **Caution:** *Don't turn the rod counterclockwise or it may separate from the tensioner. If this happens it can't be reassembled.*
7 With the screwdriver still in the tensioner, place the tensioner in position on the engine. Push it firmly against the engine, remove the screwdriver, and install the mounting nuts finger-tight. **Caution:** *If the tensioner moves away from the engine before you tighten the nuts, the rod will extend too far. If this happens (or you think it might have happened), remove the tensioner and repeat Step 6, then continue with Step 7.*
8 Tighten the mounting nuts securely, but don't overtighten them and strip the threads.

New tensioner

9 New tensioners come with a keeper that fits in the tensioner rod slot and holds the rod in the correct position for installation **(see illustration)**.

9.9 New tensioners come with a keeper (arrow) to hold the rod in position for installation

10.1a Unscrew the tensioner cap . . .

10.1b . . . and remove it, together with the spring

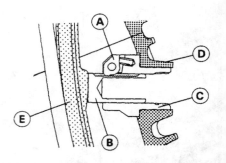

10.8 Cam chain tensioner details (Vulcan 800 models)

A Latch
B Pushrod
C Tensioner body
D Cylinder
E Camshaft chain guide

10 Place the tensioner on the engine. Install the mounting nuts and tighten them securely.

11 Pull the keeper out with needle nosed pliers. **Note:** *Save the keeper and place it in your toolbox for future use. You can use it to hold the tensioner rod in position next time you install the tensioner, leaving both hands free.*

Original or new tensioner

12 Install the tensioner cap and O-ring. Tighten the cap securely, but don't over-tighten it and strip the threads.

Chain tension spring removal

13 Unscrew the tension spring cap bolt **(see illustration 9.1)**. Remove the cap bolt and its O-ring and pull the spring out of the bore **(see illustration 8.5)**.

14 Check the O-ring for damage or deteri-oration and replace it if necessary.

15 Installation is the reverse of the removal steps. Be sure to place the spring over the protruding boss on the chain tensioner.

Tighten the cap bolt to the torque listed in this Chapter's Specifications.

---

10 Camshaft chain tensioner (Vulcan 800 models) - removal and installation

Cap and spring

Removal

Refer to illustrations 10.1a and 10.1b

1 Unscrew the cap and remove the seal-ing washer and spring **(see illustrations)**.

2 Temporarily install the cap without the spring to prevent the tensioner from falling out.

Installation

3 Installation is the reverse of the removal steps. Use a new sealing washer and tighten the cap to the torque listed in this Chapter's Specifications.

Tensioner

Removal

Refer to illustration 10.8

4 Remove the engine from the vehicle (see Section 6).

5 Remove the valve cover from the engine (see Section 8).

6 Unscrew the timing chain tensioner cap and remove the spring.

7 Remove the camshaft and timing chain guide (see Section 12).

8 Lift the latch, compress the timing chain tensioner piston into the tensioner body and release the latch **(see illustration)**. Pull the tensioner body out of the engine.

Installation

9 Installation is the reverse of the removal steps, with the following additions:

a) *Lift the latch on the tensioner and com-press the tensioner pushrod into the*

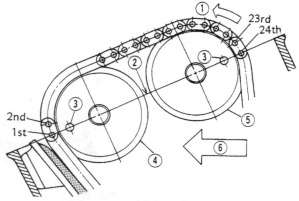

11.3a Front cylinder camshaft chain timing (Vulcan 700/750 models)

1	Direction of rotation	4	Exhaust camshaft
2	Cylinder head top surface	5	Intake camshaft
3	Sprocket marks	6	Front of engine

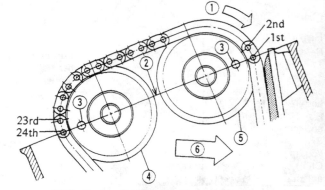

11.3b Rear cylinder camshaft chain timing (Vulcan 700/750 models)

1	Direction of rotation	4	Exhaust camshaft
2	Cylinder head top surface	5	Intake camshaft
3	Sprocket marks	6	Front of engine

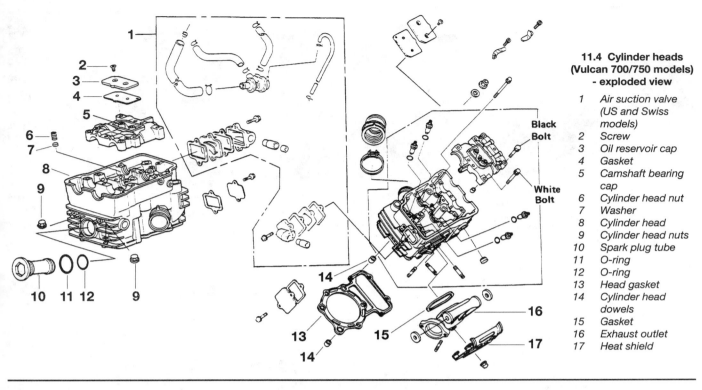

**11.4 Cylinder heads
(Vulcan 700/750 models)
- exploded view**

1   Air suction valve
    (US and Swiss
    models)
2   Screw
3   Oil reservoir cap
4   Gasket
5   Camshaft bearing
    cap
6   Cylinder head nut
7   Washer
8   Cylinder head
9   Cylinder head nuts
10 Spark plug tube
11 O-ring
12 O-ring
13 Head gasket
14 Cylinder head
    dowels
15 Gasket
16 Exhaust outlet
17 Heat shield

**Black
Bolt**

**White
Bolt**

body, then install the tensioner in its
bore.

b) Lift the latch again and push the ten-
    sioner piston lightly against the timing
    chain guide using a screwdriver blade or
    similar tool, then release the latch .

c) Install the spring in the tensioner, then
    install the cap and sealing washer.
    Tighten the cap to the torque listed in
    this Chapter's Specifications.

---

11 Camshafts, rocker arms and hydraulic lifters (Vulcan 700/750 models) - removal, inspection and installation

Camshafts

Removal

*Refer to illustrations 11.3a, 11.3b, 11.4 and
11.6*

1   Remove the engine from the motorcycle
and remove the valve covers (see Sections 6
and 8).
2   Remove the camshaft chain tensioner
and tension spring (see Section 9).
3   Turn the engine to position the cylinder
you're working on at TDC compression (see
Chapter 1 - Valve clearances - check and
adjustment). When the engine is positioned
correctly, the punch marks on the camshafts
will align with the cylinder head top surface
(see illustrations). To ease reassembly,
mark the sprockets and chain with felt pen.
4   Remove the screws and take the oil
reservoir cover off the camshaft cap **(see
illustration)**.

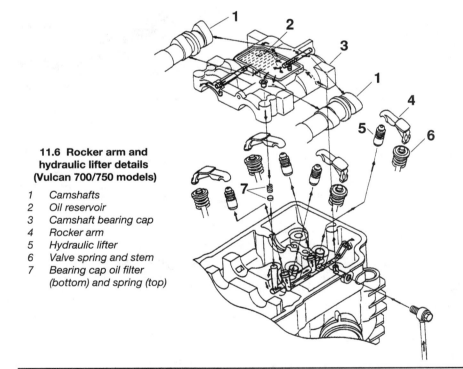

**11.6 Rocker arm and
hydraulic lifter details
(Vulcan 700/750 models)**

1   Camshafts
2   Oil reservoir
3   Camshaft bearing cap
4   Rocker arm
5   Hydraulic lifter
6   Valve spring and stem
7   Bearing cap oil filter
    (bottom) and spring (top)

5   Unscrew the camshaft bearing cap
bolts in stages, a little at a time, until they are
all loose. **Caution:** *If the bearing cap bolts
aren't loosened evenly, the camshaft may
bind.* Remove the bolts and label them with
their locations; the light-colored bolts are
longer than the dark-colored bolts. Lift off

the bearing cap, then locate the two bearing
cap dowels (they may have come off with the
cap or remained in the cylinder head).
6   Remove the oil filter and spring for the
hydraulic lifters from their bore in the cylinder
head, under the camshaft bearing cap **(see
illustration)**.

2

11.10a Check the lobes of the camshaft for wear - here's a good example of damage which will require replacement (or repair) of the camshaft

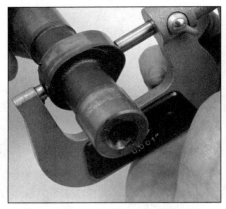

11.10b Measure the height of the camshaft lobes with a micrometer

11.12 Position a strip of Plastigage on each cam bearing journal, parallel with the centerline of the crankshaft

7   Lift one camshaft and disengage its sprocket from the chain. With the chain still held taut, remove the other camshaft. The intake camshaft is longer than the exhaust camshaft; label the camshafts to ensure they are installed in their original locations. Also, the rear cylinder's camshafts, both intake and exhaust, have grooves in the sprocket end of the camshaft just outboard of the sprocket center hole. Be careful not to mix up the front and rear cylinders' camshafts. **Note:** *The sprockets can't be removed from the camshafts.*

8   While the camshafts are out, don't allow the chain to go slack - the chain may bind between the idler sprocket and crankcase, which could damage these components. Wire the chain to another component to prevent it from dropping down. Also, cover the top of the cylinder head with a rag to prevent foreign objects from falling into the engine.

Inspection

Refer to illustrations 11.10a, 11.10b, 11.12, 11.15a and 11.15b

Note: *Before replacing camshafts or the cylinder head and bearing caps because of damage, check with local machine shops specializing in motorcycle engine work. In the case of the camshafts, it may be possible for cam lobes to be welded, reground and hardened, at a cost far lower than that of a new camshaft. If the bearing surfaces in the cylinder head are damaged, it may be possible for them to be bored out to accept bearing inserts. Due to the cost of a new cylinder head it is recommended that all options be explored before condemning it as trash!*

9   Inspect the cam bearing surfaces of the head and the bearing caps. Look for score marks, deep scratches and evidence of spalling (a pitted appearance).

10   Check the camshaft lobes for heat discoloration (blue appearance), score marks, chipped areas, flat spots and spalling **(see illustration)**. Measure the height of each lobe with a micrometer **(see illustration)** and compare the results to the minimum lobe height listed in this Chapter's Specifications.

11.15a Compare the width of the crushed Plastigage to the scale on the Plastigage envelope to obtain the clearance

If damage is noted or wear is excessive, the camshaft must be replaced. Also, be sure to check the condition of the rocker arms, as described later in this Section.

11   Next, check the camshaft bearing oil clearances. Clean the camshafts, the bearing surfaces in the cylinder head and the bearing caps with a clean, lint-free cloth, then lay the cams in place in the cylinder head, with the punch marks on the sprockets facing away from each other and level with the valve cover gasket surface of the cylinder head **(see illustrations 11.3a and 11.3b)**. Engage the cam chain with the cam sprockets, so the camshafts don't turn as the bearing caps are tightened.

12   Cut six strips of Plastigage (type HPG-1) and lay one piece on each bearing journal, parallel with the camshaft centerline **(see illustration)**.

13   Make sure the bearing cap dowels are installed. Install the bearing caps in their proper positions (the arrows on the caps must face toward the front of the engine and the letters on the caps must correspond with those on the cylinder head) and install the bolts. Tighten the bolts in three steps, follow-

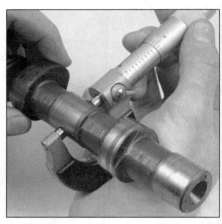

11.15b Measure the cam bearing journal with a micrometer

ing the numerical sequence cast in the bearing cap, to the torque listed in this Chapter's Specifications. While doing this, DO NOT let the camshafts rotate!

14   Now unscrew the bolts, a little at a time, and carefully lift off the bearing caps.

15   To determine the oil clearance, compare the crushed Plastigage (at its widest point) on each journal to the scale printed on the Plastigage container **(see illustration)**. Compare the results to this Chapter's Specifications. If the oil clearance is greater than specified, measure the diameter of the cam bearing journal with a micrometer **(see illustration)**. If the journal diameter is less than the specified limit, replace the camshaft with a new one and recheck the clearance. If the clearance is still too great, replace the cylinder head and bearing caps with new parts (see the Note that precedes Step 9). Remove all traces of Plastigage from the components without scratching their surfaces.

16   Except in cases of oil starvation, the camshaft chain wears very little. If the chain has stretched excessively, which makes it difficult to maintain proper tension, replace it with a new one (see Section 24).

17   Check the sprockets for wear, cracks

and other damage, replacing them if necessary (which means replacing the camshafts). If the sprockets are worn, the chain is also worn, and also the idler sprocket that connects the upper and lower timing chains. If wear this severe is apparent, the entire engine should be disassembled for inspection.

18 Check the chain guide for wear or damage. If it is worn or damaged, the chain is worn out or improperly adjusted. Replacement of the guide requires removal of the cylinder head and cylinder block.

Installation

19 Install the spring and oil filter for the hydraulic lifters in their bore in the cylinder head **(see illustration 11.6)**.

20 Make sure the bearing surfaces in the cylinder head and the bearing caps are clean, then apply a light coat of engine assembly lube or moly-based grease to each of them.

21 Apply a coat of moly-based grease to the camshaft lobes. Make sure the camshaft bearing journals are clean, then lay the camshafts in the cylinder head (do not mix them up), ensuring the marks on the cam sprockets are aligned properly **(see illustrations 11.3a and 11.3b)**.

22 Make sure the timing marks are aligned as described in Step 11, then mesh the chain with the camshaft sprockets. Count the number of chain link pins between the punch marks **(see illustrations 11.3a and 11.3b)**. There should be no slack in the chain between the two sprockets.

23 Carefully set the bearing cap in place and install the bolts, making sure to place the longer and shorter bolts in the correct locations. Tighten them in the sequence cast in the bearing cap, to the torque listed in this Chapter's Specifications.

24 Insert your finger or a wood dowel into the cam chain tensioner hole and apply pressure to the cam chain. Check the timing marks to make sure they are aligned (see Step 3) and there are still the correct number of link pins between the punch marks on the cam sprockets. If necessary, change the position of the sprocket(s) on the chain to bring all of the marks into alignment. **Caution:** *If the marks are not aligned exactly as described, the valve timing will be incorrect and the valves may contact the pistons, causing extensive damage to the engine.*

25 Install the tensioner as described in Section 10.

26 Turn the engine with a socket on the crankshaft rotation bolt. If you feel a sudden increase in resistance, stop turning. The valves may be hitting the pistons due to incorrect assembly. Find the problem and fix it before turning the engine any further, or serious damage may occur.

27 The remainder of installation is the reverse of removal.

28 Before installing the valve cover, fill the reservoir on top of the camshaft bearing cap with clean engine oil **(see illustration 11.6)**.

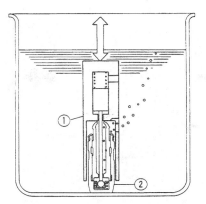

11.35 This special tool is used to bleed air from the Vulcan 700/750 hydraulic lifters

1   Bleeder (tool no. 57001-1200)
2   Hydraulic lifter

Rocker arms and hydraulic lifters

Removal

29 Remove the camshafts following the procedure given above. Be sure to keep tension on the camshaft chain.

30 Unscrew the plate spring bolts and remove the plate springs.

31 Remove the rocker arms and pull the hydraulic lifters out of their bores **(see illustration 11.6)**. Keep all of the parts in order so they can be reinstalled in their original locations. **Note:** *A container such as an egg carton with numbers written on the compartment is a convenient way to keep the parts in order.*

Inspection

Refer to illustrations 11.35 and 11.36

32 Clean all of the components with solvent and dry them off. Blow through the oil passages in the rocker arms with compressed air, if available. Inspect the rocker arm faces for pits, spalling, score marks and rough spots. Look for cracks in each rocker arm. If the faces of the rocker arms are damaged, the rocker arms and the camshafts should be replaced as a set.

33 Make sure the oil holes in the hydraulic lifters are clear. Check the lifters and their bores for wear, scuff marks, scratches and other damage. Kawasaki doesn't provide specifications or wear tolerances for the lifters or their bores. If wear or damage is found, replace the worn parts.

34 Lifter performance can be tested, but it requires a dial indicator and a special Kawasaki fixture for which there is no good substitute. The fixture holds open the adjuster check valve, allowing it to be bled of air. The procedure is described below, but you can have it done by a dealer service department or motorcycle shop if you don't have the equipment.

35 Place the lifter in a tappet bleeder

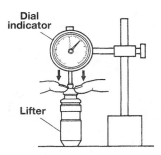

11.36 Push down on the lifter and measure the stroke

Leak-down Distance
Standard: 0 to 0.2 mm
Service Limit: 0.2 mm

(Kawasaki tool no. 57001-1200) **(see illustration)**. Immerse the fixture in a pan of kerosene with the lifter in an upright position. Slowly compress and extend the bleeder until no more air bubbles can be seen coming from the lifter.

36 Take the lifter out of the fixture and place it on a workbench with a dial indicator contacting its end **(see illustration)**. Compress the lifter suddenly with fingers and measure its stroke. If it's more than listed in this Chapter's Specifications, repeat Step 35 to bleed the lifter, then measure the stroke again. If the stroke is still more than the specification, replace the lifter.

37 If the lifters can be reused, rinse them with clean kerosene and blow them dry with compressed air. Don't wipe them with a rag or paper towel, as even small pieces of lint can affect their performance. Keep the lifters upright and don't let the kerosene from the bleeding procedure (if they were bled) spill out.

Installation

38 Pour clean engine oil into the lifter bores in the cylinder head.

39 Install the lifters in their bores, taking care not to get them mixed up.

40 Install the rocker arms in their original locations (if you're reusing the old ones). Install the plate springs and tighten their bolts securely, but don't overtighten them and strip the threads.

41 The remainder of installation is the reverse of the removal steps.

---

12 Camshafts, rocker arm shafts and rocker arms (Vulcan 800 models) - removal, inspection and installation

---

Camshafts

Removal

Refer to illustrations 12.5a, 12.5b, 12.6a, 12.6b, 12.7, 12.8a and 12.8b

1   Remove the valve cover from the cylin-

12.5a Mark the camshaft bearing caps so they can be returned to the correct cylinders

12.5b Unscrew the bearing cap bolts in a criss-cross pattern

12.6a Lift the bearing cap off the cylinder head and locate the dowel (arrow)

12.6b The rear cylinder's cam sprocket is identified by a groove (arrow); the front cylinder's cam sprocket doesn't have a groove

12.7 Lift the valve adjusting shims off and label them so they can be returned to their original locations

12.8a Lift the cam chain, disengage the sprocket and lift the camshaft out

der you're working on (see Section 8).

2   Turn the engine to position the cylinder you're working on at TDC compression (see Valve clearances (Vulcan 800 models) - check and adjustment in Chapter 1).

3   To ease reassembly, mark the sprocket

12.8b Lift the white timing chain guide out of the engine

and chain with felt pen. Label the sprockets for front or rear cylinder, and push the camshaft sprocket bolt plug out of the cylinder head.

4   Remove the timing chain tensioner cap bolt and spring (see Section 10). Lift the tensioner latch, compress the tensioner piston into the tensioner body, then reinstall the cap bolt without the spring so the tensioner can't fall into the engine.

5   Label the camshaft bearing cap so it can be reinstalled on the correct cylinder (see illustration). Loosen the camshaft cap bolts in stages, in a criss-cross pattern (see illustration).

6   Once the bolts are all loose, lift the bearing cap/rocker assembly off the engine and locate the cap dowels (see illustrations).

7   Make sure the valve adjusting shims haven't fallen out of their positions on top of the valves (see illustration). It's a good idea to remove them (labeling them so they can be reinstalled in the correct positions) so they don't fall into the engine.

8   Pull up on the camshaft chain and carefully guide the camshaft out (see illustra-

tion). Note: *Don't remove the sprockets from the camshafts unless absolutely necessary.* Lift the white timing chain guide out of the cylinder head (see illustration).

9   Repeat Steps 1 through 7 to remove the camshaft from the other cylinder if necessary. Caution: *While the camshafts are out, don't allow the chain to go slack - the chain may bind between the crankshaft and case, which could damage these components. Wire the chain to another component to prevent it from dropping down. Also, cover the top of the cylinder head with a rag to prevent foreign objects from falling into the engine.*

Inspection

10   Inspection is basically the same as for Vulcan 700/750 models, described in Section 11, with the following additions:

a)   *When you check the bearing oil clearance, align the sprocket line with the top surface of the cylinder head (see illustration 19.6c in Chapter 1). Tighten the bearing cap bolts in a criss-cross pattern to the torque listed in this Chapter's Specifications.*

b)   *The camshaft sprockets can be replaced separately from the camshafts*

12.11 Make sure the sprocket locating dowel is in position (arrow)

12.17 Make sure the rocker arms align with the valve stems before tightening the bearing cap bolts

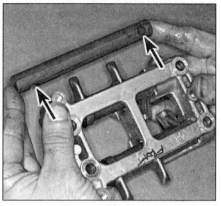

12.25 The shaft bolt hole and notch (arrows) align with the bolt holes in the bearing cap

if they're worn or damaged. Don't forget to install the sprocket locating pin. Use non-permanent thread locking agent on the sprocket bolt threads and tighten the sprocket bolt to the torque listed in this Chapter's Specifications.

c) *The sprockets are identical, but if you reuse the old ones, be sure to return them to the camshafts they came from.*

Installation

Refer to illustrations 12.11 and 12.17

11   If you removed the sprocket from the camshaft, install it, making sure the locating pin is in place **(see illustration)**.

12   Install the valve adjusting shims on top of the valves, making sure they're returned to their correct locations.

13   Make sure the timing marks are aligned as described in Step 3.

14   Make sure the bearing surfaces in the cylinder head and the bearing cap/rocker assembly are clean, then apply a light coat of engine assembly lube or moly-based grease to each of them.

15   Apply a coat of moly-based grease to the camshaft lobes. Make sure the camshaft bearing journals are clean.

16   Mesh the chain with the camshaft sprocket, then lay the camshaft in the cylinder head ensuring the line on the cam sprocket is aligned properly with the upper surface of the cylinder head (see Valve clearances (Vulcan 800 models) - check and adjustment in Chapter 1).

Note: *Do not mix up the front and rear camshafts; the rear camshaft has a groove machined in the outer edge of the sprocket mounting flange* **(see illustration 12.6b)**.

17   Make sure the bearing cap dowels are in position, then carefully set the bearing cap in place and make sure the rocker arms align with the valve stems **(see illustration)**. Install the bolts and tighten them in a criss-cross pattern **(see illustration 12.5b)**, to the torque listed in this Chapter's Specifications.

18   Remove the cam chain tensioner cap. Lift the tensioner latch, insert your finger or a wood dowel into the cam chain tensioner

hole, push the tensioner against the cam chain and release the latch.

19   Check the timing marks to make sure they are aligned (see Step 3). If necessary, change the position of the sprocket in the chain to bring all of the marks into alignment. **Caution:** *If the marks are not aligned exactly as described, the valve timing will be incorrect and the valves may contact the pistons, causing extensive damage to the engine.*

20   Install the tensioner spring and cap as described in Section 10.

21   Turn the engine with a socket on the crankshaft rotation bolt. If you feel a sudden increase in resistance, stop turning. The valves may be hitting the pistons due to incorrect assembly. Find the problem and fix it before turning the engine any further, or serious damage may occur.

22   Adjust the valve clearances (see Chapter 1).

23   The remainder of installation is the reverse of removal.

Rocker arm shafts and rocker arms

Removal

Refer to illustrations 12.25, 12.26a and 12.26b

24   Remove the camshaft bearing cap/rocker arm assembly following the procedure given above.

25   Push the rocker shafts out of the cap **(see illustration)**. Note the arrangement of the bolt hole and bolt notch in each shaft.

26   Unhook the long end of one of the rocker arm springs **(see illustration)**. Remove the rocker arm and disengage the spring from it **(see illustration)**. Note the positions of the red paint marks on two of the springs.

27   Repeat Step 26 to remove the other rocker arm and spring. Keep all of the parts in order so they can be reinstalled in their original locations.

Inspection

28   Clean all of the components with sol-

vent and dry them off. Blow through the oil passages in the rocker arms with compressed air, if available. Inspect the rocker arm faces for pits, spalling, score marks and rough spots. Check the rocker arm-to-shaft contact areas, as well. Look for cracks in each rocker arm. If the faces of the rocker arms are damaged, the rocker arms and the

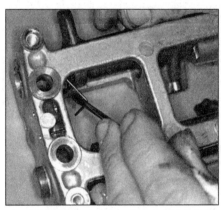

12.26a Disengage the long end of the rocker arm spring from the bearing cap . . .

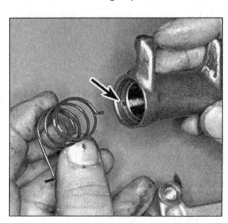

12.26b . . . and disengage the other end from the hole in the rocker arm (arrow)

2

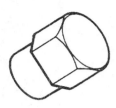

13.7 This special tool is used to unscrew the spark plug tube on Vulcan 700/750 models

13.10a Remove the 8 mm nut from the underside of the cylinder head . . .

13.10b . . . and do the same thing on the other side (arrow)

camshafts should be replaced as a set.

29   Inspect the surfaces of the rocker arm shafts, in the area where the rocker arms ride. If either the shaft or the rocker arms are visibly worn or damaged, replace them as a set.

Installation

30   Position the short end of a rocker arm and spring in the rocker arm **(see illustration 12.26b)**. Install the rocker arm and spring in the cap, then engage the long end of the spring with the cap **(see illustration 12.26a)**.

31   Lubricate the rocker arm shaft with engine oil and slide it into the cap and through the rocker arm and spring, making sure the bolt hole and notch are aligned with the bolt holes in the cap.

32   Repeat Steps 30 and 31 to install the remaining rocker arm and shaft.

33   Install the camshaft bearing cap/rocker assembly following the procedure described earlier in this Section.

13.11a Cylinder head upper nuts and bolt (Vulcan 800 model)

A)   *Small bolt*
B)   *Internal hex nuts*
C)   *10 mm nuts*

---

13   Cylinder head - removal and installation

Caution: *The engine must be completely cool before beginning this procedure, or the cylinder head may become warped.*

Note: *This procedure can be performed with the engine in the frame. If the engine has been removed, ignore the steps which don't apply.*

Removal

1   Set the bike on its centerstand (if equipped) or support it securely upright.

2   Remove the engine from the motorcycle (see Section 6).

3   Remove the valve cover from the cylinder you're working on (see Section 8).

4   Remove the cam chain tensioner (see Section 9 or 10).

5   Remove the camshaft(s) (see Section 11 or 12).

Vulcan 700/750 models

Refer to illustration 13.7

6   Remove the external oil pipe from the engine (see Section 22).

7   Unscrew the spark plug tube from the

cylinder head using a hexagonal adapter (Kawasaki tool no. 57001-1210) **(see illustration 11.4 and the accompanying illustration)**. If you don't have the special tool, you can grind a large bolt head to fit and weld it to a 3/8-inch drive socket adapter.

8   Remove the cylinder head nuts in the following order:

a)   *From below, two 6 mm nuts (thread diameter, not hex size) below the spark plug tube* **(see illustration 11.4)**.

b)   *On top of the head, the two 6 mm nuts, one on each side of the camshaft bearing journals at the sprocket end.*

13.11b Remove the small bolt first . . .

c)   *From below, the two 8 mm nuts, one below the intake manifold and one on the opposite side of the head*

d)   *On top of the head, the four 10 mm nuts (in stages, in a criss-cross pattern).*

Vulcan 800 models

Refer to illustrations 13.10a, 13.10b, 13.11a, 13.11b, 13.11c and 13.11d

9   Remove the intake manifold (see Chapter 4).

10   Remove the 8 mm nuts from the underside of the cylinder head **(see illustrations)**.

11   On top of the head, remove the single small bolt, then the two internal-hex nuts **(see**

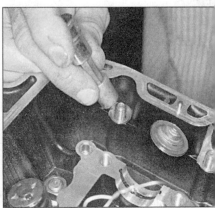

13.11c . . . then the internal hex nuts . . .

13.11d . . . then the 10 mm nuts and washers

13.12 Lift the cylinder head off the cylinder (Vulcan 800 shown)

13.13 Lift off the head gasket and on Vulcan 800 models, remove the oil tube

illustrations). Loosen the four 10 mm nuts in stages, in a criss-cross pattern, then remove the nuts and washers **(see illustration)**.

All models

Refer to illustrations 13.12, 13.13 and 13.15

12   Lift the cylinder head off the cylinder **(see illustration)**. If the head is stuck, use two wooden dowels inserted into the intake or exhaust ports to lever the head off. Don't attempt to pry the head off by inserting a screwdriver between the head and the cylinder block - you'll damage the sealing surfaces.

13   Lift the head gasket off the cylinder **(see illustration)**. If you're working on a Vulcan 800 model, pull out the oil tube.

14   Stuff a clean rag into the cam chain tunnel to prevent the entry of debris.

15   Locate the two dowel pins to make sure they haven't fallen into the engine. If they are in the head, put them in their holes in the cylinder **(see illustration)**, or else put them in a plastic bag for safekeeping.

16   Check the cylinder head gasket and the mating surfaces on the cylinder head and block for signs of leakage, which could indicate warpage. Refer to Section 15 and check the flatness of the cylinder head.

17   Clean all traces of old gasket material from the cylinder head and block. Be careful not to let any of the gasket material fall into the crankcase, the cylinder bores or the water passages.

Installation

18   If you're working on a Vulcan 800 model, place new O-rings on the oil tube **(see illustration 13.13)**. Coat the O-rings with oil and push the oil tube into place in the cylinder.

19   Make sure the dowels are in place, then lay the new gasket in place on the cylinder. Never reuse the old gasket and don't use any type of gasket sealant.

20   Carefully lower the cylinder head over the studs. It is helpful to have an assistant support the camshaft chain with a piece of

wire so it doesn't fall and become kinked or detached from the crankshaft. When the head is resting against the cylinder, wire the cam chain to another component to keep tension on it.

Vulcan 750 models

21   Install the head nuts and tighten them with fingers. Tighten them to the specified torque in the following stages:

a) *Main (10 mm) nuts (in a criss-cross pattern) to 25 Nm (18 ft-lbs)*
b) *8 mm nuts on underside of head to 18 Nm (156 inch-lbs)*
c) *6 mm nuts on top of head to 6.9 Nm (61 inch-lbs)*
d) *6 mm nuts on underside of head to 8.8 Nm (78 inch-lbs)*
e) *Main (10 mm) nuts to 39 Nm (29 ft-lbs)*
f) *8 mm nuts on underside of head to 25 Nm (18 ft-lbs)*
g) *6 mm nuts on top of head to 12 Nm (102 inch-lbs)*
h) *6 mm nuts on underside of head to 15 Nm (132 inch-lbs)*

Vulcan 800 models

22   Install the head nuts and bolt and tighten them with fingers.

23   Tighten the nuts and bolts on top of the head a little at a time, working in stages to the specified torque, using the following sequence:

a) *Main (10 mm) nuts (in a criss-cross pattern) to 39 Nm (29 ft-lbs)*
b) *Hex nuts on top of head to 25 Nm (18 ft-lbs)*
c) *Single bolt on top of head to 12 Nm (104 inch-lbs)*

24   Once all of the nuts and the single bolt on top of the head are tightened to the final torque, tighten the two 8 mm nuts on the underside of the head to their final torque of 25 Nm (18 ft-lbs).

All models

25   The remainder of installation is the reverse of the removal steps.

26   Change the engine oil (see Chapter 1).

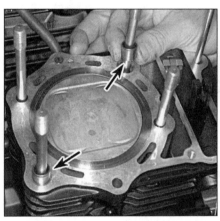

13.15 Locate the dowels (arrows)

14   Valves/valve seats/valve guides - servicing

1   Because of the complex nature of this job and the special tools and equipment required, servicing of the valves, the valve seats and the valve guides (commonly known as a valve job) is best left to a professional.

2   The home mechanic can, however, remove and disassemble the head, do the initial cleaning and inspection, then reassemble and deliver the head to a dealer service department or properly equipped motorcycle repair shop for the actual valve servicing. Refer to Section 15 for those procedures.

3   The dealer service department will remove the valves and springs, recondition or replace the valves and valve seats, replace the valve guides, check and replace the valve springs, spring retainers and keepers (as necessary), replace the valve seals with new ones and reassemble the valve components.

4   After the valve job has been performed, the head will be in like-new condition. When the head is returned, be sure to clean it again very thoroughly before installation on the

2

15.7a Compressing the valve springs with a valve spring compressor

15.7b Remove the valve keepers with needle-nose pliers or tweezers

engine to remove any metal particles or abrasive grit that may still be present from the valve service operations. Use compressed air, if available, to blow out all the holes and passages.

15 Cylinder head and valves - disassembly, inspection and reassembly

1   As mentioned in the previous Section, valve servicing and valve guide replacement should be left to a dealer service department or motorcycle repair shop. However, disassembly, cleaning and inspection of the valves and related components can be done (if the necessary special tools are available) by the home mechanic. This way no expense is incurred if the inspection reveals that service work is not required at this time.

2   To properly disassemble the valve components without the risk of damaging them, a valve spring compressor is absolutely necessary. This special tool can usually be rented, but if it's not available, have a dealer service department or motorcycle repair shop handle the entire process of disassembly,

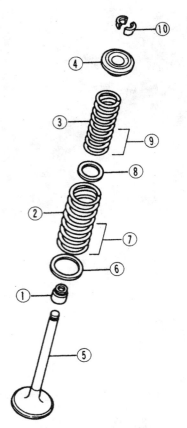

15.7c Valve components - exploded view

1   Oil seal
2   Outer spring
3   Inner spring (Vulcan 700/750 models)
4   Valve spring retainer
5   Valve
6   Outer spring seat
7   Tightly wound coils
8   Inner spring seat (Vulcan 700/750 models)
9   Tightly wound coils
10   Keepers

inspection, service or repair (if required) and reassembly of the valves.

Disassembly

Refer to illustrations 15.7a, 15.7b, 15.7c and 15.7d

3   Remove the cylinder head from the engine (see Section 13).

4   Before the valves are removed, scrape away any traces of gasket material from the head gasket sealing surface. Work slowly and do not nick or gouge the soft aluminum of the head. Gasket removing solvents, which work very well, are available at most motorcycle shops and auto parts stores.

5   Carefully scrape all carbon deposits out of the combustion chamber area. A hand held wire brush or a piece of fine emery cloth can be used once the majority of deposits have been scraped away. Do not use a wire brush mounted in a drill motor, or one with

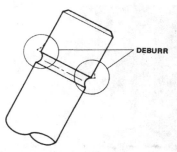

15.7d If the valve binds in the guide, deburr the area above the keeper groove

extremely stiff bristles, as the head material is soft and may be eroded away or scratched by the wire brush.

6   Before proceeding, arrange to label and store the valves along with their related components so they can be kept separate and reinstalled in the same valve guides they are removed from (again, plastic bags work well for this).

7   Compress the valve spring on the first valve with a spring compressor, then remove the keepers **(see illustrations)** and the retainer from the valve assembly. Do not compress the springs any more than is absolutely necessary. Carefully release the valve spring compressor and remove the springs and the valve from the head **(see illustration)**. If the valve binds in the guide (won't pull through), push it back into the head and deburr the area around the keeper groove with a very fine file or whetstone **(see illustration)**.

8   Repeat the procedure for the remaining valves. Remember to keep the parts for each valve together so they can be reinstalled in the same location.

9   Once the valves have been removed and labeled, pull off the valve stem seals with pliers and discard them (the old seals should never be reused), then remove the spring seats.

10   Next, clean the cylinder head with solvent and dry it thoroughly. Compressed air will speed the drying process and ensure that all holes and recessed areas are clean.

11   Clean all of the valve springs, keepers, retainers and spring seats with solvent and dry them thoroughly. Do the parts from one valve at a time so that no mixing of parts between valves occurs.

12   Scrape off any deposits that may have formed on the valve, then use a motorized wire brush to remove deposits from the valve heads and stems. Again, make sure the valves do not get mixed up.

Inspection

Refer to illustrations 15.14a, 15.14b, 15.15, 15.16, 15.17, 15.18a, 15.18b, 15.19a and 15.19b

13   Inspect the head very carefully for cracks and other damage. If cracks are found, a new head will be required. Check the cam bearing surfaces for wear and evidence of seizure. Check the camshaft(s) and

15.14a Lay a precision straightedge across the cylinder head and try to slide a feeler gauge of the specified thickness (equal to the maximum allowable warpage) under it

15.14b Measure in the directions shown

15.15 Measuring the valve seat width

rocker arms for wear as well (see Section 11 or 12).

14   Using a precision straightedge and a feeler gauge, check the head gasket mating surface for warpage. Lay the straightedge lengthwise, across the head and diagonally (corner-to-corner), intersecting the head bolt holes. Try to slip a feeler gauge of the same thickness as the warpage limit listed in this Chapter's Specifications under it, on either side of the combustion chamber **(see illustrations)**. If the feeler gauge can be inserted between the head and the straightedge, the head is warped and must either be machined or, if warpage is excessive, replaced with a new one.

15   Examine the valve seats **(see illustration)**. If they are pitted, cracked or burned, the head will require valve service that is beyond the scope of the home mechanic. Measure the valve seat width and compare it to this Chapter's Specifications. If it is not within the specified range, or if it varies around its circumference, valve service work is required.

16   Clean the valve guides to remove any carbon buildup, then measure the inside diameters of the guides (at both ends and the center of the guide) with a small hole gauge and a 0-to-1-inch micrometer **(see illustration)**. If the guides exceed the maximum value given in the Chapter's Specifications, they must be replaced. The guides are measured at the ends and at the center to determine if they are worn in a bell-mouth pattern (more wear at the ends). If they are, guide replacement is an absolute must.

17   Carefully inspect each valve face for cracks, pits and burned spots. Check the valve stem and the keeper groove area for cracks **(see illustration)**. Rotate the valve and check for any obvious indication that it is bent. Check the end of the stem for pitting and excessive wear. The presence of any of the above conditions indicates the need for valve servicing.

18   Measure the valve stem diameter and

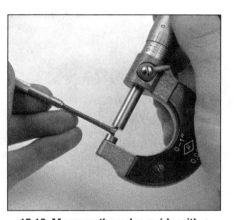

15.16   Measure the valve guide with a small hole gauge, then measure the gauge with a micrometer

replace if it exceeds the minimum value listed in this Chapter's Specifications **(see illustration)**. Also check the valve stem for bending. Set the valve in a V-block with a dial indicator touching the middle of the stem **(see illustration)**. Rotate the valve and note the reading on the gauge. If the stem runout exceeds the value listed in this Chapter's Specifications, replace the valve.

19   Check the end of each valve spring for wear and pitting. Measure the free length **(see illustration)** and compare it to this Chapter's Specifications. Any springs that are shorter than specified have sagged and

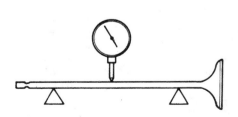

15.18b   Check the valve stem for bends with a V-block (or blocks, as shown here) and a dial indicator

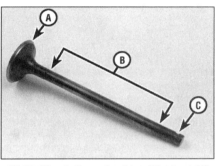

15.17   Check the valve face (A), stem (B) and keeper groove (C) for signs of wear and damage

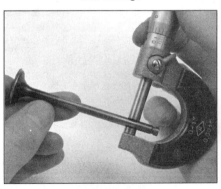

15.18a   Measure the valve stem diameter with a micrometer

2

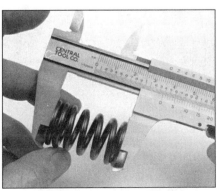

15.19a   Measure the free length of the valve springs

15.19b Check the valve springs for squareness

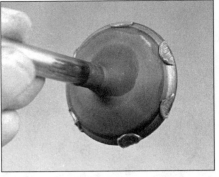

15.23 Apply the lapping compound very sparingly, in small dabs, to the valve face only

15.24a After lapping, the valve face should exhibit a uniform, unbroken contact pattern (arrow). . .

15.24b . . .and the seat should be the specified width (arrow) with a smooth, unbroken appearance

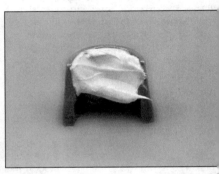

15.27 A small dab of grease will help hold the keepers in place on the valve spring while the valve is released

should not be reused. Stand the spring on a flat surface and check it for squareness (**see illustration**).

20   Check the spring retainers and keepers for obvious wear and cracks. Any questionable parts should not be reused, as extensive damage will occur in the event of failure during engine operation.

21   If the inspection indicates that no service work is required, the valve components can be reinstalled in the head.

Reassembly

Refer to illustrations 15.23, 15.24a, 15.24b and 15.27

22   Before installing the valves in the head, they should be lapped to ensure a positive seal between the valves and seats. This procedure requires fine valve lapping compound (available at auto parts stores) and a valve lapping tool. If a lapping tool is not available, a piece of rubber or plastic hose can be slipped over the valve stem (after the valve has been installed in the guide) and used to turn the valve.

23   Apply a small amount of fine lapping compound to the valve face (**see illustration**), then slip the valve into the guide. **Note:** *Make sure the valve is installed in the correct guide and be careful not to get any lapping compound on the valve stem.*

24   Attach the lapping tool (or hose) to the valve and rotate the tool between the palms of your hands. Use a back-and-forth motion rather than a circular motion. Lift the valve off the seat and turn it at regular intervals to distribute the lapping compound properly. Continue the lapping procedure until the valve face and seat contact area is of uniform width and unbroken around the entire circumference of the valve face and seat (**see illustrations**).

25   Carefully remove the valve from the guide and wipe off all traces of lapping compound. Use solvent to clean the valve and wipe the seat area thoroughly with a solvent soaked cloth. Repeat the procedure for the remaining valves.

26   Lay the spring seats in place in the cylinder head, then install new valve stem seals on each of the guides. Use an appropriate size deep socket to push the seals into place until they are properly seated. Don't twist or cock them, or they will not seal properly against the valve stems. Also, don't remove them again or they will be damaged.

27   Coat the valve stems with assembly lube or moly-based grease, then install one of them into its guide. Next, install the spring seats, springs and retainers, compress the springs and install the keepers. **Note:** *On Vulcan 700/750 models, install the inner and outer springs with the tightly wound coils at the bottom (next to the spring seat).* When compressing the springs with the valve spring compressor, depress them only as far as is absolutely necessary to slip the keepers into place. Apply a small amount of grease to the keepers (**see illustration**) to help hold them in place as the pressure is released from the springs. Make certain that the keepers are securely locked in their retaining grooves.

28   Support the cylinder head on blocks so the valves can't contact the workbench top, then very gently tap each of the valve stems with a soft-faced hammer. This will help seat the keepers in their grooves.

29   Once all of the valves have been installed in the head, check for proper valve sealing by pouring a small amount of solvent into each of the valve ports. If the solvent leaks past the valve(s) into the combustion chamber area, disassemble the valve(s) and repeat the lapping procedure, then reinstall the valve(s) and repeat the check. Repeat the procedure until a satisfactory seal is obtained.

16   Cylinders - removal, inspection and installation

Removal

1   Remove the engine from the motorcycle (see Section 6).

2   Following the procedure given in Section 13, remove the cylinder head. Make sure the crankshaft is positioned at Top Dead Center (TDC) for the cylinder you're working on.

Vulcan 700/750 models

Refer to illustration 16.5

3   If you're working on the front cylinder, remove the alternator (see Chapter 5). If you're working on the rear cylinder, remove the clutch and primary drive gear (see Sections 20 and 23).

4   Remove the upper and lower timing chains, chain guides and idler sprocket (see Section 24).

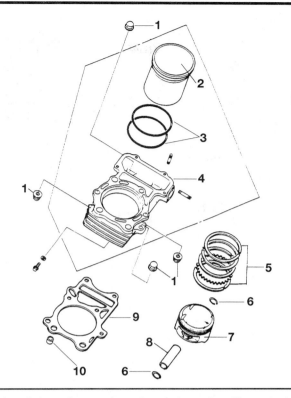

16.5 Cylinder details (Vulcan 700/750 models)

1 Cylinder nuts
2 Cylinder liner
3 O-rings
4 Cylinder
5 Piston rings
6 Circlips
7 Piston
8 Piston pin
9 Cylinder base gasket
10 Dowel

16.8 Remove the cylinder base nut

16.9a Lift the cylinder off the crankcase . . .

5 Working inside the timing chain cavity, remove two nuts that attach the cylinder to the crankcase (see illustration).

6 Lift the cylinder straight up to remove it. If it's stuck, tap around its perimeter with a soft-faced hammer. Don't attempt to pry between the block and the crankcase, as you will ruin the sealing surfaces. As you lift, note the location of the dowel pins. Be careful not to let these drop into the engine.

7 Stuff clean shop towels around the piston and remove the gasket and all traces of old gasket material from the surfaces of cylinder and crankcase.

Vulcan 800 models

Refer to illustrations 16.8, 16.9a, 16.9b and 16.10

8 Remove the nut that secures the cylin-

der to the crankcase (see illustration).

9 Lift the cylinder straight up to remove it (see illustration). If it's stuck, tap around its perimeter with a soft-faced hammer. Don't attempt to pry between the block and the crankcase, as you will ruin the sealing surfaces. As you lift, note the location of the dowel pins (see illustration). Be careful not to let these drop into the engine.

10 Stuff clean shop towels around the piston (see illustration) and remove the gasket and all traces of old gasket material from the surfaces of the cylinder and crankcase.

Inspection

Refer to illustration 16.12
Caution: *Don't attempt to separate the liners from the cylinder block.*

11 Check the cylinder walls carefully for

scratches and score marks.

12 Using the appropriate precision measuring tools, check each cylinder's diameter 10 mm down from the top, 60 mm down from the top, and 20 mm up from the bottom of the cylinder bore, parallel to the crankshaft axis (see illustration). Next, measure each cylinder's diameter at the same three locations across the crankshaft axis. Compare the results to this Chapter's Specifications. If the cylinder walls are tapered,

16.9b . . . and locate the dowels (arrows)

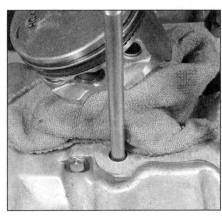

16.10 Pack clean rags into the crankcase opening to keep out debris

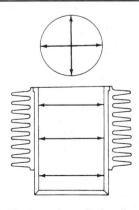

16.12 Measure the cylinder diameter in two directions, at the top, center and bottom of travel

2

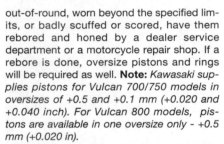

16.21 If you're experienced and very careful, the cylinder can be installed over the rings without a ring compressor, but a compressor is recommended

17.3a Using a sharp scribe, scratch the cylinder position (front or rear) into the piston crowns - also note the arrow, which must point to the front

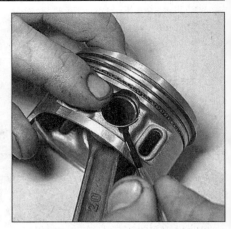

17.3b Wear eye protection and pry the circlip out of the groove with a pointed tool

out-of-round, worn beyond the specified limits, or badly scuffed or scored, have them rebored and honed by a dealer service department or a motorcycle repair shop. If a rebore is done, oversize pistons and rings will be required as well. **Note:** *Kawasaki supplies pistons for Vulcan 700/750 models in oversizes of +0.5 and +0.1 mm (+0.020 and +0.040 inch). For Vulcan 800 models, pistons are available in one oversize only - +0.5 mm (+0.020 in).*

13   As an alternative, if the precision measuring tools are not available, a dealer service department or motorcycle repair shop will make the measurements and offer advice concerning servicing of the cylinders.

14   If they are in reasonably good condition and not worn to the outside of the limits, and if the piston-to-cylinder clearances can be maintained properly (see Section 17), then the cylinders do not have to be rebored; honing is all that is necessary.

15   To perform the honing operation you will need the proper size flexible hone with fine stones, or a "bottle brush" type hone, plenty of light oil or honing oil, some shop towels and an electric drill motor. Hold the cylinder block in a vise (cushioned with soft jaws or wood blocks) when performing the honing operation. Mount the hone in the drill motor, compress the stones and slip the hone into the cylinder. Lubricate the cylinder thoroughly, turn on the drill and move the hone up and down in the cylinder at a pace which will produce a fine crosshatch pattern on the cylinder wall with the crosshatch lines intersecting at approximately a 60-degree angle. Be sure to use plenty of lubricant and do not take off any more material than is absolutely necessary to produce the desired effect. Do not withdraw the hone from the cylinder while it is running. Instead, shut off the drill and continue moving the hone up and down in the cylinder until it comes to a complete stop, then compress the stones and withdraw the hone. Wipe the oil out of the cylinder and repeat the procedure on the

remaining cylinder. Remember, do not remove too much material from the cylinder wall. If you do not have the tools, or do not desire to perform the honing operation, a dealer service department or motorcycle repair shop will generally do it for a reasonable fee.

16   Next, the cylinders must be thoroughly washed with warm soapy water to remove all traces of the abrasive grit produced during the honing operation. Be sure to run a brush through the bolt holes and flush them with running water. After rinsing, dry the cylinders thoroughly and apply a coat of light, rust-preventative oil to all machined surfaces.

Installation

Refer to illustration 16.21

17   Lubricate the cylinder bore with plenty of clean engine oil. Apply a thin film of moly-based grease to the piston skirt.

18   Install the dowel pins, then place a new cylinder base gasket on the crankcase.

19   Slowly rotate the crankshaft until the pistons is at top dead center.

20   Attach a piston ring compressor to the piston and compress the piston rings. A large hose clamps can be used instead - just make sure it doesn't scratch the piston, and don't tighten it too much.

21   Install the cylinder over the piston and carefully lower it down until the piston crown fits into the cylinder liner **(see illustration)**. While doing this, pull the camshaft chain up, using a hooked tool or a piece of coat hanger. Push down on the cylinder, making sure the piston doesn't get cocked sideways, until the bottom of the cylinder liner slides down past the piston rings. A wood or plastic hammer handle can be used to gently tap the cylinder down, but don't use too much force or the piston will be damaged.

22   Remove the piston ring compressor or hose clamp, being careful not to scratch the piston.

23   The remainder of installation is the reverse of removal.

17 Pistons - removal, inspection and installation

1   The pistons are attached to the connecting rods with piston pins that are a slip fit in the pistons and rods.

2   Before removing the pistons from the rods, stuff a clean shop towel into each crankcase hole, around the connecting rod **(see illustration 16.10)**. This will prevent the circlips from falling into the crankcase if they are inadvertently dropped.

Removal

Refer to illustrations 17.3a, 17.3b, 17.3c and 17.3d

3   Using a sharp scribe, scratch the position of each piston (front or rear cylinder) into its crown. Each piston should also have an arrow pointing toward the front of the engine **(see illustration)**. If not, scribe an arrow into the piston crown before removal. Support the piston and remove the circlip with needle-nose pliers or a pointed tool **(see illustration)**. Push the piston pin out with fingers

17.3c Push the piston pin part-way out, then pull it the rest of the way

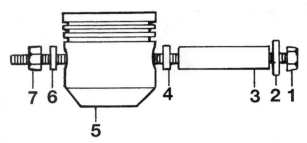

1	Bolt
2	Washer
3	Pipe (A)
4	Padding (A)
5	Piston
6	Washer (B)
7	Nut (B)
A)	Large enough for piston pin to fit inside
B)	Small enough to fit through piston pin bore

17.3d The piston should come out with hand pressure - if it doesn't, this tool can be fabricated from readily available parts

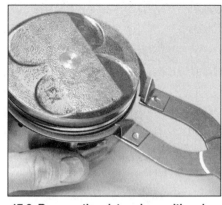

17.6 Remove the piston rings with a ring removal and installation tool

(see illustration). If the pin won't come out, fabricate a piston pin removal tool from threaded stock (stud), nuts, washers and a piece of pipe (see illustration).

4   Push the piston pin out from the opposite end to free the piston from the rod. You may have to deburr the area around the groove to enable the pin to slide out (use a triangular file for this procedure). Repeat the procedure for the other piston.

Inspection

Refer to illustrations 17.6, 17.11, 17.13, 17.14, 17.15 and 17.16

5   Before the inspection process can be carried out, the pistons must be cleaned and the old piston rings removed.

6   Using a piston ring installation tool, carefully remove the rings from the pistons (see illustration). Do not nick or gouge the pistons in the process.

7   Scrape all traces of carbon from the tops of the pistons. A hand-held wire brush or a piece of fine emery cloth can be used once most of the deposits have been scraped away. Do not, under any circumstances, use a wire brush mounted in a drill motor to remove deposits from the pistons; the piston material is soft and will be eroded away by the wire brush.

8   Use a piston ring groove cleaning tool to remove any carbon deposits from the ring grooves. If a tool is not available, a piece broken off the old ring will do the job. Be very careful to remove only the carbon deposits. Do not remove any metal and do not nick or gouge the sides of the ring grooves.

9   Once the deposits have been removed, clean the pistons with solvent and dry them thoroughly. Make sure the oil return holes below the oil ring grooves are clear.

10   If the pistons are not damaged or worn excessively and if the cylinders are not rebored, new pistons will not be necessary. Normal piston wear appears as even, vertical wear on the thrust surfaces of the piston and slight looseness of the top ring in its groove. New piston rings, on the other hand, should always be used when an engine is rebuilt.

11   Carefully inspect each piston for cracks around the skirt, at the pin bosses and at the ring lands (see illustration).

12   Look for scoring and scuffing on the thrust faces of the skirt, holes in the piston crown and burned areas at the edge of crown. If the skirt is scored or scuffed, the engine may have been suffering from overheating and/or abnormal combustion, which caused excessively high operating temperatures. The oil pump and cooling system should be checked thoroughly. A hole in the piston crown, an extreme to be sure, is an

indication that abnormal combustion (preignition) was occurring. Burned areas at the edge of the piston crown are usually evidence of spark knock (detonation). If any of the above problems exist, the causes must be corrected or the damage will occur again.

13   Measure the piston ring-to-groove clearance by laying a new piston ring in the ring groove and slipping a feeler gauge in beside it (see illustration). Check the clearance at three or four locations around the groove. Be sure to use the correct ring for each groove; they are different. If the clearance is greater than specified, new pistons will have to be used when the engine is reassembled.

14   Check the piston-to-bore clearance by measuring the bore (see Section 16) and the piston diameter. Make sure that the pistons and cylinders are correctly matched. Measure the piston across the skirt on the thrust faces at a 90-degree angle to the piston pin, about 1/2-inch (13 mm) up from the bottom of the skirt (see illustration). Subtract the piston diameter from the bore diameter to obtain the clearance. If it is greater than specified, the cylinders will have to be rebored and new oversized pistons and rings installed. If the appropriate precision mea-

2

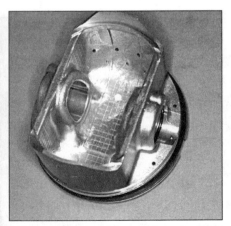

17.11 Check the piston pin bore and the piston skirt for wear, and make sure the internal holes are clear

17.13 Measure the piston ring-to-groove clearance with a feeler gauge

17.14 Measure the piston diameter with a micrometer

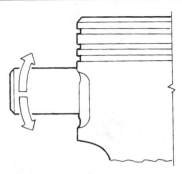

17.15 Slip the pin into the piston and try to wiggle it back-and-forth; if it's loose, replace the piston and pin

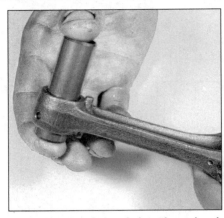

17.16 Slip the piston pin into the rod and try to rock it back-and-forth to check for looseness

17.18 Make sure both piston pin circlips are securely seated in the piston grooves

suring tools are not available, the piston-to-cylinder clearances can be obtained, though not quite as accurately, using feeler gauge stock. Feeler gauge stock comes in 12-inch lengths and various thicknesses and is generally available at auto parts stores. To check the clearance, select a piece of 0.002 in (0.07 mm) feeler gauge stock for Vulcan 700/750 models or 0.001 inch (0.37 mm) feeler gauge for Vulcan 800 models. Slip the gauge into the cylinder alongside of the piston. The cylinder should be upside down and the piston must be positioned exactly as it normally would be. Place the feeler gauge between the piston and cylinder on one of the thrust faces (90-degrees to the piston pin bore). The piston should slip through the cylinder (with the feeler gauge in place) with moderate pressure. If it falls through, or slides through easily, the clearance is excessive and a new piston will be required. If the piston binds at the lower end of the cylinder and is loose toward the top, the cylinder is tapered, and if tight spots are encountered as the feeler gauge is placed at different points around the cylinder, the cylinder is out-of-round. Repeat the procedure for the remaining piston and cylinder. Be sure to have the cylinders and pistons checked by a dealer service department or a motorcycle repair shop to confirm your findings before purchasing new parts.

15   Apply clean engine oil to the pin, insert it into the piston and check for freeplay by rocking the pin back-and-forth **(see illustration)**. If the pin is loose, new pistons and pins must be installed.

16   Repeat Step 15, this time inserting the pin into the connecting rod **(see illustration)**. If the pin is loose, measure the pin diameter and the pin bore in the connecting rod (or have this done by a dealer service department or machine shop). Replace the piston and pin if the pin is worn; replace the connecting rod if the pin bore is worn.

17   Refer to Section 18 and install the rings on the pistons.

Installation

Refer to illustration 17.18

18   Install the piston in its original location

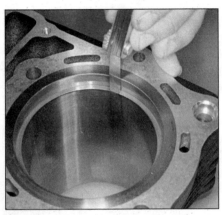

18.3 Check the piston ring end gap with a feeler gauge -measure at the bottom of the ring travel area if the cylinder looks worn

(front or rear cylinder) with the arrow pointing to the front of the engine. Lubricate the pin and the rod bore with clean engine oil. Install a new circlip in the piston groove on one side of the pistons (don't reuse the old circlips). Push the pin into position from the opposite side and install a new circlip. Compress the circlips only enough for them to fit in the piston. Make sure the circlips are properly seated in the grooves **(see illustration)**.

19   Repeat the procedure to install the other piston.

18 Piston rings - installation

Refer to illustrations 18.3, 18.5, 18.9a, 18.9b, 18.9c, 18.11a, 18.11b, 18.15a and 18.15b

1   Before installing the new piston rings, the ring end gaps must be checked.

2   Lay out the pistons and the new ring sets so the rings will be matched with the same piston and cylinder during the end gap measurement procedure and engine assembly.

3   Insert the top (No. 1) ring into the bot-

18.5 If the end gap is too small, clamp a file in a vise and file the ring ends (from the outside in only) to enlarge the gap slightly

tom of the cylinder and square it up with the cylinder walls by pushing it in with the top of the piston **(see illustration)**. The ring should be about one inch above the bottom edge of the cylinder. To measure the end gap, slip a feeler gauge between the ends of the ring and compare the measurement to the Specifications.

4   If the gap is larger or smaller than specified, double check to make sure that you have the correct rings before proceeding.

5   If the gap is too small, it must be enlarged or the ring ends may come in contact with each other during engine operation, which can cause serious damage. The end gap can be increased by filing the ring ends very carefully with a fine file **(see illustration)**. When performing this operation, file only from the outside in.

6   Excess end gap is not critical unless it is greater than 0.040 in (1 mm). Again, double check to make sure you have the correct rings for your engine.

7   Repeat the procedure for each ring that will be installed in the first cylinder and for each ring in the remaining cylinder. Remember to keep the rings, pistons and cylinders

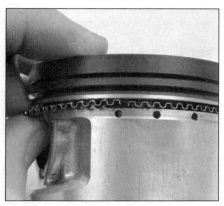

18.9a Installing the oil ring expander - make sure the ends don't overlap

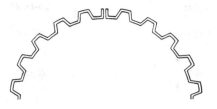

18.9b Butt the ends of the oil ring expander together like this - don't overlap them

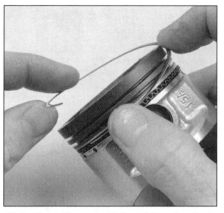

18.9c Installing an oil ring side rail - don't use a ring installation tool to do this

matched up.

8   Once the ring end gaps have been checked/corrected, the rings can be installed on the pistons.

9   The oil control ring (lowest on the piston) is installed first. It is composed of three separate components. Slip the expander into the groove, then install the upper side rail **(see illustrations)**. Do not use a piston ring installation tool on the oil ring side rails as they may be damaged. Instead, place one end of the side rail into the groove between the spacer expander and the ring land. Hold it firmly in place and slide a finger around the piston while pushing the rail into the groove. Next, install the lower side rail in the same manner.

10   After the three oil ring components have been installed, check to make sure that both the upper and lower side rails can be turned smoothly in the ring groove.

11   Install the second compression ring (middle ring) next. It can be readily distinguished from the top compression ring by its cross-section shape **(see illustrations)**. Do not mix the top and middle rings.

12   To avoid breaking the ring, use a piston ring installation tool and make sure that the identification mark is facing up. Fit the ring into the middle groove on the piston. Do not expand the ring any more than is necessary to slide it into place.

13   Finally, install the top compression ring in the same manner. Make sure the identifying mark is facing up.

14   Repeat the procedure for the remaining piston and rings. Be very careful not to confuse the middle and top rings.

15   Once the rings have been properly installed, stagger the end gaps, including those of the oil ring side rails **(see illustrations)**.

19 Clutch cable - replacement

Vulcan 700/750 models

Refer to illustration 19.4

1   Loosen the midline cable adjuster and the handlebar cable adjuster to provide as

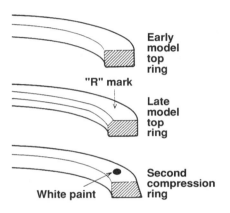

18.11a Piston ring profiles (Vulcan 700/750 models)

much slack as possible in the cable (see Chapter 1).

2   Disconnect the upper end of the clutch cable from the lever (see Chapter 1).

3   Free the cable from the retainer just above the midline cable adjuster.

2

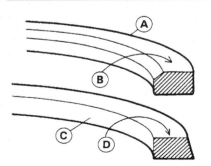

18.11b Piston ring profiles (Vulcan 800 models)

A   Top compression ring
B   Top mark
C   Second compression ring
D   Top mark

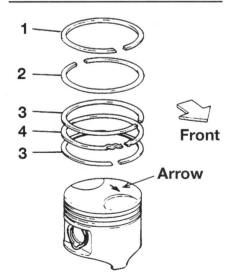

18.15a Piston and piston ring details (Vulcan 700/750 models)

1   Top compression ring
2   Second compression ring
3   Oil ring side rails
4   Oil ring expander

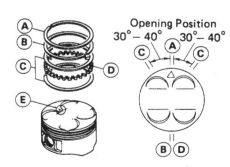

18.15b Piston and piston ring details (Vulcan 800 models)

A   Top compression ring
B   Second compression ring
C   Oil ring side rails
D   Oil ring expander
E   Piston front mark

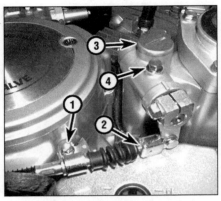

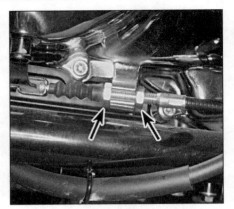

19.4 Clutch cable and release lever details (Vulcan 700/750 models)

1 Bracket bolt
2 Cable end
3 Plastic plug
4 Release shaft bolt

4 Unbolt the cable bracket near the release lever **(see illustration)**.
5 Slip the end of the cable out of the fitting on the release lever **(see illustration 19.4)**. If necessary, carefully widen the fitting slot with a screwdriver just enough to slip the cable out.

Vulcan 800 models

Refer to illustrations 19.6 and 19.8

6 Loosen the handlebar cable adjuster to provide as much slack as possible in the cable (see Chapter 1). Loosen the locknuts on the side of the engine as much as possible **(see illustration)**.
7 Disconnect the upper end of the clutch cable from the lever (see Chapter 1).
8 Push the release lever forward and disengage the cable from the bracket **(see illustration)**.
9 Slip the end of the cable out of the fitting on the release lever **(see illustration 19.6)**. If necessary, carefully widen the fitting slot with a screwdriver just enough to slip the cable out.

19.6 Loosen the locknuts (arrows) to create as much slack as possible

10 Secure the release lever in the forward position by taping it to the engine so the clutch pushrod can't fall out.

All models

11 Before removing the cable from the bike, tape the lower end of the new cable to the upper end of the old cable. Slowly pull the lower end of the old cable out, guiding the new cable down into position. Using this method will ensure the cable is routed correctly.
12 Lubricate the cable (see Chapter 1). Reconnect the ends of the cable by reversing the removal procedure, then adjust the cable following the procedure given in Chapter 1.

---

20 Clutch and release mechanism - removal, inspection and installation

---

Clutch removal

1 Set the bike on its centerstand (if equipped).
2 Drain the engine oil (see Chapter 1).

19.8 Unscrew the rear locknut, push the lever and cable housing forward and slip the cable out of the bracket

Vulcan 700/750 models

Refer to illustrations 20.5, 20.8 and 20.11

3 The clutch plates and discs can be removed without removing the engine from the motorcycle, but removal of the clutch housing does require engine removal. Unless you're sure there's a problem with the clutch housing, it's a good idea to start the procedure by removing just the clutch plates and discs, which will allow you to inspect the clutch housing to see if needs to be removed.
4 Support the bike securely upright.
5 Remove the outer clutch cover **(see illustration)**. **Caution:** *Use a wrench, not a socket, to remove the bottom bolt so the bolt won't be damaged.* As you remove the cover, separate the coolant tube from the engine.
6 Loosen the clutch spring bolts in a criss-cross pattern. Remove the clutch springs, spring plate and bearing.
7 If you're working on an early model, note the direction of the radial grooves in the friction plate. If you're looking at the top of the friction plate, the uppermost groove should slant from left (bottom) to right (top) (all of the grooves slant in the same direction). If they slant in the opposite direction, the friction plate is installed inside-out. Later friction plates have straight-cut grooves and can be installed with either face out.
8 Remove the pushrod, friction plates and steel plates from the clutch housing **(see illustration)**.
9 Inspect the plates and the clutch housing as described below to decide whether you need to remove the clutch housing (which means removing the engine from the motorcycle).
10 If you're planning to remove the clutch housing, remove the engine from the vehicle (see Section 6). Remove the right crankcase cover **(see illustration 20.5)**.
11 Remove the clutch center nut, using a special holding tool (Kawasaki tool no. 57001-1243) to prevent the clutch housing from turning. An alternative to this tool can

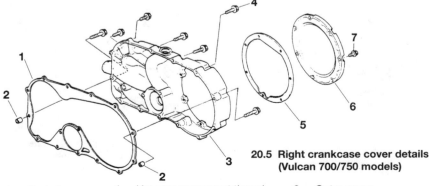

20.5 Right crankcase cover details (Vulcan 700/750 models)

1 Gasket
2 Dowels
3 Inner cover
4 Use non-permanent thread locking agent on this bolt
5 Gasket
6 Outer cover
7 Use non-permanent thread locking agent on this bolt

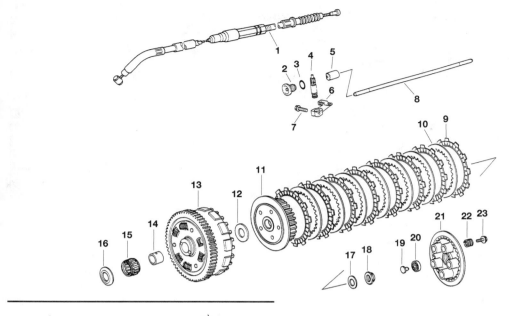

20.8 Clutch (Vulcan 700/750 models) - exploded view

1	Clutch cable
2	Plastic plug
3	O-ring
4	Release shaft
5	Release rack
6	Release lever
7	Pinch bolt
8	Long pushrod
9	Friction plates
10	Metal plates
11	Clutch center
12	Thrust washer
13	Clutch housing
14	Collar
15	Needle roller bearing
16	Thrust washer
17	Washer
18	Locknut
19	Short pushrod
20	Bearing
21	Pressure plate
22	Pressure plate spring
23	Spring bolt

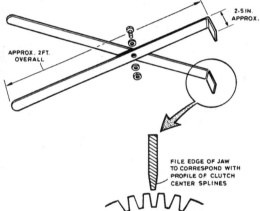

20.11 You can make your own clutch holding tool out of steel strap

be fabricated from some steel strap, bent at the ends and bolted together in the middle **(see illustration)**. The nut is self-locking, so discard it and replace it with a new one during installation.

12   Remove the washer, clutch housing and thrust washer **(see illustration 20.5)**. Remove the clutch housing bushing, needle roller bearing and thrust washer from the transmission output shaft.

Vulcan 800 models

Refer to illustrations 20.15a, 20.15b, 20.15c and 20.16

13   Disconnect the clutch cable from the release lever (see Section 19).

14   Drain the cooling system (see Chapter 3).

15   Remove the clutch cover bolts and take the cover off together with the release lever and coolant tube **(see illustrations)**. If the cover is stuck, tap around its perimeter with a soft-face hammer.

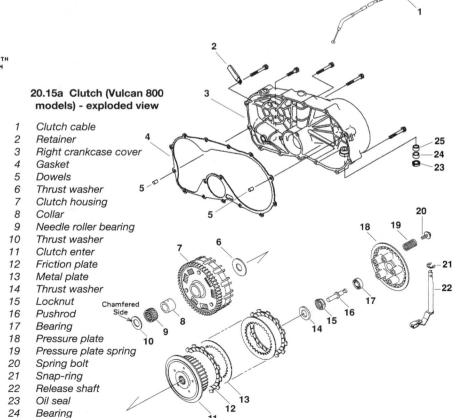

20.15a Clutch (Vulcan 800 models) - exploded view

1	Clutch cable
2	Retainer
3	Right crankcase cover
4	Gasket
5	Dowels
6	Thrust washer
7	Clutch housing
8	Collar
9	Needle roller bearing
10	Thrust washer
11	Clutch enter
12	Friction plate
13	Metal plate
14	Thrust washer
15	Locknut
16	Pushrod
17	Bearing
18	Pressure plate
19	Pressure plate spring
20	Spring bolt
21	Snap-ring
22	Release shaft
23	Oil seal
24	Bearing
25	Bearing

2

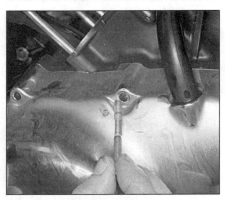

20.15b If you re-use this bolt, use non-permanent thread locking agent on the threads

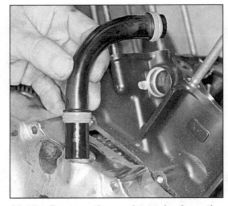

20.15c Remove the coolant tube from the cover and engine

20.16 Remove the spring bolts and springs and take off the pressure plate

20.19 Check the clutch center splines (arrows) for wear and distortion

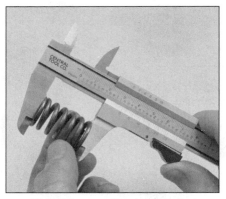

20.20 Measure the clutch spring free length

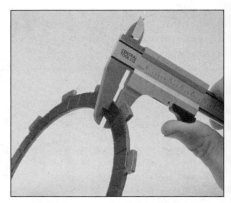

20.21 Measure the thickness of the friction plates

16   Loosen the clutch spring bolts in a criss-cross pattern **(see illustration)**. Remove the clutch springs, spring plate and bearing **(see illustration 20.15a)**.
17   Remove the pushrod, friction plates and steel plates from the clutch housing **(see illustration 20.15a)**.
18   Remove the clutch housing and related components as described in Steps 11 and 12 above.

Clutch inspection

Refer to illustrations 20.19, 20.20, 20.21, 20.22, 20.24 and 20.25

19   Examine the splines on both the inside and the outside of the clutch center **(see illustration)**. If any wear is evident, replace the hub with a new one.
20   Measure the free length of the clutch springs **(see illustration)** and compare the results to this Chapter's Specifications. If the springs have sagged, or if cracks are noted, replace them with new ones as a set.
21   If the lining material of the friction plates smells burnt or if it is glazed, new parts are required. If the metal clutch plates are scored or discolored, they must be replaced with new ones. Measure the thickness of each friction plate **(see illustration)** and compare the results to this Chapter's Specifications. Replace the friction plates as a set if they are near the wear limit.

22   Lay all metal and friction plates, one at a time, on a perfectly flat surface (such as a piece of plate glass) and check for warpage by trying to slip a 0.012-inch (0.3 mm) feeler gauge between the flat surface and the plate **(see illustration)**. Do this at several places around the plate's circumference. If the feeler gauge can be slipped under the plate, it is warped and should be replaced with a new one.
23   Check the tabs on the friction plates for excessive wear and mushroomed edges. They can be cleaned up with a file if the deformation is not severe.
24   Check the edges of the slots in the clutch housing for indentations made by the friction plate tabs **(see illustration)**. If the indentations are deep they can prevent clutch release, so the housing should be replaced with a new one. If the indentations can be removed easily with a file, the life of the housing can be prolonged to an extent.
25   Check the clutch spring plate for wear and damage and make sure the pushrod is not bent (roll it on a perfectly flat surface or use V-blocks and a dial indicator). Check the fit of the pushrod in the spring plate bearing **(see illustration)**. Check the bearing for wear or damage. Replace the pushrod and bearing if they're worn.
26   Clean all traces of old gasket material from the right crankcase cover (and the outer

cover on Vulcan 700/750 models). If the release shaft seal has been leaking, replace it as described under *Release mechanism* below.

Clutch installation

Refer to illustrations 20.27 and 20.31
Note: *This procedure includes installation of the clutch housing and right crankcase cover. If you didn't remove them, ignore the Steps which don't apply.*
27   Install the clutch housing thrust washer with its chamfered side toward the engine **(see illustration)**. Lubricate the needle roller bearing with clean engine oil and install it on the transmission output shaft, then install the clutch housing bushing.
28   Lubricate the clutch housing bushing with clean engine oil and install the clutch housing over the bushing.
29   Install the clutch center thrust washer over the transmission output shaft, against the clutch housing, then install the clutch center.
30   Install the clutch center washer and a new clutch center nut and tighten it to the torque listed in this Chapter's Specifications. Use the technique described in Step 8 to prevent the hub from turning.
31   Coat the clutch friction plates with engine oil. Install the clutch plates, starting with a friction plate and alternating them. If

20.22 Check all plates for warpage

20.24 Check the slots on the clutch housing for indentations - if they're worn, replace the clutch housing

20.25 Check the pushrod and the bearing in the pressure plate for wear and damage

20.27 Install the thrust washer with its chamfered side toward the engine

20.31 Place the tabs of the outer friction plate in the short grooves (arrow); all of the other friction plate tabs go in deep grooves

you're working on an early Vulcan 700/750 model, be sure the radial grooves in the friction plates are pointed in the correct direction (see Step 7 above). On all but the last friction plate, position the friction plate tabs in the clutch housing main grooves **(see illustration)**. The tabs of the last friction plate go in the shallow grooves.

32   If you're working on a Vulcan 700/750 model, lubricate the long pushrod and install it in the output shaft (through the spring plate). Install the short pushrod (all models) through the spring plate bearing, inserting it from the inside.

33   Install the spring plate on the clutch assembly and install the springs and bolts, tightening them to the torque listed in this Chapter's Specifications in a criss-cross pattern.

34   Install two new O-rings on each end of the coolant tube that fits into the right crankcase cover **(see illustration 20.15c)**. Lubricate the O-rings with soapy water only; do not use oil. Install the tube in the cover. Make sure the clutch cover dowels are in place **(see illustration 20.5 or 20.12a)**. Install a new gasket. Position the cover on the engine, pushing the coolant tube into its bore at the same time. Note that one of the upper bolts is coated with non-permanent thread locking agent **(see illustration 20.5 for Vulcan 700/750 models or illustration**

20.15b for Vulcan 800 models). Tighten the bolts, in a criss-cross pattern, to the torque listed in this Chapter's Specifications.

35   Connect the clutch cable to the release lever and adjust the freeplay (see Chapter 1).

36   Fill the crankcase with the recommended type and amount of engine oil (see Chapter 1).

Release mechanism removal

Vulcan 700/750 models

37   These models use a long pushrod that transfers release lever motion through the transmission output shaft to the clutch. It's removed as part of the clutch removal procedure described earlier in this section.

38   To remove the release shaft and rack, disconnect the clutch cable (see Section 19). Unscrew the plastic plug with an Allen wrench and remove the shaft guide bolt **(see illustration 19.4)**.

39   Lower the release shaft out of the engine, taking care not to let the upper portion scratch the oil seal **(see illustration 20.5)**.

40   Pull the release rack out of the hole the plastic plug was removed from, using a magnet if necessary.

41   If necessary, unscrew the release lever bolt completely (don't just loosen it) and

remove the release lever from the shaft.

42   Inspect all parts for wear or damage and replace as needed. Replace the plastic plug's O-ring if it's flattened or deteriorated.

43   Installation is the reverse of the removal steps, with the following additions:

a) *Lubricate the release rack and shaft with clean engine oil.*

b) *Make sure the release shaft engages with the rack teeth.*

c) *Align the split in the release lever with the cast rib on the engine (see Chapter 1).*

d) *Tighten the release lever pinch bolt securely, but don't overtighten it and strip the threads.*

e) *Check the engine oil and add some if necessary (see Chapter 1).*

f) *Adjust the clutch cable freeplay (see Chapter 1).*

Vulcan 800 models

Refer to illustration 20.46

44   Disconnect the clutch cable from the release lever (see Section 19).

45   Remove the right crankcase cover as described above.

46   Remove the snap-ring and slide the release shaft out of the crankcase cover **(see illustration)**.

20.46 Remove the snap-ring (arrow) and slide the release shaft out of the crankcase cover

2

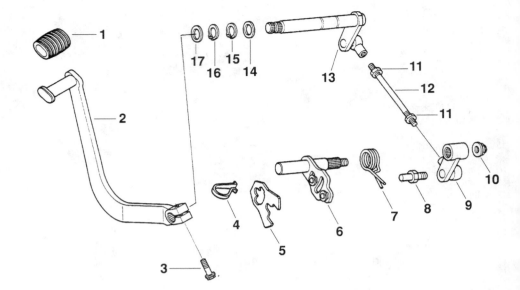

21.2 Shift pedal and linkage (Vulcan 700/750 models) - exploded view

1. Pedal pad
2. Pedal
3. Pinch bolt
4. Pawl spring
5. Shift pawl
6. Shift shaft
7. Return spring
8. Return spring post
9. Shift shaft lever
10. Nut
11. Linkage rod locknuts
12. Linkage rod
13. Pedal shaft
14. Seal
15. Snap-ring
16. Snap-ring
17. Seal

47 If the oil seal has been leaking, pry it out of the crankcase cover.

48 Remove the bearings from the crankcase cover if they're worn or damaged.

49 Installation is the reverse of the removal steps, with the following additions:

a) If the bearings were removed, lubricate the new ones with clean engine oil.

b) Press a new oil seal into the bore with your thumbs or a socket the same diameter as the seal.

21 External shift mechanism - removal, inspection and installation

Shift lever and pedal

Refer to illustrations 21.2, 21.3a, 21.3b, 21.3c and 21.4

Removal

1 Set the bike on its centerstand (if equipped) or prop it securely upright. Drain the engine oil (see Chapter 1).

2 If you're working on a Vulcan 750 model, mark the shift pedal shaft next to the split in the pedal, then remove the shift pedal bolt **(see illustration)**. Take the shift pedal off the shaft.

3 If you're working on a Vulcan 800 model (except Drifter), mark the shift shaft next to the split in the linkage lever, then remove the shift linkage pinch bolt **(see illustration)**. Remove the shift pedal nut, then unscrew the pedal pivot bolt **(see illustrations)**. Remove the pedal from the footpeg bracket together with the shift linkage.

4 If you're working on a Vulcan 800 Drifter model, mark the front shift pedal shaft next to the split in the pedal, then remove the front shift pedal pinch bolt **(see illustration)**. Take the shift pedal off the shaft. Mark the

21.3a Remove the shift linkage bolt

21.3b Remove the shift pedal nut (left arrow), then unscrew the shift pedal bolt (right arrow)

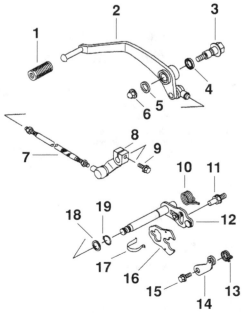

21.3c External shift linkage (Vulcan 800 models except Drifter) - exploded view

1. Pedal pad
2. Shift pedal
3. Pivot bolt
4. Seal
5. Washer
6. Pivot bolt nut
7. Linkage rod and locknuts
8. Linkage lever
9. Pinch bolt
10. Return spring
11. Return spring pin
12. Shift shaft
13. Positioning lever spring
14. Positioning lever
15. Positioning lever bolt
16. Pawl
17. Pawl spring
18. Washer
19. Snap-ring

21.4 Shift pedal and external shift linkage details (Vulcan 800 Drifter models)

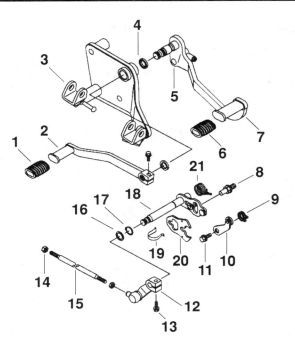

1   Pedal pad
2   Front shift pedal
3   Footpeg bracket
4   Seal
5   Rear shift pedal
6   Pedal pad
7   Rear shift pedal
8   Return spring pin
9   Positioning lever spring
10 Positioning lever
11 Bolt
12 Linkage lever
13 Pinch bolt
14 Linkage rod locknuts
15 Linkage rod
16 O-ring
17 O-ring
18 Shift shaft
19 Pawl spring
20 Shift pawl
21 Return spring

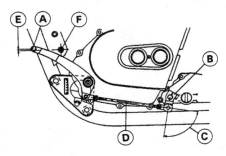

21.5a Shift linkage adjustment details (Vulcan 800 models except Drifter)

A   Shift pedal
B   Linkage lever
C   90-degrees
D   Shift linkage rod
E   Shift pedal height
F   Engine mounting bracket lower bolt

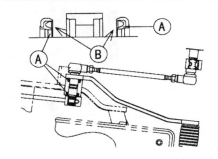

21.5b Shift linkage seals (Vulcan 800 Drifter models)

A   Seals
B   Open side (facing inward)

shift shaft next to the split in the linkage lever, then remove the lever pinch bolt and detach the linkage lever from the shaft. Slide the rear shift pedal out of the footpeg bracket and remove it together with the shift linkage. Check the pedal seals in the footpeg bracket and replace them if they're worn or damaged.

Installation

Refer to illustrations 21.5a, 21.5b, 21.5c and 21.5d

5   Installation is the reverse of removal, plus the following additions:

a) *If you're working on a Vulcan 700/750 model, align the match marks and slip the pedal onto the shaft. Install the bolt and tighten it securely.*

b) *If you're working on a Vulcan 800 model (except Drifter), install the pedal and tighten its pivot bolt with fingers. Install the linkage lever on its shaft so the lever and linkage rod are at right angles to each other* **(see illustration)**. *Tighten the pedal pivot bolt, pivot bolt nut and linkage lever pinch bolt to the torques listed in this Chapter's Specifications. If necessary, adjust pedal position as described below.*

c) *If you're working on a Vulcan 800 Drifter model, install new oil seals if the old ones were removed* **(see illustration)**. *Lubricate the seal lips with high-temperature grease. Install the rear shift pedal in the pedal bracket, slip the linkage lever over the shaft, install the pinch bolt and tighten it to the torque listed in this Chapter's Specifications* **(see illustration)**.

d) *If you're working on a Vulcan 800 Drifter model, align the match marks and install*

the front pedal onto the shaft of the rear pedal **(see illustration)**. *Install the pinch bolt and tighten it securely.*

Adjustment

6   Adjustment of the linkage rod position on Vulcan 700/750 models requires splitting the crankcase (see Section 27).

7   The standard setting on Vulcan 800 models (except Drifter) places the center of the shift pedal about 4 mm (5/32-inch) above the center of the lower bolt in the engine mounting bracket **(see illustration 21.5a)**. To raise or lower the pedal to suit your personal taste, loosen the locknuts on the linkage rod, rotate the rod to shorten or lengthen it, then tighten the locknuts. **Note:** *the lock-*

nut next to the knurled part of the linkage rod has left-hand threads.

8   If you're working on a Vulcan 800 Drifter model, the length of the linkage rod should be 130 +/- 1 mm (5.118 +/- 0.039 inch) **(see illustration 21.5b)**. If necessary, loosen the locknuts on the linkage rod, rotate the rod to

2

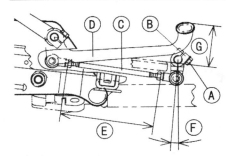

21.5c Rear shift pedal and linkage adjustment (Vulcan 800 Drifter models)

A   Pinch bolt
B   Linkage lever
C   Linkage rod
D   Rear shift pedal
E   130 mm (5.118 inches)
F   5-degrees
G   59 mm (2.323 inches)

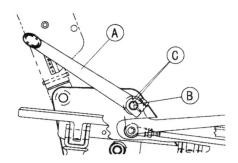

21.5d Front shift pedal adjustment (Vulcan 800 Drifter models)

A   Shift pedal
B   Pedal shaft
C   Alignment marks

21.14 Remove the cover bolts (arrows) (Vulcan 800 shown)

21.15a Remove the washer from the shift shaft

21.15b Disengage the pawl from the shift drum cam and pull the shift shaft out of the engine

21.16a Note how the spring engages the positioning lever (arrow), then unbolt the positioning lever . . .

21.16b . . . note how the other end of the spring (arrow) rests against the crankcase, then lift the lever off

shorten or lengthen it, then tighten the locknuts. **Note:** *the locknut next to the knurled part of the linkage rod has left-hand threads.*

Shift mechanism
Removal

Refer to illustrations 21.14, 21.15a, 21.15b, 21.16a, 21.16b, 21.17a and 21.17b

9   The shift shaft on Vulcan 700/750 models can't be removed without splitting the crankcase, as the nut that secures it is inside. However, the remainder of the external shift linkage (shift pawl, springs, return spring post and shift drum cam) can be removed without removing the engine from the motorcycle.

10   Drain the engine oil (see Chapter 1).

11   Remove the shift pedal and linkage (Steps 1 through 4).

12   If you're working on a Vulcan 700/750 model, remove the front bevel gear case (see Chapter 6).

13   If you're working on a Vulcan 800 model, remove the engine sprocket cover (see Chapter 6).

14   Remove the external shift linkage cover (see illustration). **Note:** *On Vulcan 800 models, it's a good idea to pull the cover off together with the shift shaft if you don't plan to*

replace the seal; that way, the seal won't be damaged by pulling the shift shaft through it. The illustrations in this Section show removing the cover and shift shaft separately for clarity.

15   If you're working on a Vulcan 800 model, remove the washer from the shift shaft (see illustration). Note how the shift shaft is installed, then pull it out of the crankcase together with the pawl, pawl spring and return spring (see illustration).

21.17a Remove the shift drum cam screw (arrow) . . .

16   Remove the bolt from the gear positioning lever (see illustration). Note how the spring engages the lever and crankcase, then remove the lever (see illustration).

17   If the shift drum cam needs to be removed, loosen its screw with an impact driver (see illustration). Remove the screw, then pull off the shift drum cam and O-ring, taking care not to lose its small dowel pin (see illustration).

21.17b . . . lift off the shift drum cam and O-ring; don't lose the dowel pin (arrow)

21.24 The assembled external shift linkage should look like this

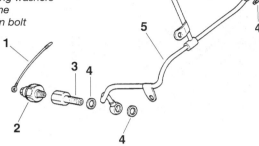

22.2 External oil line details (Vulcan 700/750 models)

1 Oil pressure switch wire
2 Oil pressure switch
3 Switch fitting/union bolt
4 Sealing washers
5 Oil line
6 Union bolt

Inspection

18 Check the shift shaft for bends and damage to the splines. If either condition is found it will have to be replaced.

19 Check the condition of the gear positioning lever, spring and shift drum cam. Replace them if they are cracked or distorted.

20 Check the shift mechanism arm for cracks, distortion and wear. Pay special attention to the tips of the pawl where they engage the shift drum cam. If any of these conditions are found, replace the shift mechanism.

21 Make sure the return spring pin isn't loose. If it is, unscrew it, apply a non-permanent locking compound to the threads, then reinstall the pin and tighten it securely.

22 Check the condition of the seal in the cover. If it has been leaking, drive it out with a hammer and punch. Drive a new seal in with a socket.

Installation

Refer to illustration 21.24

23 If you removed the shift drum cam, install it. Be sure to install the dowel pin and O-ring and use non-permanent thread locking agent on the threads of the screw. Tighten the screw securely.

24 Install the positioning lever **(see illustration)**. The shift drum should be in neutral so that the positioning lever roller locates in the neutral detent. Ensure that the leg of the return spring is correctly located against the casing web **(see illustration 21.16b)**.

25 Slide the shift shaft into place, compressing the pawl against the spring to clear the shift drum cam. Once the shaft is in place, release the pawl and let it engage with the shift drum cam **(see illustration 21.24)**.

26 Apply high-temperature grease to the lip of the cover seal. Wrap the splines of the shift shaft with electrical tape, so the splines won't damage the seal as the cover is installed.

27 Install a new gasket on the crankcase. Carefully guide the cover into place and install the screws, tightening them securely.

22.3a Pump-to-filter line and oil passage details

1 Pump-to-filter line
2 Oil passage
3 Oil pressure relief valve location (Vulcan 700/750 models)

28 The remainder of installation is the reverse of the removal steps.

29 Install and adjust the shift pedal and linkage (see Steps 1 through 5).

30 Refill the engine with oil (see Chapter 1).

22 External oil lines and passage - removal and installation

Removal

Refer to illustrations 22.2, 22.3a and 22.3b

1 Vulcan 700/750 models have an external oil line that runs from the lower right front of the engine to each cylinder head to lubricate the rocker arms and camshafts. All models have an external oil line mounted inside the left crankcase cover that routes oil from the pump to the filter.

2 To remove the cylinder head oil line on Vulcan 700/750 models, disconnect the electrical connector from the oil pressure switch **(see illustration)**. Unscrew the union bolts at each of the three fittings, remove the retainer bolts and take the oil line off together with its sealing washers.

3 To remove the pump-to-filter line, remove the alternator rotor (see Chapter 9). Remove the mounting screws, pull the line

off the engine and remove the O-rings **(see illustrations)**.

4 To remove the oil passage, remove the pump-to-filter line as described above. Remove the passage mounting screws **(see illustration 22.3a)**, then take off the oil passage together with the gasket.

Installation

5 Installation is the reverse of the removal steps, with the following additions:

a) Use a new gasket on the oil passage and new sealing washers or O-rings on the oil lines.

b) Tighten the union bolts or screws to the torque listed in this Chapter's Specifications if specified. If not, tighten them securely, but don't overtighten them and strip the threads. Use non-permanent thread locking agent on the threads of the oil passage screws and left external oil line mounting bolts.

23 Primary drive gear

Removal

Refer to illustrations 23.2a, 23.2b, 23.3, 23.4a and 23.4b

1 Remove the right crankcase cover (see Section 20).

2

22.3b Remove the line from the crankcase and pull off the O-rings

23.2a Wedge a copper washer or penny between the gears (arrow), then unscrew the primary drive gear bolt

23.2b Remove the bolt and washer

23.3 Mark the outside of the gear so it can be reinstalled facing the same way

23.4a Pull the gear off the shaft . . .

23.4b . . . and remove the Woodruff key

2   Slip a copper washer or penny between the primary gear and the gear on the clutch housing to keep the primary gear from turning **(see illustration)**. Unscrew the primary gear bolt and remove the washer **(see illustration)**.
3   Mark the outside of the primary gear so it can be installed in its original orientation **(see illustration)**.
4   Pull off the gear and remove the Woodruff key **(see illustration)**. If necessary, tap the key out of its slot with a hammer and chisel **(see illustration)**.

Inspection

5   Check the gear for worn or damaged teeth and replace it if necessary. If the primary gear is worn or damaged, also check the clutch housing gear. You may need to replace the clutch housing as well.

Installation

6   Installation is the reverse of the removal steps. Be sure to install the Woodruff key and tighten the bolt to the torque listed in this Chapter's Specifications.

24 Camshaft chains and guides (Vulcan 700/750 models) - removal, inspection and installation

Refer to illustration 24.1
1   Each cylinder on Vulcan 700/750 models uses upper and lower camshaft chains connected by an idler sprocket **(see illustration)**.

Removal

Refer to illustrations 24.2, 24.5a, 24.5b, 24.6a and 24.6b
2   Loosen the idler shaft plug and the upper camshaft chain guide bolts while the engine is still in the motorcycle **(see illustration)**.
3   Remove the engine from the motorcycle (see Section 6). If you're working on the front cylinder, remove the alternator (see Chapter 9). If you're working on the rear cylinder, remove the clutch housing and primary drive gear (see Sections 20 and 23).
4   Remove the camshaft chain tensioner and upper tension spring, camshafts and cylinder head (see Sections 8, 11 and 13).
5   Unscrew the upper chain guide bolts

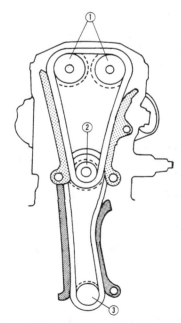

24.1 Camshaft chain layout (Vulcan 700/750 models)

1   *Cam sprockets*
2   *Idler sprockets*
3   *Crankshaft sprocket*

24.2 Loosen the idler shaft plug (A) and camshaft chain guide bolts (B)

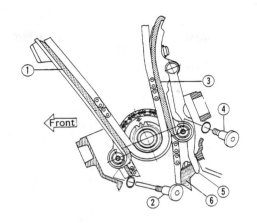

24.5a Vulcan 700/750 upper camshaft chain guides (front cylinder)

1   Upper chain guide
2   Long mounting bolt
3   Upper chain guide
4   Short mounting bolt
5   Upper chain guide contact pad
6   Lower chain guide

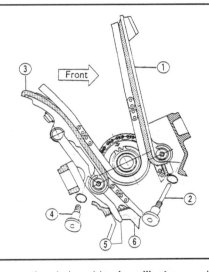

24.5b Vulcan 700/750 upper camshaft chain guides (rear cylinder)

1   Upper chain guide
2   Long mounting bolt
3   Upper chain guide
4   Short mounting bolt
5   Upper chain guide contact pad
6   Lower chain guide

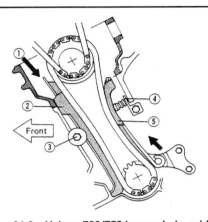

24.6a Vulcan 700/750 lower chain guide (front cylinder)

1   Direction of installation
2   Front chain guide
3   Chain guide bolt
4   Tension spring
5   Rear chain guide

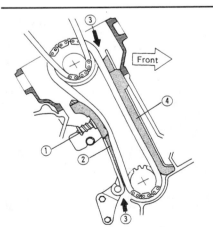

24.6b Vulcan 700/750 lower chain guide (front cylinder)

1   Tension spring
2   Rear chain guide
3   Direction of installation
4   Front chain guide

and remove the chain guides **(see illustration 8.5 and the accompanying illustrations)**.

6   On the front cylinder only, unbolt the lower front chain guide from the crankcase **(see illustrations)**. The rear cylinder's lower front chain guide is not bolted. Pull the rear run of the lower chain rearward (not too hard). This will cause the slack in the rear run of the chain to rotate around the sprocket to the front run, providing removal clearance for the guide. Put a finger under the bottom end of the guide and push it upward out of the engine.

7   Unbolt the rear lower chain guide from the crankcase. Unbolt the lower rear chain guide's tension spring and remove it, then remove the lower rear chain guide downward out of the engine.

8   Unscrew the idler shaft plug. Thread a 6x1.0 mm bolt into the shaft and use the bolt as a handle to pull the shaft out of the engine.

9   Disengage the lower chain from the crankshaft sprocket, then lift both chains and the idler sprocket out of the engine as a unit. Separate the chains from the sprocket and set them aside for inspection.

Inspection

Refer to illustration 24.10

10   Pull the chain tight to eliminate all slack and measure the length of twenty links, pin-to-pin **(see illustration)**. Compare your findings to this Chapter's Specifications. The measurement is the same for upper and lower chains.

2

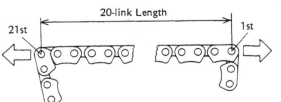

24.10 Stretch the chain and measure the length of 20 links

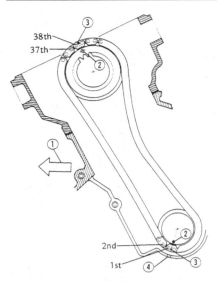

24.17 Lower camshaft chain timing marks (Vulcan 700/750 models)

1   Front of engine
2   Sprocket timing marks
3   Chain timing marks
4   Crankcase timing mark

11   Also check the chains for binding and obvious damage.
12   If the twenty-link length is not as specified, or there is visible damage, replace the chain.
13   Check the chain guides for deep grooves, cracking and other obvious damage, replacing them if necessary.
14   Check the idler sprocket for worn or damaged teeth and replace it if problems are found. If the sprocket needs to replaced, the timing chains should also be replaced.

Installation

Refer to illustration 24.17
15   Make sure the piston of the cylinder you're working on is at Top Dead Center.
16   Look for timing marks on the lower camshaft chain. If they're visible, go to Step 17. If you can't see any marks, go to Step 18.
17   Install the lower camshaft chain on the crankshaft sprocket, aligning the timing mark on the chain with the mark on the sprocket **(see illustration)**. **Note:** *The lower chain is narrower than the upper chain.* Engage the idler sprocket with the upper part of the chain, aligning the idler sprocket mark with the timing mark on the chain.
18   If marks aren't visible (early chains weren't marked), install the chain on the crankshaft sprocket and mark it next to the crankshaft sprocket mark **(see illustration 24.17)**. Pull the chain taut, count 38 pins along the front run and mark the chain at the 38th pin. Engage the idler sprocket with the chain, aligning the idler sprocket mark with the space after the 38th pin. Hold the idler sprocket up to keep the chain taut during the next Step.

25.4 Unbolt the front guide (left arrow) (front cylinder only) and the rear guide (both cylinders)

19   Coat the idler shaft with moly-based grease and place it within easy reach. Place the upper camshaft chain on its sprocket. Align the sprocket bore with the shaft hole and slip the shaft through the sprocket into the engine. Unscrew the bolt you used as a handle, install the shaft plug and tighten it securely.
20   The remainder of installation is the reverse of the removal steps, with the following additions:

a) *The front lower chain guide for the front cylinder is marked with the letter F, and the front lower chain guide for the rear cylinder is marked with the letter R. Be sure not to mix them up; the front cylinder's guide is shorter than the rear cylinder's guide.*
b) *If you're reusing the chain guide bolts, coat their threads with non-permanent thread locking agent.*
c) *Compress the lower tensioner spring onto its shaft and slip a bent paper clip or similar wire through the shaft hole to keep the spring compressed. After the tensioner is installed, remove the paper clip to release the spring.*
d) *Use new O-rings on the upper chain guide bolts. Position the lower end of the upper rear chain guide behind the top of the lower rear chain guide, so the flat pads contact each other.*

25   Camshaft chains and guides (Vulcan 800 models) - removal, inspection and installation

Removal

Refer to illustrations 25.4 and 25.5
1   Remove the camshaft chain tensioner and camshaft (see Sections 10 and 12).
2   If you're working on a front cylinder, remove the alternator (see Chapter 9).
3   If you're working on a rear cylinder, remove the clutch housing and primary gear (see Sections 20 and 23).

25.5 Unbolt the rear guide (arrow) from the rear cylinder

4   Remove the front (white) chain guide. On the front cylinder, the guide is bolted in **(see illustration)**. On the rear cylinder, it isn't bolted and can just be lifted out.
5   Label the rear (black) chain guide for front or rear cylinder so they don't get mixed up **(see illustration)**. Unbolt the chain guide and lift it out.

Inspection

6   Inspect the chain and sprockets as described in Section 24.

Installation

7   Installation is the reverse of the removal steps.

26   Balancers, starter clutch and torque limiter - removal, inspection and installation

Left balancer

Removal

Refer to illustrations 26.1, 26.2, 26.3a, 26.3b, 26.4a, 26.4b and 26.5
Note: *If you're working on a Vulcan 700/750 model, remove the engine from the motorcycle (see Section 6).*

26.1 Wedge a copper washer or penny between the balancer and alternator gears (arrow) (alternator gear hidden)

26.2 Remove the balancer bolt and washer

26.3a Note how the balancer pegs fit in the gear holes

1   Large hole (no peg)
2   Medium hole (large peg)
3   Small holes (small pegs)

26.3b Remove the gear and note the arrangement of the dampers and metal collars

26.4a Place a small bolt in the balancer . . .

26.4b . . . and set up a puller like this to remove the balancer

26.5 Pull the balancer off; the alignment marks (arrows) must be lined up during installation

1   Wedge a copper washer or penny between the balancer gear and the gear on he back of the alternator rotor **(see illustration)**. Loosen the balancer bolt, then remove the alternator rotor (see Chapter 9). **Note:** *The bolt has left-hand threads (turn it clockwise to loosen it).*
2   Unscrew the balancer bolt and remove the washer **(see illustration)**.
3   Note how the gear fits over the balancer, then lift the gear and rubber dampers off the balancer **(see illustrations)**.
4   Remove the balancer from its shaft with a puller. Place a small bolt in the balancer for the puller to push against **(see illustration)**. Install the puller and tighten it against the bolt **(see illustration)**.
5   Tighten the puller to remove the balancer and collar from the shaft. Note the punch marks on the balancer and shaft **(see illustration)**; they must be aligned on installation.

Inspection

6   Check the balancer gear for wear or damage and repealed it if problems are found.
7   Check the rubber dampers for wear or deterioration and replace them if their condition is in doubt.

Installation

8   Installation is the reverse of the removal steps, with the following additions:
a) Align the punch marks on balancer and shaft **(see illustration 26.5)**.
b) Install the rubber dampers in the gear and install metal collars in four of the six

26.10 Remove the torque limiter washer

dampers (the two dampers that fit over balancer pegs don't have collars **(see illustration 26.3b)**.
c) Place the gear over the damper with its holes correctly aligned; the largest goes over the straight edge of the damper. The next smallest goes over the large damper peg. The two smallest holes (which contain rubber dampers without metal collars) go over two of the small damper pegs.
d) Use non-permanent thread locking agent on the balancer bolt and tighten it to the torque listed in this Chapter's Specifications.

Right balancer, starter clutch and torque limiter

Refer to illustrations 26.10, 26.11, 26.12, 26.13, 26.14, 26.15, 26.16a, 26.15b and 26.17

Removal

9   Remove the right crankcase cover (see Section 20).
10   Remove the washer from the starter torque limiter **(see illustration)**.
11   Wedge a piece of hardwood into the

26.11 Wedge a piece of hardwood between the gears (arrow) and unscrew the balancer bolt

26.12 Remove the bolt and washer; the chamfered side of the washer faces the engine

26.13 Remove the starter torque limiter from its bore

26.14 Slip the needle roller bearing off the balancer shaft

26.15 If the starter clutch/balancer is stuck, use a puller to remove it

space between the primary drive gear and balancer gear so the balancer won't turn **(see illustration)**.

12   Unscrew the balancer bolt, remove the washer and take the balancer gear off **(see illustration)**.

13   If the starter torque limiter needs to be removed, pull it out of its bore **(see illustration)**.

14   Slip the needle roller bearing off the bal-

ancer shaft **(see illustration)**.

15   Pull the starter clutch/balancer and collar off the shaft. If they're difficult to remove, use a puller **(see illustration)**.

16   Once the starter clutch/balancer balancer is loose from the shaft, remove the collar and thrust washer **(see illustrations)**.

17   Note the alignment marks on the starter clutch/balancer and shaft **(see illustration)**. Pull the starter clutch/balancer off the shaft.

Inspection

18   Check the gears for wear or damage. Replace them if problems are found.

19   Check the rollers inside the starter clutch for scoring or wear. Check their retainer for damage and make sure all the rollers are securely retained. Place the starter clutch on the alternator rotor and try to turn it in both directions. It should turn freely in one direction and not at all in the other direction.

26.16a Remove the collar . . .

26.16b . . . and thrust washer

26.17 Note the positions of the alignment marks, then remove the starter clutch/balancer from the shaft

27.6a Unbolt the oil filter base . . .

27.6b . . . then remove the gasket, small O-ring (right arrow) and large O-ring (left arrow)

27.7a Be sure to remove all of the crankcase bolts; these two (arrows) . . .

27.7b . . . this one (arrow) . . .

27.7c . . . and this one (arrow) are hidden in recesses

27.8a Pry only at the pry points; here's one . . .

If it turns both ways or neither way, or if wear or damage can be seen, replace it. Remove the Allen bolts that secure the starter clutch to the balancer and take it off. Install a new starter clutch on the balancer, using non-permanent thread locking agent on the bolts, and tighten them to the torque listed in this Chapter's Specifications.

20   Check the torque limiter for wear on the gear teeth, damage or discoloration (indicating overheating). Replace it if problems are found.

Installation

21   Installation is the reverse of the removal steps, with the following additions:

a) Align the balancer and shaft marks **(see illustration 26.17)**.

b) Make sure the chamfered side of the balancer bolt washer faces the engine **(see illustration 26.12)**. Use non-permanent thread locking agent on the threads of the balancer bolt and tighten it to the torque listed in this Chapter's Specifications.

c) Lubricate the needle roller bearing with clean engine oil.

27 Crankcase - disassembly and reassembly

1   To examine and repair or replace the crankshaft, connecting rods, bearings, transmission components, oil pump, balancer shaft and starter motor clutch, the crankcase must be split into two parts.

2   Remove the right and left crankcase covers (see Section 20 and Chapter 9) and the external shift mechanism (see Section 21).

Disassembly

Refer to illustrations 27.6a, 27.6b, 27.7a, 27.7b, 27.7c, 27.8a, 27.8b, 27.9a and 27.9b

3   Remove the camshafts, cylinder heads, camshaft chains, cylinders and pistons (see Sections 11 or 12, 13, 16 and 17).

4   Remove the left balancer and alternator rotor (see Section 26 and Chapter 9).

5   Remove the clutch, primary drive gear and right balancer (see Sections 20, 23 and 26).

6   Remove the oil filter (see Chapter 1). Remove the oil filter base, gasket and O-

27.8b . . . and here's the other

rings **(see illustrations)**.

7   Remove the crankcase bolts from both sides of the crankcase, in the reverse of the tightening sequence **(see illustrations 27.19 and 27.20)**. Some of the bolts are hidden in crankcase recesses; be sure not to miss any **(see illustrations)**.

8   Carefully pry the crankcase apart. Pry ONLY in the areas indicated **(see illustrations)**.

2

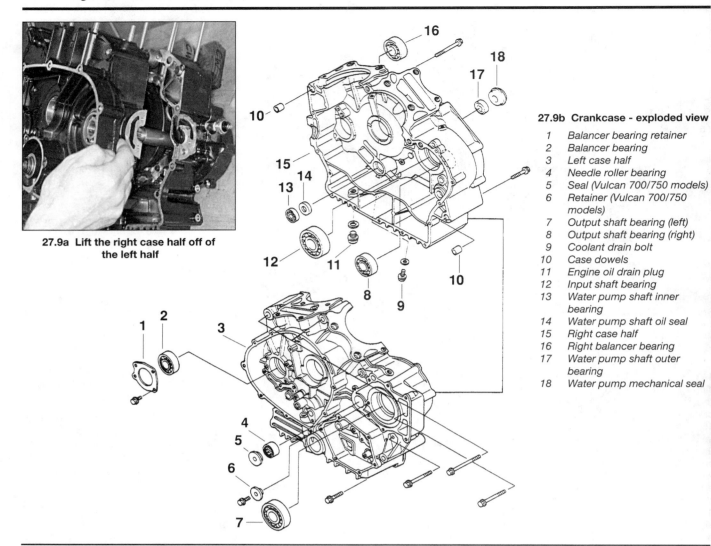

27.9a Lift the right case half off of the left half

27.9b Crankcase - exploded view

1   Balancer bearing retainer
2   Balancer bearing
3   Left case half
4   Needle roller bearing
5   Seal (Vulcan 700/750 models)
6   Retainer (Vulcan 700/750 models)
7   Output shaft bearing (left)
8   Output shaft bearing (right)
9   Coolant drain bolt
10 Case dowels
11 Engine oil drain plug
12 Input shaft bearing
13 Water pump shaft inner bearing
14 Water pump shaft oil seal
15 Right case half
16 Right balancer bearing
17 Water pump shaft outer bearing
18 Water pump mechanical seal

9   Separate the crankcase halves **(see illustrations)**.
10   Refer to Sections 28 through 37 for information on the internal components of the crankcase.

Reassembly

Refer to illustrations 27.12, 27.13, 27.15, 27.17, 27.19 and 27.20

11   Remove all traces of sealant from the crankcase mating surfaces. Be careful not to let any fall into the case as this is done.
12   Check to make sure the two dowel pins are in place in their holes in the mating surface of the crankcase half **(see illustration)**.
13   Make sure the following components are in place inside the crankcase:

27.12 Make sure the dowels (arrows) are in position

27.13 Don't forget to install the oil filter adapter

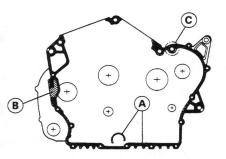

27.15 Place thin coat of silicone sealant on the mating surface (A); DO NOT put sealant in the oil passage (B) or hole (C)

27.17 Fit the notch in the water pump shaft over the oil pump tab (arrows)

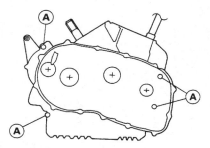

27.19 Start by tightening the 6 mm bolts in the right crankcase half (A) . . .

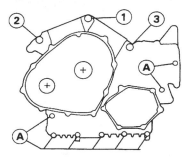

27.20 . . . then tighten the 10 mm bolts in the left crankcase half in order (1-2-3), then tighten the remaining 6 mm bolts (A)

a) Oil filter adapter fitting (see illustration)
b) Transmission shafts, shift drum and forks
c) Balancer shaft
d) Crankshaft and connecting rods
e) Oil pump
f) Internal oil lines
g) Oil pressure relief valve
h) Water pump shaft

14   Pour some engine oil over the transmission gears, the crankshaft main bearings and the shift drum. Don't get any oil on the crankcase mating surface.

15   Apply a thin, even bead of silicone sealant to the crankcase mating surface (see illustration). Caution: Don't apply an excessive amount of sealant, as it will ooze out when the case halves are assembled. Don't apply sealant to the oil passage at the front of the crankcase or the hole at the top rear.

16   Check the position of the shift drum, shift forks and transmission shafts - make sure they're in the neutral position.

17   Carefully assemble the crankcase halves, making sure the slot in the water pump engages the slot in the oil pump driveshaft (see illustration).

18   Install the crankcase bolts and tighten them so they are just snug.

19   In two steps, tighten the 6 mm bolts in the right case half to the torque listed in this Chapter's Specifications (see illustration).

20   In two steps, tighten the 10 mm bolts in the left case half to the torque listed in this Chapter's Specifications, following the sequence (see illustration). Once the 10 mm bolts are tight, tighten the 6 mm bolts to the torque listed in this Chapter's Specifications.

21   Turn the balancer shaft, input shaft and the output shaft to make sure they turn freely. Also make sure the crankshaft turns freely.

22   The remainder of installation is the reverse of removal, with the following additions:

a) Once the external shift linkage is installed, shift the transmission through all the gear positions and back to Neutral. Because the positive neutral finder locks out second through fifth gears when the output shaft isn't spinning, you'll have to spin the output shaft to shift into second through fifth gears.
b) Be sure to refill the engine oil and coolant.

28 Crankcase components - inspection and servicing

Refer to illustrations 28.2a and 28.2b

1   After the crankcases have been separated and the crankshaft, shift drum and forks, balancer shaft, oil pump and transmission components removed, the crankcases should be cleaned thoroughly with new solvent and dried with compressed air.

2   Remove the internal oil lines and the oil pressure relief valve. All oil passages and lines should be blown out with compressed air (see illustrations). Use new O-rings when installing the oil lines and tighten their

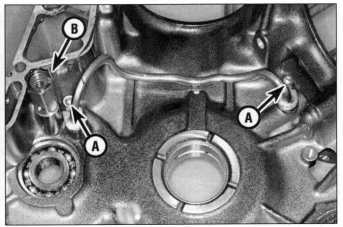

28.2a Unscrew the oil line bolts (A); The Vulcan 800 oil pressure relief valve (B) is inside the crankcase

28.2b Left case half oil line and bearings

28.5 Right case half bearings

bolts to the torque listed in this Chapter's Specifications.

3   All traces of old gasket sealant should be removed from the crankcase mating surfaces. Minor damage to the surfaces can be cleaned up with a fine sharpening stone. **Caution:** *Be very careful not to nick or gouge the crankcase mating surfaces or leaks will result. Check both crankcase sections very*

28.12 Remove the snap-ring (arrow) from the water pump shaft and push the shaft out of the case

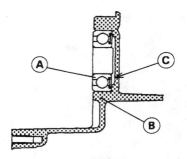

28.9 The right case half output shaft bearing (A) is installed in the crankcase (B) with its sealed side (C) into the bearing bore

carefully for cracks and other damage.
4   If any damage is found that can't be repaired, replace the crankcase halves as a set.

Bearing replacement

Refer to illustrations 28.5 and 28.9

5   Check the crankcase bearings for wear or damage **(see illustration 28.2b and the accompanying illustration)**. Inspection of the crankshaft main bearings, which are replaced as a unit with the case halves, is described in Section 30. Rotate the other bearings with fingers and check for roughness, looseness or noise. Replace bearings that are in doubtful condition.
7   Unbolt the bearing retainer from bearings so equipped. For water pump shaft bearing replacement, see Step 9. Drive the remaining bearings out with a socket or bearing driver having a diameter slightly smaller than the bearing outer race.
8   Before installing the bearings, allow them to sit in the freezer overnight, and about fifteen minutes before installation, place the case half in an oven heated to about 200-degrees F and allow it to heat up. The bearings are an interference fit and this will ease installation. **Warning:** *Before heating the case, wash it thoroughly with soap and water so that no explosive fumes are*

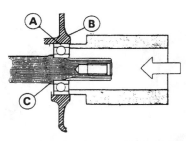

28.11 Press the right balancer bearing (A) in until it's flush with the case (B); after the balancer shaft is installed, press the bearing against the shaft shoulder (C)

present. Also, don't use a flame to heat the case.
9   Install all of the bearings except the output shaft bearing in the right case half with the marked side facing out. The sealed side of the output shaft bearing faces the crankcase **(see illustration)**.
10   Install all of the bearings except the right balancer bearing and water pump bearings with a socket or bearing driver that bears against the bearing outer race. Refer to the next Steps to install the right balancer bearing and water pump bearings.

Balancer bearing

Refer to illustration 28.11

11   Drive the right balancer in until it's flush with the outer edge of the bearing housing **(see illustration)**. Once the balancer shaft and left balancer are installed, finish the job by driving the bearing in until it stops against the shoulder on the balancer shaft.

Water pump mechanical seal and bearings

Refer to illustrations 28.12, 28.13 and 28.14

12   Remove the snap-ring and pull the water pump shaft out of the crankcase **(see illustration)**.
13   Insert a thin punch into the shaft bore and tap out the sealed bearing and oil seal **(see illustration)**. Insert the punch from the

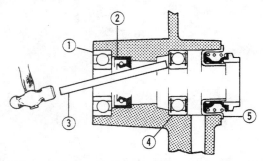

28.13 Tap out the water pump bearings and seals with a hammer and punch

1	Inner bearing	4	Outer (sealed) bearing
2	Oil seal	5	Mechanical seal
3	Punch		

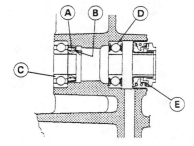

28.14 Water pump seal and bearing details

A	Oil seal	D	Outer (sealed) ball bearing
B	Marked side of seal		
C	Inner (unsealed) ball bearing	E	Mechanical seal

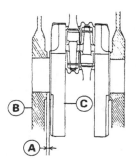

30.1a Crankshaft side clearance measurement

A   Side clearance
B   Crankcase
C   Crankshaft

other direction and tap out the oil seal and left bearing. **Note:** *the mechanical seal can be reused if it's not worn and if it wasn't damaged during removal. However, it's highly recommended that you install a new one.*

14   Install a new water pump oil seal with its marked side facing in the proper direction **(see illustration)**. Install the unsealed ball bearing against the seal. Install the sealed ball bearing in the other end of the bore, then tap in the mechanical seal with a socket that bears against the outer diameter of the seal.

29   Connecting rod bearings - general note

1   Even though connecting rod bearings are generally replaced with new ones during the engine overhaul, the old bearings should be retained for close examination as they may reveal valuable information about the condition of the engine.
2   Bearing failure occurs mainly because of lack of lubrication, the presence of dirt or other foreign particles, overloading the engine and/or corrosion. Regardless of the cause of bearing failure, it must be corrected before the engine is reassembled to prevent it from happening again.
3   When examining the bearings, remove them from the connecting rods and caps and lay them out on a clean surface in the same general position as their location on the crankshaft journals. This will enable you to match any noted bearing problems with the corresponding side of the crankshaft journal.
4   Dirt and other foreign particles get into the engine in a variety of ways. It may be left in the engine during assembly or it may pass through filters or breathers. It may get into the oil and from there into the bearings. Metal chips from machining operations and normal engine wear are often present. Abrasives are sometimes left in engine components after reconditioning operations such as cylinder honing, especially when parts are not thoroughly cleaned using the proper

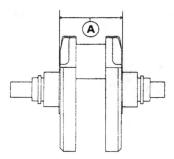

30.1b Measure crankshaft web length (A) with a vernier caliper

cleaning methods. Whatever the source, these foreign objects often end up imbedded in the soft bearing material and are easily recognized. Large particles will not imbed in the bearing and will score or gouge the bearing and journal. The best prevention for this cause of bearing failure is to clean all parts thoroughly and keep everything spotlessly clean during engine reassembly. Frequent and regular oil and filter changes are also recommended.
5   Lack of lubrication or lubrication breakdown has a number of interrelated causes. Excessive heat (which thins the oil), overloading (which squeezes the oil from the bearing face) and oil leakage or throw off (from excessive bearing clearances, worn oil pump or high engine speeds) all contribute to lubrication breakdown. Blocked oil passages will also starve a bearing and destroy it. When lack of lubrication is the cause of bearing failure, the bearing material is wiped or extruded from the steel backing of the bearing. Temperatures may increase to the point where the steel backing and the journal turn blue from overheating.
6   Riding habits can have a definite effect on bearing life. Full throttle low speed operation, or lugging the engine, puts very high loads on bearings, which tend to squeeze out the oil film. These loads cause the bearings to flex, which produces fine cracks in the bearing face (fatigue failure). Eventually the bearing material will loosen in pieces and tear away from the steel backing. Short trip riding leads to corrosion of bearings, as insufficient engine heat is produced to drive off the condensed water and corrosive gases produced. These products collect in the engine oil, forming acid and sludge. As the oil is carried to the engine bearings, the acid attacks and corrodes the bearing material.
7   Incorrect bearing installation during engine assembly will lead to bearing failure as well. Tight fitting bearings which leave insufficient bearing oil clearances result in oil starvation. Dirt or foreign particles trapped behind a bearing insert result in high spots on the bearing which lead to failure.
8   To avoid bearing problems, clean all parts thoroughly before reassembly, double check all bearing clearance measurements

30.2 Lift the crankshaft out of the case

and lubricate the new bearings with engine assembly lube or moly-based grease during installation.

30   Crankshaft and main bearings - removal, inspection and installation

Crankshaft removal

Refer to illustrations 30.1a, 30.1b and 30.2
1   Before removing the crankshaft check the side clearance. Insert a feeler gauge between the crankshaft and crankcase thrust surface **(see illustration)**. Compare your findings with this Chapter's Specifications. If the side clearance is excessive, measure the crankshaft web length **(see illustration)** and compare it to the value listed in this Chapter's Specifications. If the web length is below the specified limit, replace the crankshaft. If it's within the specified range, replace the case halves as a set.
2   Lift the crankshaft out and set it on a clean surface **(see illustration)**.

Inspection

Refer to illustrations 30.6, 30.7 and 30.9
3   If you haven't already done so, mark and remove the connecting rods from the crankshaft (see Section 31).
4   Clean the crankshaft with solvent, using a rifle-cleaning brush to scrub out the oil passages. If available, blow the crank dry with compressed air. Check the main and connecting rod journals for uneven wear, scoring and pits. Rub a copper coin across the journal several times - if a journal picks up copper from the coin, it's too rough. Replace the crankshaft.
5   Check the camshaft chain sprockets on the crankshaft for chipped teeth and other wear. If any undesirable conditions are found, replace the crankshaft. Check the chains as described in Section 24. Check the rest of the crankshaft for cracks and other damage. It should be magnafluxed to reveal hidden cracks - a dealer service department

2

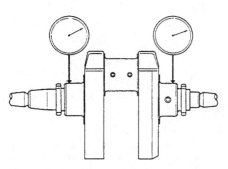

30.6 Measure crankshaft journal runout with a pair of dial indicators

or motorcycle machine shop will handle the procedure.

6   Set the crankshaft on V-blocks and check the runout with a dial indicator touching each of the main journals **(see illustration)**. Compare your findings with this Chapter's Specifications. If the runout exceeds the limit, replace the crank.

7   Measure the diameter of the crankshaft journals with a micrometer **(see illustration)** and compare your findings with this Chapter's Specifications. Also, by measuring the

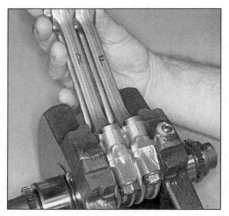

30.12a Use the Front and Rear labels on the connecting rods . . .

30.12b . . . to guide the rods into the correct cylinder openings

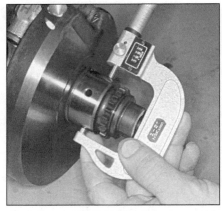

30.7 Measure main journal diameter with a micrometer

diameter at a number of points around each journal's circumference, you'll be able to determine whether or not the journal is out-of-round. Take the measurement at each end of the journal to determine if the journal is tapered.

8   If any crank journal has worn down past the service limit, replace the crankshaft.

9   Using a telescoping gauge and a micrometer, measure the diameters of the main bearing bores, then compare the measurements with those listed in this Chapter's Specifications **(see illustration)**. If the measurements are beyond the specified limit, the crankcase halves must be replaced as a set.

Crankshaft installation

Refer to illustration 30.12a and 30.12b

10   Lubricate the bearings with engine assembly lube or moly-based grease.

11   Install the connecting rods on the crankshaft at this point (see Section 31).

12   Carefully lower the crankshaft into place. Guide the connecting rods into the correct cylinders **(see illustrations)**.

13   Assemble the case halves (see Section 27) and check to make sure the crankshaft and the transmission shafts turn freely.

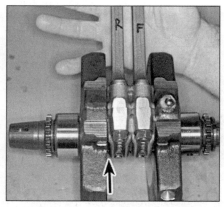

31.1 Measure connecting rod side clearance (arrow) with a feeler gauge

30.9 Measure main bearing diameter with a hole gauge

31   Connecting rods and bearings - removal, inspection, bearing selection and installation

Removal

Refer to illustrations 31.1, 31.2, 31.3a and 31.3b

1   Before removing the connecting rods from the crankshaft, measure the side clearance of the rods with a feeler gauge **(see illustration)**. If the clearance on either rod is greater than that listed in this Chapter's Specifications, the rods will have to be replaced with new ones.

2   Label the rods with cylinder letters, F for front and R for rear **(see illustration 30.12a)**. Also mark the caps. The weight grade letters on the rods can be used to determine which cap goes on which rod, since the letters are stamped across the parting line of rod and cap **(see illustration)**. If the halves of the letter don't line up perfectly, the cap is on the wrong rod.

3   Unscrew the bearing cap nuts, separate the cap from the rod, then detach the rod from the crankshaft **(see illustrations)**. If the cap is stuck, tap on the ends of the rod bolts with a soft face hammer to free them.

31.2 The letter stamped across the rod and cap is a weight grade; it should be the same for both rods

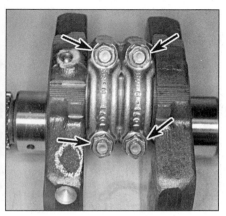

31.3a Unscrew the cap nuts (arrows) . . .

4   Separate the bearing inserts from the rods and caps, keeping them in order so they can be reinstalled in their original locations. Wash the parts in solvent and dry them with compressed air, if available.

Inspection

Refer to illustration 31.5

5   Check the connecting rods for cracks and other obvious damage. Lubricate the piston pin for each rod, install it in the proper rod and check for play **(see illustration)**. If it is loose, replace the connecting rod and/or the pin.

6   Refer to Section 29 and examine the connecting rod bearing inserts. If they are scored, badly scuffed or appear to have been seized, new bearings must be installed. Always replace the bearings in the connecting rods as a set. If they are badly damaged, check the corresponding crankshaft journal. Evidence of extreme heat, such as discoloration, indicates that lubrication failure has occurred. Be sure to thoroughly check the oil pump and pressure relief valve as well as all oil holes and passages before reassembling the engine.

7   Have the rods checked for twist and bending at a dealer service department or other motorcycle repair shop.

31.11 Lay a Plastigage strip (arrow) on the journal, parallel to the crankshaft centerline

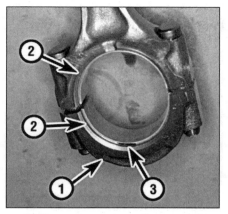

31.3b . . . then remove the cap and bearing halves

1   Cap
2   Bearing halves
3   Bearing size mark (color)

Bearing selection

Refer to illustrations 31.11, 31.13, 31.18, 31.20a, 31.20b and 31.21

8   If the bearings and journals appear to be in good condition, check the oil clearances as follows:

9   Start with the rod for the number one cylinder. Wipe the bearing inserts and the connecting rod and cap clean, using a lint-free cloth.

10   Install the bearing inserts in the connecting rod and cap. Make sure the tab on the bearing engages with the notch in the rod or cap.

11   Wipe off the connecting rod journal with a lint-free cloth. Lay a strip of Plastigage (type HPG-1) across the top of the journal, parallel with the journal axis **(see illustration)**.

12   Install the rod cap and nuts. Tighten the nuts to the torque listed in this Chapter's Specifications, but don't allow the connecting rod to rotate at all.

13   Unscrew the nuts and remove the connecting rod and cap from the journal, being very careful not to disturb the Plastigage.

31.13 Measuring the width of the crushed Plastigage (be sure to use the correct scale - standard and metric are included)

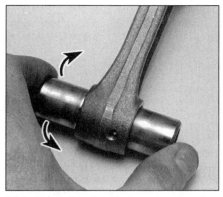

31.5 Check the piston pin and connecting rod bore for wear

Compare the width of the crushed Plastigage to the scale printed in the Plastigage envelope **(see illustration)** to determine the bearing oil clearance.

14   If the clearance is within the range listed in this Chapter's Specifications and the bearings are in perfect condition, they can be reused. If the clearance is beyond the standard range, but within the service limit, replace the bearing inserts with inserts that have blue paint marks, then check the oil clearance once again (these are the thickest bearing inserts, and may be thick enough to bring bearing clearance with the specified range). Always replace all of the inserts at the same time.

15   The clearance might be slightly greater than the standard clearance, but that doesn't matter, as long as it isn't greater than the maximum clearance or less than the minimum clearance.

16   If the clearance is greater than the service limit listed in this Chapter's Specifications, measure the diameter of the connecting rod journal with a micrometer and compare your findings with this Chapter's Specifications. Also, by measuring the diameter at a number of points around the journal's circumference, you'll be able to determine whether or not the journal is out-of-round. Take the measurement at each end of the journal to determine if the journal is tapered.

17   If any journal has worn down past the service limit, replace the crankshaft.

18   If the diameter of the journal isn't less

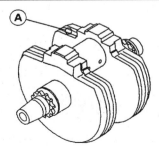

31.18 The number 1 (or no mark) in this location indicates the crankpin diameter

2

than the service limit but differs from the original markings on the crankshaft **(see illustration)**, apply new marks with a hammer and punch.

- If the journal measures within the **"no mark"** range listed in this Chapter's Specifications, don't make any marks on the crank (there shouldn't be one there anyway).
- If the journal measures within the **"1"** mark range listed in this Chapter's Specifications, make a "1" mark on the crank in the area indicated (if not already there).

19 . Remove the bearing inserts from the connecting rod and cap, then assemble the cap to the rod. Tighten the nuts to the torque listed in this Chapter's Specifications.

20 Using a telescoping gauge and a micrometer, measure the inside diameter of the connecting rod **(see illustration)**. The mark on the connecting rod (if any) should coincide with the measurement, but if it doesn't, make a new mark **(see illustration)**.

- If the inside diameter measures within the **"no mark"** range listed in this Chapter's Specifications, don't make any mark on the rod (there shouldn't be one there anyway).
- If the inside diameter measures within the **"0"** mark range, make a "0" mark on the rod (it should already be there).

21 By referring to the accompanying chart **(see illustration)**, select the correct connecting rod bearing inserts.

22 Repeat the bearing selection procedure for the remaining connecting rod.

Installation

23 Wipe off the bearing inserts, connecting rods and caps. Install the inserts into the rods and caps, using your hands only, making sure the tabs on the inserts engage with the notches in the rods and caps. When all the inserts are installed, lubricate them with engine assembly lube or moly-based grease. Don't get any lubricant on the mating surfaces of the rod or cap.

24 Assemble each connecting rod to its proper journal, making sure the previously applied matchmarks correspond to each

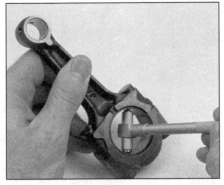

31.20a Assemble the connecting rod and measure the bore diameter with a hole gauge and micrometer

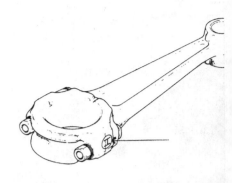

31.20b Connecting rod bore diameter is indicated by a circle around the weight grade letter (or the absence of a circle)

Connecting Rod Big End Bearing Insert Selection

Con-rod Big End Bore Diameter	Crankpin Diameter	Bearing Insert	
Marking	Marking	Size Color	Part Number
None	1	Brown	13034-1059
None	None	Black	13034-1058
○	1		
○	None	Blue	13034-1057

31.21 Use this chart to select connecting rod bearings

other and the arrow casting on the piston points to the front of the engine **(see illustration 17.3a)**. Also, the letter present at the rod/cap seam on one side of the connecting rod is a weight mark. If new rods are being installed, they should both have the same letter on them to minimize vibration.

25 When you're sure the rods are positioned correctly, tighten the nuts to the torque listed in this Chapter's Specifications.

26 Turn the rods on the crankshaft. If either of them feels tight, tap on the bottom of the connecting rod caps with a hammer - this should relieve stress and free them up. If it doesn't, recheck the bearing clearance.

27 As a final step, recheck the connecting rod side clearances (see Step 1). If the clearances aren't correct, find out why before proceeding with engine assembly.

32 Oil pump and balancer shaft - removal, inspection and installation

Note: *Oil pump and balancer shaft removal requires that the engine be removed, the crankcase disassembled and the crankshaft removed.*

Removal

Refer to illustrations 32.2, 32.3, 32.4, 32.5a and 32.5b

1 Remove the engine, disassemble the crankcase and remove the crankshaft (see Sections 6, 27 and 30).

2 Remove the snap-ring that secures the oil pump sprocket **(see illustration)**.

32.2 Remove the snap-ring from the oil pump shaft . . .

32.3 . . . and remove the sprocket, chain and balancer shaft together

32.4 Remove the screws or bolts and lift out the pump body, noting the dowel location (arrow) . . .

32.5a . . . the shaft and inner rotor . . .

32.5b . . . with the drive pin (DO NOT forget to reinstall it) and the outer rotor

32.7 Measure the oil pump clearances with a feeler gauge

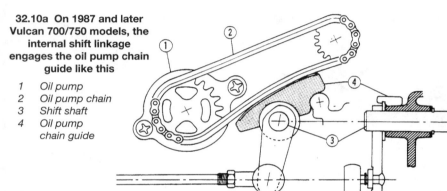

32.10a On 1987 and later Vulcan 700/750 models, the internal shift linkage engages the oil pump chain guide like this

1   Oil pump
2   Oil pump chain
3   Shift shaft
4   Oil pump chain guide

32.10b The assembled oil pump should look like this (Vulcan 800 shown)

3   Lift the oil pump sprocket, chain and balancer shaft out of the engine together **(see illustration)**.
4   Remove the screws or bolts that attach the oil pump body to the crankcase and lift it out with its O-ring **(see illustration)**. Note the location of the pump body dowel.
5   Lift out the shaft, inner rotor and drive pin **(see illustrations)**.
6   Lift the outer rotor out of the crankcase.

Inspection

Refer to illustration 32.7
7   Wash all the components in solvent, then dry them off. Check the pump body, the rotors and the shaft for scoring and wear. Measure clearance between the rotors with a feeler gauge **(see illustration)**. Also measure the clearance between the outer rotor and pump body. Lay a straightedge across the pump body and rotors and measure the clearance between the straightedge and rotors (rotor side clearance). If the measurements exceed the amount listed in this Chapter's Specifications, replace the oil pump (individual parts aren't available).
Note: *Kawasaki doesn't provide wear tolerances for Vulcan 800 models, but the Vulcan 700/750 specifications can be used as a guide. If you're rebuilding the engine, it's a good idea to install a new oil pump, even if the old one is within the Specifications.*

8   Check the bearing journals on the balancer shaft for wear or damage. Also check the sprocket for worn or damaged teeth. Replace the balancer shaft if problems are found.
9   Check the chain guide in the crankcase for wear or damage and replace it if any problems are found **(see illustration 32.5a)**.

Installation

Refer to illustrations 32.10a and 32.10b
10   Installation is the reverse of removal, with the following additions:
a) *Reassemble the pump by reversing the disassembly steps, but before installing the pump body, prime it by pouring oil between the rotors while turning the shaft by hand - this will ensure that it begins to pump oil quickly.*
b) *Make sure the pump body O-ring is in place.*
c) *Use non-permanent thread locking agent on the pump mounting bolts and tighten them to the torque listed in this Chapter's Specifications.*
d) *If you're working on a 1987 or later Vulcan 700/750 model, position the oil pump chain guide in the correct relationship with the internal shift linkage* **(see illustration)**.
e) *Use a new snap-ring and place it securely in the groove* **(see illustration)**.

33 Oil pressure relief valve - removal, inspection and installation

Removal

1   Remove the engine from the motorcycle (see Section 6).

Vulcan 700/750 models

2   Remove the left crankcase cover (see Chapter 9).
3   Remove the left side external oil line (see Section 22).
4   Unscrew the relief valve from the side of the engine, just beneath the alternator rotor.

Vulcan 800 models

5   Disassemble the crankcase (see Section 27).
6   Unscrew the relief valve from the crankcase **(see illustration 28.2a)**.

Inspection

7   Clean the valve with solvent and dry it, using compressed air if available.
8   Using a wood or plastic tool, depress the steel ball inside the valve and see if it moves smoothly. Make sure it returns to its seat completely. If it doesn't, replace it with a new one (don't attempt to disassemble and repair it).

Installation

9   Apply a non-permanent thread locking

2

34.2a Grasp the fork rod (arrow) . . .

34.2b . . . and pull it out of the forks

34.3 Remove the upper fork . . .

34.4 . . . the center fork . . .

34.5 . . . the shift drum . . .

34.6 . . . and the lower fork

compound to the threads of the valve and install it, tightening it to the torque listed in this Chapter's Specifications.
10 The remainder of installation is the reverse of removal.

34 Shift drum and forks - removal, inspection and installation

Removal

Refer to illustrations 34.2a, 34.2b, 34.3, 34.4, 34.5, 34.6 and 34.7

1 Remove the engine. Remove the external shift linkage and separate the crankcase halves (see Sections 6, 21 and 27).
2 Support the shift forks and pull the shift rod out **(see illustrations)**.
3 Remove the upper fork, noting how it engages its gear **(see illustration)**.
4 Remove the center fork **(see illustration)**.
5 Lift the shift drum out of the crankcase **(see illustration)**. If the shift drum cam is still installed on the shift drum, rotate it to align with the crankcase hole.
6 Remove the remaining shift fork **(see illustration)**.
7 It's a good idea to reassemble the forks on the shaft and engage them with the shift

drum grooves so you won't forget how they're installed **(see illustration)**.

Inspection

Refer to illustration 34.10

8 Check the edges of the grooves in the drum for signs of excessive wear. Measure the widths of the grooves and compare your findings to this Chapter's Specifications. Check the cam and bearing on the end of the shift drum for wear and damage. If undesirable conditions are found, replace the cam

34.7 Install the forks on the rod in the correct order; here's how they engage the shift drum

or bearing.
9 Check the pin plate, retainer and snapring on the other end of the shift drum for wear or damage. Replace worn or damaged parts.
10 Check the shift forks for distortion and wear, especially at the fork ears. Measure the thickness of the fork ears and compare your findings with this Chapter's Specifications **(see illustration)**. If they are discolored or severely worn they are probably bent. If damage or wear is evident, check the shift

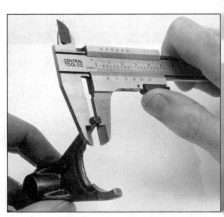

34.10 Measure the thickness of the shift fork ears

34.12a The shift forks engage with the shift drum like this (front view) . . .

34.12b . . . and here's a rear view

35.2 Lift the input shaft out of the case

fork groove in the corresponding gear as well. Inspect the guide pins and the shaft bore for excessive wear and distortion and replace any defective parts with new ones.

11 Check the shift fork rod for evidence of wear, galling and other damage. Make sure the shift forks move smoothly on the rod. If the rod is worn or bent, replace it with a new one.

Installation

Refer to illustration 34.12a and 34.12b

12 Installation is the reverse of removal, noting the following points:

a) *Lubricate all parts with engine oil before installing them.*

b) *Use a new pin plate snap-ring on the shift drum if you removed the old one.*

c) *Install the shift drum bearing with its sealed side away from the shift drum.*

d) *If you removed the shift drum bearing, use non-permanent thread locking agent on the threads of the retainer screws.*

e) *Make sure the shift forks are engaged correctly with the gear grooves* **(see illustrations)**.

35 Transmission shafts - removal and installation

Removal

Refer to illustration 35.2

1 Remove the engine and separate the case halves (see Sections 6 and 27).

2 Lift the input shaft out of the case **(see illustration)**, then lift out the output shaft.

3 Refer to Section 36 for information pertaining to transmission shaft service and Section 34 for information pertaining to the shift drum and forks.

Installation

Refer to illustration 35.4

4 Carefully lower each shaft into place and make sure the gears engage each other correctly **(see illustration)**.

5 The remainder of installation is the reverse of removal.

36 Transmission shafts - disassembly, inspection and reassembly

Note: *When disassembling the transmission shafts, place the parts on a long rod or thread a wire through them to keep them in order and facing the proper direction.*

1 Remove the shafts from the crankcase (see Section 35).

Disassembly

Refer to illustrations 36.2a and 36.2b

2 All of the input shaft parts are held on

35.4 The gears engage each other like this when they're installed correctly

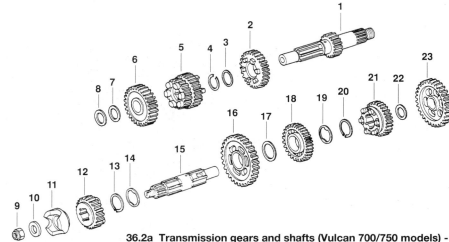

36.2a Transmission gears and shafts (Vulcan 700/750 models) - exploded view

1	Input shaft/first gear	8	Thrust washer	16	Second gear
2	Fourth gear	9	Locknut	17	Thrust washer
3	Thrust washer	10	Washer	18	Third gear
4	Snap-ring	11	Damper coupling	19	Splined washer
5	Third/second cluster gear	12	Fifth gear	20	Snap-ring
		13	Snap-ring	21	Fourth gear
6	Fifth gear	14	Splined washer	22	Thrust washer
7	Thrust washer	15	Output shaft	23	First gear

2

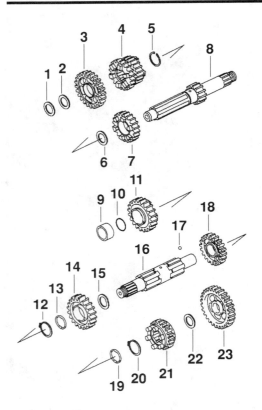

36.2b Transmission gears and shafts (Vulcan 800 models) - exploded view

1   Thrust washer
2   Thrust washer
3   Input shaft fifth gear
4   Input shaft second/third cluster gear
5   Snap-ring
6   Thrust washer
7   Input shaft fourth gear
8   Input shaft/first gear
9   Bushing
10 O-ring
11 Output shaft fifth gear
12 Snap-ring
13 Splined washer
14 Output shaft second gear
15 Thrust washer
16 Output shaft
17 Steel ball (for positive neutral finder)
18 Output shaft third gear
19 Splined washer
20 Snap-ring
21 Output shaft fourth gear
22 Thrust washer
23 Output shaft first gear

36.9 Check the slots (left arrow) and dogs (right arrow) for wear, especially at the corners; rounded corners cause the transmission to jump out of gear - new gears (bottom) have sharp corners

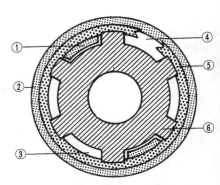

36.10 Center snap-ring gaps within a shaft groove; don't align splined washer teeth with snap-ring gaps

1	Splined washer teeth	3	Shaft groove
2	Splined washer	4	Snap-ring gap
		5	Snap-ring
		6	Shaft

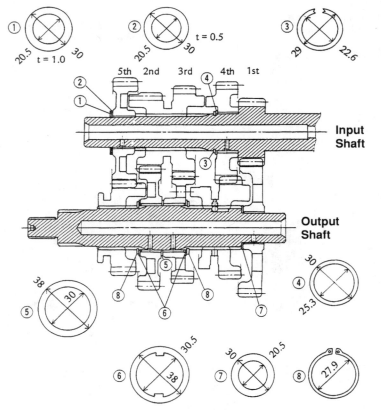

36.11a Snap-ring and thrust washer details (Vulcan 700/750 models)

the shaft by snap-rings, except first gear, which is integral with the shaft **(see illustrations)**.

3   All of the output shaft parts are held on the shaft by snap-rings **(see illustration 36.2a or 36.2b)**. Fourth gear is secured to the shaft by three steel balls, installed in channels in the gear, which must be spun outward by centrifugal force. To do this, spin the shaft with one hand, and at the same time, lift the gear with the other hand (the gear will spin with the shaft). This may take several tries.

4   Each freewheeling gear is secured with a toothed washer and snap-ring. Use snap-ring pliers to remove the snap-rings. **Caution:** *There are several sizes of snap-ring, with only a small difference between them. Be sure to keep the snap rings in their original locations and to replace them with ones of the same size.*

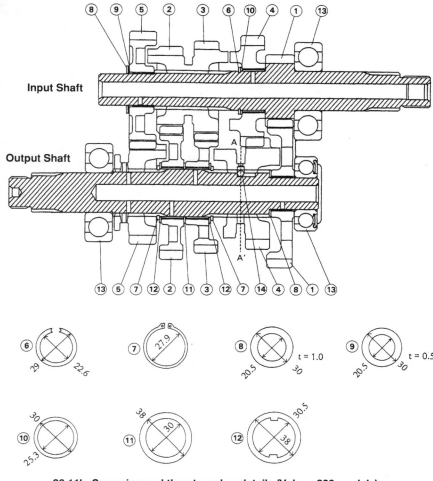

Input Shaft

Output Shaft

A

A'

36.11b Snap-ring and thrust washer details (Vulcan 800 models)

1	Output shaft first gear	8	Thrust washer (20.5x30x1.0)
2	Output shaft second gear	9	Thrust washer (20.5x30x0.5)
3	Output shaft third gear	10	Thrust washer (20.5x30x1.0)
4	Output shaft fourth gear	11	Thrust washer (30x38.x1.0)
5	Output shaft fifth gear	12	Splined washer
6	Snap-ring	13	Ball bearing
7	Snap-ring	14	Steel ball (for positive neutral finder)

5   To disassemble the shafts, refer to the appropriate illustrations **(see illustrations 36.2a and 36.2b)**.

Inspection

Refer to illustration 36.9

6   Wash all of the components in clean solvent and dry them off.

7   Measure the shift fork grooves in the gears. If the groove width exceeds the figure listed in this Chapter's Specifications, replace the gear assembly, and also check the shift fork (see Section 34).

8   Check the gear teeth for cracking and other obvious damage. Check the gear bushings for scoring or heat discoloration. If a gear or bushing is damaged, replace the gear. Also give a close look to its corresponding gear on the other shaft.

9   Inspect the dogs and the dog holes in the gears for excessive wear **(see illustration)**. Replace the paired gears as a set if necessary.

Reassembly

Refer to illustrations 36.10, 36.11a, 36.11b, 36.12a, 36.12b, 36.13 and 36.14

10   During reassembly, always use new snap-rings and align the opening of the ring with a spline groove **(see illustration)**.

11   To reassemble the shafts, refer to the exploded views **(see illustrations 36.2a and 36.2b)**. Make sure the snap-rings and thrust washers are in the correct positions **(see illustrations)**. Lubricate the components with engine oil before assembling them.

12   When installing fourth gear, don't use grease to hold the balls in place - to do so would impair the positive neutral finder mechanism. Just set the balls in their holes (the holes that they can't pass through), keep the gear in a vertical position and carefully set it on the shaft (engine oil will help keep them in place). The spline grooves that contain the holes with the balls must be aligned with the slots in the shaft spline grooves **(see illustrations)**.

2

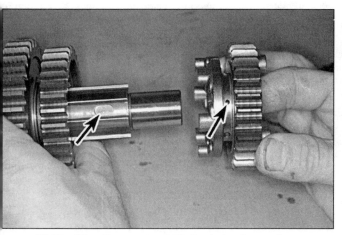

36.12a Align the grooves with the holes (arrows) . . .

36.12b . . . there are six holes inside the gear (arrow); place the centrifugal balls in the three holes that they can't pass all the way through

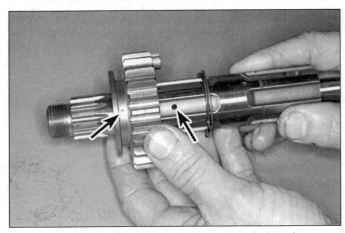

36.13 Align the oil holes in the output shaft and fifth gear (arrows)

36.14 The gears mesh like this when the shafts are properly assembled

13   When installing the output shaft fifth gear, align the oil holes in the shaft and gear **(see illustration)**.

14   Check the assembled shafts to make sure all parts are installed correctly and the gears mesh correctly with each other **(see illustration)**.

15   Lubricate the components with engine oil before assembling them.

37   Internal shift linkage (Vulcan 700/750 models) - removal, inspection and installation

1   Remove the engine and disassemble the crankcase (see Sections 6 and 27).

2   Remove the nut that secures the shift arm to the shift shaft **(see illustration 21.1)**. Pull the shift shaft out of the engine, disengaging it from the shift arm.

3   Pull the pedal shaft out of the crankcase together with the shift arm and linkage rod.

4   Check the linkage rod ends for wear and damage. Don't disassemble them unless necessary, but if problems are found, loosen the locknuts and unscrew the rod from the ends. **Note:** *The rear end of the linkage rod has left-hand threads (turn clockwise to loosen).*

5   Apply non-permanent thread locking agent to the linkage rod threads. Reassemble the linkage rod and ends so the space between the ends is 88 to 92 mm (3.464 to 3.622 inches). Tighten the locknuts securely.

6   The remainder of assembly is the reverse of the disassembly steps. Tighten the shift shaft nut securely, but don't overtighten it and strip the threads.

7   The remainder of installation is the reverse of the removal steps.

38   Initial start-up after overhaul

Note: *Make sure the cooling system is checked carefully (especially the coolant level) before starting and running the engine.*

1   Make sure the engine oil level is correct, then remove the spark plugs from the engine. Place the engine STOP switch in the Off position and unplug the primary (low tension) wires from the coil.

2   Turn on the key switch and crank the engine over with the starter until the oil pressure indicator light goes off (which indicates that oil pressure exists). Reinstall the spark plugs, connect the wires and turn the switch to On. **Note:** *If the oil pressure light won't go out, remove the oil filter (see Chapter 1). Hold the filter with the open end upright and pour oil into the center hole until the filter is full. Let the oil settle, then top it off again (you may need to do this twice). Reinstall the filter (a small amount of oil may leak out when you install it).*

3   Make sure there is fuel in the tank, then turn the fuel tap to the On position and operate the choke.

4   Start the engine and allow it to run at a moderately fast idle until it reaches operating temperature. **Warning:** *If the oil pressure indicator light doesn't go off, or it comes on while the engine is running, stop the engine immediately.*

5   Check carefully for oil leaks and make sure the transmission and controls, especially the brakes, function properly before road testing the machine. Refer to Section 39 for the recommended break-in procedure.

6   Upon completion of the road test, and after the engine has cooled down completely, recheck the valve clearances (see Chapter 1).

39   Recommended break-in procedure

1   Any rebuilt engine needs time to break-in, even if parts have been installed in their original locations. For this reason, treat the machine gently for the first few miles to make sure oil has circulated throughout the engine and any new parts installed have started to seat.

2   Even greater care is necessary if the engine has been rebored or a new crankshaft has been installed. In the case of a rebore, the engine will have to be broken in as if the machine were new. This means greater use of the transmission and a restraining hand on the throttle until at least 500 miles (800 km) have been covered. There's no point in keeping to any set speed limit - the main idea is to keep from lugging the engine and to gradually increase performance until the 500 mile (800 km) mark is reached. These recommendations can be lessened to an extent when only a new crankshaft is installed. Experience is the best guide, since it's easy to tell when an engine is running freely.

3   If a lubrication failure is suspected, stop the engine immediately and try to find the cause. If an engine is run without oil, even for a short period of time, severe damage will occur.

Chapter 3
Cooling system

Contents

Specifications

General

Coolant type and mixture ratio	See Chapter 1
Coolant capacity..	See Chapter 1
Radiator cap pressure rating	1.0 to 1.2 Bar (14 to 18 psi)
Thermostat rating	
Opening temperature	
Vulcan 700/750 models	80 to 84-degrees C (176 to 183-degrees F)
Vulcan 800 models	58 to 62-degrees C (136 to 144-degrees F)
Valve travel (when fully open)...	Not less than 8 mm (5/16-inch) at 95-degrees C (203-degrees F)

Torque specifications

Thermostatic fan switch	7.8 Nm (69 inch-lbs)
Coolant temperature sender unit	
Vulcan 700/750 models..	7.8 Nm (69 inch-lbs)
Vulcan 800 models	18 Nm (156 inch-lbs)

1 General information

Refer to illustrations 1.1a and 1.1b

1   The models covered by this manual are equipped with a liquid cooling system, which utilizes a water/antifreeze mixture to carry away excess heat produced during the combustion process **(see illustrations)**. The cylinders are surrounded by water jackets, through which the coolant is circulated by the water pump. The pump is mounted to the right side of the crankcase and is driven by a shaft that connects it to the oil pump, which in turn is driven by the balancer shaft through a chain. The coolant passes up through a coolant pipe, which distributes water around the cylinders. It flows through the water passages in the cylinder heads, through a pair of tubes and hoses and into the thermostat housing. The hot coolant then flows down

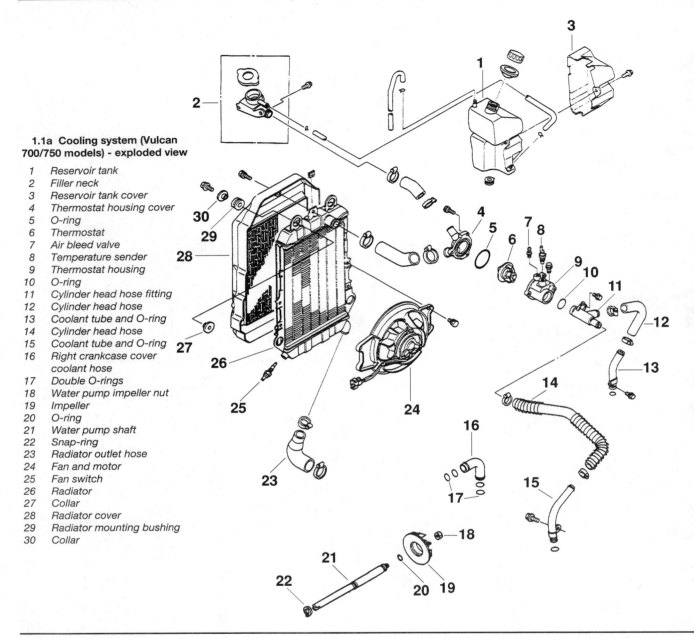

1.1a Cooling system (Vulcan 700/750 models) - exploded view

1 Reservoir tank
2 Filler neck
3 Reservoir tank cover
4 Thermostat housing cover
5 O-ring
6 Thermostat
7 Air bleed valve
8 Temperature sender
9 Thermostat housing
10 O-ring
11 Cylinder head hose fitting
12 Cylinder head hose
13 Coolant tube and O-ring
14 Cylinder head hose
15 Coolant tube and O-ring
16 Right crankcase cover coolant hose
17 Double O-rings
18 Water pump impeller nut
19 Impeller
20 O-ring
21 Water pump shaft
22 Snap-ring
23 Radiator outlet hose
24 Fan and motor
25 Fan switch
26 Radiator
27 Collar
28 Radiator cover
29 Radiator mounting bushing
30 Collar

into the radiator (which is mounted on the frame downtubes to take advantage of maximum air flow), where it is cooled by the passing air, through another hose and back to the water pump, where the cycle is repeated.

2 An electric fan, mounted behind the radiator and automatically controlled by a thermostatic switch, provides a flow of cooling air through the radiator when the motorcycle is not moving. Under certain conditions, the fan may come on even after the engine is stopped, and the ignition switch is off, and may run for several minutes.

3 The coolant temperature sending unit, threaded into the thermostat housing on Vulcan 700/750 models and into the radiator on Vulcan 800 models, senses the temperature of the coolant and controls the coolant tem-

perature gauge or light on the instrument cluster.

4 The entire system is sealed and pressurized. The pressure is controlled by a valve which is part of the radiator cap. By pressurizing the coolant, the boiling point is raised, which prevents premature boiling of the coolant. An overflow hose, connected between the radiator and reservoir tank, directs coolant to the tank when the radiator cap valve is opened by excessive pressure. The coolant is automatically siphoned back to the radiator as the engine cools.

5 Many cooling system inspection and service procedures are considered part of routine maintenance and are included in Chapter 1.

Warning: *Do not allow antifreeze to come in*

contact with your skin or painted surfaces o[f] the motorcycle. Rinse off spills immediately with plenty of water. Antifreeze is highly toxic if ingested. Never leave antifreeze lying around in an open container or in puddles on the floor; children and pets are attracted by its sweet smell and may drink it. Check with local authorities about disposing of used antifreeze. Many communities have collec tion centers which will see that antifreeze is disposed of safely.

Warning: *Do not remove the pressure cap from the thermostat housing when the engine and radiator are hot. Scalding ho[t] coolant and steam may be blown out under pressure, which could cause serious injury. To open the pressure cap, wait until the engine has cooled. When the engine has*

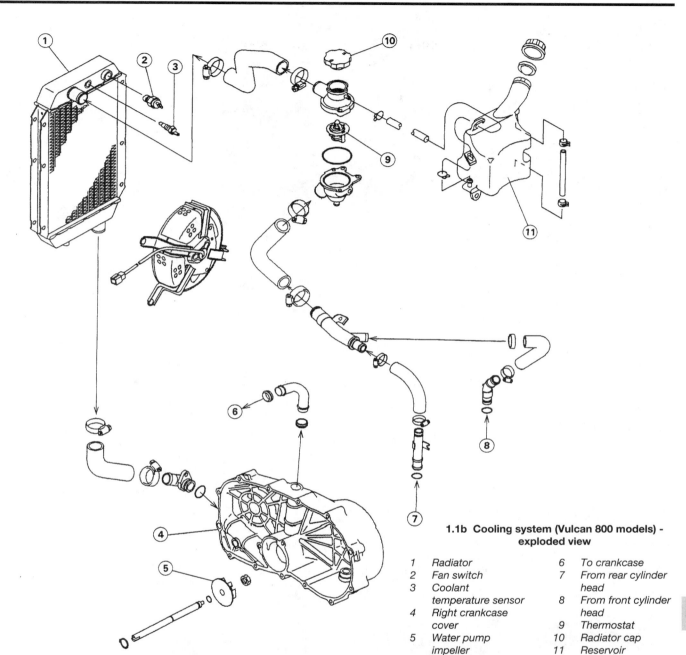

1.1b Cooling system (Vulcan 800 models) - exploded view

1	Radiator	6	To crankcase
2	Fan switch	7	From rear cylinder head
3	Coolant temperature sensor	8	From front cylinder head
4	Right crankcase cover	9	Thermostat
5	Water pump impeller	10	Radiator cap
		11	Reservoir

3

cooled, place a thick rag, like a towel, over the radiator cap; slowly rotate the cap counterclockwise to the first stop. This procedure allows any residual pressure to escape. When the steam has stopped escaping, press down on the cap while turning counterclockwise and remove it.

2   Radiator cap - check

If problems such as overheating and loss of coolant occur, check the entire system as described in Chapter 1. The radiator cap opening pressure should be checked by

a dealer service department or service station equipped with the special tester required to do the job. If the cap is defective, replace it with a new one.

3   Coolant reservoir - removal and installation

Vulcan 700/750 models

1   Remove the right side cover (see Chapter 8).
2   Unscrew the tank mounting bolt and remove the filler cap. Take the cover off the

tank **(see illustration 1.1a)**.
3   Lift the tank, with the hoses still attached, off the bottom mount. Pour the coolant into a suitable container, then disconnect the hoses and remove the tank from the motorcycle.
4   Installation is the reverse of the removal steps. Fill the tank with the specified coolant (see Chapter 1).

Vulcan 800 models

Refer to illustrations 3.6 and 3.7

5   Remove the seat, fuel tank and rear wheel (see Chapters 8, 4 and 7).
6   Disconnect the coolant hose from the

3.6 Disconnect the coolant hose (arrow)

3.7 Unbolt the mounting bracket (arrow) and remove the mounting bolts from the rear side of the tank

tank and plug it to prevent the loss of coolant **(see illustration)**.

7 Remove the mounting bolts at the rear of the tank and unbolt the tank bracket **(see illustration 3.6 and the accompanying illustration)**. Lift the tank out.

8 Installation is the reverse of the removal steps. Fill the tank with the specified coolant (see Chapter 1).

4 Cooling fan and thermostatic switch - check and replacement

Check

1 If the engine is overheating and the cooling fan isn't coming on, first check the fuses (see Chapter 9). If the fuse is blown, check the fan circuit for a short to ground (see the *Wiring diagrams* at the end of this book). If the fuses are all good, disconnect the fan electrical connector **(see illustration 11.a or 1.1b)**. Using two jumper wires, apply battery voltage to the terminals in the fan motor side of the electrical connector. If the fan doesn't work, replace the motor.

2 If the fan does come on, the problem lies in the thermostatic fan switch, the junction block, or the wiring that connects the components. Remove the jumper wires and reconnect the electrical connector to the fan.

3 If you're working on a Vulcan 700/750 model (with a single-wire fan switch harness), disconnect the electrical connector from the fan switch, attach a jumper wire to the harness side of the connector and ground the other end of the jumper wire. If the fan comes on, the circuit to the motor is good, and the thermostatic fan switch is defective.

4 If you're working on a Vulcan 800 model (with a double-wire fan switch connector), disconnect the connector. Connect the terminals in the harness side of the connector together with a jumper wire. If the fan comes on, the circuit to the motor is good and the switch is defective.

5 If you're working on Vulcan 700/750 model and the fan still doesn't work, trace the fan relay (located under the seat on the junction box - use its wire colors for identification) and place your hand on it. Repeat-

edly touch the jumper wire to ground as detailed in Step 3 - if you feel and hear a clicking inside the relay, the relay is good and the fault must lie in the wiring from the relay to the fan motor. If no clicking is heard in the relay, the fault lies in the wiring from the thermostatic fan switch to the relay. If all wiring checks out OK, the fan relay is likely to be the problem and should be replaced. Since the fan relay is an integral part of the junction box, then entire junction box must be replaced. For this reason, it's a good idea to have your diagnosis confirmed by a dealer service department or other qualified shop before buying the new part.

6 If you're working on a Vulcan 800 model and the fan still doesn't work, check the wiring back to the junction box fuse.

Replacement

Fan motor

Refer to illustrations 4.8 and 4.9

Warning: *The engine must be completely cool before beginning this procedure.*

7 Disconnect the cable from the negative terminal of the battery and remove the radiator (see Section 7).

8 Remove the three bolts securing the fan bracket to the radiator **(see illustration)**. On early models, note which bolt secures the fan motor ground wire. Separate the fan and bracket from the radiator.

9 Remove the nut that retains the blades to the fan motor shaft **(see illustration)** and remove the fan blade assembly from the motor.

10 Remove the screws that attach the fan motor to the bracket and detach the motor from the bracket.

11 Installation is the reverse of the removal steps.

Thermostatic fan switch

Refer to illustration 4.13

Warning: *The engine must be completely cool before beginning this procedure.*

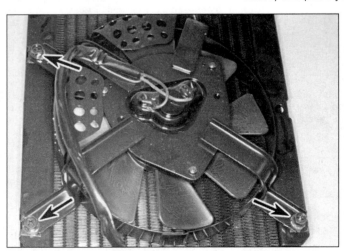

4.8 Remove the bolts (arrows) to detach the fan shroud from the radiator

4.9 The fan blade assembly is retained to the motor shaft by a single nut (arrow)

4.13 Disconnect the electrical connector and unscrew the fan switch (arrow) from the radiator

5.4a The Vulcan 700/750 coolant temperature sender (arrow) is located in the thermostat housing

5.4b Disconnect the wires from the temperature sender

12 If you're working on a Vulcan 700/750 model with a single-wire fan switch harness, don't place Teflon tape or silicone sealer on the switch threads. If you're working on a Vulcan 800 model with a two-wire fan switch harness, prepare the new switch by wrapping the new threads with Teflon tape or by coating the threads with RTV sealant.

13 Unscrew the switch from the radiator **(see illustration 1.1a or the accompanying illustration)**.

14 Quickly install the new switch, tightening it to the torque listed in this Chapter's Specifications.

15 Connect the electrical connector to the switch. Check, and if necessary, add coolant to the system (see Chapter 1).

5   Coolant temperature gauge/light and sender unit - check and replacement

Refer to illustrations 5.4a and 5.4b

Check

1 These motorcycles may be equipped with a coolant temperature gauge or a warning light.

2 If the engine has been overheating but the coolant temperature gauge hasn't been indicating a hotter than normal condition (or the warning light hasn't been coming on), begin with a check of the coolant level (see Chapter 1). If it's low, add the recommended type of coolant and be sure to locate the source of the leak.

3 Remove the seat and the fuel tank (see Chapter 4).

4 Locate the coolant temperature sender unit, which is screwed into the thermostat housing on Vulcan 700/750 models or the radiator on Vulcan 800 models **(see illustrations)**. Disconnect the electrical connector from the sender unit and turn the ignition key to the Run position (don't crank the engine over). If you're working on a model with a

temperature gauge, the gauge should read Cold. If you're working on a model with a warning light, the light should stay out.

5 With the ignition key still in the Run position, connect one end of a jumper wire to the sender unit wire and connect the other end of the jumper wire to ground. The needle on the temperature gauge should swing over to the Hot mark or the warning light should come on. **Caution:** *If the motorcycle has a gauge, don't ground the wire any longer than necessary or the gauge may be damaged.*

6 If the gauge or light passes both of these tests but doesn't operate correctly under normal riding conditions, the temperature sender unit is defective and must be replaced.

7 If the gauge or light didn't respond to the tests properly, either the wire to the gauge is bad, the gauge itself is defective or the bulb is burned out.

Replacement
Sender unit
Warning: *The engine must be completely cool before beginning this procedure.*

6.5 Loosen the clamp (arrow) and disconnect the filler neck hose from the thermostat housing

8 Unscrew the sender unit from the thermostat housing or radiator and quickly install the new unit, tightening to the torque listed in this Chapter's Specifications.

9 Connect the electrical connector to the sender unit. Check, and if necessary, add coolant to the system (see Chapter 1).

Coolant temperature gauge or bulb
10 Refer to Chapter 9 for the coolant temperature gauge or bulb replacement procedure.

6   Thermostat - removal, check and installation

Warning: *The engine must be completely cool before beginning this procedure.*

Removal

1 If the thermostat is functioning properly, the coolant temperature gauge should rise to the normal operating temperature quickly and then stay there, only rising above the normal position occasionally when the engine gets abnormally hot. If the engine does not reach normal operating temperature quickly, or if it overheats, the thermostat should be removed and checked, or replaced with a new one.

2 Refer to Chapter 1 and drain the cooling system.

3 Remove the seat and the fuel tank (see Chapter 4).

Vulcan 700/750 models
Refer to illustration 6.5

4 Disconnect the radiator hoses, reservoir tank hose and temperature sensor wire from the thermostat housing **(see illustration 5.4a)**.

5 Loosen the clamp on the filler neck hose **(see illustration)** and unbolt the thermostat housing from the frame. Work the filler neck free of the hose and remove the thermostat housing.

6 Remove the thermostat housing cover

3

6.8 Note the position of the alignment tabs (upper arrow); the thermostat bridge (arrow) fits between them

6.9 Lift the thermostat out of the housing, noting which end goes in first

7.5a Remove the radiator mounting bolt (arrow) from each side of the radiator

(see illustration 1.1a).
7   Note the position of the relief hole, then lift out the thermostat.

Vulcan 800 models

Refer to illustrations 6.8 and 6.9
8   Unbolt the cover from the thermostat housing and lift it off **(see illustration)**. Note how the thermostat fits into the alignment tabs in the housing.
9   Lift the thermostat out of the housing **(see illustration)**.

All models

10   Check the cover O-ring and replace it if its condition is in doubt. It's a good idea to replace the O-ring as a matter of course.

Check

11   Remove any coolant deposits, then visually check the thermostat for corrosion, cracks and other damage. If it was open when it was removed, the thermostat is defective.
12   To check the thermostat operation, submerge it in a container of the specified coolant (50/50 antifreeze and water) along with a thermometer. The thermostat should be suspended so it does not touch the sides of the container. **Warning:** *Antifreeze is poisonous. Do not use a cooking pan to test the thermostat.*
13   Gradually heat the water in the container with a hot plate or stove and check the temperature when the thermostat first starts to open.
14   Compare the opening temperature to the values listed in this Chapter's Specifications.
15   Continue heating the water until the valve is fully open.
16   Measure how far the thermostat valve has opened and compare to the value listed in this Chapter's Specifications.
17   If these specifications are not met, or if the thermostat doesn't open while the water is heated, replace it with a new one.

Installation

18   Install the thermostat into the housing. If you're working on a Vulcan 700/750 model, position the relief hole upward. If you're working on a Vulcan 800 model, place the thermostat so it will align with the cover tabs when the cover is installed.
19   Install a new O-ring in the groove in the thermostat cover.
20   Place the cover on the housing and install the bolts, tightening them securely.
21   The remainder of installation is the reverse of the removal steps. Fill the cooling system with the recommended coolant (see Chapter 1).

7   Radiator - removal and installation

Refer to illustrations 7.5a, 7.5b and 7.5c
Warning: *The engine must be completely cool before beginning this procedure.*
1   Set the bike on its centerstand (if equipped). Remove the fan (see Section 4). Drain the cooling system (see Chapter 1).
2   Disconnect the fan motor connector.

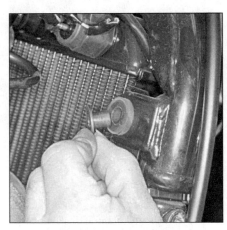

7.5b Remove the collars from the mounting bushings

Disconnect the electrical connector from the fan switch. If you're working on a Vulcan 800 model, disconnect the temperature sensor connector wires at the top of the radiator **(see illustration 5.4b)**.
3   Loosen the radiator hose clamps. Work the hoses free from the fittings, taking care not to damage the fittings in the process.
4   If you're working on a Vulcan 700/750 model, remove three bolts that secure the radiator cover. Remove the radiator mounting bolts (two at the top and two at the bottom). Take the radiator out.
5   If you're working on a Vulcan 800 model, remove the two mounting bolts at the top of the radiator, then lift the radiator bottom posts out of the mounting bushings **(see illustrations)**.
6   Inspect the mounting bushings. Replace them if they're cracked or deteriorated.
7   Installation is the reverse of the removal steps, with the following additions:
a) *Don't forget to connect the fan switch connector.*
b) *On all models, fill the cooling system with the recommended coolant (see Chapter 1).*

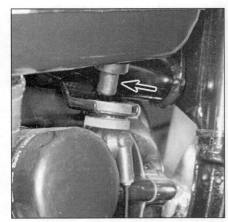

7.5c Lift the bottom posts out of the lower mounting bushings

8.10a Unscrew the impeller nut . . .

8.10b . . . and pull the impeller off the shaft; the mechanical seal (arrow) can be pried out if it's worn or damaged

8.11 Remove the sealing seat and O-ring from inside the impeller

8 Water pump - check, removal, inspection and installation

Warning: *The engine must be completely cool before beginning this procedure.*

Check

1   Visually check the area around the water pump for coolant leaks. Try to determine if the leak is simply the result of a loose hose clamp or deteriorated hose.
2   Set the bike on its centerstand (if equipped).
3   Drain the engine oil and coolant following the procedure in Chapter 1.
4   Remove the right crankcase cover (see Chapter 2).
5   Try to wiggle the pump impeller back-and-forth and in-and-out. If you can feel movement, the water pump must be replaced.
6   Check the impeller blades for corrosion. If they are heavily corroded, replace the impeller and flush the system thoroughly (it would also be a good idea to check the internal condition of the radiator).
7   If the cause of the leak was just a defective cover gasket, remove the old gasket and install a new one.

Removal

Refer to illustrations 8.10a, 8.10b and 8.11

8   Drain the engine oil and coolant and remove the right crankcase cover (if it hasn't already been removed).
9   Shift the transmission into first gear and, with the rear tire in firm contact with the floor, press the brake pedal to keep the engine from turning.
10   Unscrew the impeller nut and take the impeller off the shaft **(see illustrations)**.
11   Remove the O-ring and sealing seat from the impeller **(see illustration)**.

Inspection

Refer to illustration 8.14

12   Check all parts for wear and damage

and replace as necessary.
13   Wiggle the water pump shaft to check for looseness in the bearings. If the shaft bearings or internal oil seal need to be replaced, the crankcase must be disassembled (see Chapter 2).
14   If the mechanical seal needs to be replaced, pry its flange loose from the bore with a sharp screwdriver and pull the seal out

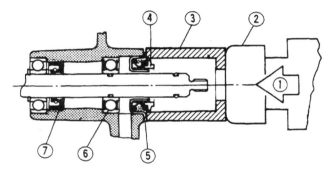

8.14 Mechanical seal installation details

1   Direction of installation
2   Bearing driver
3   28 mm socket
4   Seal
5   Seal flange
6   Water pump shaft bearing
7   Internal oil seal

9.2 Unbolt the tube brackets from the head and pull the tubes out

with pliers. Tap a new one in with a seal driver or 28 mm socket **(see illustration)**.
Note: *The new seal is coated with adhesive on the outside. Don't apply sealant to the seal or its bore.*
15   Inspect the impeller's self-locking nut. Replace it if the insert looks worn or if the nut turns easily on the threads.

Installation

16   Install a new O-ring and sealing seat on the back side of the impeller **(see illustration 8.11)**.
17   Install the impeller on the shaft and tighten the nut listed in this Chapter's Specifications.
18   The remainder of installation is the reverse of the removal steps.

9 Coolant tubes - removal and installation

Refer to illustrations 9.2, 9.3 and 9.6
Warning: *The engine must be completely cool for this procedure.*
1   Remove the seat and fuel tank (see Chapter 4).
2   Remove the screws that secure the tubes to the engine **(see illustration)**.

3

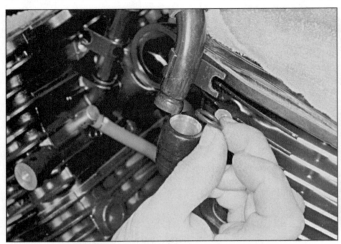

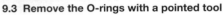

9.3 Remove the O-rings with a pointed tool

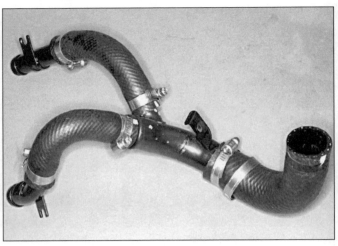

9.6 Vulcan 800 center tube and hoses

3   Pull the tubes out of the engine **(see illustration)**.

4   Remove the O-ring from each tube with a pointed tool. Lightly coat new O-rings with high-temperature grease and install them on the tubes.

5   If the tubes are being removed to provide access for other work, suspend them with their ends up.

6   Vulcan 800 models have a center tube that connects the coolant outlet hoses **(see illustration)**. The tube is secured to the hoses by clamps.

7   Installation is the reverse of the removal steps.

Chapter 4
Fuel and exhaust systems

Contents

Specifications

General

Fuel tank capacity	See General Specifications
Fuel grade	Unleaded or low-lead (subject to local regulations), minimum octane rating 91 RON
Carburetor type	
Vulcan 700/750 models	Keihin CVK34 (two)
Vulcan 800 models	Keihin CVK36 (one)
Idle speed	See Chapter 1

Jet sizes

Vulcan 700

Main jet	
Standard	135
Optional	125, 128, 130, 132, 138, 140
Main air jet	100
Jet needle	
Front carburetor	N27H
Rear carburetor	N27M
Pilot jet	38
Pilot air jet	95
Pilot screw (turns out)	Not specified
Starter (choke) jet	52

Vulcan 750

Main jet	
1985	132
1986	
US, Canada	132
Germany, Switzerland	108
All others	110
1987 through 1993	
US, Canada	132
Germany	108
Switzerland	105
All others	110
1994 and later	
US, Canada	132
Germany, Austria and Switzerland	108
All others	110

4

Jet sizes (continued)

Vulcan 750 (continued)

Main air jet 100
Jet needle
  1985
    Front carburetor N27J
    Rear carburetor N27K
  1986
    US
      Front carburetor N27U
      Rear carburetor N27V
    Canada
      Front carburetor N27J
      Rear carburetor N27K
    All others (front and rear) N31F
  1987
    US, Canada
      Front carburetor N53A
      Rear carburetor N53B
    All others (front and rear) N31F
  1988 through 1992
    US, Canada
      Front carburetor N53A
      Rear carburetor N53B
    Switzerland (front and rear) N60D
    All others (front and rear) N31F
  1993 and later
    US, Canada
      Front carburetor N53A
      Rear carburetor N53B
    Austria and Switzerland (front and rear) N96E
    All others (front and rear) N31F
Pilot jet.. 38
Pilot air jet 95
Pilot screw (turns out)
  1985 and 1986 .... 1-5/8
  1987
    All except Canada.. 1-5/8
    Canada.. 2
  1988 through 1992
    All except Canada and Switzerland 1-5/8
    Canada.. 2
    Switzerland .... Not specified
  1993 and later
    All except Canada and Switzerland 1-1/2
    Canada.. 2
    Switzerland .... Not specified
Starter (choke) jet 52

Vulcan 800

Main jet
  All except Drifter California models.. 135
  Drifter California models.. 138
Main air jet
  All except Drifter.. 100
  Drifter 70
Jet needle
  All except Drifter.. N2PE
  Drifter N8GT
Pilot jet... 48
Pilot air jet
  All except Drifter.. 70
  Drifter 110
Pilot screw (turns out).. 1-3/4
Starter (choke) jet
  All except Drifter.. 70
  Drifter 75

Fuel level

Vulcan 700/750 models

Front carburetor	0.8 mm (0.031 inch) below to 1.2 mm (0.047 inch) above upper edge of screw
Rear carburetor	1.2 mm (0.047 inch) below to 0.8 mm (0.031 inch) above upper edge of screw

Vulcan 800 models

All except Drifter...	1 to 3 mm (0.039 to 0.118 inch) above upper edge of float chamber
Drifter	0.5 +/-1 mm (0.020 +/- 0.039 inch) below float bowl mating surface

Float level

Vulcan 700/750 models	Align marks (see text)
Vulcan 800 models	
All except Drifter..	16.5 +/-2 mm (0.649 +/- 0.079 inch)
Drifter	11.0 +/-2 mm (0.433 +/- 0.079 inch)

Air switching valve test vacuum

Vulcan 700/750 models	39 to 47 kPa (11.4 to 13.8 in-Hg)
Vulcan 800 models	57 to 65 kPa (16.9 to 19.3 in-Hg)

1 General information

The fuel system consists of the fuel tank, the fuel tap and filter, the carburetor(s) and the connecting lines, hoses and control cables.

The carburetors used on Vulcan 700/750 models are two constant vacuum Keihins with butterfly-type throttle valves. The Vulcan 800 uses a single constant vacuum Keihin. For cold starting, an enrichment circuit is actuated either by a cable and the choke lever mounted on the left handlebar (Vulcan 700/750 models), or by a hand-control on the left side of the carburetor (Vulcan 800 models).

The exhaust system uses separate pipes for each cylinder. On Vulcan 700/750 models, one pipe is routed along each side of the bike. On Vulcan 800 models except Drifter, two separate pipes are routed along the right side of the bike. The Vulcan 800 Drifter is similar, but the two pipes blend into a single fishtail muffler.

Many of the fuel system service procedures are considered routine maintenance items and for that reason are included in Chapter 1.

2 Fuel tank - removal and installation

Refer to illustrations 2.1a, 2.1b, 2.3a, 2.3b, 2.3c, 2.5, 2.6, 2.7a and 2.7b

Warning: *Gasoline is extremely flammable, so take extra precautions when you work on any part of the fuel system. Don't smoke or allow open flames or bare light bulbs near the* work area, and don't work in a garage where a natural gas-type appliance (such as a water heater or clothes dryer) is present. Since gasoline is carcinogenic, wear fuel-resistant gloves when there's a possibility of being exposed to fuel, and, if you spill any fuel on your skin, rinse it off immediately with soap and water. Mop up any spills immediately and do not store fuel-soaked rags where they could ignite. When you perform any kind of work on the fuel system, wear safety glasses and have a fire extinguisher suitable for a Class B type fire (flammable liquids) on hand.

1 The fuel tank on Vulcan 700/750 models is held in place at the forward end by two bolts, one on each side of the tank, which pass through metal collars and rubber mounting grommets **(see illustration)**. The fuel tank on Vulcan 800 models is held in place at the forward end by two rubber dampers, one on each side of the tank, which fit into cups on the frame **(see illustration)**. The rear of the tank on all models is fastened to a bracket by a bolt, collar and rubber insulator, which fit through a flange projecting from the tank.

2 Remove the seat (see Chapter 8) and disconnect the cable from the negative terminal of the battery. If you're working on a Vulcan 800 model, remove the instrument

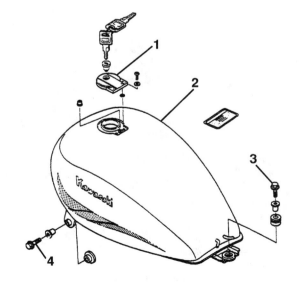

2.1a Fuel tank details (Vulcan 700/750 models)

1 *Locking cap*
2 *Fuel tank*
3 *Rear mounting bolt and grommet*
4 *Front mounting bolt and grommet (left side shown)*

4

2.1b Fuel tank details (Vulcan 800 models)

1   Instrument cluster
2   Fuel cap
3   Fuel tank
4   Rear mounting bolt and grommet
5   Front mounting bolt and grommet
6   Mounting dampers

2.3a Note how the hoses are routed (Vulcan 800 model shown)

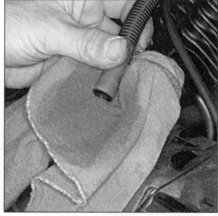

2.3b Look for color codes on the hoses and tank (arrows)

2.3c It's a good idea to have a rag handy to catch dripping fuel

2.5 Remove the bolt at the rear of the tank (Vulcan 700/750 model shown)

cluster from the top of the tank (see Chapter 9).
3   Note the routing of the tank hoses through their retainers **(see illustration)**. Mark and disconnect the breather hose and, on California models, the evaporative emission control system hoses from the tank.

Note any color code markings on the hoses; if they're obscured, make your own so the hoses can be reconnected properly **(see illustration)**. It's a good idea to have a rag ready to catch any dripping fuel **(see illustration)**.
4   Disconnect the fuel lines from the fit-

tings on the fuel tap (see Chapter 1).
5   Remove the bolt securing the rear of the tank to the bracket **(see illustration)**.
6   If you're working on a Vulcan 700/750 model, remove the front mounting bolt on each side of the tank **(see illustration)**.
7   If you're working on a Vulcan 800

2.6 On Vulcan 700/750 models, remove the bolt on each side of the tank at the front (arrow)

2.7a On Vulcan 800 models, remove the mounting bolt at the front of the tank - it's below the instrument cluster

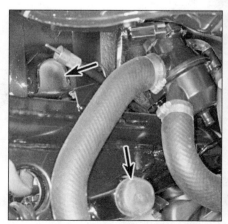

2.7b On Vulcan 800 models, pull the tank cups off the mounting dampers (arrows)

model, remove the mounting bolt at the front of the tank **(see illustration)**. Slide the tank to the rear to disengage the rubber dampers from the cups, then carefully lift the tank away from the machine **(see illustration)**.

8   Before installing the tank, check the condition of the rubber mounting dampers and grommets and the hoses on the underside of the tank - if they're hardened, cracked, or show any other signs of deterioration, replace them.

9   When installing the tank, reverse the above procedure. Make sure the tank seats properly and does not pinch any control cables or wires. If difficulty is encountered when trying to slide the tank dampers into the cups on Vulcan 800 models, a small amount of light oil should be used to lubricate them.

3   Fuel tank - cleaning and repair

1   All repairs to the fuel tank should be carried out by a professional who has experience in this critical and potentially dangerous work. Even after cleaning and flushing of the fuel system, explosive fumes can remain and ignite during repair of the tank.

2   If the fuel tank is removed from the vehicle, it should not be placed in an area where sparks or open flames could ignite the fumes coming out of the tank. Be especially careful inside garages where a natural gas-type appliance is located, because the pilot light could cause an explosion.

4   Idle fuel/air mixture adjustment - general information

1   Due to the increased emphasis on controlling motorcycle exhaust emissions, certain governmental regulations have been formulated which directly affect the carburetion of this machine. In order to comply with the regulations, the carburetors on some models have a metal sealing plug pressed into the hole over the pilot screw (which controls the idle fuel/air mixture) on each carburetor, so they can't be tampered with. These should only be removed in the event of a complete carburetor overhaul (described in Section 8), and even then the screws should be returned to their original settings. The pilot screws on other models are accessible, but the use of an exhaust gas analyzer is the only accurate way to adjust the idle fuel/air mixture and be sure the machine doesn't exceed the emissions regulations.

2   If the engine runs extremely rough at idle or continually stalls, and if a carburetor overhaul does not cure the problem, take the motorcycle to a Kawasaki dealer service department or other repair shop equipped with an exhaust gas analyzer. They will be able to properly adjust the idle fuel/air mixture to achieve a smooth idle and restore low speed performance.

5   Carburetor overhaul - general information

1   Poor engine performance, hesitation, hard starting, stalling, flooding and backfiring are all signs that major carburetor maintenance may be required.

2   Keep in mind that many so-called carburetor problems are really not carburetor problems at all, but mechanical problems within the engine or malfunctions within the ignition system. Try to establish for certain that the carburetors are in need of a major overhaul before beginning.

3   Check the fuel tap filter, the fuel lines, the tank cap vent, the intake manifold hose clamps, the vacuum hoses, the air filter element, the cylinder compression, the spark plugs, the air suction system (if equipped) and the carburetor synchronization before assuming that a carburetor overhaul is required.

4   Most carburetor problems are caused by dirt particles, varnish and other deposits which build up in and block the fuel and air passages. Also, in time, gaskets and O-rings shrink or deteriorate and cause fuel and air leaks which lead to poor performance.

5   When the carburetor is overhauled, it is generally disassembled completely and the parts are cleaned thoroughly with a carburetor cleaning solvent and dried with filtered, unlubricated compressed air. The fuel and air passages are also blown through with compressed air to force out any dirt that may have been loosened but not removed by the solvent. Once the cleaning process is complete, the carburetor is reassembled using new gaskets, O-rings and, generally, a new inlet needle valve and seat.

6   Before disassembling the carburetor(s), make sure you have a carburetor rebuild kit (which will include all necessary O-rings and other parts), some carburetor cleaner, a supply of rags, some means of blowing out the carburetor passages and a clean place to work. It is recommended that only one car-

buretor be overhauled at a time to avoid mixing up parts.

6   Carburetors - removal and installation

Warning: *Gasoline is extremely flammable, so take extra precautions when you work on any part of the fuel system (see the Warning in Section 2).*

Vulcan 700/750 models
Removal
Refer to illustrations 6.8a, 6.8b, 6.8c, 6.8d and 6.9

1   Remove the seat, fuel tank and fuel tank front trim covers (see Chapter 8 and Section 2).

2   Remove both air cleaner housings (see Section 12).

3   Disconnect the upper ends of both throttle cables at the handlebar (see Section 10). Free the lower ends of the cables from their brackets at the carburetors, but don't disconnect the cables from the carburetors yet.

4   Drain the cooling system (see Chapter 1). Remove the thermostat housing and coolant filler neck from the motorcycle (see Chapter 3).

5   Free the main wiring harness from its retainers.

6   Disconnect the right air suction hose and the vent hose from the surge tank (see Section 14).

7   Disconnect the choke cable from the rear carburetor (see Section 11).

8   Loosen the clamping bands on the carburetor air intake ducts. Detach the ducts from the carburetors and surge tank **(see illustrations)**. **Note:** *You'll need to lift the rear end of the surge tank up as far as possible to detach the air intake tubes.*

9   Loosen both intake manifold clamping bands on the rear carburetor. Loosen the

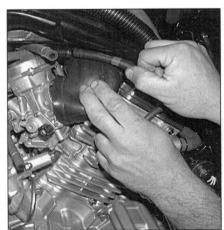

6.8a Separate the rear carburetor's air intake tube from the carburetor . . .

6.8b . . . and from the surge tank, then remove it

6.8c Separate the front carburetor's air intake tube from the carburetor . . .

6.8d . . . and from the surge tank; the notch in each tube (arrow) aligns with the tab on the surge tank

6.9 Use a long screwdriver to loosen the intake manifold clamping bands

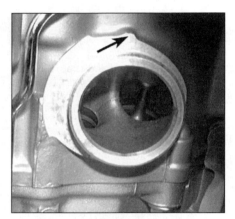

6.14 The tab on the intake manifold should align with the mark above the intake port (arrow)

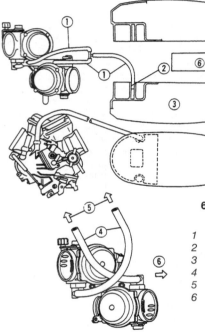

6.19 Carburetor hose details (Vulcan 700/750 models)

1   *Vent hoses*
2   *Insert hose, but not too deep*
3   *Right air cleaner housing*
4   *Fuel hoses*
5   *To fuel tap*
6   *Front of motorcycle*

band that secures the front intake manifold to the carburetor, but not the band that secures the front intake manifold to the cylinder head **(see illustration)**.

10   Pull the carburetor assembly clear of the intake manifolds. Disconnect the throttle cables from the throttle pulley using long forceps or a similar tool, then remove the carburetors from the right side of the motorcycle.

11   After the carburetors have been removed, stuff clean rags into the intake manifold tubes to prevent the entry of dirt or other objects.

12   The intake manifolds aren't interchangeable. Look for the cylinder marks (F and R for front and rear). Make your own marks if they aren't visible. Loosen the clamps and remove the manifolds from the engine.

Installation

Refer to illustrations 6.14 and 6.19

13   Install the front intake manifold on the front cylinder. Align the tab on the manifold with the cast mark at the top of the intake port on the cylinder head.

14   Install the rear intake manifold on the rear carburetor with the alignment tab

approximately 15 mm outboard of the straight-up position, so it will align with the cast mark at the top of the rear intake port when the carburetor is installed **(see illustration)**. **Warning:** *The screw heads of both clamps on the rear carburetor intake tube must face inward (toward the center of the motorcycle) or the screws may interfere with the operation of the throttle linkage.*

15   Position the carburetor assembly on the engine. Check to make sure the intake manifolds and their clamping band screws are positioned correctly, then tighten their screws.

16   Lightly lubricate the ends of the throttle cables with multi-purpose grease and attach them to the throttle pulley. Make sure the accelerator and decelerator cables are in

their proper positions.

17   Install the air intake ducts between the carburetors and surge tank, making sure to align the notches in the ducts with the tabs on the tank **(see illustration 6.8d)**.

18   Connect the choke cable to the assembly and adjust it (see Section 11).

19   The remainder of installation is the reverse of the removal steps, with the following additions:

a) *Be sure the vent and fuel hoses are routed correctly* **(see illustration)**.
b) *Adjust the throttle grip freeplay and choke lever freeplay (see Chapter 1).*
c) *Check for fuel leaks.*
d) *Check and, if necessary, adjust the idle speed and carburetor synchronization (see Chapter 1).*

6.22a Disconnect the vent line . . .

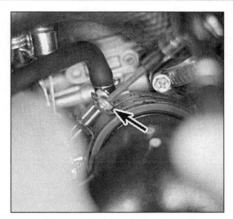

6.22b . . . and the vacuum line, then loosen the intake manifold clamping bands

6.23 Unbolt the carburetor mounting bracket

6.24 Pull the carburetor out partway for access to the throttle cables

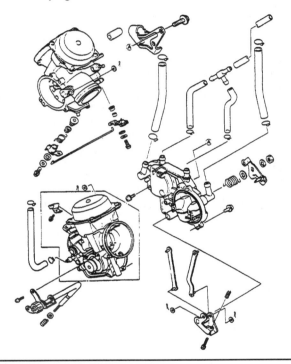

7.2a Carburetor assembly details (Vulcan 700/750 models)

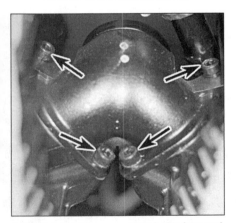

6.26 Remove the mounting bolts (arrows) and take the intake manifold off

Vulcan 800 models

Removal

Refer to illustrations 6.22a, 6.22b, 6.23, 6.24 and 6.26

20 Remove the seat (see Chapter 9).
21 Remove the fuel tank and air cleaner housing (see Sections 2 and 12).
22 Disconnect the vacuum hoses from the carburetor and loosen the intake manifold clamp screw **(see illustrations)**.

23 Unbolt the carburetor bracket from the engine **(see illustration)**.
24 Pull the carburetor out of the intake duct so you can get at the throttle cables **(see illustration)**.
25 Disconnect the throttle and choke cables from the carburetor (see Sections 10 and 11). Take the carburetor out.
26 If necessary, remove the intake manifold bolts and take the manifold off the engine **(see illustration)**.

Installation

27 Installation is the reverse of the removal steps, with the following additions:

a) *Adjust the throttle grip freeplay and choke lever freeplay (see Chapter 1).*
b) *Check for fuel leaks.*
c) *Check and, if necessary, adjust the idle speed (see Chapter 1).*

7 Carburetor separation (Vulcan 700/750 models)

1 The carburetor diaphragms and jets can be removed for cleaning and inspection without separating the carburetors from each other. The float chambers are contained within the center section of the carburetor assembly, so individual carburetor bodies must be removed from the center section to inspect the floats.

Rear carburetor separation

Refer to illustrations 7.2a, 7.2b, 7.2c, 7.3, 7.4a , 7.4b and 7.4c

2 Remove the screw and detach the choke link collar from the choke plunger **(see illustrations)**.

4

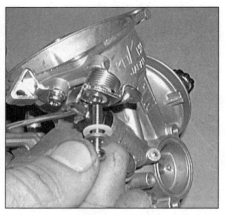

7.2b Remove the choke link screw . . .

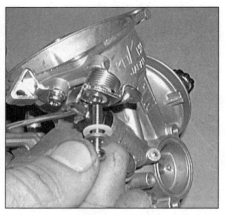

7.2c . . . metal washer and nylon washer, then disconnect the throttle link

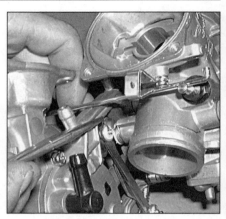

7.3 Pull out the cotter pin, remove the washer and disconnect the throttle link

7.4a Remove the screws (arrows) (note the R mark indicating the rear carburetor) . . .

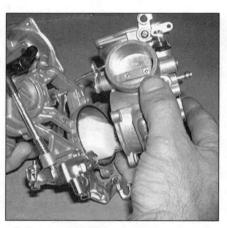

7.4b . . . and lift the rear carburetor off the center section . . .

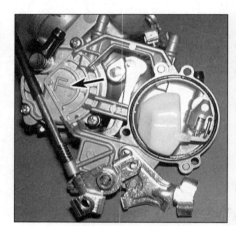

7.4c . . . for access to the float - note the F mark (arrow) indicating the front carburetor

3   Remove the cotter pin and plastic washer, then detach the throttle link from the carburetor (see illustration).
4   Remove the float chamber screws and separate the rear carburetor body from the center section (see illustrations).

Front carburetor separation

Refer to illustrations 7.5 and 7.7
5   Remove the screw and detach the idle speed knob bracket from the carburetor (see illustration).

6   Remove the cotter pin and plastic washer, then detach the throttle link from the carburetor (see illustration 7.3).
7   Remove the float chamber screws and separate the front carburetor body from the center section (see illustration).

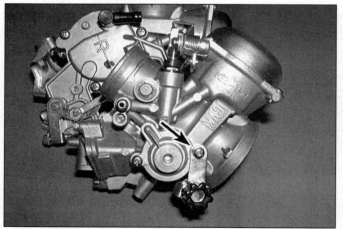

7.5 Remove the screw (arrow) and detach the idle speed knob bracket

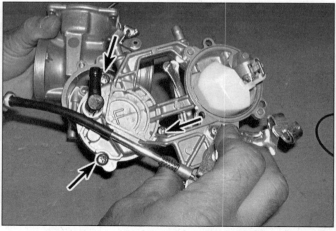

7.7 Remove the screws (arrows) to detach the front carburetor from the center section

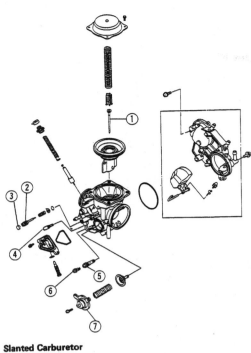

Slanted Carburetor

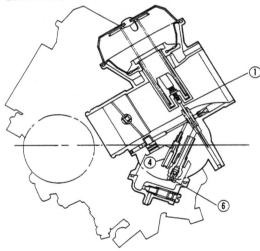

8.2a Carburetor (Vulcan 700/750 models) - exploded and cross-section views

1	Jet needle	4	Pilot jet
2	Pilot (fuel mixture) screw	5	Needle jet holder
3	Pilot screw plug	6	Main jet
		7	Coasting enricher

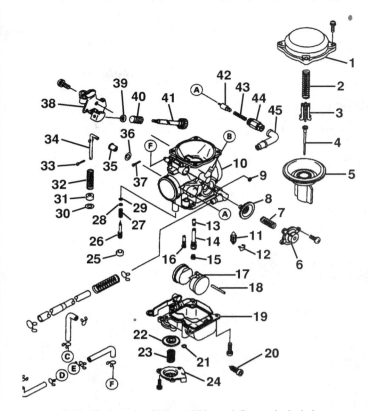

8.2b Carburetor (Vulcan 800 model) - exploded view

1	Cover	23	Spring
2	Piston spring	24	Diaphragm cover
3	Jet needle holder	25	Pilot (fuel mixture) screw plug
4	Jet needle	26	Pilot (fuel mixture) screw
5	Vacuum piston	27	Spring
6	Coasting enricher diaphragm cover	28	Washer
7	Spring	29	O-ring
8	Diaphragm	30	Washer
9	O-ring	31	Collar
10	Carburetor body	32	Spring
11	Needle valve	33	Cotter pin
12	Clip	34	Link
13	Needle jet	35	Bushing
14	Needle jet holder	36	Washer
15	Main jet	37	Cotter pin
16	Pilot jet	38	Bracket
17	Floats	39	Washer
18	Pivot pin	40	Spring
19	Float bowl	41	Idle speed screw
20	Drain screw	42	Choke plunger tip
21	O-ring	43	Spring
22	Accelerator pump diaphragm	44	Choke plunger body
		45	Cable housing

4

8 Carburetors - disassembly, cleaning and inspection

Warning: *Gasoline is extremely flammable, so take extra precautions when you work on any part of the fuel system (see the Warning in Section 2).*

Disassembly

Refer to illustrations 8.2a, 8.2b, 8.2c, 8.2d, 8.3, 8.4a and 8.4b

1   Remove the carburetor(s) from the machine as described in Section 6. Set the assembly on a clean working surface. If you're planning to work on the floats of a Vulcan 700/750 model, or if the float chamber O-rings have been leaking, separate the carburetors (see Section 7).

2   Remove the four screws securing the top cover to the carburetor body **(see illustrations)**. Lift the cover off and remove the piston spring **(see illustration)**.

8.2c Remove the cover screws . . .

8.2d . . . lift off the cover and remove the spring and diaphragm

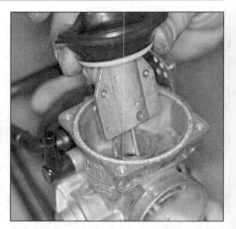

8.3 Lift the vacuum piston and jet needle from the carburetor

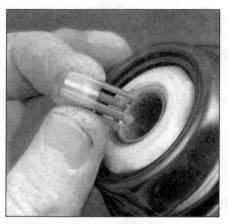

8.4a Remove the vacuum piston spring seat from the piston

8.4b Remove the needle from the piston

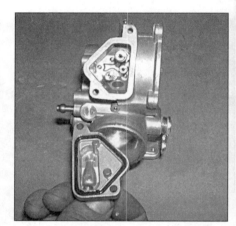

8.7 Remove the cover and O-ring for access to the jets (Vulcan 700/750 models)

3 Peel the diaphragm away from its groove in the carburetor body, being careful not to tear it. Lift out the diaphragm/piston assembly **(see illustration)**.
4 Remove the piston spring seat and separate the needle from the piston **(see illustrations)**.

Vulcan 700/750 models

Refer to illustrations 8.7, 8.8, 8.9, 8.10 and 8.11

5 Refer to the exploded view **(see illustration 7.3a)** and note the following:
6 Make sure the screwdrivers fit their slots.

7 Remove the cover and O-ring for access to the jets **(see illustration)**.
8 Pull out the float pin with needle-nosed pliers to remove the floats **(see illustration)**.
9 When removing the diaphragm covers, do not lose the small O-ring in the passage next to the diaphragm **(see illustration)**.

8.8 Pull out the float pivot pin

8.9 Don't forget to reinstall the O-ring under the diaphragm cover (arrow)

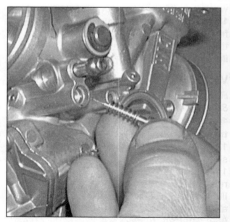

8.10 Unscrew the pilot screw and remove its spring, washer and O-ring

8.11 Unscrew the choke plunger

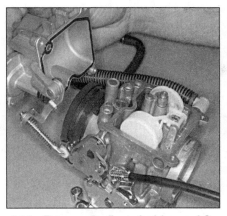

8.14a Remove the float chamber and O-ring for access to the jest and floats

8.14b Hold the needle jet holder/air bleed tube with a wrench while you unscrew the main jet

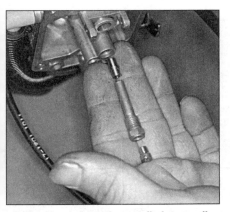

8.14c Here's how the needle jet, needle jet holder and main jet are arranged

8.15a Push the float pivot pin partway out . . .

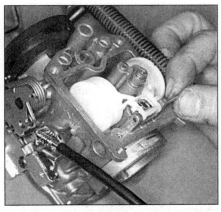

8.15b . . . then pull it the rest of the way

10 The pilot (idle mixture) screw is located in a passage in the carburetor body. On US models, this screw is hidden behind a plug which will have to be removed if the screw is to be taken out. The usual way to do this is to drill a hole in the plug, then pry it out. Be careful not to drill into the screw. Turn the pilot screw in, counting the number of turns until it bottoms lightly. Record that number for use when installing the screw. Now remove the pilot screw along with its spring, washer and O-ring **(see illustration)**.

11 The choke plunger can be removed from each carburetor by unscrewing the nut that retains it to the carburetor body **(see illustration)**.

Vulcan 800 models

Refer to illustrations 8.14a, 8.14b, 8.14c, 8.15a, 8.15b, 8.16, 8.18a and 8.18b

12 Refer to the exploded view **(see illustration 7.3b)** and note the following:

13 Make sure the screwdrivers fit their slots.

14 Remove the float chamber cover and O-ring for access to the jets and floats **(see illustration)**. Hold the needle jet holder with a wrench while you unscrew the main jet **(see illustration)**. Note which way the needle jet goes in the bore **(see illustration)**.

15 Push out the float pin to remove the

8.16 Don't forget the O-rings (arrow) - there's one under each diaphragm cover

floats **(see illustrations)**.

16 When removing the diaphragm covers, do not lose the small O-ring in the passage next to the diaphragm **(see illustration)**.

17 The pilot (idle mixture) screw is located in a passage in the carburetor body. On US models, this screw is hidden behind a plug which will have to be removed if the screw is to be taken out. The usual way to do this is to drill a hole in the plug, then pry it out. Be

8.18a Compress the spring . . .

careful not to drill into the screw. Turn the pilot screw in, counting the number of turns until it bottoms lightly. Record that number for use when installing the screw. Now remove the pilot screw along with its spring, washer and O-ring.

18 The choke plunger is part of the choke cable **(see illustration)**. To remove it, unscrew it from the carburetor, then compress the spring and slip the cable end out of the plunger **(see illustration)**.

4

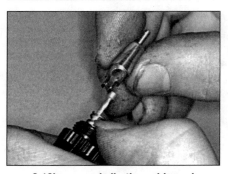

8.18b . . . and slip the cable end out of the plunger

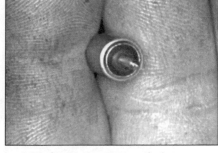

8.21 Check the plunger tip for wear

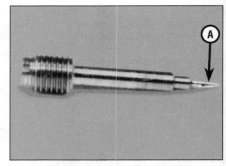

8.22 Check the tapered portion of the pilot screw (A) for wear or damage

Cleaning

Caution: *Use only a carburetor cleaning solution that is safe for use with plastic parts (be sure to read the label on the container).*

19   Submerge the metal components in the carburetor cleaner for approximately thirty minutes (or longer, if the directions recommend it).

20   After the carburetor has soaked long enough for the cleaner to loosen and dissolve most of the varnish and other deposits, use a brush to remove the stubborn deposits. Rinse it again, then dry it with compressed air. Blow out all of the fuel and air passages in the main and upper body. **Caution:** *Never clean the jets or passages with a piece of wire or a drill bit, as they will be enlarged, causing the fuel and air metering rates to be upset.*

Inspection

Refer to illustrations 8.21, 8.22 and 8.27

21   Check the operation of the choke plunger. If it doesn't move smoothly, replace it, along with the return spring. Check the tapered end of plunger for wear and replace if it's worn **(see illustration)**.

22   Check the tapered portion of the pilot screw for wear or damage **(see illustration)**. Replace the pilot screw if necessary.

23   Check the carburetor body, float bowl and top cover for cracks, distorted sealing surfaces and other damage. If any defects are found, replace the faulty component, although replacement of the entire carburetor will probably be necessary (check with your parts supplier for the availability of separate components).

24   Check the diaphragms for splits, holes and general deterioration. Holding it up to a light will help to reveal problems of this nature.

25   Insert the vacuum piston in the carburetor body and see that it moves up-and-down smoothly. Check the surface of the piston for wear. If it's worn excessively or doesn't move smoothly in the bore, replace the carburetor.

26   Check the jet needle for straightness by rolling it on a flat surface (such as a piece of glass). Replace it if it's bent or if the tip is worn.

27   Check the tip of the fuel inlet valve nee-

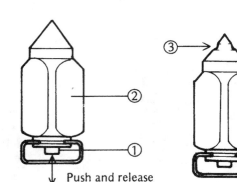

8.27 Check the tip of the fuel inlet valve needle for grooves or scratches - also make sure the rod in the end of the needle pops back out quickly after it's pushed in

1   *Rod*
2   *Valve needle*
3   *Groove in tip*

Push and release

dle. If it has grooves or scratches in it, it must be replaced. Push in on the rod in the other end of the needle, then release it - if it doesn't spring back, replace the valve needle **(see illustration)**.

28   Check the O-rings. Replace them if they're damaged.

29   Operate the throttle shaft to make sure the throttle butterfly valve opens and closes smoothly. If it doesn't, replace the carburetor.

30   Check the floats for damage. This will usually be apparent by the presence of fuel inside one of the floats. If the floats are damaged, they must be replaced.

9.4 Don't let the jet needle retainer block the vacuum hole (arrow)

9   Carburetors - reassembly and fuel level adjustment

Caution: *When installing the jets, be careful not to over-tighten them - they're made of soft material and can strip or shear easily.*
Note: *When reassembling the carburetors, be sure to use the new O-rings, gaskets and other parts supplied in the rebuild kit.*

Reassembly

Refer to illustration 9.4

1   If the choke plunger was removed, install it in its bore, followed by its spring and nut. Tighten the nut securely and install the cap.

2   Install the pilot screw (if removed) along with its spring, washer and O-ring, turning it in until it seats lightly. Now, turn the screw out the number of turns that was previously recorded. If you're working on a US model, install a new metal plug in the hole over the screw. Apply a little bonding agent around the circumference of the plug after it has been seated.

3   Install the pilot jet, needle jet, needle jet holder/air bleed pipe and main jet. If you're working on a Vulcan 700/750 model, install the O-ring and jet cover.

4   Drop the jet needle down into its hole in the vacuum piston and install the spring seat over the needle. Make sure the spring seat doesn't cover the hole at the bottom of the vacuum piston - reposition it if necessary **(see illustration)**.

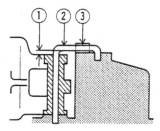

9.7 Float pivot pin details (Vulcan 700/750 models)

1 Clearance 0.2 to 0.4 mm
2 Don't tap on this part
3 Tap on this part

5   Install the diaphragm/vacuum piston assembly into the carburetor body. Lower the spring into the piston. Seat the bead of the diaphragm into the groove in the top of the carburetor body, making sure the diaphragm isn't distorted or kinked **(see illustration 7.3d)**. This isn't always an easy task. If the diaphragm seems too large in diameter and doesn't want to seat in the groove, place the top cover over the carburetor diaphragm, insert your finger into the throat of the carburetor and push up on the vacuum piston. Push down gently on the top cover - it should drop into place, indicating the diaphragm has seated in its groove.
6   Install the top cover, tightening the screws securely.

Vulcan 700/750 models

Refer to illustrations 9.7 and 9.8

7   Place the floats in their installed position and push the float pin into place. Tap the pin over the carburetor body until it's fully installed **(see illustration)**.
8   To check the float height, hold the center section so the float hangs down, then tilt it back until the valve needle is just seated (the rod in the end of the valve shouldn't be compressed) **(see illustration)**. The float

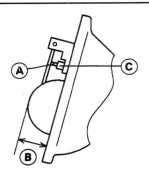

9.9 Let the float hang down so its tang touches the needle valve but doesn't compress it

A   Needle valve plunger
B   Float level
C   Needle valve body

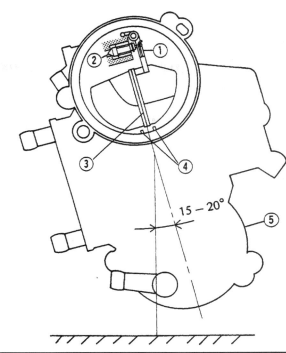

9.8 Float level adjustment (Vulcan 700/750 models)

1 Float tang
2 Needle valve
3 Float seam
4 Float level marks
5 Carburetor center section

seam should be between the two cast marks on the center section. If not, bend the float tang in small increments to adjust the float position. Repeat the procedure for the other float.

Vulcan 800 models

Refer to illustration 9.9

9   Invert the carburetor. Attach the fuel inlet valve needle to the float. Set the float into position in the carburetor, making sure the valve needle seats correctly. Install the float pivot pin. To check the float height, hold the carburetor so the float hangs down, then tilt it back until the valve needle is just seated (the rod in the end of the valve shouldn't be compressed). Measure the distance from the carburetor body to the top of the float **(see illustration)** and compare your measurement to the float height listed in this Chapter's Specifications. If it isn't as specified, carefully bend the tang that contacts the valve needle up or down until the float height is correct.
10   Install the O-ring into the groove in the float bowl. Place the float bowl on the carburetor and install the screws, tightening them securely.

Fuel level adjustment

Vulcan 700/750 models

Refer to illustrations 9.13a and 9.13b
Warning: *Gasoline is extremely flammable, so take extra precautions when you work on any part of the fuel system (see the Warning in Section 2).*
11   The carburetors must be installed on the engine for this procedure.
12   Place the motorcycle in a perfectly upright position. Set the fuel tap to the PRI

position so fuel will flow into the carburetors. **Note:** *This can also be done if the engine has been removed from the motorcycle - place the engine in an upright position and temporarily connect the fuel tank to the carburetors.*
13   Attach Kawasaki service tool no. 57001-1017 to the drain fitting on the bottom of the carburetor assembly (both will be checked) **(see illustrations)**. This is a clear plastic tube graduated in millimeters. An alternative is to use a length of clear plastic tubing and an accurate ruler. Hold the gradu-

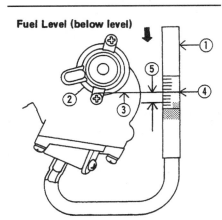

9.13a Fuel level measurement (Vulcan 700/750 front carburetor)

1 Fuel level gauge
2 Coasting enricher
3 Upper edge of diaphragm cover screw
4 Zero line
5 Fuel level

4

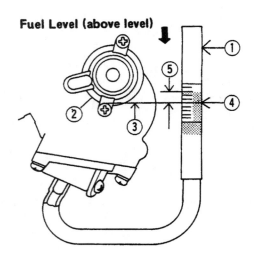

Fuel Level (above level)

**9.13b Fuel level measurement
(Vulcan 700/750 front carburetor)**

1   Fuel level gauge
2   Coasting enricher
3   Upper edge of
    diaphragm cover screw
4   Zero line
5   Fuel level

9.18 Checking the fuel level in a carburetor

1   Kawasaki tool no. 57001-1017
2   Fuel hose
3   Bottom edge of carburetor body
4   Zero line
5   Fuel level

ated tube (or the free end of the clear plastic tube) against the carburetor body, as shown in the accompanying illustration. If the Kawasaki tool is being used, raise the zero mark to a point several millimeters above the upper edge of the coasting enricher diaphragm screw (the zero point). If a piece of clear plastic tubing is being used, make a mark on the tubing at this point.

14   Unscrew the drain screw at the bottom of the float bowl a couple of turns, then let fuel flow into the tube. Wait for the fuel level to stabilize, then slowly lower the tube until the zero mark is level with the upper edge of the coasting enricher diaphragm screw (the zero point). **Note:** *Don't lower the zero mark below the zero point, then bring it back up - the reading won't be accurate. If this happens accidentally, dump the fuel out of the hose and start over.*

15   Measure the distance between the mark and the top of the fuel in the tube or gauge. This distance is the fuel level - write it down on a piece of paper, screw in the drain screw, close off the fuel supply, then move on to the next carburetor and check it the same way.

16   Compare your fuel level readings to the value listed in this Chapter's Specifications. If the fuel level in either carburetor is not correct, separate the carburetors for access to the float bowl and bend the tang (see Step 8), as necessary, then recheck the fuel level.

Vulcan 800 models

Refer to illustration 9.18

Warning: *Gasoline is extremely flammable, so take extra precautions when you work on*

any part of the fuel system (see the Warning in Section 2).

17   Place the motorcycle in a perfectly upright position. Set the fuel tap to the PRI position so fuel will flow into the carburetor. **Note:** *This can also be done if the engine has been removed from the motorcycle - place the engine in an upright position and temporarily connect the fuel tank to the carburetor.*

18   Attach Kawasaki service tool no. 57001-1017 to the drain fitting on the bottom of the carburetor assembly (both will be checked) **(see illustration)**. This is a clear plastic tube graduated in millimeters. An alternative is to use a length of clear plastic tubing and an accurate ruler. Hold the graduated tube (or the free end of the clear plastic tube) against the carburetor body, as shown in the accompanying illustration. If the Kawasaki tool is being used, raise the zero mark to a point several millimeters above the upper edge of the coasting enricher diaphragm screw (the zero point). If a piece of clear plastic tubing is being used, make a mark on the tubing at this point.

19   Unscrew the drain screw at the bottom of the float bowl a couple of turns, then let fuel flow into the tube. Wait for the fuel level to stabilize, then slowly lower the tube until the zero mark is level with the upper edge of the coasting enricher diaphragm screw (the zero point). **Note:** *Don't lower the zero mark below the zero point, then bring it back up - the reading won't be accurate. If this happens accidentally, dump the fuel out of the hose and start over.*

20   Measure the distance between the mark and the top of the fuel in the tube or

gauge. This distance is the fuel level - write it down on a piece of paper, screw in the drain screw, close off the fuel supply, then move on to the next carburetor and check it the same way.

21   Compare your fuel level readings to the value listed in this Chapter's Specifications. If the fuel level is not correct, remove the float bowl and bend the tang up or down (see Step 10), as necessary, then recheck the fuel level. **Note:** *Bending the tang up increases the float height and lowers the fuel level - bending it down decreases the float height and raises the fuel level.*

10   Throttle cables - removal, installation and adjustment

Removal

Refer to illustrations 10.3 and 10.4

1   Remove the fuel tank (see Section 2).

2   Loosen the locknuts on the accelerator cable and decelerator cable at the handlebar and screw the cable adjusters in to create as much slack as possible (see Chapter 1).

3   Remove the screws and separate the throttle housing halves **(see illustration)**.

4   Lift each cable out of its grooves in the throttle pulley, align the cables with the pulley slots and slip the cable ends out of the throttle pulley **(see illustration)**.

Vulcan 700/750 models

Refer to illustrations 10.5 and 10.6

5   Loosen the locknuts and free the cables from their brackets at the carburetor **(see illustration)**.

10.3 Remove the throttle housing screw at the top (shown) and bottom of the housing

10.4 Rotate the cable to align it with the slot, then slip the cable out of the pulley

10.5 Pull the cable housings out of the brackets, then slip the cables through the bracket slots

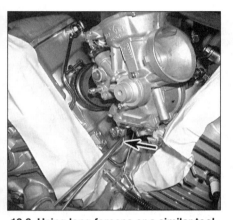

10.6 Using long forceps or a similar tool, rotate the cable to align it with the slot, then slip the cable out of the pulley

10.9a Push back the lower end of the clip (arrow) . . .

10.9b . . . pull the cable housings out of the brackets, then slip the cables through the bracket slots . . .

6   Using long forceps or a similar tool, rotate each cable so it aligns with the slot in the pulley, then slide the end plug out of the pulley **(see illustration)**.
7   Remove the cables, noting how they are routed.

Vulcan 800 models

Refer to illustrations 10.9a, 10.9b and 10.10

8   Remove the carburetor from the engine (see Section 6).
9   Release the lower end of the bracket clip from the throttle cable bracket at the carburetor **(see illustration)**. Slip the cable housings up out of the bracket, then slide the cables through the gaps in the bracket **(see illustration)**.
10   Rotate the end of each cable so it aligns with the slot in the pulley, then slide the end plug out of the pulley **(see illustration)**.
11   Remove the cables, noting how they are routed.

Installation

12   Route the cables into place. Make sure they don't interfere with any other components and aren't kinked or bent sharply.

13   Lubricate the end of the accelerator cable with multi-purpose grease and connect it to the throttle pulley at the carburetor. Pass the inner cable through the slot in the bracket, then seat the cable housing in the bracket.
14   Repeat the previous step to connect the decelerator cable.
15   If you're working on a Vulcan 800 model, reinstall the carburetor (see Section 6).
16   Connect the cables to the throttle grip pulley and position them in their slots.
17   Install the cable/switch housing and tighten its screws securely.

Adjustment

18   Follow the procedure outlined in Chapter 1, Throttle operation/grip freeplay - check and adjustment, to adjust the cables.
19   Turn the handlebars back and forth to make sure the cables don't cause the steering to bind.
20   Operate the throttle and check the cable action. The cables should move freely and the throttle pulley at the carburetor should move back and forth in response to both acceleration and deceleration. If the

10.10 . . . then rotate each cable to align it with the slot and slip the cable end out of the pulley

cables don't operate properly, find and fix the problem before you put the fuel tank back on.
21   Install the fuel tank (see Section 2).
22   Start the engine. With the engine idling, turn the handlebars all the way to left and

4

11.3a Pull the choke cable housing out of the bracket . . .

11.3b . . . then rotate the cable to align it with the slot and slip the cable end out of the lever

11.5 Unbolt the cable bracket . . .

right while listening for changes in idle speed. If idle speed increases as the handlebars turn, the cables are improperly routed. This is dangerous. Find the problem and fix it before riding the bike.

11.6a Pass the cable through the frame . . .

11.6b . . . and unscrew the choke plunger from the carburetor to free the cable

11 Choke cable - removal, installation and adjustment

Removal

Vulcan 700/750 models

Refer to illustrations 11.3a and 11.3b

1   Remove the seat and fuel tank (see Chapter 9 and Section 2).

2   Remove the screws securing the choke cable/switch housing halves to the left handlebar. Pull the front half of the housing off and separate the choke cable from the lever.

3   Pull the choke cable housing away from its mounting bracket at the carburetor and pass the inner cable through the opening in the bracket **(see illustration)**. Detach the cable end from the carburetor choke lever **(see illustration)**.

4   Remove the cable, noting how it's routed.

Vulcan 800 models

Refer to illustrations 11.5, 11.6a and 11.6b

5   Unbolt the cable bracket from the motorcycle **(see illustration)**.

6   Pass the cable under the frame, then unscrew the choke plunger from the carburetor **(see illustrations)**. Remove the cable and choke plunger together.

7   If necessary, separate the choke plunger from the cable (see Section 11).

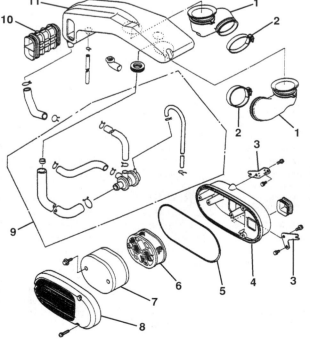

12.2 Air cleaner housing details (Vulcan 700/750 models)

1   Air intake duct
2   Clamp
3   Bracket
4   Air cleaner housing
5   O-ring
6   Air filter element core
7   Air filter element
8   Air cleaner cover
9   Air suction system (US and Swiss models)
10   Air duct
11   Surge tank

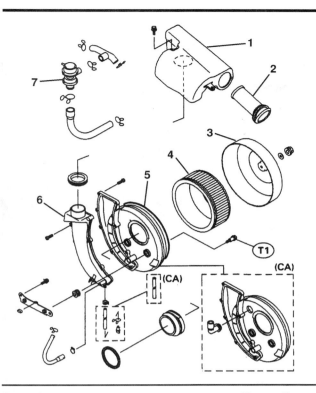

12.6b Unbolt the housing from the bracket

12.6a Air cleaner housing details (Vulcan 800 models)

1 Surge tank
2 Duct
3 Air cleaner cover
4 Air filter element
5 Air cleaner housing
6 Surge tank duct
7 Air suction valve (US and Swiss models)

12.6c Disconnect the hoses at the top of the air cleaner housing . . .

Installation

8   Installation is the reverse of the removal steps.

Adjustment

9   Refer to Chapter 1 for cable adjustment procedures.
10   Install the fuel tank and all of the other components that were previously removed.

12 Air filter housing (air box) - removal and installation

Vulcan 700/750 models

Refer to illustration 12.2
1   Remove the air cleaner element (see

Chapter 1).
2   Unbolt the air cleaner housing from the engine **(see illustration)**.
3   If it's necessary to remove the surge tank, remove the engine from the motorcycle (see Chapter 2). Disconnect the surge tank hoses and remove it from the frame.
4   Installation is the reverse of the removal steps. The left and right air cleaner housings are interchangeable, but the mounting brackets are different. If the brackets don't seem to align with their mounting points, the housings may be on the wrong side of the bike.

Vulcan 800 models

Refer to illustrations 12.6a through 12.6e and 12.7
5   Remove the air cleaner element (see

Chapter 1).
6   Unbolt the air cleaner housing from its mounting bracket **(see illustrations)**. Disconnect the hoses from the back and top of the housing and remove it.
7   If it's necessary to remove the surge tank, remove the seat and fuel tank (see Chapter 9 and Section 2. Remove the bolts

12.6d . . . at the top of the back side . . .

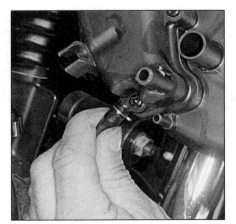

12.6e . . . and at the bottom of the back side

12.7 Remove the surge tank mounting bolts at the front and at the rear (arrow) and lift the surge tank off the duct

4

13.1 Remove the exhaust pipe nuts at the cylinder head (arrows)

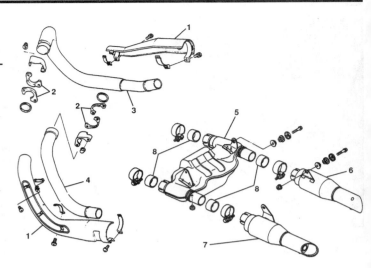

13.2 Exhaust system (Vulcan 700/750 models) - exploded view

1 Heat shield
2 Clamps
3 Front cylinder exhaust pipe
4 Rear cylinder exhaust pipe
5 Power chamber
6 Front cylinder muffler
7 Rear cylinder muffler
8 Gaskets

at front and rear of the surge tank and lift it from the air cleaner housing **(see illustration)**.

8 Installation is the reverse of removal.

13 Exhaust system - removal and installation

Vulcan 700/750 models

Refer to illustrations 13.1 and 13.2

1 Remove the nuts that secure the right (front cylinder) exhaust pipe holder to the cylinder head, then remove the holders **(see illustration)**.
2 Loosen the clamp that secures the right exhaust pipe and remove the pipe **(see illustration)**.
3 Loosen the right muffler's clamp and detach the muffler from the power chamber.
4 Remove the nuts that secure the left (rear cylinder) muffler to the cylinder head.

Remove the left muffler mounting bolt and power chamber mounting bolt, then remove the exhaust system from the motorcycle.
5 Installation is the reverse of the removal steps, with the following additions:
   a) Tighten all of the nuts and bolts until they're snug, but don't torque them yet.
   b) Tighten the exhaust pipe holder nuts at the cylinder heads evenly.
   c) Tighten the remaining nuts and bolts securely.
   d) Warm up the engine to normal operating temperature, let it cool, then retighten all of the nuts and bolts.

Vulcan 800 models (except Drifter)

Refer to illustrations 13.6, 13.7, 13.8a, 13.8b, 13.10a and 13.10b

6 Unbolt the cover from the front exhaust pipe **(see illustration)**.

7 Unscrew the exhaust pipe holder bolts from the cylinders heads **(see illustration)**.
8 Remove the front muffler mounting bolts and the clamp bolt that secures it to the crossover pipe **(see illustrations)**. Remove the front muffler from the motorcycle.
9 Unbolt the rear exhaust pipe cover. Detach the rear exhaust pipe from the bracket, then remove it from the motorcycle **(see illustration 13.8b)**.
10 Installation is the reverse of removal, with the following additions:

13.7 Unscrew the Allen bolts at the cylinder head

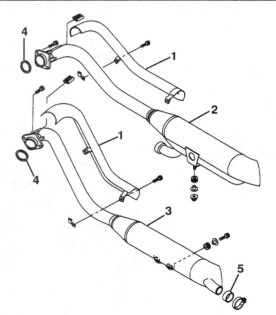

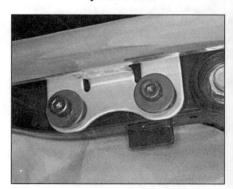

13.8a Remove the mounting bolts

13.6 Exhaust system (Vulcan 800 models) - exploded view

1 Heat shield
2 Front cylinder exhaust pipe
3 Rear cylinder exhaust pipe
4 Gaskets
5 Gasket

13.8b Loosen the clamp and remove the mounting nut (arrows)

13.10a Don't forget to reinstall the collars in the mounting bushings

13.10b Use a new gasket (arrow) on the crossover connection

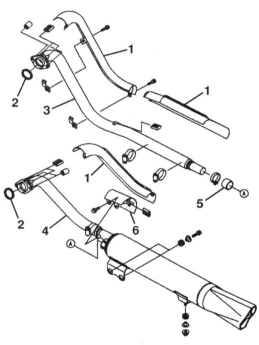

13.11 Exhaust system (Vulcan 800 Drifter models) - exploded view

1	Heat shield	4	Rear cylinder exhaust
2	Gaskets		pipe/muffler
3	Front cylinder exhaust	5	Gasket
	pipe	6	Fitting cover

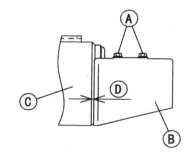

13.17a Fitting cover installation details (Vulcan 800 Drifter model)

A   Bolts
B   Fitting cover
C   Muffler
D   3 mm (1/8-inch) gap

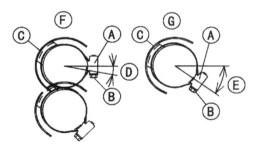

13.17b Rear exhaust pipe clamp positioning details (Vulcan 800 Drifter model)

A	Rear exhaust pipe cover clamps	D	0 to 10-degrees
		E	0 to 35-degrees
B	Bolt head (note position)	F	Lower
C	Rear exhaust pipe heat shield	G	Upper

a) Install new gaskets at the cylinder head. Replace the crossover clamp gasket if it's damaged **(see illustration)**.
b) Be sure to reinstall the collars in the grommets **(see illustration)**.
c) Tighten the exhaust pipe holder nuts at the cylinder heads evenly.
d) Tighten the remaining nuts and bolts securely.
d) Warm up the engine to normal operating temperature, let it cool, then retighten all of the nuts and bolts.

Vulcan 800 Drifter

Refer to illustrations 13.11, 13.17a, 13.17b, 13.17c and 13.17d

11   Remove the bolts and clamps that secure the heat shield to the front exhaust pipe **(see illustration)**.
12   Remove the right footrest and rear master cylinder as an assembly (see Chapters 7 and 8).
13   Slide the upper end of the heat shield along the front exhaust pipe.
14   Loosen the clamp at the rear end of the front exhaust pipe. Remove the nuts that secure the front exhaust pipe to the cylinder head, then pull the pipe out.
15   Remove the bolts and clamps that secure the heat shield to the rear exhaust pipe. Slide the upper end of the heat shield along the rear exhaust pipe.
16   Remove the nuts that secure the rear exhaust pipe to the cylinder head, then pull the pipe out. Remove the muffler mounting bolts and nuts and remove the muffler and rear exhaust pipe from the motorcycle.
17   Installation is the reverse of the removal

steps, with the following additions:

a) *Leave a 3 mm (1/8-inch) gap between the fitting cover and the muffler (see illustration).*

b) *Position the clamps correctly (see illustrations).*

c) *Tighten the exhaust pipe holder nuts at the cylinder heads evenly.*

d) *Tighten the remaining nuts and bolts securely.*

e) *Warm up the engine to normal operating temperature, let it cool, then retighten all of the nuts and bolts.*

14 Air switching valve (US models) - operational test

1   The air switching valve is part of the air suction system used on US models. Routine checking procedures are described in Chapter 1. If you suspect the valve has failed (for example, if the bike runs poorly at low speed or backfires during deceleration), test it as follows:

2   Remove the seat (see Chapter 8). Remove the valve and its hoses from the motorcycle **(see illustration 12.2 or 12.6a)**.

3   Connect a vacuum pump to the thin vacuum hose on top of the valve.

4   Try to blow air into the large air hose on the bottom of the valve. It should flow easily when there's no vacuum applied to the vacuum line.

5   Operate the vacuum pump and raise

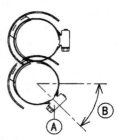

13.17c Front heat shield lower clamp positioning details (Vulcan 800 Drifter model)

A   *Clamp bolt*   B   *45-degrees*

13.17d Front heat fitting clamp positioning details (Vulcan 800 Drifter model)

A   *Clamp*   C   *45-degrees*
B   *Bolt head*

vacuum to the value listed in this Chapter's Specifications. The valve should close, making it impossible to blow air into the hose.

6   If the valve doesn't perform as described, replace it.

15 Evaporative emission control system (California models) - removal and installation

Refer to illustration 15.1a and 15.1b

1   The evaporative emission control system used on California models prevents fuel vapor from escaping into the atmosphere. When the engine isn't running, the vapor is stored in a canister, then routed into the combustion chambers for burning when the engine starts **(see illustrations)**.

2   The hoses should be checked periodically for loose connections, damage and deterioration. Tighten or replace the hoses as needed.

3   To remove the canister, remove the side cover (see Chapter 8). Disconnect the hoses and lift the canister out of its holder.

4   To remove the liquid/vapor separator, disconnect its hoses and remove it from the mounting strap. Keep the separator in an upright position while it's out of the bike. **Note:** *This will be easier on Vulcan 800 models if you remove the cover from the storage box first.*

5   Installation is the reverse of the removal steps.

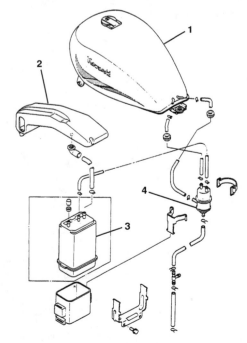

15.1a Evaporative emission control system details (Vulcan 700/750 models)

1   *Fuel tank*   3   *Canister*
2   *Surge tank*   4   *Liquid-vapor separator*

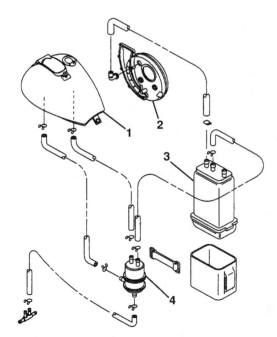

15.1b Evaporative emission control system details (Vulcan 700/750 models)

1   *Fuel tank*   3   *Canister*
2   *Air cleaner housing*   4   *Liquid-vapor separator*

Chapter 5
Ignition system

Contents

Specifications

Ignition coil

Vulcan 700/750 models
    Primary resistance.. 1.8 to 2.2 ohms
    Secondary resistance.. 19 to 29 k-ohms
Vulcan 800 models
    Primary resistance.. 2.3 to 3.5 ohms
    Secondary resistance.. 12 to 18 k-ohms
Arcing distance .... 7 mm (1/4 in) or more

Pickup coil resistance

Vulcan 700/750 models .... 355 to 535 ohms
Vulcan 800 models .... 380 to 570 ohms

Ignition timing .... Not adjustable

1   General information

These motorcycles are equipped with a battery operated, fully transistorized, break-erless ignition system. The system consists of the following components:

Pickup coil(s)
IC igniter unit
Battery and fuse
Ignition coils
Spark plugs (two per cylinder on Vulcan 700/750 models)
Stop and main (key) switches
Primary and secondary circuit wiring

The transistorized ignition system functions on the same principle as a breaker point DC ignition system with the pickup unit and igniter performing the tasks previously associated with the breaker points and mechanical advance system. As a result, adjustment and maintenance of ignition components is eliminated (with the exception of spark plug replacement).

Because of their nature, the individual ignition system components can be checked but not repaired. If ignition system troubles occur, and the faulty component can be isolated, the only cure for the problem is to replace the part with a new one. Keep in mind that most electrical parts, once purchased, can't be returned. To avoid unnecessary expense, make very sure the faulty component has been positively identified before buying a replacement part.

2   Ignition system - check

Refer to illustrations 2.5 and 2.13
Warning: *Because of the very high voltage generated by the ignition system, extreme care should be taken to avoid electrical shock when these checks are performed.*
1   If the ignition system is the suspected cause of poor engine performance or failure to start, a number of checks can be made to isolate the problem.
2   Make sure the ignition stop switch is in the Run or On position.

Engine will not start

3   Disconnect one of the spark plug wires, connect the wire to a spare spark plug and

5

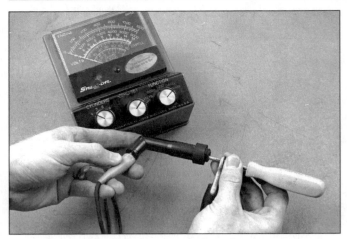

2.5 Unscrew the spark plug caps from the plug wires and measure their resistance with an ohmmeter

2.13 A simple spark gap testing fixture can be made from a block of wood, a large alligator clip, two nails, a screw and a piece of wire

lay the plug on the engine with the threads contacting the engine. If it's necessary to hold the spark plug, use an insulated tool. Crank the engine over and make sure a well-defined, blue spark occurs between the spark plug electrodes. **Warning:** *DO NOT remove one of the spark plugs from the engine to perform this check - atomized fuel being pumped out of the open spark plug hole could ignite, causing severe injury!*

4   If no spark occurs, the following checks should be made:

5   Unscrew a spark plug cap from a plug wire and check the cap resistance with an ohmmeter **(see illustration)**. If the resistance is infinite, replace it with a new one. Repeat this check on the other plug cap.

6   Make sure all electrical connectors are clean and tight. Refer to the wiring diagrams at the end of this book and check all wires for shorts, opens and correct installation.

7   Check the battery voltage with a voltmeter and the specific gravity with a hydrometer (see Chapter 1). If the voltage is less than 12-volts or if the specific gravity is low, recharge the battery.

8   Check the ignition fuse and the fuse connections. If the fuse is blown, replace it with a new one; if the connections are loose or corroded, clean or repair them.

9   Refer to Section 3 and check the ignition coil primary and secondary resistance.

10   Refer to Section 4 and check the pickup coil resistance.

11   If the preceding checks produce positive results but there is still no spark at the plug, have the IC igniter checked by a Kawasaki dealer service department or other repair shop equipped with the special tester required.

Engine starts but misfires

12   If the engine starts but misfires, make the following checks before deciding that the ignition system is at fault.

13   The ignition system must be able to produce a spark across a seven millimeter

(1/4-inch) gap (minimum). A simple test fixture **(see illustration)** can be constructed to make sure the minimum spark gap can be jumped. Make sure the fixture electrodes are positioned seven millimeters apart.

14   Connect one of the spark plug wires to the protruding test fixture electrode, then attach the fixture's alligator clip to a good engine ground.

15   Crank the engine over (it may start and run on the remaining cylinder) and see if well-defined, blue sparks occur between the test fixture electrodes. If the minimum spark gap test is positive, the ignition coil for that cylinder is functioning properly. Repeat the check on the spark plug wire that is connected to the other coil. If the spark will not jump the gap during either test, or if it is weak (orange colored), refer to Steps 5 through 11 of this Section and perform the component checks described.

3   Ignition coils - check, removal and installation

Check

Refer to illustrations 3.4a and 3.4b

1   In order to determine conclusively that the ignition coils are defective, they should be tested by an authorized Kawasaki dealer service department which is equipped with the special electrical tester required for this check.

2   However, the coils can be checked visually (for cracks and other damage) and the primary and secondary coil resistances can be measured with an ohmmeter. If the coils are undamaged, and if the resistances are as specified, they are probably capable of proper operation.

3   To check the coils for physical damage, they must be removed (see Step 9). To check the resistances, simply remove the fuel tank (see Chapter 4), unplug the primary circuit electrical connectors from the coil(s) and

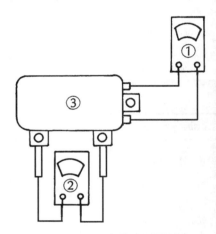

3.4a Ignition coil test (Vulcan 700/750 models)

1   *Measure primary winding resistance*
2   *Measure secondary winding resistance*
3   *Ignition coil*

remove the spark plug wire from the plug that is connected to the coil being checked. Mark the locations of all wires before disconnecting them.

4   To check the coil primary resistance, attach one ohmmeter lead to one of the primary terminals and the other ohmmeter lead to the other primary terminal **(see illustrations)**.

5   Place the ohmmeter selector switch in the Rx1 position and compare the measured resistance to the value listed in this Chapter's Specifications.

6   If the coil primary resistance is as specified, check the coil secondary resistance by disconnecting the meter leads from the primary terminals and attaching one of them to the spark plug wire terminal and the other to either of the primary terminals **(see illustration 3.4a or 3.4b)**.

7   Place the ohmmeter selector switch in

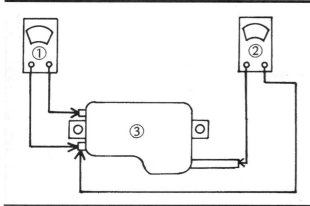

3.4b Ignition coil test (Vulcan 800 models)

1 Measure primary winding resistance
2 Measure secondary winding resistance
3 Ignition coil

the Rx100 position and compare the measured resistance to the values listed in this Chapter's Specifications.

8 If the resistances are not as specified, unscrew the spark plug wire retainers from the coil, detach the wires and check the resistance again. If it is now within specifications, one or both of the wires are bad. If it's still not as specified, the coil is probably defective and should be replaced with a new one.

Removal and installation

Refer to illustrations 3.11a, 3.11b, 3.11c and 3.11d

9 Remove the fuel tank and fuel tank trim cover for access to the front coil (see Chapters 4 and 8). Remove the left side cover for access to the rear coil (see Chapter 8).
10 To remove the coils, disconnect the spark plug wires from the plugs. After labeling them with tape to aid in reinstallation,

unplug the coil primary circuit electrical connectors.
11 Support the coil with one hand and remove the coil mounting screws **(see illustrations)**, then remove the coil.
12 Installation is the reverse of removal. If a new coil is being installed, disconnect the spark plug wire terminal from the coil, disconnect the wire and transfer it to the new coil. Make sure the primary circuit electrical connectors are attached to the proper terminals.

4 Pickup coils - check, removal and installation

Refer to illustrations 4.2a and 4.2b

Check

1 Remove the left side cover (see Chapter 8).
2 Follow the pickup coil wiring harness from the point where it leaves the alternator cover to the electrical connector, then disconnect the connector for the pickup coil(s) **(see illustrations)**.

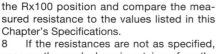

3.11a Here's the front ignition coil (Vulcan 700/750 models) . . .

3.11b . . . the rear ignition coil (Vulcan 700/750 models) . . .

3.11c . . . the front ignition coil (Vulcan 800 models) . . .

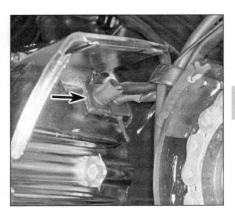

3.11d . . . and the rear ignition coil (Vulcan 800 models)

4.2a The Vulcan 700/750 pickup coil wiring connectors are located in this area (arrow) - they can be identified by their wire colors

4.2b The Vulcan 800 pickup coil harness leaves the alternator cover at this grommet (arrow); follow the harness to the connector (apply silicone sealer to the grommet whenever it's removed and reinstalled)

5

4.9 To remove the pickup coils, remove the mounting screws (left arrows) (Vulcan 800 model shown); also remove the screws that secure the harness clip (right arrows)

5.2a The Vulcan 700/750 IC igniter is mounted behind the battery (arrow)

3   If you're working on a Vulcan 700/750 model, probe each pair of terminals in the pickup coil connector with an ohmmeter (the black and black/yellow wire terminals, then the black/red and black/white wire terminals) and compare the resistance reading with the value listed in this Chapter's Specifications.

4   If you're working on a Vulcan 800 model, connect the wires between the yellow and black/yellow wires and compare the resistance reading with the value listed in this Chapter's Specifications.

5   Set the ohmmeter on the highest resistance range. Measure the resistance between a good ground and each terminal in the electrical connector. The meter should read infinity.

6   If a pickup coil fails either of the above tests, it must be replaced. On Vulcan 700/750 models, replace both coils as a set.

Removal

Refer to illustration 4.9

7   If you're working on a Vulcan 700/750 model, remove the outer alternator cover (see Chapter 9).

8   If you're working on a Vulcan 800 model, remove the right crankcase cover (see Chapter 9).

9   Unscrew the pickup coil mounting screws and remove the pickup coils **(see**

illustration)**. Remove the wiring harness retainer, slip the grommet out of its slot and remove the pickup coil(s) together with the wiring harness.

Installation

10   Position the pickup coil(s)s in the alternator cover and install the screws, tightening them securely. If you're working on a Vulcan 800 model, apply a small amount of silicone sealant to the grommet on the wiring harness and seat the grommet securely in the notch in the alternator cover **(see illustration 4.2b)**.

11   Install the alternator cover and connect the electrical connector.

---

5   IC igniter - removal, check and installation

Refer to illustrations 5.2a and 5.2b

Removal

1   Remove the seat.

2   Disconnect the igniter electrical connector and remove the two mounting bolts **(see illustrations)**. Lift out the igniter.

Check

3   A special tester is required to accurately

measure the resistance values across the various terminals of the IC igniter. Take the unit to a Kawasaki dealer service department or other repair shop equipped with this tester.

Installation

4   Installation is the reverse of the removal steps.

5.2b The Vulcan 800 IC igniter is mounted forward of the battery (arrow)

Chapter 6
Steering, suspension and final drive

Contents

Specifications

Front suspension

Fork oil type, amount and level .... See Chapter 1

Vulcan 700/750 models

Fork spring length.. Not specified

Front Fork air pressure (early Vulcan 700/750 models only)

    Standard.. 0 psi (0 Bar)

    Maximum.. 7 psi (0.48 Bar)

Vulcan 800 models

Fork spring free length

    All except Classic and Drifter

        Standard .... 469.6 mm (18.488 inches)

        Minimum .... 460 mm (18.110 inches)

    Classic

        Standard .... 547.2 mm (21.543 inches)

        Minimum .... 540 mm (21.259 inches)

    Drifter (C1, 1999 and later)

        Standard .... 450.6 mm (17.740 inches)

        Minimum .... 442 mm (17.401 inches)

    Drifter (E1, 2001)

        Standard .... 465.5 mm (18.326 inches)

        Minimum .... 456 mm (17.952 inches)

Rear suspension and final drive

Shock absorber (Vulcan 700/750 models)

    Air pressure .... 0 to 43 psi (2.97 Bar)

    Damper setting

        US, Canada.. 2

        All others 3

Shock absorber preload setting (Vulcan 800 models)

    Standard

        All except Drifter 1

        Drifter 4

    Useable range .... 1 to 7

Drive chain 20-link length

    Standard... 317.5 to 318.2 mm (12.5 to 12.53 inches)

    Limit .... 323 mm (12.716 inches)

6

Torque specifications

Vulcan 700/750 models

Handlebar bracket bolts	39 Nm (29 ft-lbs)
Steering head bolt	39 Nm (29 ft-lbs)
Steering stem adjusting nut	
Initial torque	39 Nm (29 ft-lbs)
Final torque	Hand tight (approximately 4.9 Nm/43 inch-lbs)
Fork upper triple clamp bolts	20 Nm (174 inch-lbs)
Fork lower triple clamp bolts	25 Nm (18 ft-lbs)
Fork drain bolt	Not specified
Fork damper rod bolt	20 Nm (174 inch-lbs)*
Rear shock absorber mounting bolts/nuts	30 Nm (22 ft-lbs)
Swingarm pivot shaft locknuts	13 Nm (113 inch-lbs)
Swingarm retainer plate bolts	Not specified
Differential to driveshaft housing nuts	24 Nm (288 inch-lbs)
Front bevel housing bolts	12 Nm (104 inch-lbs)

Vulcan 800 models

Handlebar clamps (1995 and 1996 standard models A1, A2)	
Clamp pinch bolts	59 Nm (43 ft-lbs)
Clamp stud nuts	34 Nm (25 ft-lbs)
Handlebar brackets (all except (1995 and 1996 standard models A1, A2)	
Bracket bolts	34 Nm (25 ft-lbs)
Bracket stud nuts	34 Nm (25 ft-lbs)
Steering stem bolt	44 Nm (33 ft-lbs)
Steering stem adjusting nut	
Initial torque	39 Nm (29 ft-lbs)
Final torque	Hand tight (approximately 4.9 Nm/43 inch-lbs)
Fork upper triple clamp bolts	20 Nm (174 inch-lbs)
Fork lower triple clamp bolts	25 Nm (18 ft-lbs)
Fork damper rod bolt	20 Nm (174 inch-lbs)*
Rear shock absorber mounting bolts/nuts	59 Nm (43 ft-lbs)
Suspension linkage tie-rod nuts/bolts	59 Nm (43 ft-lbs)
Suspension linkage rocker arm pivot bolt/nut	98 Nm (72 ft-lbs)
Swingarm pivot shaft nut	98 Nm (72 ft-lbs)
Driven sprocket-to-wheel coupling nuts	74 Nm (59 ft-lbs)
Engine sprocket nut	125 Nm (94 ft-lbs)

Apply non-permanent thread locking agent to the threads.

1 General information

The front forks on these models are of the conventional coil spring, hydraulically-damped telescopic type. Early Vulcan 700/750 forks include an air pressure adjustment mechanism.

The rear suspension on Vulcan 700/750 models consists of two coil spring/shock absorbers and a swingarm, which contains a passage for the driveshaft.

The rear suspension on Vulcan 800 models is a simulated rigid frame, consisting of a rocker-type swingarm, single coil-over shock absorber and progressive rising rate linkage.

The final drive on Vulcan 700/750 models uses a bevel gear at the engine, a driveshaft and a rear differential. Final drive on Vulcan 800 models uses a chain. A rubber damper is installed between the rear wheel coupling and the wheel on all models.

2 Handlebars - removal and installation

Refer to illustrations 2.2, 2.4a and 2.4b

1   These motorcycles use a one-piece handlebar, secured to the upper triple clamp by an upper and lower bracket.

2   Before removing the handlebars, look for a punch mark indicating the position of the handlebar in the brackets **(see illustration)**. Make your own mark if you can't see one.

3   If you're working on a Vulcan 700/750 model or a 1997 or later Vulcan 800 model, pry the trim plugs out of the handlebar bolt holes **(see illustration 2.2)**.

4   If the handlebars must be removed for access to other components, such as the forks or the steering head, simply remove the bracket nuts (1995 and 1996 Vulcan 800 models) or the upper bolts (all others) and lift the handlebar off **(see illustrations)**. It's not necessary to disconnect the cables, wires or hoses, but it is a good idea to support the assembly with a piece of wire or rope, to avoid unnecessary strain on the cables, wires and (on the right side) the brake hose.

5   Check the handlebar for cracks and distortion and replace it if any undesirable conditions are found.

6   Installation is the reverse of the removal steps, with the following additions:

  a) *If you're working on a 1995 or 1996 Vulcan 800 model, tighten the bracket nuts to the torque listed in this Chapter's Specifications.*

  b) *If you're working on a Vulcan 700/750 model or a 1997 or later Vulcan 800 model, tighten the forward bolt on each bracket to the torque listed in this Chapter's Specifications, then tighten the rear bolt. This will leave a gap at the rear of the bracket **(see illustration 2.2)**. Don't try to close the gap by tightening the bolts further or the brackets will break.*

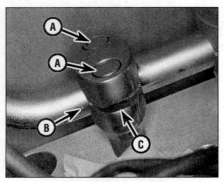

**2.2 Handlebar details
(Vulcan 800 model shown)**

A   *Caps (bolts underneath)*
B   *Alignment mark*
C   *Gap at rear*

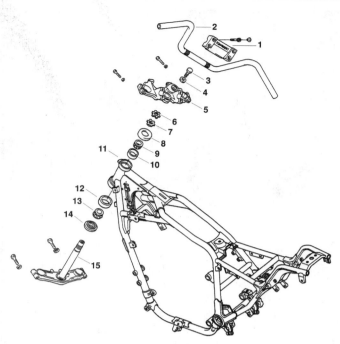

2.4a Handlebar and steering stem (Vulcan 700/750 models) - exploded view

1	Handlebar clamp	10	Upper bearing outer race
2	Handlebar	11	Steering head (part of
3	Steering head bolt		frame)
4	Washer	12	Lower bearing outer race
5	Upper triple clamp	13	Lower bearing
6	Bearing locknut	14	Grease seal
7	Bearing adjusting nut	15	Steering stem/lower
8	Bearing cover		triple clamp
9	Upper bearing		

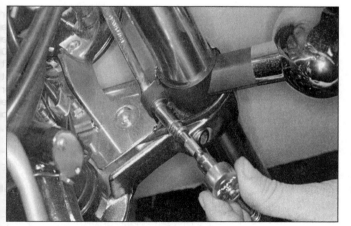

3.6a Remove the bolt . . .

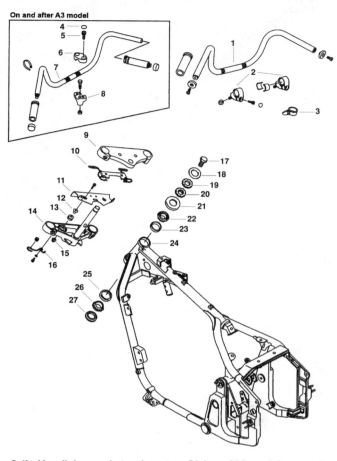

2.4b Handlebar and steering stem (Vulcan 800 models except Drifter) - exploded view

1	Handlebar (1995 and 1996 models)	13	Handlebar mounting bushing
2	Handlebar clamps (1995 and 1996 models)	14	Lower triple clamp/steering stem
3	Harness retainer	15	Nut
4	Trim plug	16	Hose retainer
5	Handlebar bracket bolt	17	Steering head bolt
6	Handlebar clamp (1997 and later models)	18	Washer
7	Handlebar (1997 and later models)	19	Bearing locknut
8	Handlebar bracket (1997 and later models)	20	Bearing adjusting nut
9	Upper triple clamp	21	Bearing cover
10	Brake hose retainer	22	Upper bearing
11	Triple clamp front cover	23	Upper bearing outer race
12	Collar	24	Steering head (part of frame)
		25	Lower bearing outer race
		26	Lower bearing
		27	Grease seal

6

3   Forks - removal and installation

Removal

Refer to illustrations 3.6a, 3.6b, 3.7a and 3.7b

1   Set the bike on its centerstand (if equipped).

2   If you're working on an early Vulcan 700/750 model, release the front fork air pressure (see Chapter 1).

3   Remove the brake caliper (Vulcan 700/750 models, both fork legs; Vulcan 800 models, left fork leg only) and hang it from the bike with a piece of rope or wire (see Chapter 7). It's not necessary to disconnect the caliper brake hose for fork removal.

4   Remove the wheel (see Chapter 7).

5   Remove the front fender (see Chapter 8).

6   Remove any wiring harness clamps or straps from the fork tubes. If you're working on a Vulcan 800 model, unbolt the turn signal

3.6b . . . and the trim cover, then take the turn signal off the fork leg

3.7a Loosen the upper triple clamp pinch bolt . . .

3.7b . . . and the lower triple clamp pinch bolt

3.10 When installed, the top of the inner fork tube should be flush with the upper triple clamp (arrow) (fork cap removed for clarity)

3.11 Don't forget to reinstall the metal collar in the turn signal clamp

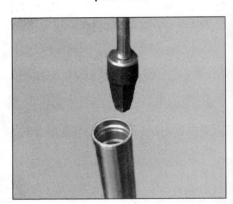

4.4a This is the Kawasaki tool that keeps the damper rod from turning - the corners of the tapered section bite into the round hole in the damper rod to hold it

4.4b Hold the damper rod and remove the screw with an Allen wrench

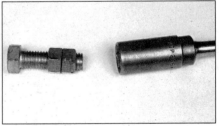
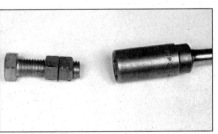

4.4c To make a damper rod holder, thread two nuts onto a bolt with a head that will wedge inside the damper rod and tighten the nuts against each other . . .

4.4d . . . then install the nut-end into a socket (connected to a long extension) and tape it into place

clamp and remove it from the fork leg **(see illustrations)**.

7   Loosen the upper triple clamp bolt **(see illustration)**. Loosen the lower triple clamp bolt **(see illustration)**, then twist the fork tubes and slide them downward and out of the triple clamps.

Installation

Refer to illustrations 3.10 and 3.11

8   If you're working on a Vulcan 800 Drifter model, apply soapy water to the rubber dampers inside the upper fork leg cover.
9   Slide each fork leg into the lower triple clamp.
10   Slide the fork legs up, installing the tops of the tubes into the upper triple clamp. The end of each tube should be flush with the top surface of the upper triple clamp **(see illustration)**.

11   The remainder of installation is the reverse of the removal steps, with the following additions:

a)   *Be sure to tighten the triple clamp bolts to the torque listed in this Chapter's Specifications.*

b)   *Tighten the caliper mounting bolts to the torque listed in the Chapter 7 Specifications.*

c)   *Don't forget to install the metal bushing in the Vulcan 800 turn signal clamp* **(see illustration)**.

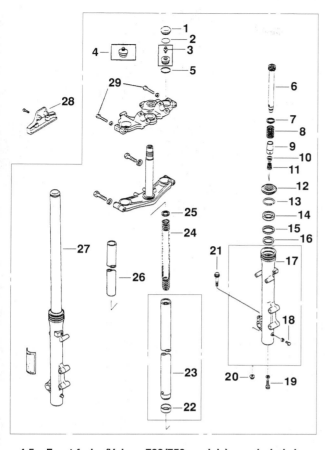

4.5a Front forks (Vulcan 700/750 models) - exploded view

1	Fork cap	14	Oil seal
2	O-ring	15	Bushing
3	Air valve and spring retainer (1985 through 1988 models)	16	Bushing
		17	Outer fork tube
4	Spring retainer (1989 and later models)	18	Drain bolt and washer
		19	Damper rod bolt and washer
5	Retainer ring	20	Axle pinch bolt nut
6	Damper rod	21	Axle pinch bolt
7	Teflon ring	22	Bushing
8	Rebound spring	23	Inner fork tube
9	Base (oil lock piece)	24	Spring
10	Valve	25	Spring seat
11	Spring	26	Spacer
12	Dust seal	27	Fork leg (complete)
13	Retainer	28	Bracket

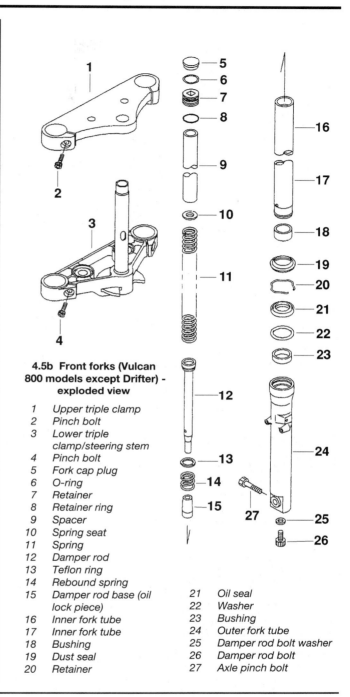

4.5b Front forks (Vulcan 800 models except Drifter) - exploded view

1	Upper triple clamp		
2	Pinch bolt		
3	Lower triple clamp/steering stem		
4	Pinch bolt		
5	Fork cap plug		
6	O-ring		
7	Retainer		
8	Retainer ring		
9	Spacer		
10	Spring seat		
11	Spring		
12	Damper rod		
13	Teflon ring		
14	Rebound spring		
15	Damper rod base (oil lock piece)	21	Oil seal
16	Inner fork tube	22	Washer
17	Inner fork tube	23	Bushing
18	Bushing	24	Outer fork tube
19	Dust seal	25	Damper rod bolt washer
20	Retainer	26	Damper rod bolt
		27	Axle pinch bolt

12 Pump the front brake lever several times to bring the pads into contact with the disc(s).

4   Forks - disassembly, inspection and reassembly

Disassembly

Refer to illustrations 4.4a, 4.4b, 4.4c, 4.4d, 4.5a, 4.5b, 4.5c, 4.6, 4.7 and 4.10

1   Remove the forks following the proce-

dure in Section 3. Work on one fork leg at a time to avoid mixing up the parts.

2   Remove the retaining ring, top plug, spacer, spring seat and fork spring (see Chapter 1).

3   Invert the fork assembly over a container and allow the oil to drain out.

4   Prevent the damper rod from turning using a holding handle (Kawasaki tool no. 57001-183) and adapter (Kawasaki tool no. 57001-1057) or equivalents **(see illustration)**. Unscrew the Allen bolt at the bottom of the outer tube and retrieve the copper washer **(see illustration)**. **Note:** *If you don't*

have access to these special tools, you can fabricate your own using a bolt with a head that fits inside the damper rod, two nuts, a socket (to fit on the nuts), a long extension and a ratchet. Thread the two nuts onto the bolt and tighten them against each other **(see illustration)**. *Insert the assembly into the socket and tape it into place* **(see illustration)**. *Now, insert the tool into the fork tube and engage the bolt head (or the special Kawasaki tool) into the round hole in the damper rod.*

5   Pull out the damper rod and its spring **(see illustrations)**. Don't remove the Teflon

6

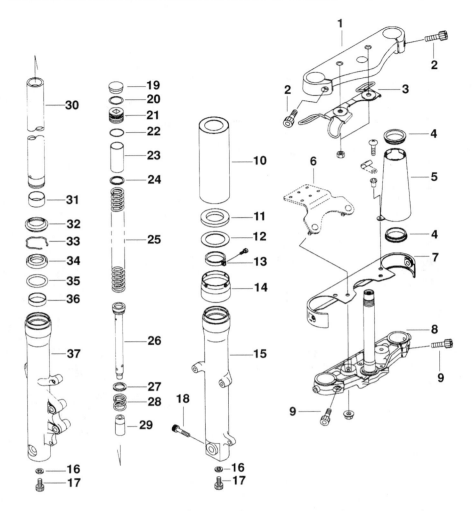

4.5c Front forks (Vulcan 800 Drifter shown; Classic similar) - exploded view

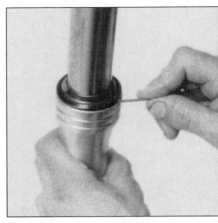

4.6 Pry the dust seal out of the outer tube with a small screwdriver

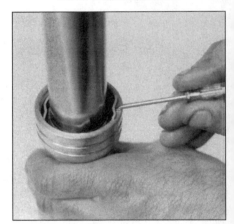

4.7 Pry the retaining ring out of its groove

1	Upper triple clamp	11	Washer	24	Spring seat
2	Pinch bolt	12	Washer	25	Spring
3	Hose bracket	13	Clamp	26	Damper rod
4	Rubber damper	14	Boot	27	Teflon ring
5	Fork cover (upper	15	Outer fork tube	28	Damper rod spring
	section)	16	Damper rod bolt	29	Damper rod base (oil
6	Bracket		washer		lock piece)
7	Triple clamp front	17	Damper rod bolt	30	Inner fork tube
	cover	18	Axle pinch bolt	31	Bushing
8	Lower triple	19	Fork cap	32	Dust seal
	clamp/steering stem	20	O-ring	33	Retainer
9	Pinch bolt	21	Spring retainer	34	Oil seal
10	Fork cover (lower	22	Wire ring	35	Washer
	section)	23	Spacer	36	Bushing
				37	Outer fork tube

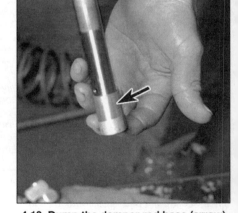

4.10 Dump the damper rod base (arrow) out of the fork tube and put it back on the damper rod

ring from the damper rod unless you plan to replace it.

6　Pry the dust seal from the outer tube **(see illustration)**.

7　Pry the retaining ring from its groove in the outer tube **(see illustration)**.

8　Hold the outer tube and yank the inner tube upward, repeatedly (like a slide hammer), until the seal, washer and outer tube guide bushing pop loose.

9　Slide the seal, washer and outer tube guide bushing from the inner tube **(see illustrations 4.5a, 4.5b and 4.5c)**.

10　Invert the outer tube and remove the damper rod base **(see illustration)**.

Inspection

11　Clean all parts in solvent and blow them dry with compressed air, if available. Check the inner and outer fork tubes, the guide

bushings and the damper rod for score marks, scratches, flaking of the chrome and excessive or abnormal wear. Look for dents in the tubes and replace them if any are found. Check the fork seal seat for nicks, gouges and scratches. If damage is evident, leaks will occur around the seal-to-outer tube junction. Replace worn or defective

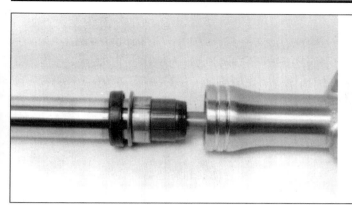

4.17a Install the assembled inner fork tube into the outer fork tube. . .

4.17b . . . place a new washer on the damper rod bolt . . .

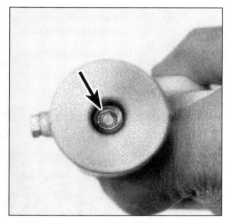

4.17c . . . and thread it into the damper rod (arrow)

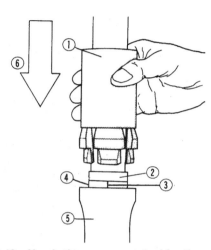

4.18a Here's the proper way to drive the outer guide bushing into place

1   Tool no. 57001-1219
2   Used bushing
3   Slit
4   New guide bushing
5   Outer tube
6   Tap downward

4.18b If you don't have the proper tool, a section of pipe can be used the same way the special tool would be used - as a slide hammer (be sure to tape the ends of the pipe so it doesn't scratch the fork tube)

parts with new ones.

12   Have the fork inner tube checked for runout at a dealer service department or other repair shop. **Warning:** *If it is bent, it should not be straightened; replace it with a new one.*

13   Measure the overall length of the long spring and check it for cracks and other damage. Compare the length to the minimum length listed in this Chapter's Specifications. If it's defective or sagged, replace both fork springs with new ones. Never replace only one spring.

Reassembly

Refer to illustrations 4.17a, 4.17b, 4.17c, 4.18a, 4.18b, 4.21 and 4.25

14   If it's necessary to replace the inner guide bushing (the one that won't come off that's on the bottom of the inner tube), pry it apart at the slit and slide it off. Make sure the new one seats properly.

15   Place the rebound spring over the damper rod and slide the rod assembly into the inner fork tube until it protrudes from the lower end of the tube.

16   If you haven't already done so, install the damper rod base onto the end of the damper rod **(see illustration 4.10)**.

17   Insert the inner tube/damper rod assembly into the outer tube **(see illustra-**

tion) until the Allen-head bolt (with copper washer) can be threaded into the damper rod from the lower end of the outer tube **(see illustrations)**. **Note:** *Apply a non-permanent thread locking compound to the threads of the bolt. Keep the two tubes fairly horizontal so the damper rod base doesn't fall off. Using the tool described in Step 4, hold the damper rod and tighten the Allen bolt to the torque listed in this Chapter's Specifications.*

18   Slide the outer guide bushing down the inner tube. On Vulcan 700/750 models, the slit in the bushing must point to the left or right - not to the front or rear. Using a special bushing driver (Kawasaki tool no. 57001-1219) or equivalent and a used guide bushing placed on top of the guide bushing being installed, drive the bushing into place until it is fully seated **(see illustration)**. If you don't have access to one of these tools, it is highly recommended that you take the assembly to a Kawasaki dealer service department or other

motorcycle repair shop to have this done. It is possible, however, to drive the bushing into place using a section of tubing and an old guide bushing **(see illustration)**. Wrap tape around the ends of the tubing to prevent it from scratching the fork tube.

19   Slide the washer down the inner tube, into position over the guide bushing.

20   Lubricate the lips and the outer diameter of the fork seal with the recommended fork oil (see Chapter 1) and slide it down the inner tube, with the lips facing down. Drive the seal into place with a special seal driver (Kawasaki tool no. 57001-1091). If you don't have access to one of these, it is recommended that you take the assembly to a Kawasaki dealer service department or other motorcycle repair shop to have the seal driven in. If you are very careful, the seal can be driven in with a hammer and a drift punch. Work around the circumference of the seal, tapping gently on the outer edge of the seal until it's seated. Be careful - if you distort the seal, you'll have to disassemble the fork again and end up taking it to a dealer anyway!

6

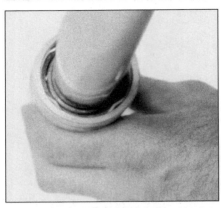

4.21 Install the retaining ring and make sure it seats in its groove

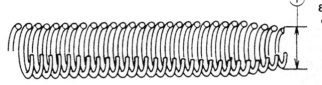

4.25 On Vulcan 700/750 and Vulcan 800 Drifter models, the end of the spring with small-diameter coils goes downward

1   Smaller diameter
2   Top of fork
3   Bottom of fork

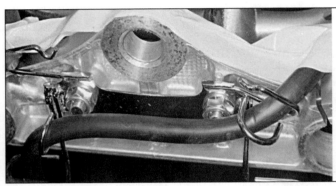

5.10b Lift off the triple clamp; note the tape used to protect it from scratches

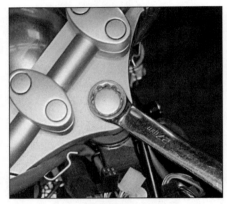

5.10a Unscrew the steering head bolt

21   Install the retaining ring, making sure the ring is completely seated in its groove **(see illustration)**.
22   Install the dust seal, making sure it seats completely.
23   Install the drain screw and a new gasket, if it was removed.
24   Compress the fork fully and add the recommended type and quantity of fork oil (see Chapter 1).
25   Install the fork spring, with the small-diameter end at the bottom on Vulcan 700/750 and 800 Drifter models **(see illustration)**. Install the spring seat and spacer, then install the top plug and secure it with the retaining ring (see Chapter 1).
26   Install the fork by following the procedure outlined in Section 3. If you won't be installing the fork right away, store it in an upright position to prevent leakage.

5   Steering head bearings - replacement

Refer to illustrations 5.10a, 5.10b, 5.11a, 5.11b, 5.12, 5.15a, 5.15b, 5.17a, 5.17b, 5.21, 5.22 and 5.24

1   If the steering head bearing check/adjustment (see Chapter 1) does not remedy excessive play or roughness in the

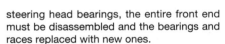

5.11a Unscrew the locknut and adjusting nut . . .

steering head bearings, the entire front end must be disassembled and the bearings and races replaced with new ones.
2   On all models except Vulcan 800 Drifter, refer to Chapter 4 and remove the fuel tank.
3   Refer to Chapter 7 and remove the front wheel.
4   If you're working on a Vulcan 700/750 model, disconnect the speedometer cable (see Chapter 9).
5   If you're working on a Vulcan 800 model (except Drifter), remove the headlight assembly and the front turn signals (see Chapter 9 and Section 3).
6   If you're working on a Vulcan 800 Drifter model, remove the headlight assembly (see Chapter 9). Remove the bolts from the underside of the upper triple clamp and remove the turn signal bracket.
7   Remove the cover from the front of the lower triple clamp.

5.11b . . . lift off the bearing cover and upper bearing . . .

8   Refer to Section 3 and remove the front forks. **Note:** *You can remove both fork legs together with the front fender as an assembly. If you choose this option, ignore the Steps in Section 3 that don't apply.*
9   Refer to Section 2 and remove the handlebars. For this procedure, remove the handlebars by unscrewing the nuts below the triple clamp and lifting the handlebar out together with the brackets.
10   Remove the steering stem bolt **(see illustration)**, then lift off the upper triple clamp (sometimes called the fork bridge or crown) **(see illustration)**.
11   Remove the stem locknut **(see illustration)**. Using an adjustable spanner wrench, remove the stem adjusting nut while supporting the steering head from the bottom. Lift off the race cover and upper bearing **(see illustration 2.4a, 2.4b, 2.4c and the accompanying illustration)**.
12   Remove the steering stem and lower

5.12 . . . and lower the steering stem and bearing out of the steering head

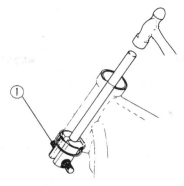

5.15a This special Kawasaki tool expands to grip the bearing race, then is driven out with a hammer and punch

1   Kawasaki tool 57001-1107

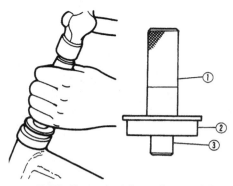

5.15b If you don't have the special Kawasaki tools, drive in the bearing races with a bearing driver or a socket the same diameter as the bearing race

1   Bearing driver handle
2   Bearing driver
3   Bearing driver

5.17a Remove the lower bearing with a bearing splitter like this one (if it will fit on the steering stem) and a puller or hydraulic press . . .

5.17b . . . and if a bearing splitter won't fit, use the pry slot (arrow)

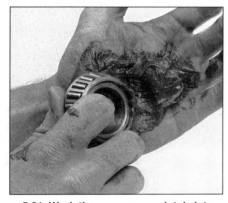

5.21 Work the grease completely into the rollers

triple clamp assembly together with the lower bearing **(see illustration)**. If it's stuck, gently tap on the top of the steering stem with a plastic mallet or a hammer and a wood block.

13   Clean all the parts with solvent and dry them thoroughly, using compressed air, if available. If you do use compressed air, don't let the bearings spin as they're dried - it could ruin them. Wipe the old grease out of the frame steering head and bearing races.

14   Examine the races in the steering head for cracks, dents, and pits. If even the slightest amount of wear or damage is evident, the races should be replaced with new ones.

15   To remove the races, drive them out of the steering head with Kawasaki tool no. 57001-1107 or equivalent **(see illustration)**. A slide hammer with the proper internal-jaw puller will also work. Since the races are an interference fit in the frame, installation will be easier if the new races are left overnight in a refrigerator. This will cause them to contract and slip into place in the frame with very little effort. When installing the races, use Kawasaki press shaft no. 57001-1075 and drivers no. 57001-1106 and 57001-1076, or

tap them gently into place with a hammer and bearing driver or a large socket **(see illustration)**. Do not strike the bearing surface or the race will be damaged.

16   Check the bearings for wear. Look for cracks, dents, and pits in the races and flat spots on the bearings. Replace any defective parts with new ones. If a new bearing is required, replace both of them as a set.

17   To remove the lower bearing from the steering stem, use a bearing puller (Kawasaki tool no. 57001-135 or equivalent) **(see illustration)**. **Note:** *The shape of the triple clamp will block access for the puller shown on some Vulcan 800 models. In this case, use a puller that catches the bearing in the triple clamp slot* **(see illustration)**. Don't remove this bearing unless it, or the grease seal underneath, must be replaced.

18   Check the grease seal under the lower bearing and replace it with a new one if necessary.

19   Inspect the steering stem/lower triple clamp for cracks and other damage. Do not attempt to repair any steering components. Replace them with new parts if defects are found.

20   Check the bearing cover - if it's worn or deteriorated, replace it.

21   Pack the bearings with high-quality grease (preferably a moly-based grease) **(see illustration)**. Coat the outer races with grease also.

22   Install the grease seal and lower bearing onto the steering stem. Drive the lower bear-

5.22 Drive the grease seal and bearing lower race on with a hollow driver (or an equivalent piece of pipe) and a hammer

6

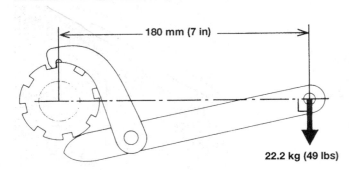

5.24 To get a precise torque setting for the bearing adjusting nut, apply a measured pulling force to the handle at a measured distance from the center of the nut

6.2a Here are the Vulcan 700/750 upper and lower shock mounting bolts (arrows)

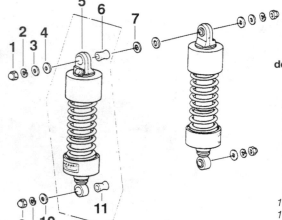

6.2b Rear shock absorber details (Vulcan 700/750 models)

1 Upper nut
2 Lockwasher
3 Washer
4 Bushing washer
5 Shock absorber
6 Bushing
7 Washer
8 Lower nut
9 Lockwasher
10 Bushing washer
11 Bushing

ing onto the steering stem using Kawasaki stem bearing driver no. 57001-137 and adapter no. 57001-1074 (see illustration). If you don't have access to these tools, a section of pipe with a diameter the same as the inner race of the bearing can be used. Drive the bearing on until it is fully seated.

23 Insert the steering stem/lower triple clamp into the frame head. Install the upper bearing and the race cover (see illustration 5.11).

24 Install the adjusting nut with its shoulder down (against the bearing). Using the adjustable wrench, tighten the nut while moving the lower triple clamp back and forth. Continue to tighten the nut (to approximately 29 ft-lbs/39 Nm) until the steering head becomes tight, then back off until there is some play in the bearings. You can calculate the torque by applying a measured amount of force to the wrench handle at a measured distance from the center of the nut (see illustration). Once the nut is tightened to the initial torque, make sure there is no more play (don't overtighten, though, or the steering will be too tight and the bearings may be damaged). Make sure the steering head turns smoothly.

25 Install the locknut, then adjust the bearings (see Chapter 1).

26 The remainder of installation is the reverse of removal.

6 Rear shock absorbers - removal and installation

Vulcan 700/750 models

Removal

Refer to illustrations 6.2a and 6.2b

1 Set the bike on its centerstand (if equipped). If the bike doesn't have a centerstand, support it in an upright position so it can't be knocked over during this procedure.

2 Remove the shock absorber upper and lower nuts and lift the shock off the motorcycle (see illustrations).

Installation

3 Installation is the reverse of the removal procedure. Position the shock with the air valves at the top and facing outward. Tighten the shock absorber nuts to the torque values listed in this Chapter's Specifications.

6.7a Remove the bolts from the suspension linkage tie-rod and the lower end of the shock absorber (arrows)

Vulcan 800 models

Removal

Refer to illustrations 6.7a, 6.7b and 6.8

4 Set the bike on its centerstand (if equipped). If the bike doesn't have a centerstand, support it in an upright position so it can't be knocked over during this procedure.

5 Remove the exhaust system (see Chapter 4).

6 Remove the storage and tool kit box (see Chapter 8).

7 Remove the bolts from the suspension linkage tie-rod and the lower end of the shock absorber (see illustrations).

8 Remove the upper shock bolt and nut and take the shock out of the motorcycle (see illustration).

9 Installation is the reverse of the removal steps. Be sure the bolt heads are facing in the proper directions. Tighten the bolts to the torque listed in this Chapter's Specifications.

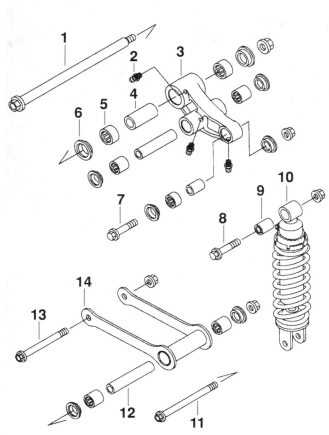

6.7b Rear shock absorber and suspension linkage (Vulcan 800 models) - exploded view

1   Rocker arm pivot bolt
2   Grease fitting
3   Rocker arm
4   Collar
5   Needle bearing
6   Grease seal
7   Rocker arm bolt
8   Shock absorber upper bolt
9   Bushing
10 Shock absorber
11 Tie-rod pivot bolt
12 Collar
13 Tie-rod pivot bolt
14 Tie-rod

6.8 Note which way the bolt is installed and remove the nut and bolt

7.3a Pry the cap off the bolt and nut . . .

7.3b . . then unscrew the nut and remove the bolt

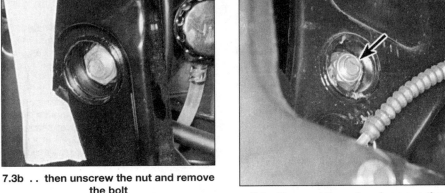

7.4a Unscrew the nut and remove the rocker arm pivot bolt . . .

7.4b . . . then remove the rocker arm

7   Rear suspension linkage (Vulcan 800 models) - removal, inspection and installation

Removal

Refer to illustrations 7.3a, 7.3b, 7.4a and 7.4b

1   Perform Steps 4 through 7 of Section 6.

2   Support the tie-rod, remove the bolt and take the tie-rod out.
3   Pry the cover off of the nut on the swingarm pivot shaft **(see illustration)**. Loosen, but don't remove, the nut **(see illustration)**.
4   Remove the rocker arm pivot bolt and

nut and detach the rocker arm from the frame **(see illustrations)**.

Inspection

Refer to illustrations 7.5a, 7.5b and 7.5c

5   Pry out the seals and slip the collars out

6

7.5a Here are the rocker arm grease seals and bearings . . .

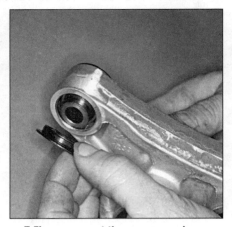

7.5b . . . pry out the grease seals . . .

7.5c . . . and remove the collars for access to the bearings

of the needle bearings **(see illustrations)**. Check the bearings for wear or damage. If the bearings are good, pack them with molybdenum disulfide grease and install the collars.

6   If the seals are worn or appear to have been leaking, replace them. Press the seals in with a seal driver or socket the same diameter as the seals.

7   If the bearings need to be replaced, press them out and press new ones in. To prevent damage to the new bearings, you'll need a shouldered drift with a narrow diameter the same size as the inside diameter of the bearings. If you don't have the proper tool, have the bearings replaced by a dealer service department or other qualified shop. A well-equipped automotive machine shop should also be able to do the job.

Installation

8   Installation is the reverse of the removal steps. Tighten the nuts and bolts to the torque listed in this Chapter's Specifications.

8   Swingarm bearings - check

1   Refer to Chapter 7 and remove the rear wheel, then refer to Section 6 and remove the rear shock absorbers.

2   Grasp the rear of the swingarm with one hand and place your other hand at the junction of the swingarm and the frame. Try to move the rear of the swingarm from side-to-side. Any wear (play) in the bearings should be felt as movement between the swingarm and the frame at the front. The swingarm will

actually be felt to move forward and backward at the front (not from side-to-side). If any play is noted, the bearings should be replaced with new ones (see Section 10).

3   Next, move the swingarm up and down through its full travel. It should move freely, without any binding or rough spots. If it does not move freely, refer to Section 10 for servicing procedures.

9   Swingarm - removal and installation

Vulcan 700/750 models

Removal

Refer to illustration 9.6

1   Raise the bike and set it on its centerstand (if equipped). If the bike doesn't have a centerstand, support it securely so it can't be knocked over during this procedure.

2   Remove the right shock absorber (see Section 6).

3   Remove the rear wheel (see Chapter 7).

4   Remove the mufflers (see Chapter 4).

5   Remove the front bevel gear case, differential and driveshaft (see Sections 11 and 12).

6   Pry the caps off the swingarm pivots **(see illustration)**. Unbolt the shaft retainers.

7   Support the swingarm. Thread a bolt (5 mm x 0.8) into each of the pivot shafts and pull the shafts out.

8   Remove the swingarm to the rear of the vehicle.

9   Check the pivot bearings in the swingarm for dryness or deterioration. If they're in need of lubrication or replacement, refer to Section 10.

Installation

Refer to illustration 9.13

10 Support the swing arm so its pivot holes are aligned with the holes in the frame. Install the pivot shafts.

11 Install the shaft retainers and tighten their bolts to the torque listed in this Chap-

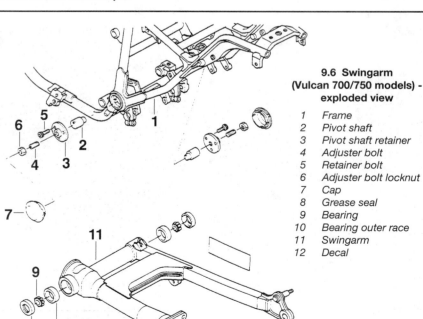

9.6 Swingarm (Vulcan 700/750 models) - exploded view

1   *Frame*
2   *Pivot shaft*
3   *Pivot shaft retainer*
4   *Adjuster bolt*
5   *Retainer bolt*
6   *Adjuster bolt locknut*
7   *Cap*
8   *Grease seal*
9   *Bearing*
10   *Bearing outer race*
11   *Swingarm*
12   *Decal*

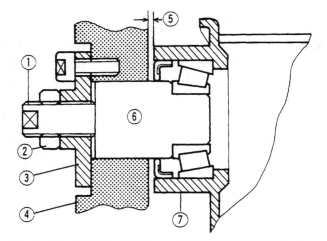

9.13 Swingarm adjustment details (Vulcan 700/750 models)

1   Adjuster bolt
2   Locknut
3   Pivot shaft retainer
4   Frame gusset
5   Swingarm
    clearance
6   Pivot shaft
7   Swingarm

9.28a Support the swingarm with a bungee cord while you pull it out

19   Remove the rear wheel (see Chapter 7).
20   Remove the upper tie-rod bolt from the suspension linkage (see Section 7).
21   Remove the shock absorber (see Section 6).
22   Remove the inner rear fender (see Chapter 8).
23   On all except Drifter models, remove the nut and detach the rear brake cable from the right side of the frame.

Vulcan 800 Drifter models

24   Remove the seat (see Chapter 8). Remove the cover from the electrical components, disconnect the electrical connectors for the rear lights and free the wiring harness from its retainer.
25   Remove the rear fender.
26   Remove the regulator/rectifier (see Chapter 9).
27   Disconnect the brake hose from the rear caliper (see Chapter 7). Cover the end of the hose with a plastic bag secured with a rubber band, then place the end of the hose up to prevent brake fluid loss.

All models

28   Support the swingarm **(see illustration)**. Remove the swingarm pivot bolt and nut and remove it from the frame **(see illustration)**.
29   Installation is the reverse of the removal steps, with the following additions:
  a) *Tighten all fasteners to the torques listed in this Chapter's Specifications.*
  b) *On all except Drifter models, adjust the rear brake (see Chapter 1).*
  c) *On Drifter models, bleed the rear brake (see Chapter 7).*

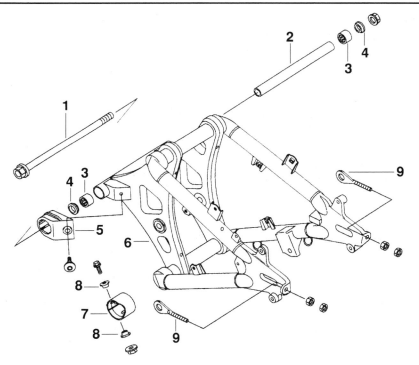

9.28b Swingarm (Vulcan 800 models) - exploded view

1	Swingarm pivot bolt	4	Grease seal	7	Chain slider
2	Collar	5	Chain slider	8	Grommet
3	Needle bearing	6	Swingarm	9	Chain adjuster bolt

ter's Specifications.
12   Install the adjuster bolts and locknuts (leave the locknuts loose).
13   Place a 2.5 mm (0.984 inch) shim between the left side of the swingarm and the frame **(see illustration)**. **Note:** *You can stack up feeler gauges to reach the correct thickness.*
14   Thread the right adjuster bolt in, pushing the swingarm against the shim. Tighten the locknut on the right adjuster bolt while holding the bolt with a screwdriver.
15   Remove the shim. Thread in the left adjuster bolt until it stops, then hold it with a

screwdriver and tighten the locknut.
16   Raise and lower the swingarm to make sure it moves freely without binding or interference. Check swingarm bearing play as described in Section 8.
17   The remainder of installation is the reverse of the removal steps.

Vulcan 800 models

Removal

Refer to illustrations 9.28a and 9.28b
18   Remove the exhaust system (see Chapter 4).

10   Swingarm bearings - replacement

1   Bearing replacement isn't complicated, but it requires a blind hole (expanding) puller and a slide hammer. The puller and slide hammer can be rented if you don't have them, but compare the cost of having the

6

10.6a There's a grease seal on the outside of each bearing . . .

10.6b . . . pry the seal out . . .

10.7 . . . and pull out the collar . . .

bearings replaced by a dealer service department or other qualified shop to that of renting the equipment before you proceed.

2   Remove the swingarm (see Section 9).

Vulcan 700/750 models

3   Pry out the seals **(see illustration 9.6)**.

4   Remove the bearing inner races, then remove the outer races with a blind hole

10.8 . . . for access to the bearings

11.5 Remove the nuts (arrows) (lower two nuts hidden) to detach the differential from the driveshaft tube

(expanding) puller and slide hammer.

5   Drive new inner races into the swingarm with a bearing driver or socket the same diameter as the bearing outer race.

Vulcan 800 models

Refer to illustrations 10.6a, 10.6b, 10.7 and 10.8

6   Pry out the swingarm seals **(see illustrations)**.

7   Remove the swingarm shaft collar **(see illustration)**.

8   Remove the bearings with a blind hole puller **(see illustration)**. To prevent distorting the new bearing, drive it in the with a shouldered drift with a narrow diameter that just fits inside the bearing. The marked side of the bearing faces outward.

9   Pack the bearing with molybdenum disulfide grease. Coat the pivot shaft with the same grease and install it, then install the seals and apply grease to the seal lips.

---

11 Rear differential (Vulcan 700/750 models) - removal, inspection and installation

---

Removal

Refer to illustration 11.5

1   Raise the bike and set it on its centerstand (if equipped). If the bike doesn't have a centerstand, support it securely so it can't be knocked over during this procedure.

2   Remove the left shock absorber (see Section 6).

3   Remove the rear wheel (see Chapter 7).

4   Remove the left muffler (see Chapter 4).

5   Remove the differential mounting nuts and take the differential off the driveshaft housing **(see illustration)**. The spring that's installed on the rear end of the driveshaft will come off with the differential.

Inspection

6   Check for signs of oil leakage around the pinion and drive coupling. Turn the pinion by hand and check for rough or noisy movement. Remove the filler plug and look into the hole, using a flashlight if necessary, for obvious signs of damage such as broken gear teeth.

7   Differential overhaul is a complicated procedure that requires several special tools, for which there are no readily available substitutes. If there's visible wear or damage, or if differential rotation is rough or noisy, take it to a Kawasaki dealer for disassembly and further inspection.

Installation

Refer to illustrations 11.8a, 11.8b and 11.8c

8   Installation is the reverse of the removal steps, with the following additions:

a) *Don't forget to reinstall the spring between the differential pinion and the rear end of the driveshaft* **(see illustration)**.

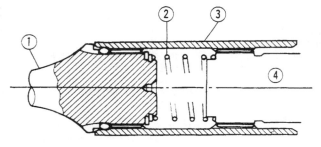

11.8a Don't forget to reinstall the spring between the rear end of the driveshaft and the differential pinion

1   Driveshaft
2   Spring
3   Joint
4   Differential pinion

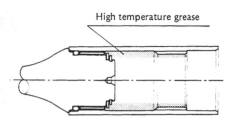

11.8b Coat the area indicated with high-temperature grease

b) *Wipe all the old grease off the differential pinion and put a coating of high-temperature grease on the splines* **(see illustration)**.
c) *If the driveshaft pulled off of the front pinion when the differential was removed, pull back the rubber cover at the front end of the driveshaft* **(see illustration)**. *Align the splines of the driveshaft and front bevel housing and push the driveshaft back on.*
d) *Tighten the mounting nuts to the torque listed in this Chapter's Specifications.*
e) *Fill the differential with oil (see Chapter 1).*

12 Front bevel gear housing and driveshaft - removal, inspection and installation

Removal

Refer to illustrations 12.3a, 12.3b and 12.4

1   Raise the bike and set it on its centerstand (if equipped). If the bike doesn't have a centerstand, support it securely so it can't be knocked over during this procedure.
2   Disconnect the clutch cable from the release mechanism (see Chapter 2).
3   Loosen the bolts in the reverse order of the tightening sequence, then remove the bolts and take the front bevel gear case off the engine **(see illustrations)**. Disengage it from the driveshaft splines and from the damper coupling on the engine.

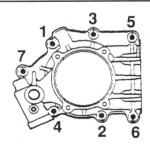

12.3b Housing bolts TIGHTENING sequence; apply non-permanent thread locking agent to the 95 mm bolts (1, 2, and 4)

11.8c Pull back the rubber cover at the front end of the driveshaft (arrow)

4   Pull the driveshaft forward out of the swingarm **(see illustration)**. If the spring on the rear end of the driveshaft falls off inside the swingarm, pull it out with a gripper tool or magnet.

Inspection

5   Rotate the pinion coupling on the bevel gear housing with fingers and check for rough or noisy movement. Check for signs of oil leakage around the pinion and drive coupling. Visual inspection of the internal components isn't possible without disassembling the unit.
6   Bevel gear housing overhaul is a complicated procedure that requires several special tools, for which there are no readily available substitutes. If there's visible wear or damage, or if differential rotation is rough or noisy, take it to a Kawasaki dealer for disassembly and further inspection.
7   Check the driveshaft for bending or other visible damage such as step wear of the splines. If the shaft is bent, replace it. If the splines at either end of the shaft are worn, replace the shaft.
8   Hold the driveshaft firmly in one hand and try to twist the universal joint. If there's play in the joint, replace the shaft (but don't

12.3a Here's the front bevel gear housing (arrow)

confuse play in the joint with its normal motion).

Installation

9   Installation is the reverse of the removal steps, with the following additions:
a) *Install the driveshaft spring and lubricate the splines at the rear end with high-temperature grease* **(see illustrations 11.8a and 11.8b)**.
b) *Make sure both dowel pins are in place and use a new gasket when installing the front bevel gear housing. Tighten the bolts in order* **(see illustration 12.3b)**. *If you reuse the three 95 mm bolts, apply non-permanent thread locking agent to their threads.*
c) *Check the engine oil level and add some if necessary (see Chapter 1).*

13 Drive chain - removal, cleaning, inspection and installation

Warning: *These motorcycles use an endless chain. Kawasaki recommends against cutting the chain to install a master link. If the chain breaks in operation, it could cause loss of control of the motorcycle.*

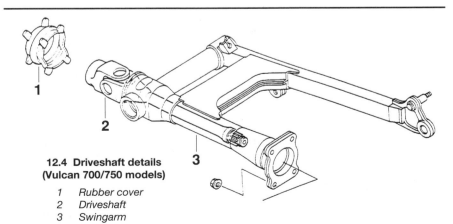

12.4 Driveshaft details (Vulcan 700/750 models)

1   *Rubber cover*
2   *Driveshaft*
3   *Swingarm*

6

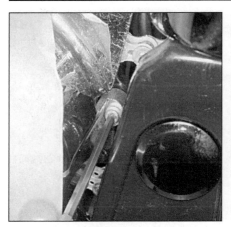

13.4a Remove the sprocket cover Allen bolt . . .

13.4b . . . and separate the cover from the left crankcase cover

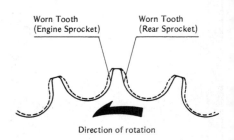

14.3 Check the sprockets in the areas indicated to see if they're worn excessively

Removal

Refer to illustrations 13.4a and 13.4b
1   Remove the chain guard.
2   Remove the rear wheel (see Chapter 7).
3   Remove the swingarm (see Section 9).
4   Remove the Allen bolt that secures the engine sprocket cover **(see illustration)**. Pull the cover rearward to detach it from the left crankcase cover **(see illustration)**.
5   Lift the chain off the sprockets and remove it from the bike.
6   Check the chain guard on the swingarm for wear or damage and replace it as necessary.

Cleaning and inspection

7   Soak the chain in a high flash point solvent for approximately five or six minutes. Use a brush to work the solvent into the spaces between the links and plates.
8   Wipe the chain dry, then check it carefully for worn or damaged links. Replace the chain if wear or damage is found at any point.
9   Stretch the chain taut and measure its

length between the number of pins listed in this Chapter's Specifications. Compare the measured length to the specified value replace the chain if it's beyond the limit. If the chain needs to be replaced, refer to Section 14 and check the sprockets. If they're worn, replace them also. If a new chain is installed on worn sprockets, it will wear out quickly.
10   Lubricate the chain with spray chain lube compatible with O-ring chains.

Installation

11   Installation is the reverse of the removal steps. Refer to Chapter 1 and adjust the chain.

14 Sprockets - check and replacement

Refer to illustrations 14.3, 14.5, 14.6a, 14.6b, 14.6c, 14.7a, 14.7b and 14.7c
1   Support the bike securely so it can't be knocked over during this procedure.

2   Whenever the sprockets are inspected, the chain should be inspected also and replaced if it's worn. Installing a worn chain on new sprockets will cause them to wear quickly.
3   Remove the engine sprocket cover (see Section 13). Check the teeth on the engine sprocket and rear sprocket for wear **(see illustration)**.
4   If the sprockets are worn, remove the rear wheel (see Chapter 7) and the chain (Section 13).
5   Remove the nuts and detach the

14.6a Bend back the lockwasher . . .

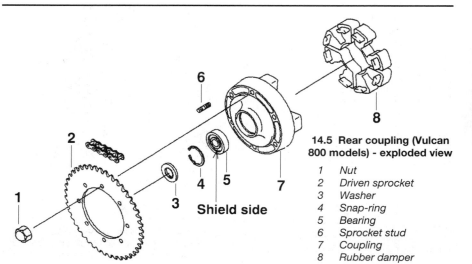

14.5 Rear coupling (Vulcan 800 models) - exploded view

1   Nut
2   Driven sprocket
3   Washer
4   Snap-ring
5   Bearing
6   Sprocket stud
7   Coupling
8   Rubber damper

Shield side

14.6b . . . unscrew the nut and remove the lockwasher . . .

14.6c . . . then pull the sprocket off and disengage it from the chain

14.7a Remove the rubber damper (it covers on of the bearing cover bolts . . .

14.7b . . . if the seal has been leaking, remove the bolts (arrows) . . .

14.7c . . . and take off the cover, gasket and dowels (arrows)

15.2 Lift the coupling off the wheel for access to the damper

15.3 Check the damper for wear or deterioration

sprocket from the rear wheel hub **(see illustration)**.
6 Bend back the lockwasher, then unscrew the nut from the transmission shaft and remove the lockwasher **(see illustrations)**. Pull the sprocket off the transmission shaft, together with the chain **(see illustration)**.
7 Inspect the seal behind the engine sprocket **(see illustration)**. If it has been leaking, remove the seal cover, its gasket and dowel **(see illustrations)**. Pry the seal out (taking care not to scratch the seal bore) and tap in a new seal with a socket the same diameter as the seal. Reinstall the cover, using a new gasket.
8 Installation is the reverse of the removal steps, with the following additions:
a) If you removed the seal cover, reinstall the dowel and use a new gasket **(see illustration 14.7c)**. Tighten the sprocket cover bolts to the torque listed in this Chapter's Specifications, then reinstall the chain guard.
b) Tighten the sprocket nuts at the engine and wheel to the torques listed in this Chapter's Specifications. Use a new lockwasher on the engine sprocket and

bend it against the nut.
c) Refer to Chapter 1 and adjust the chain.
d) If you removed the seal cover, check the engine oil level and add some if necessary (see Chapter 1).

15 Rear wheel coupling/rubber damper - check and replacement

Refer to illustrations 15.2, 15.3 and 15.5
1 Remove the rear wheel (see Chapter 7). If you're working on a Vulcan 700/750 model, remove the differential (see Section 11).
2 If you're working on a Vulcan 700/750 model, remove the large snap-ring that secures the coupling to the wheel (see Chapter 7). Lift the rear wheel coupling from the wheel **(see illustration)**.
3 Lift the rubber damper from the wheel **(see illustration)** and check it for cracks, hardening and general deterioration. Replace it with a new one if necessary.
4 Checking and replacement procedures for the coupling bearing on Vulcan 800 models are similar to those described for the wheel bearings. Refer to Chapter 7.

5 Installation is the reverse of the removal procedure. **Caution:** On Vulcan 800 models, be sure not to forget the spacer **(see illustration)**; if the axle nut is tightened without the spacer in position, the rear wheel bearings may be damaged.

15.5 DO NOT lose the coupling collar or the bearings will be damaged when you tighten the axle nut; note which end fits into the bearing

6

16 Suspension adjustments

Front forks (early Vulcan 700/750 models)

1 The front forks on early Vulcan 700/750 models are equipped with air pressure valves. Later Vulcan 700/750 models and all Vulcan 800 models have non-adjustable forks. The recommended air pressure setting is listed in this Chapter's Specifications. **Warning:** *Never exceed the maximum pressure listed in this Chapter's Specifications. Never remove the fork springs and rely on air pressure alone to support the forks or unstable handling may occur. Ensure that the pressure is equal in both legs.*

Rear shock absorbers (Vulcan 700/750 models)

2 The rear shocks on Vulcan 700/750 models are equipped with air pressure valves. The recommended air pressure setting is listed in this Chapter's Specifications. **Caution:** *Don't exceed the maximum pressure listed in this Chapter's Specifications or the shock seals may be damaged.* **Warning:** *Ensure that the pressure is equal in both shocks or unstable handling may occur.*

Rear spring preload adjustment (Vulcan 800 models)

Refer to illustration 16.3

3 The rear spring preload is adjusted by turning the adjusting sleeve with the hook wrench included in the bike's tool kit **(see illustration)**. Compare preload with the values listed in this Chapter's Specifications and adjust as needed.

16.3 Turn the adjuster ring to change the shock preload

Chapter 7
Brakes, wheels and tires

Contents

Specifications

Brakes

Brake fluid type	See Chapter 1
Brake pad minimum thickness	See Chapter 1
Front disc thickness (single-piston calipers)*	
Standard	4.8 to 5.1 mm (0.189 to 0.200 inch)
Minimum*	4.5 mm (0.177 inch)
Front disc thickness (dual-piston calipers)*	
Standard	5.8 to 6.2 mm (0.228 to 0.244 inch)
Minimum*	5.5 mm (0.217 inch)
Rear disc thickness (Drifter)*	
Standard	6.8 to 7.2 mm (0.268 to 0.283 inch)
Minimum*	6.0 mm (0.236 inch)

Refer to marks stamped into the disc (they supersede information printed here)

Disc runout (maximum)	0.3 mm (0.012 inch)
Brake pedal position and freeplay	See Chapter 1
Rear drum brake lining thickness	
Standard	
Vulcan 700/750 models	Not specified
Vulcan 800 models	4.9 to 5.5 mm (0.193 to 0.217 inch)
Minimum	
Vulcan 700/750 models	Not specified
Vulcan 800 models	2.6 mm (0.102 inch)
Brake drum diameter	
Standard	180.00 to 180.16 mm (7.087 to 7.093 inch)
Maximum	180.75 mm (7.116 inch)

7

Wheels and tires

Vulcan 700/750 models

Wheel runout limit
    Axial (side-to-side).. 0.5 mm (0.020 inch)
    Radial (out-of-round).. 0.8 mm (0.031 inch)
Axle runout limit (front and rear) .... 0.05 mm (0.002 inch)
Tire pressures .... See Chapter 1

Vulcan 800 models (except Drifter)

Wheel runout limit
    Axial (side-to-side).. 2.0 mm (0.078 inch)
    Radial (out-of-round).. 2.0 mm (0.078 inch)
Axle runout limit (front and rear) .... 0.2 mm (0.008 inch) per 100 mm (3.94 inches) of axle length
Tire pressures .... See Chapter 1

Vulcan 800 Drifter

Wheel runout limit
    Axial (side-to-side).. 1.5 mm (0.059 inch)
    Radial (out-of-round).. 1.5 mm (0.059 inch)
Axle runout limit (front and rear) .... 0.2 mm (0.008 inch) per 100 mm (3.94 inches) of axle length
Tire pressures .... See Chapter 1

Torque specifications

Vulcan 700/750 models

Caliper mounting bolts .... 32 Nm (24 ft-lbs)
Union bolts .... 25 Nm (18 ft-lbs)
Brake disc-to-wheel bolts .... 23 Nm (16.5 ft-lbs)
Master cylinder mounting bolts .... Not specified
Front brake lever pivot pin locknut .... Not specified
Caliper bleed valve .... 7.8 Nm (69 inch-lbs)
Brake pedal pinch bolt .... 25 Nm (18 ft-lbs)
Front axle nut .... 59 Nm (43 ft-lbs)
Front axle pinch bolt .... 13 Nm (113 inch-lbs)
Rear axle nut .... 110 Nm (80 ft-lbs)

Vulcan 800 models

Caliper mounting bolts .... 34 Nm (25 ft-lbs)
Union bolts .... 25 Nm (18 ft-lbs)
Brake disc-to-wheel bolts
    Single-piston caliper .... 23 Nm (16.5 ft-lbs)
    Dual-piston caliper .... 27 Nm (20 ft-lbs)
Master cylinder mounting bolts
    All except Drifter... 11 Nm (95 inch-lbs)
    Drifter .... 8.8 Nm (78 inch-lbs)
Front brake lever pivot pin locknut .... 5.9 Nm (52 inch-lbs)
Caliper bleed valve .... 7.8 Nm (69 inch-lbs)
Brake pedal lever pinch bolt
    All except Drifter... 23 Nm (16.5 ft-lbs)
    Drifter .... 27 Nm (20 ft-lbs)
Front axle nut .... 110 Nm (80 ft-lbs)
Front axle pinch bolt .... 34 Nm (25 ft-lbs)
Rear axle nut .... 98 Nm (72 ft-lbs)

1   General information

The motorcycles covered by this manual are equipped with hydraulic disc brakes on the front wheel. Vulcan 700/750 models use a pair of single-piston calipers. Vulcan 800 models use a single caliper; on standard models the caliper has a single piston, while on Classic and Drifter models it has dual pistons.

All models except the Vulcan 800 Drifter use a mechanical drum brake on the rear wheel. The Vulcan 800 Drifter uses a rear disc brake with a dual-piston caliper.

Vulcan 700/750 models are equipped with cast aluminum wheels, which require very little maintenance and allow tubeless tires to be used. Vulcan 800 models use wire wheels at front and rear. **Caution:** *Disc brake components rarely require disassembly. Do not disassemble components unless abso-*

lutely necessary. If any hydraulic brake line connection in the system is loosened, the entire system should be disassembled, drained, cleaned and then properly filled and bled upon reassembly. Do not use solvents on internal brake components. Solvents will cause seals to swell and distort. Use only clean brake fluid or alcohol for cleaning. Use care when working with brake fluid as it can injure your eyes and it will damage painted surfaces and plastic parts.

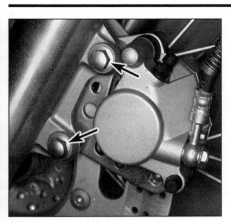

2.2 Remove the caliper mounting bolts (arrows) and support the caliper so it doesn't hang by the brake hose

2.3 It's a good idea to wrap the caliper so the caliper and fork aren't scratched

2.4 Slide the caliper bracket toward the pistons so it clears the inner pad, then remove the pad

2.5 Disengage the clips on the outer pad from the caliper and remove the pad

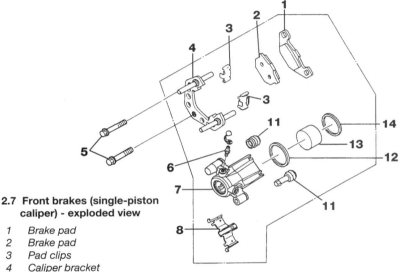

2.7 Front brakes (single-piston caliper) - exploded view

1   Brake pad
2   Brake pad
3   Pad clips
4   Caliper bracket
5   Caliper mounting bolts
6   Bleed valve and dust cap
7   Caliper body
8   Anti-rattle spring
9   Brake disc mounting bolt
10 Brake disc
11 Slider pin boots
12 Piston seal
13 Piston
14 Dust seal

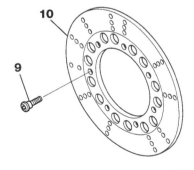

2.6 Remove the anti-rattle spring

A   Anti-rattle spring
B   Piston insert

2   Brake pads - replacement

Warning: *The dust created by the brake system may contain asbestos, which is harmful to your health. Never blow it out with compressed air and don't inhale any of it. An approved filtering mask should be worn when working on the brakes.*

1   Set the bike on its centerstand (if equipped).

Single-piston calipers

Refer to illustrations 2.2, 2.3, 2.4, 2.5, 2.6 and 2.7

2   Remove the caliper mounting bolts **(see illustration)**. Slide the caliper and pads off the disc.

3   Support the caliper with rope or wire so it doesn't hang by the brake hose **(see illustration)**. It's a good idea to wrap the caliper with rags and tape to protect the caliper and wheel from scratches.

4   Push the caliper bracket in (toward the piston) until the pins on the bracket clear the holes in the pad backing plate, then remove the inner pad **(see illustration)**.

5   Remove the outer brake pad from the caliper **(see illustration)**.

6   Remove the anti-rattle spring **(see illustration)**. If it appears damaged, replace it.

7   Check the pad support clips on the caliper bracket **(see illustration)**. If they are

7

missing or distorted, replace them.

8   Check the condition of the brake disc (see Section 4). If it is in need of machining or replacement, follow the procedure in that Section to remove it. If it is okay, deglaze it with sandpaper or emery cloth, using a swirling motion.

9   Remove the cap from the master cylinder reservoir and siphon out some fluid. Push the piston into the caliper as far as possible, while checking the master cylinder reservoir to make sure it doesn't overflow. If you can't depress the piston with thumb pressure, try using a C-clamp. If the piston sticks, remove the caliper and overhaul it as described in Section 3.

10   Install the anti-rattle spring in the caliper.

11   Install both pads in the caliper and pull the caliper bracket out, so the pins on the bracket engage with the holes in the pad backing plate.

12   Install the caliper, tightening the mounting bolts to the torque listed in this Chapter's Specifications.

13   Refill the master cylinder reservoir (see Chapter 1) and install the diaphragm and cap.

14   Operate the brake lever several times to bring the pads into contact with the disc. Check the operation of the brakes carefully before riding the motorcycle.

15   If you're working on a Vulcan 700/750 model, repeat the procedure to replace the pads in the other caliper.

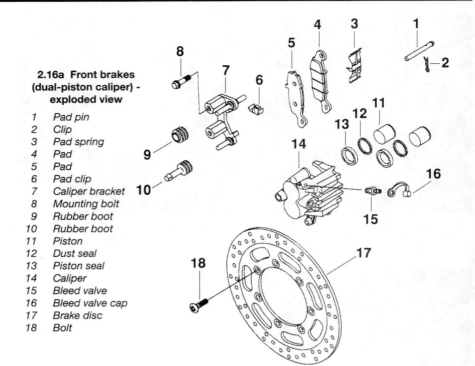

2.16a Front brakes (dual-piston caliper) - exploded view

1   Pad pin
2   Clip
3   Pad spring
4   Pad
5   Pad
6   Pad clip
7   Caliper bracket
8   Mounting bolt
9   Rubber boot
10   Rubber boot
11   Piston
12   Dust seal
13   Piston seal
14   Caliper
15   Bleed valve
16   Bleed valve cap
17   Brake disc
18   Bolt

Dual-piston calipers

Note: *Pad replacement procedures are the same for front and rear dual-piston calipers.*

Refer to illustrations 2.16a, 2.16b, 2.18a and 2.18b

16   Remove the caliper mounting bolts **(see illustrations)**. Slide the caliper and pads off the disc.

17   Support the caliper with rope or wire so it doesn't hang by the brake hose. It's a good idea to wrap the caliper with rags and tape to protect the caliper and wheel from scratches.

18   Remove the clip and pad pin **(see illustration)**. Swivel the outer pad out of the caliper and slip it off the pin, then remove the inner pad **(see illustration)**.

19   Remove the anti-rattle spring **(see illustration 2.16a or 2.16b)**. If it appears damaged, replace it.

20   Check the pad support clips on the caliper bracket **(see illustration 2.16a or 2.16b)**. If they are missing or distorted, replace them.

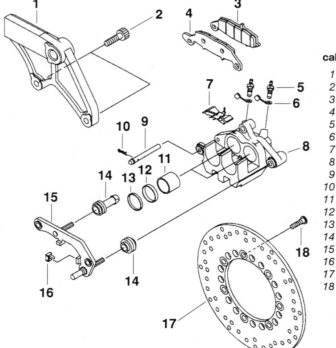

2.16b Rear brake caliper - exploded view

1   Mounting bracket
2   Bolt
3   Pad
4   Pad
5   Bleed valves
6   Bleed valve caps
7   Pad spring
8   Caliper
9   Pad pin
10   Clip
11   Piston
12   Piston seal
13   Dust seal
14   Rubber boot
15   Caliper bracket
16   Pad clip
17   Brake disc
18   Bolt

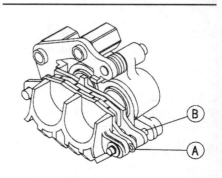

2.18a Remove the clip (A) and pad pin (B)

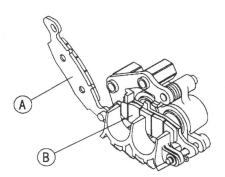

2.18b Rotate the outer pad (A) and slide it off, then remove the inner pad (B)

21   Check the condition of the brake disc (see Section 4). If it is in need of machining or replacement, follow the procedure in that Section to remove it. If it is okay, deglaze it with sandpaper or emery cloth, using a swirling motion.
22   Remove the cap from the master cylinder reservoir and siphon out some fluid. Push the piston into the caliper as far as possible, while checking the master cylinder reservoir to make sure it doesn't overflow. If you can't depress the piston with thumb pressure, try using a C-clamp. If the piston sticks, remove the caliper and overhaul it as described in Section 3.
23   Install the anti-rattle spring in the caliper.
24   Install the inner pad in the caliper.
25   Slip the outer pad onto its pivot pin and swivel it into position. Install the retaining pin and clip.
26   Install the caliper, tightening the mounting bolts to the torque listed in this Chapter's Specifications.
27   Refill the master cylinder reservoir (see Chapter 1) and install the diaphragm and cap.
28   Operate the brake lever several times to bring the pads into contact with the disc. Check the operation of the brakes carefully before riding the motorcycle.

3   Brake caliper - removal, overhaul and installation

Warning: *If a caliper indicates the need for an overhaul (usually due to leaking fluid or sticky operation), all old brake fluid should be flushed from the system. Also, the dust created by the brake system may contain asbestos, which is harmful to your health. Never blow it out with compressed air and don't inhale any of it. An approved filtering mask should be worn when working on the brakes. Do not, under any circumstances, use petroleum-based solvents to clean brake parts. Use clean brake fluid, brake cleaner or denatured alcohol only!*

3.2 Remove the brake hose banjo fitting bolt - there's a sealing washer on each side of the fitting

Note: *If you are removing the caliper only to replace or inspect the brake pads, don't disconnect the hose from the caliper.*

Removal
Refer to illustration 3.2
1   Place the bike on its centerstand (if equipped). If you're planning to overhaul the caliper and don't have a source of compressed air to blow out the piston, use the bike's hydraulic system instead. To do this, remove the pads (see Section 2) and operate the brake lever or pedal to force the piston out of the cylinder. On dual-piston calipers, block one piston with a piece of wood in the brake pad cavity, then push the other piston almost all the way out. Hold the exposed piston with a C-clamp, then operate the brake lever or pedal to push the other piston all the way out. Grip the exposed piston with a rag and twist and pull it out the rest of the way. **Note**: *Brake fluid will run out of the caliper if you remove the piston(s) in this manner. Try to keep it off of the bike by holding the caliper over a pan. Be sure to wipe any spilled fluid off painted or plastic surfaces immediately and clean the area with soap and water.*
2   Remove the brake hose banjo fitting bolt and separate the hose from the caliper **(see illustration)**. Discard the sealing washers. Plug the end of the hose or wrap a plastic bag tightly around it to prevent excessive fluid loss and contamination.
3   Remove the caliper (see Section 2).

Overhaul
Refer to illustrations 3.8, 3.15 and 3.16
4   Remove the brake pads and anti-rattle spring from the caliper (see Section 2, if necessary).
5   Clean the exterior of the caliper with denatured alcohol or brake system cleaner.
6   Remove the caliper bracket and the slider pin boots from the caliper **(see illustration 2.7, 2.16a or 2.16b)**.
7   If you didn't force out the piston with

3.8 Remove the dust seal with a plastic or wooden tool to avoid damage to the bore and seal groove (a pencil works well) - remove the piston seal the same way

the bike's hydraulic system in Step 1, place a few rags between the piston and the caliper frame to act as a cushion, then use compressed air, directed into the fluid inlet, to remove the piston. Use only enough air pressure to ease the piston out of the bore. If a piston is blown out, even with the cushion in place, it may be damaged. **Warning:** *Never place your fingers in front of the piston in an attempt to catch or protect it when applying compressed air, as serious injury could occur.*
8   Using a wood or plastic tool, remove the dust seal **(see illustration)**. Metal tools may cause bore damage.
9   Using a wood or plastic tool, remove the piston seal from the groove in the caliper bore.
10   Clean the piston and the bore with denatured alcohol, clean brake fluid or brake system cleaner and blow dry them with filtered, unlubricated compressed air. Inspect the surface of the piston for nicks and burrs and loss of plating. Check the caliper bore, too. If surface defects are present, the caliper must be replaced. If the caliper is in bad shape, the master cylinder should also be checked.
11   Temporarily reinstall the caliper bracket. Make sure it slides smoothly in-and-out of the caliper. If it doesn't, check the slider pins for burrs or excessive wear. Also check the slider pin bores in the caliper for wear and scoring. Replace the caliper bracket, the caliper, or both if necessary.
12   Lubricate the new piston seal with clean brake fluid and install it in its groove in the caliper bore. Make sure it seats completely and isn't twisted.
13   Lubricate the new dust seal with clean brake fluid and install it in its groove, making sure it seats correctly.
14   Lubricate the piston with clean brake fluid and install it in the caliper bore. Using your thumbs, push the piston all the way in, making sure it doesn't get cocked in the bore.

7

3.15 Install the slider pin boots

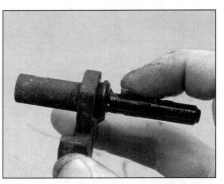

3.16 Apply a thin coat of the specified grease to the slider pins on the caliper bracket

15   Install the slider pin boots **(see illustration)**.
16   Apply a thin coat of PBC (poly butyl cuprysil) grease, or silicone grease designed for high-temperature brake applications, to the slider pins on the caliper bracket **(see illustration)**. Install the caliper bracket to the caliper and seat the boots over the lips on the bracket.

Installation

17   Install the Krattle spring and the brake pads (see Section 2).
18   Install the caliper, tightening the mounting bolts to the torque listed in this Chapter's Specifications.
19   Connect the brake hose to the caliper, using a new sealing washer on each side of the fitting. Tighten the banjo fitting bolt to the torque listed in this Chapter's Specifications.
20   Fill the master cylinder with the recommended brake fluid (see Chapter 1) and bleed the system (see Section 8). Check for leaks.
21   Check the operation of the brakes carefully before riding the motorcycle.

4   Brake disc - inspection, removal and installation

Inspection

Refer to illustration 4.4
1   Set the bike on its centerstand (if equipped). Otherwise prop it securely with the front wheel (or rear wheel on Drifter models) off the ground.
2   Visually inspect the surface of the disc for score marks and other damage. Light scratches are normal after use and won't affect brake operation, but deep grooves and heavy score marks will reduce braking efficiency and accelerate pad wear. If the disc is badly grooved it must be machined or replaced.
3   To check disc runout, mount a dial indicator to a fork leg (front disc) or frame (rear disc) with the plunger on the indicator touching the surface of the disc about 1/2-inch from the outer edge. **Note:** *The procedure is the same for both front discs on Vulcan 700/750 models.* **Note:** *You may have to remove the muffler to check the rear disc on Drifter models (see Chapter 4).* Slowly turn the wheel and watch the indicator needle, comparing your reading with the limit listed

in this Chapter's Specifications. If the runout is greater than allowed, check the hub bearings for play (see Chapter 1). If the bearings are worn, replace them and repeat this check. If the disc runout is still excessive, it will have to be replaced.
4   The disc must not be machined or allowed to wear down to a thickness less than the minimum allowable thickness listed in this Chapter's Specifications. The thickness of the disc can be checked with a micrometer. If the thickness of the disc is less than the minimum allowable, it must be replaced. The minimum thickness is also stamped into the disc **(see illustration)**.

Removal

Refer to illustration 4.6
5   Remove the wheel (see Section 11). **Caution:** *Don't lay the wheel down and allow it to rest on the disc - the disc could become warped.*
6   Mark the relationship of the disc to the wheel, so it can be installed in the same position. Remove the Allen bolts that retain the disc to the wheel **(see illustration)**. Loosen the bolts a little at a time, in a crisscross pattern, to avoid distorting the disc.
7   Take note of any paper shims that may be present where the disc mates to the wheel. If there are any, mark their position and be sure to include them when installing the disc.

Installation

8   Position the disc on the wheel, aligning the previously applied matchmarks (if you're reinstalling the original disc). Make sure the arrow (stamped on the disc) marking the direction of rotation is pointing in the proper direction.
9   Apply a non-hardening thread locking compound to the threads of the bolts. Install the bolts, tightening them a little at a time, in a criss-cross pattern, until the torque listed in this Chapter's Specifications is reached. Clean off all grease from the brake disc using acetone or brake system cleaner.

4.4   The minimum allowable thickness is stamped into the disc

4.6   Loosen the disc retaining bolts a little at a time to prevent distortion

10 Install the wheel.

11 Operate the brake lever several times to bring the pads into contact with the disc. Check the operation of the brakes carefully before riding the motorcycle.

5 Master cylinder - removal, overhaul and installation

1 If the master cylinder is leaking fluid, or if the lever does not produce a firm feel when the brake is applied, and bleeding the brakes does not help, master cylinder overhaul is recommended. Before disassembling the master cylinder, read through the entire procedure and make sure that you have the correct rebuild kit. Also, you will need some new, clean brake fluid of the recommended type, some clean rags and internal snap-ring pliers. **Caution:** *To prevent damage to the paint from spilled brake fluid, always cover the fuel tank when working on the master cylinder.*

2 **Caution:** *Disassembly, overhaul and reassembly of the brake master cylinder must be done in a spotlessly clean work area to avoid contamination and possible failure of the brake hydraulic system components.*

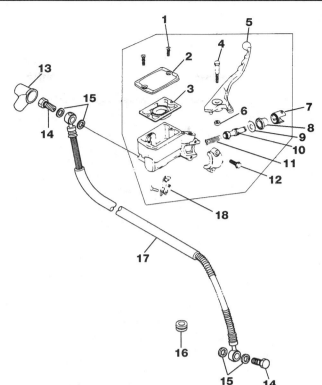

5.4a Master cylinder (early Vulcan 700/750 models) - exploded view

1 Reservoir cap screws
2 Reservoir cap
3 Diaphragm
4 Brake lever pivot bolt
5 Brake lever
6 Brake lever pivot bolt nut
7 Insert
8 Dust boot
9 Washer
10 Piston assembly
11 Spring
12 Clamp bolt
13 Rubber boot
14 Banjo bolt
15 Sealing washers
16 Grommet
17 Brake line
18 Brake light switch

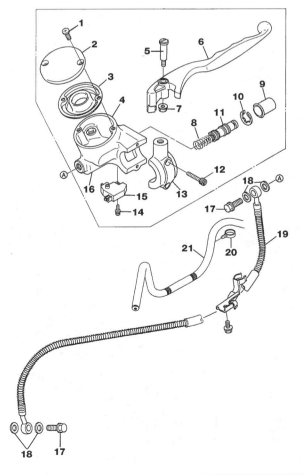

5.4b Master cylinder (later Vulcan 700/750, all Vulcan 800 models) - exploded view

1 Reservoir cap screws
2 Reservoir cap
3 Diaphragm
4 Master cylinder body
5 Lever pivot bolt
6 Brake lever
7 Lever pivot bolt nut
8 Spring
9 Dust boot
10 Snap-ring
11 Piston assembly
12 Spring
13 Clamp
14 Screw
15 Brake light switch
16 Master cylinder body
17 Banjo bolt
18 Sealing washers
19 Brake line
20 Retainer cap
21 Handlebar

Removal

Front master cylinder

Refer to illustrations 5.4a, 5.4b and 5.6

3 Loosen, but do not remove, the screws holding the reservoir cap in place.

4 Pull back the rubber boot (if equipped), loosen the banjo fitting bolt **(see illustrations)** and separate the brake hose from the master cylinder. Wrap the end of the hose in a clean rag and suspend the hose in an upright position or bend it down carefully and place the open end in a clean container. The objective is to prevent excess loss of brake fluid, fluid spills and system contamination.

5 Remove the locknut from the underside of the lever pivot bolt, then unscrew the bolt **(see illustration 5.4a or 5.4b)**.

6 Remove the master cylinder mounting

5.6 Remove master cylinder mounting bolts (arrows)

7

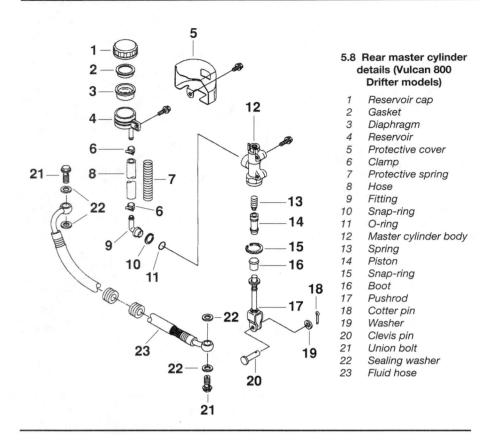

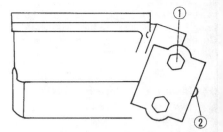

5.21 On Vulcan 700/750 models, the protrusion on the master cylinder clamp faces to the right

1	Upper mounting bolt
2	Protrusion

Note: *The secondary cups on Vulcan 800 front master cylinders can't be removed. If they're worn or damaged, replace the piston assembly.*

19   Before reassembling the master cylinder, soak the piston and the rubber cup seals in clean brake fluid for ten to fifteen minutes. Lubricate the master cylinder bore with clean brake fluid, then carefully insert the piston and related parts in the reverse order of disassembly. Make sure the lips on the cup seals do not turn inside out when they are slipped into the bore.

20   On Vulcan 700/750 models, install the washer and rubber dust boot (make sure its lip locates correctly). On Vulcan 800 models, depress the piston, then install the snap-ring (make sure the snap-ring is properly seated in the groove with the sharp edge facing out). Install the rubber dust boot (make sure the lip is seated properly in the piston groove).

Installation

Refer to illustration 5.21

21   Attach the master cylinder to the handlebar with the clamp. On Vulcan 700/750 models, the protrusion on the clamp must face to the right **(see illustration)**. On Vulcan 800 models, align the clamp seam with the dot on the handlebar. Tighten the bolts to the torque listed in this Chapter's Specifications. **Note:** *Tighten the upper bolt first, then the lower bolt. There will be a gap at the bottom between the clamp and master cylinder body.*

22   Install the brake lever and tighten the pivot bolt locknut.

23   Connect the brake hose to the master cylinder, using new sealing washers. Tighten the banjo fitting bolt to the torque listed in this Chapter's Specifications. Refer to Section 8 and bleed the air from the system.

6   Rear drum brake - removal, inspection and installation

Warning: *The dust collected by the brake system may contain asbestos, which is harmful to your health. Never blow it out with compressed air and don't inhale any of it. An*

---

bolts **(see illustration)** and separate the master cylinder from the handlebar. **Caution:** *Do not tip the master cylinder upside down or brake fluid will run out.*

7   Disconnect the electrical connectors from the brake light switch.

Rear master cylinder

Refer to illustration 5.8

8   Remove the protective cover from the brake fluid reservoir, then unbolt the reservoir from the motorcycle **(see illustration)**. If you're not planning to overhaul or replace the master cylinder, leave the reservoir hose connected. **Note:** *Keep the reservoir upright so brake fluid doesn't spill out.*

9   Loosen the fluid hose union bolt at the brake caliper. Don't unscrew it yet; leave it tight enough so fluid won't spill out.

10   Remove the master cylinder mounting bolts (don't try to remove them yet).

11   Unbolt the right floorboard from the motorcycle and support it with rope or a bungee cord.

12   Remove the cotter pin, washer and clevis pin from the master cylinder and brake pedal lever.

13   Remove the union bolt at the caliper. Cover the brake line with a plastic bag and secure it with a rubber band to prevent fluid loss.

14   Unscrew the master cylinder mounting bolts and take the master cylinder off, together with the fluid reservoir.

Overhaul

15   Detach the reservoir cap and the rubber diaphragm, then drain the brake fluid into a suitable container. Wipe any remaining fluid out of the reservoir with a clean rag.

16   Carefully remove the rubber dust boot from the end of the piston **(see illustration 5.4a, 5.4b or 5.8)**. On Vulcan 700/750 models, remove the insert, dust boot and washer. On Vulcan 800 models, remove the snap-ring and slide out the piston, the cup seals and the spring. Lay the parts out in the proper order to prevent confusion during reassembly.

17   Clean all of the parts with brake system cleaner (available at auto parts stores), denatured alcohol or clean brake fluid. **Caution:** *Do not, under any circumstances, use a petroleum-based solvent to clean brake parts. If compressed air is available, use it to dry the parts thoroughly (make sure it's filtered and unlubricated). Check the master cylinder bore for corrosion, scratches, nicks and score marks. If damage is evident, the master cylinder must be replaced with a new one. If the master cylinder is in poor condition, then the caliper should be checked as well. Make sure the ports in the bottom of the master cylinder are clear. If the small relief port is clogged, the brakes will drag.*

18   Remove the old cup seals from the piston and spring and install the new ones. If a new piston is included in the rebuild kit, use it regardless of the condition of the old one.

6.3 Pull the brake panel out of the rear wheel; on Vulcan 800 standard and Classic models, the speedometer clutch cogs (left arrow) fit into slots in the drive unit (right arrow)

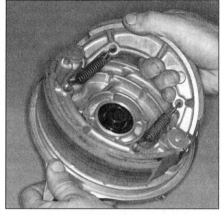

6.4 Fold the shoes off the panel to remove them

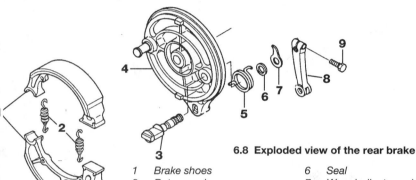

6.8 Exploded view of the rear brake

1	Brake shoes	6	Seal
2	Return springs	7	Wear indicator pointer
3	Brake cam	8	Brake cam lever
4	Brake panel	9	Pinch bolt
5	Brake cam lever spring		

6.9 The brake drum diameter limit is cast into the drum

approved filtering mask should be worn when working on the brakes.

Removal

Refer to illustrations 6.3 and 6.4

1   Before you start, inspect the rear brake wear indicator (see Chapter 1).

2   Remove the rear wheel (see Section 12).

3   Lift the brake panel out of the wheel **(see illustration)**.

4   Fold the shoes toward each other to release the spring tension **(see illustration)**. Remove the shoes and springs from the brake panel.

Inspection

Refer to illustrations 6.8 and 6.9

5   Check the linings for wear, damage, and signs of contamination from road dirt or water. If the linings are visibly defective, replace them.

6   Measure the thickness of the lining material (just the lining material, not the metal backing) and compare with the value listed in this Chapter's Specifications. Replace the shoes if the material is worn to less than the minimum.

7   Check the ends of the shoes where they

contact the brake cam and pivot post. Replace the shoes if there's visible wear.

8   Check the brake cam and pivot post for wear and damage. If necessary, make match marks on the cam and cam lever, then remove the pinch bolt, lever, wear indicator pointer, seal, spring and cam **(see illustration)**.

9   Check the brake drum (inside the wheel) for wear or damage **(see illustration)**. Measure the diameter at several points with a brake drum micrometer (or have this done by a Kawasaki dealer). If the measurements are uneven (indicating that the drum is out-of-round) or if there are scratches deep enough to snag a fingernail, have the drum turned (skimmed) by a dealer to correct the surface. If the drum has to be turned (skimmed) beyond the wear limit to remove the defects, replace it.

10   Check the brake cam for looseness in the brake panel hole. If it feels loose, measure the diameter of the cam and hole and compare them with those listed in this Chapter's Specifications. Replace worn parts.

Installation

11   Apply high temperature brake grease to the ends of the springs, the cam and the

anchor pin.

12   Hook the springs to the shoes. Position the shoes in a V on the brake panel, then fold them down into position **(see illustration 6.4)**. Make sure the ends of the shoes fit correctly in the cam and on the pivot post.

13   The remainder of installation is the reverse of the removal steps.

14   Check the position of the brake pedal (see Chapter 1) and adjust it if necessary. Check the operation of the brakes carefully before riding the motorcycle.

7   Brake hoses and lines - inspection and replacement

Inspection

Refer to illustration 7.2

1   Once a week, or if the motorcycle is used less frequently, before every ride, check the condition of the brake hose.

2   Twist and flex the rubber hose **(see illustration 5.4a or 5.4b, 5.8 or the accompanying illustration)** while looking for

7

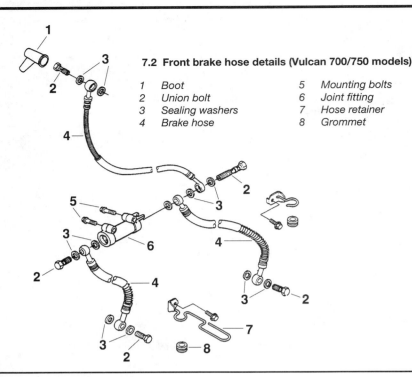

7.2 Front brake hose details (Vulcan 700/750 models)

1	Boot	5	Mounting bolts
2	Union bolt	6	Joint fitting
3	Sealing washers	7	Hose retainer
4	Brake hose	8	Grommet

8.5 Remove the bleed valve cap (arrow) and fit a length of tubing over it; place the other end in a clean glass jar and place a wrench on the bleed valve

cracks, bulges and seeping fluid. Check extra carefully around the areas where the hose connects to the banjo fittings, as these are common areas for hose failure.

Replacement

3   Each brake hose has banjo fittings on each end. Cover the surrounding area with plenty of rags and unscrew the banjo bolts on either end of the hose. Remove any retainers that secure the hose to other components, detach the hose from the clips and remove the hose.

4   Position the new hose, making sure it isn't twisted or otherwise strained, between the two components. Install the banjo bolts, using new sealing washers on both sides of the fittings, and tighten them to the torque listed in this Chapter's Specifications.

5   Flush the old brake fluid from the system, refill the system with the recommended fluid (see Chapter 1) and bleed the air from the system (see Section 8). Check the operation of the brakes carefully before riding the motorcycle.

8   Brake system bleeding

Refer to illustration 8.5

1   Bleeding the brake is simply the process of removing all the air bubbles from the brake fluid reservoir, the hose and the brake caliper. Bleeding is necessary whenever a brake system hydraulic connection is loosened, when a component or hose is replaced, or when the master cylinder or caliper is overhauled. Leaks in the system may also allow air to enter, but leaking brake fluid will reveal their presence and warn you

of the need for repair.

2   To bleed the brake, you will need some new, clean brake fluid of the recommended type (see Chapter 1), a length of clear vinyl or plastic tubing, a small container partially filled with clean brake fluid, some rags and a wrench to fit the brake caliper bleed valve.

3   Cover the fuel tank and other painted components to prevent damage in the event that brake fluid is spilled.

4   Remove the reservoir cap and slowly pump the brake lever a few times, until no air bubbles can be seen floating up from the holes at the bottom of the reservoir. Doing this bleeds the air from the master cylinder end of the line. Reinstall the reservoir cap.

5   Attach one end of the clear vinyl or plastic tubing to the brake caliper bleeder valve and submerge the other end in the brake fluid in the container **(see illustration)**.

6   Remove the reservoir cap and check the fluid level. Do not allow the fluid level to drop below the lower mark during the bleeding process.

7   Carefully pump the brake lever three or four times and hold it while opening the caliper bleeder valve. When the valve is opened, brake fluid will flow out of the caliper into the clear tubing and the lever will move toward the handlebar.

8   Retighten the bleeder valve, then release the brake lever gradually. Repeat the process until no air bubbles are visible in the brake fluid leaving the caliper and the lever is firm when applied. Remember to add fluid to the reservoir as the level drops. Use only new, clean brake fluid of the recommended type. Never reuse the fluid lost during bleeding; it absorbs moisture from the air, which can lead to brake failure.

9   Replace the reservoir cap, wipe up any spilled brake fluid and check the entire system for leaks. **Note:** *If bleeding is difficult, it may be necessary to let the brake fluid in the system stabilize for a few hours (it may be aerated). Repeat the bleeding procedure when the tiny bubbles in the system have settled out.*

10   If you're working on a rear caliper, repeat the procedure for the other bleed valve.

9   Brake pedal and linkage - removal and installation

Vulcan 700/750 models

Refer to illustrations 9.2a, 9.2b and 9.3

1   Place the motorcycle on its centerstand (if equipped).

2   Unhook the brake pedal spring **(see illustrations)**.

3   Fully unscrew the brake free play adjusting nut from the wheel end of the brake rod and disengage the threaded rod from the brake cam lever **(see illustration)**.

9.2a Unhook the brake pedal spring (arrow)

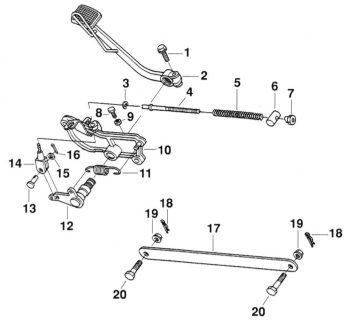

9.3 Disconnect the brake rod from the lever (arrow)

9.2b Brake pedal details (Vulcan 700/750 models)

1	Pedal pinch bolt	8	Pedal adjusting bolt	14	Brake cable/rod
2	Pedal	9	Adjusting bolt		(front end)
3	Circlip		locknut	15	Washer
4	Brake cable/rod	10	Pedal bracket	16	Cotter pin
5	Spring	11	Pedal return spring	17	Torque link
6	Adjuster pivot	12	Pedal lever	18	Cotter pin
7	Adjuster nut	13	Clevis pin	19	Nut
				20	Bolt

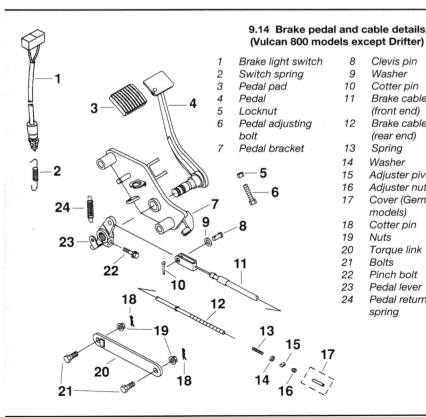

9.14 Brake pedal and cable details (Vulcan 800 models except Drifter)

1	Brake light switch	8	Clevis pin
2	Switch spring	9	Washer
3	Pedal pad	10	Cotter pin
4	Pedal	11	Brake cable/rod
5	Locknut		(front end)
6	Pedal adjusting	12	Brake cable/rod
	bolt		(rear end)
7	Pedal bracket	13	Spring
		14	Washer
		15	Adjuster pivot
		16	Adjuster nut
		17	Cover (German
			models)
		18	Cotter pin
		19	Nuts
		20	Torque link
		21	Bolts
		22	Pinch bolt
		23	Pedal lever
		24	Pedal return
			spring

4   Remove the right side cover (see Chapter 8).

5   Remove the circlip from the brake cable at the bracket. Pull the cable housing out of the bracket, then slip the cable out of the slot in the bracket.

6   If necessary, loosen the brake pedal locknut and back off the adjusting bolt to increase the clearance between the adjusting bolt and brake pedal (see Chapter 1). Look for alignment marks on the pedal and shaft and make your own if you don't see them. Remove the pedal pinch bolt and pull the pedal off the shaft.

7   Follow the wires from the brake light switch to the connector and disconnect them.

8   Unbolt the footpeg mounting bracket **(see illustration 9.2b)**.

9   Pull the cable housing out of the fitting on the brake pedal bracket **(see illustration 9.2a)**, slip the cable out of the slot and take it off.

10   Pull the shaft of the brake pedal lever out of the bracket.

11   Remove the cotter pin, washer and clevis pin that connect the brake cable to the pedal lever **(see illustration 9.2b)**.

12   Installation is the reverse of the removal steps, with the following additions:

   a) *Tighten the pedal pinch bolt to the torque listed in this Chapter's Specifications.*

   b) *Lubricate the pedal shaft with multi-purpose grease.*

   c) *Lubricate the inner brake cable with engine oil.*

   d) *Check brake pedal height and free play and adjust as necessary (see Chapter 1).*

Vulcan 800 models (except Drifter)

Refer to illustrations 9.14, 9.15, 9.16 and 9.19

13   Support the motorcycle securely upright so it can't be knocked over during this procedure.

14   Unbolt the footpeg bracket from the frame **(see illustration)**.

7

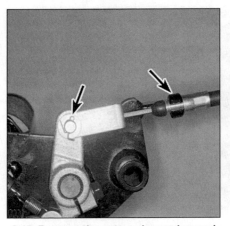

9.15 Remove the cotter pin, washer and clevis pin (left arrow) and pull the cable out of the bracket (right arrow)

9.16 Unhook the pedal return spring (arrow)

9.19 Unscrew the nut and detach the cable

9.23 Brake pedal details (Vulcan 800 Drifter models)

1   Brake light switch
2   Spring
3   Pedal pad
4   Pedal
5   Pedal bracket
6   Pedal return spring
7   Pedal lever
8   Pinch bolt
9   Clevis pin
10   Washer
11   Cotter pin

Vulcan 800 Drifter models

Refer to illustration 9.23

21   Support the motorcycle securely upright so it can't be knocked over during this procedure.

22   Unbolt the right floorboard bracket from the frame (see Chapter 8).

23   Turn the floorboard bracket around. Remove the cotter pin, washer and clevis pin and disconnect the cable from the master cylinder pushrod **(see illustration)**.

24   Unhook the brake pedal spring.

25   Look for alignment marks on the pedal shaft and lever and make your own if you don't see them. Remove the pedal pinch bolt and pull the lever off the pedal shaft.

26   Remove the floorboard circlips and spring and detach the floorboard from the bracket. Pull the brake pedal out of the bracket.

27   Installation is the reverse of the removal steps, with the following additions:

   a)   *Tighten the pedal pinch bolt to the torque listed in this Chapter's Specifications.*

   b)   *Lubricate the pedal shaft with multi-purpose grease.*

   d)   *Check brake pedal height and free play and adjust as necessary (see Chapter 1).*

10   Wheels - inspection, repair and alignment check

Inspection and repair

1   Clean the wheels thoroughly to remove mud and dirt that may interfere with the inspection procedure or mask defects. Make a general check of the wheels and tires as described in Chapter 1.

2   Place the motorcycle on the centerstand (if equipped). Otherwise, jack the bike up and support it so the wheel you're inspecting is off the ground. With the wheel in the air, attach a dial indicator to the fork slider or the swingarm and position the pointer against the side of the rim. Spin the

---

15   Turn the footpeg bracket around. Remove the cotter pin, washer and clevis pin and disconnect the cable from the pedal lever **(see illustration)**. Pull the cable housing out of the bracket, then slip the cable out of the slot.

16   Unhook the brake pedal spring **(see illustration)**.

17   If necessary, loosen the brake pedal locknut and back off the adjusting bolt to increase the clearance between the adjusting bolt and brake pedal (see Chapter 1). Look for alignment marks on the pedal shaft and lever and make your own if you don't see them **(see illustration 9.15)**. Remove the pedal pinch bolt and pull the lever off the pedal shaft.

18   Fully unscrew the brake free play adjusting nut from the wheel end of the brake rod and disengage the threaded rod from the brake cam lever **(see illustration 12.9a)**.

19   Remove the nut from the brake cable at the bracket **(see illustration)**. Pull the cable housing out of the bracket, then slip the cable out of the slot in the bracket.

20   Installation is the reverse of the removal steps, with the following additions:

   a)   *Tighten the pedal pinch bolt to the torque listed in this Chapter's Specifications.*

   b)   *Lubricate the pedal shaft with multi-purpose grease.*

   c)   *Lubricate the inner brake cable with engine oil.*

   d)   *Check brake pedal height and free play and adjust as necessary (see Chapter 1).*

11.3a Remove the axle nut (left arrow) and unscrew the speedometer cable (right arrow)

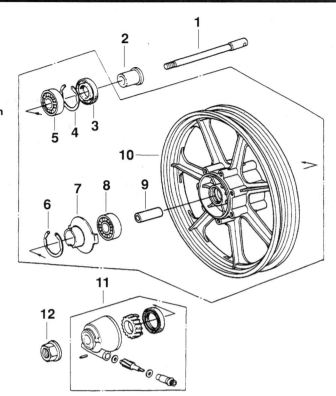

11.3b Front wheel bearing details (Vulcan 700/750 models)

1   Axle
2   Spacer
3   Grease seal
4   Snap-ring
5   Wheel bearing
6   Snap-ring
7   Speedometer clutch
8   Wheel bearing
9   Spacer
10   Wheel
11   Speedometer drive unit
12   Nut

wheel slowly and check the side-to-side (axial) runout of the rim, then compare your readings with the value listed in this Chapter's Specifications. In order to accurately check radial runout with the dial indicator, the wheel would have to be removed from the machine and the tire removed from the wheel. With the axle clamped in a vise, the wheel can be rotated to check the runout.

3   An easier, though slightly less accurate, method is to attach a stiff wire pointer to the fork slider or the swingarm and position the end a fraction of an inch from the wheel (where the wheel and tire join). If the wheel is true, the distance from the pointer to the rim will be constant as the wheel is rotated. Repeat the procedure to check the runout of the rear wheel. **Note:** *If wheel runout is excessive, refer to the appropriate Section in this Chapter and check the wheel bearings very carefully before replacing the wheel.*

4   The wheels should also be visually inspected for cracks, flat spots on the rim and other damage. Since tubeless tires are involved, look very closely for dents in the area where the tire bead contacts the rim. Dents in this area may prevent complete sealing of the tire against the rim, which leads to deflation of the tire over a period of time.

5   If damage is evident, or if runout in either direction is excessive, the wheel will have to be replaced with a new one. Never attempt to repair a damaged wheel.

Alignment check

6   Misalignment of the wheels, which may be due to a cocked rear wheel or a bent frame or triple clamps, can cause strange and possibly serious handling problems. If the frame or triple clamps are at fault, repair by a frame specialist or replacement with new parts are the only alternatives.

7   To check the alignment you will need an assistant, a length of string or a perfectly straight piece of wood and a ruler graduated in 1/64 inch increments. A plumb bob or other suitable weight will also be required.

8   Place the motorcycle on the center-stand, then measure the width of both tires at their widest points. Subtract the smaller measurement from the larger measurement, then divide the difference by two. The result is the amount of offset that should exist between the front and rear tires on both sides.

9   If a string is used, have your assistant hold one end of it about half way between the floor and the rear axle, touching the rear sidewall of the tire.

10   Run the other end of the string forward and pull it tight so that it is roughly parallel to the floor. Slowly bring the string into contact with the front sidewall of the rear tire, then turn the front wheel until it is parallel with the string. Measure the distance from the front tire sidewall to the string.

11   Repeat the procedure on the other side of the motorcycle. The distance from the front tire sidewall to the string should be equal on both sides.

12   As was previously pointed out, a perfectly straight length of wood may be substituted for the string. The procedure is the same.

13   If the distance between the string and tire is greater on one side, or if the rear wheel appears to be cocked, refer to Chapter 6, Swingarm bearings - check, and make sure the swingarm is tight. Also refer to the chain adjustment procedure in Chapter 1 and make sure the adjusters are set evenly.

14   If the front-to-back alignment is correct, the wheels still may be out of alignment vertically.

15   Using the plumb bob, or other suitable weight, and a length of string, check the rear wheel to make sure it is vertical. To do this, hold the string against the tire upper sidewall and allow the weight to settle just off the floor. When the string touches both the upper and lower tire sidewalls and is perfectly straight, the wheel is vertical. If it is not, place thin spacers under one leg of the centerstand.

16   Once the rear wheel is vertical, check the front wheel in the same manner. If both wheels are not perfectly vertical, the frame and/or major suspension components are bent.

11   Front wheel - removal, inspection and installation

Removal

1   Place the motorcycle on the center-stand (if equipped). If the bike doesn't have a centerstand, support it securely so it can't be knocked over during this procedure. Raise the front wheel off the ground by placing a floor jack, with a wood block on the jack head, under the engine.

Vulcan 700/750 models

Refer to illustrations 11.3a, 11.3b and 11.4

2   Remove one of the two front brake calipers (see Section 3).

3   Remove the axle nut and unscrew the speedometer cable from the drive unit on the left side **(see illustrations).**

7

11.4 Unscrew the pinch bolt (upper arrow), put a punch in the hole (lower arrow) and pull the axle out

11.8a Unscrew the axle nut

4   Loosen the axle clamp bolt **(see illustration)**.

5   Support the wheel, then insert a punch or similar tool into the hole in the right side of the axle and pull it out.

6   Carefully lower the wheel until the brake disc clears the remaining caliper. It will probably be necessary to tilt the wheel to one side to allow removal. Don't lose the spacer that fits into the right side of the hub **(see illustration 11.3b)**. **Caution:** *Don't lay the wheel down and allow it to rest on a disc - the disc could become warped. Set the wheel on wood blocks so the disc doesn't support the weight of the wheel. If the axle is corroded, remove the corrosion with fine emery cloth.* **Note:** *Do not operate the front brake lever with the wheel removed. To prevent accidental operation of the brake, slip a piece of wood between the brake pads.*

Vulcan 800 models

Refer to illustrations 11.8a, 11.8b, 11.8c and 11.9

7   Remove the brake caliper (see Section 2).

8   Remove the axle nut from the left side

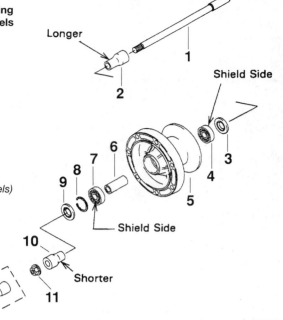

11.8b Front wheel bearing details (Vulcan 800 models except Drifter)

1   Axle
2   Spacer
3   Grease seal
4   Wheel bearing
5   Wheel hub
6   Spacer
7   Wheel bearing
8   Snap-ring
9   Grease seal
10   Spacer
11   Axle nut
12   Cover (German models)

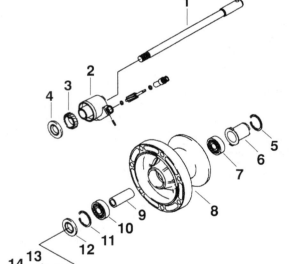

11.8c Front wheel bearing details (Vulcan 800 Drifter models)

1   Axle
2   Speedometer drive unit
3   Speedometer drive gear
4   Grease seal
5   Snap-ring
6   Speedometer clutch
7   Wheel bearing
8   Wheel hub
9   Spacer
10   Wheel bearing
11   Snap-ring
12   Grease seal
13   Spacer
14   Axle nut

(see illustrations). If you're working on a Drifter, unscrew the speedometer cable from the drive unit on the left side **(see illustration)**.

9   Loosen the axle clamp bolt **(see illustration)**.

10   Support the wheel, then insert a punch or similar tool into the hole in the right side of the axle and pull it out.

11   Carefully lower the wheel clear. If you're working on a standard or Classic model, don't lose the spacers that fit into each side of the hub. **Caution:** *Don't lay the wheel down and allow it to rest on a disc - the disc could become warped. Set the wheel on*

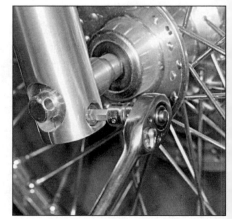

11.9 Loosen the axle clamp bolt

11.16a Be sure to put the spacers in the correct sides . . .

11.16b . . . the short spacer goes in the left side . . .

11.16c . . . and the long spacer goes in the right side

wood blocks so the disc doesn't support the weight of the wheel. If the axle is corroded, remove the corrosion with fine emery cloth. **Note:** *Do not operate the front brake lever with the wheel removed. To prevent accidental operation of the brake, slip a piece of wood between the brake pads.*

Inspection

12   Check the axle for straightness (Sec-

tion 12, Step 17).
13   Check the condition of the wheel bearings (see Section 13).

Installation

Refer to illustrations 11.16a, 11.16b and 11.16c
14   Installation is the reverse of removal.
15   If you're working on a Vulcan 700/750 model, apply a thin coat of grease to the seal

lip, then slide the spacer into the right side of the hub. Position the speedometer drive unit in place in the left side of the hub (if it was removed), then slide the wheel into place. Make sure the notches in the speedometer drive assembly in the wheel line up with the lugs in the drive unit (see Chapter 8). If the disc will not slide between the brake pads, remove the wheel and carefully pry them apart with a piece of wood.
16   On Vulcan 800 standard models, install the spacers in the hub, noting that the shorter one goes on the left side **(see illustrations)**.
17   If you're working on a Vulcan 800 Drifter model, apply a thin coat of grease to the seal lip, then slide the spacer into the right side of the hub. Position the speedometer drive unit in place in the left side of the hub (if it was removed), then slide the wheel into place. Make sure the notches in the speedometer drive assembly in the wheel line up with the lugs in the drive unit (see Chapter 9).
18   Slip the axle into place, then tighten the axle nut to the torque listed in this Chapter's Specifications. Tighten the right side axle clamp bolt to the torque listed in this Chapter's Specifications.
19   Reinstall the brake caliper.
20   If you're working on a Vulcan 700/750 or Vulcan 800 Drifter model, connect the speedometer cable (see Chapter 9).
21   Apply the front brake, pump the forks up and down several times and check for binding and proper brake operation.

12   Rear wheel - removal, inspection and installation

Removal

Vulcan 700/750 models
Refer to illustration 12.2
1   Remove the right muffler (see Chapter 4).
2   Remove the cotter pin from the axle nut and loosen the nut **(see illustration)**.

12.2 Rear wheel details (Vulcan 700/750 models)

1   Axle
2   Spacer
3   Rear brake
4   Snap-ring
5   Wheel bearing
6   Wheel
7   Spacer
8   Rubber damper
9   Wheel bearing
10   Coupling
11   Snap-ring
12   Spacer
13   Washer
14   Axle nut
15   Cotter pin

7

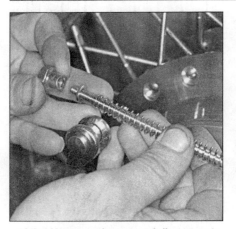

12.9a Unscrew the nut and disconnect the brake rod from the lever

12.9b Remove the clips and nuts and remove the torque link

12.13a Remove the cotter pin from the axle hole (arrow) and loosen the axle nut

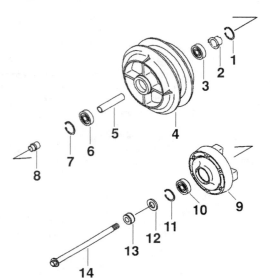

12.13b Rear wheel details (Vulcan 800 models except Drifter)

1   Snap-ring
2   Speedometer clutch
3   Wheel bearing
4   Wheel hub
5   Spacer
6   Wheel bearing
7   Snap-ring
8   Coupling collar
9   Coupling
10 Wheel bearing
11 Snap-ring
12 Washer
13 Spacer
14 Axle

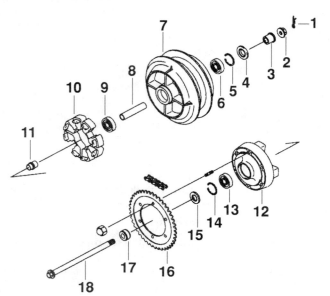
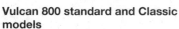

12.13c Rear wheel details (Vulcan 800 Drifter models)

1   Cotter pin
2   Axle nut
3   Spacer
4   Grease seal
5   Snap-ring
6   Wheel bearing
7   Wheel hub
8   Spacer
9   Wheel bearing
10 Rubber damper
11 Coupling collar
12 Coupling
13 Wheel bearing
14 Snap-ring
15 Washer
16 Rear sprocket
17 Spacer
18 Axle

3   Set the bike on its centerstand (if equipped). If the bike doesn't have a centerstand, support it securely so it can't be knocked over during this procedure. Raise the front wheel off the ground by placing a floor jack, with a wood block on the jack head, under the engine.

4   Unscrew the brake free play adjusting nut from the cable's threaded end **(see illustration 9.3)**. Slide out the pin and disconnect the brake cable from the cam lever. Remove the cotter pin from the torque link nut, then remove the nut and disconnect the torque link from the brake panel.

5   Remove the axle nut and the washer **(see illustration 12.2)**.

6   Support the wheel and slide the axle out. Pull the wheel to the right to clear the differential, lower the wheel and remove it from the swingarm, being careful not to lose the spacer on the right side of the hub **(see illustration 12.2)**.

Vulcan 800 models

Refer to illustrations 12.9a, 12.9b, 12.13a, 12.13b, 12.13c and 12.16

7   Set the bike on its centerstand (if equipped). If the bike doesn't have a centerstand, support it securely so it can't be knocked over during this procedure. Raise the front wheel off the ground by placing a floor jack, with a wood block on the jack head, under the engine.

Vulcan 800 standard and Classic models

8   Unscrew the speedometer cable retaining bolt and detach the speedometer cable from the rear wheel (see Chapter 9).

9   Unscrew the brake free play adjusting nut from the cable's threaded end **(see illustration)**. Slide out the pin and disconnect the brake cable from the cam lever. Remove the cotter pin from the torque link nut, then remove the nut and disconnect the torque link from the brake panel **(see illustration)**.

10 Remove the chain guard (see Chapter 6).

12.16 Don't forget the spacer in the left side of the hub

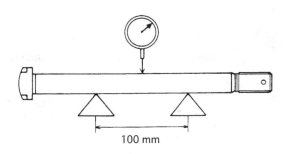

12.17 Check the axle for runout using a dial indicator and V-blocks

Vulcan 800 Drifter models

11   Remove the rear brake caliper and fender (see Chapters 6 and 8).

All Vulcan 800 models

12   Loosen the chain adjusters (see Chapter 1).

13   Remove the cotter pin from the axle nut and loosen the nut **(see illustrations)**.

14   Push the rear wheel as far forward as possible. Lift the top of the chain up off the rear sprocket and pull it to the left while rotating the wheel backwards. This will disengage the chain from the pulley. **Warning:** *Don't let your fingers slip between the chain and the pulley.*

15   Remove the axle nut and the washer. On Vulcan 800 Drifter models, note the location of the spacer on the right side of the wheel (on all except Drifter models, the brake panel occupies this space).

16   Support the wheel and slide the axle out. Lower the wheel and remove it from the swingarm, being careful not to lose the spacer on the left side of the hub **(see illustration)**. **Caution:** *On Drifter models, don't lay the wheel down and allow it to rest on the brake disc - it could become warped. Set the wheel on wood blocks so the disc doesn't support the weight of the wheel.*

Inspection

Refer to illustration 12.17

17   Before installing the wheel, check the axle for straightness. If the axle is corroded, first remove the corrosion with fine emery cloth. Set the axle on V-blocks and check it for runout using a dial indicator **(see illustration)**. If the axle exceeds the maximum allowable runout limit listed in this Chapter's Specifications, it must be replaced.

18   Check the condition of the wheel bearings (see Section 13).

Installation

19   Apply a thin coat of grease to the seal lips, then slide the spacers into their proper positions on the sides of the hub.

20   Place the axle, washer and drive chain

adjuster in the left side of the swingarm so they're ready to go when the wheel is in position.

21   Slide the wheel and spacers into place.

22   Pull the chain up over the sprocket, raise the wheel and install the axle, drive adjuster, washer and axle nut. Don't tighten the axle nut at this time.

23   Adjust the drive chain slack (see Chapter 1) and tighten the adjuster locknuts.

24   Tighten the axle nut to the torque listed in this Chapter's Specifications. Install a new cotter pin, tightening the axle nut an additional amount, if necessary, to align the hole in the axle with the castellations on the nut.

25   On all except Drifter models, tighten the torque link nut to the torque listed in this Chapter's Specifications and install a new cotter pin.

26   The remainder of installation is the reverse of the removal steps.

27   On all except Drifter models, adjust the brake pedal height and freeplay (see Chapter 1).

28   Check the operation of the brakes carefully before riding the motorcycle. On Drifter models, it shouldn't be necessary to bleed the rear brake if the hose wasn't disconnected, but verify that the rear brake works and bleed it if necessary.

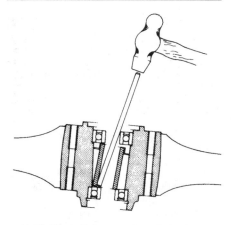

13.9a Once the snap-rings have been removed, drive the bearings from the hub with a brass drift and hammer

13   Wheel bearings - inspection and maintenance

1   The front wheel uses two ball bearings, which are permanently lubricated and sealed on both sides. The rear wheel hub uses two ball bearings, which are sealed on the outer side. On Vulcan 800 models the drive chain sprocket coupling uses one unsealed ball bearing.

2   Set the bike on its centerstand (if equipped). If the bike doesn't have a centerstand, support it securely so it can't be knocked over during this procedure. Remove the wheel (see Section 11 or 12).

3   Set the wheel on blocks so as not to allow the weight of the wheel to rest on the brake disc or drive chain sprocket.

Front wheel bearings

Refer to illustration 13.9a, 13.9b and 13.9c

Vulcan 700/750 models

4   Remove the speedometer gear housing and collar, the remaining brake disc, snapring and speedometer drive **(see illustration 11.3b)**.

5   Pry out the grease seal from the right side. Remove the remaining snap-ring.

Vulcan 800 models (except Drifter)

6   Pry out the grease seal from each side **(see illustration 11.8b)**. Remove the snapring from the left side.

Vulcan 800 Drifter models

7   Remove the speedometer gear housing, snap-ring and speedometer drive **(see illustration 11.8c)**.

8   Pry out the grease seal from the left side. Remove the remaining snap-ring.

All models

9   Insert a brass drift from the right side of the hub and tap evenly around the inner race of the opposite bearing to remove it **(see illustration)**. Remove the bearing spacer, then remove the remaining bearing in the same way. **Note:** *If there isn't room to insert a drift into the hub and push the spacer out of the way so you can catch the edge of the bearing with the drift, use a bearing remover*

7

13.9b To use this special tool, insert the split end into the bearing and drive the wedge into the split end to lock it to the bearing . . .

13.9c . . . then drive the tool out of the hub, together with the bearing

13.16 Drive the bearing out from this side

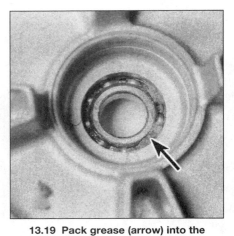

13.19 Pack grease (arrow) into the bearing until it's full

13.23a Remove the snap-ring . . .

tool (Kawasaki tool 57001-1265 and 1267) **(see illustrations)**.

10   Thoroughly clean the inside of the hub with high-flash point solvent and blow it out with compressed air, if available.

11   Drive in the new bearings with a bearing driver or a socket the same diameter as the bearing outer race. Don't forget to install the spacer after you've installed the first bearing.

12   The remainder of installation is the reverse of the removal steps. Install new snap-rings and make sure they seat securely in their grooves.

13   Tap new grease seals in evenly, using a bearing driver or a socket the same diameter as the seal.

Coupling bearing (Vulcan 800 models)

Refer to illustrations 13.16 and 13.19

14   Remove the coupling from the rear wheel and remove the coupling collar (see Chapter 6).

15   Pry the grease seal out of the coupling to expose the bearing **(see illustrations)**.

16   Tap against the back side of the bearing with a bearing driver or a socket to drive it

out of the coupling **(see illustration)**.

17   Thoroughly clean the bearing with solvent. Blow it dry with compressed air, if available, but don't spin the bearing with compressed air while it's dry. Hold the inner race with fingers and spin the outer race. If the bearing feels rough, loose, or makes noise (more than a slight whirring), replace it.

18   Drive the bearing into the coupling with a bearing driver or a socket the same diameter as the outer race.

19   Pack the bearing with grease **(see illustration)**.

20   Tap in a new grease seal with a brass or plastic mallet. Tap evenly so the seal doesn't tilt. If necessary, lay a block of wood across the seal so the hammer's force will be spread evenly.

21   Check the rubber damper in the rear wheel; if it shows signs of wear or deterioration it must be replaced.

Rear wheel bearings

Refer to illustrations 13.23a and 13.23b

22   If you haven't already done so, remove the coupling from the hub.

23   Remove the snap-ring from the right-

hand bearing **(see illustration)**. On Vulcan 800 standard and Classic models, the snap-ring secures the speedometer clutch **(see illustration)**.

13.23b . . . on Vulcan 800 models (except Drifter), the snap-ring secures the speedometer clutch as well as the bearing

TIRE CHANGING SEQUENCE - TUBELESS TIRES

Deflate tire. After releasing beads, push tire bead into well of rim at point opposite valve. Insert lever next to valve and work bead over edge of rim.

Use two levers to work bead over edge of rim. Note use of rim protectors.

When first bead is clear, remove tire as shown.

Before installing, ensure that tire is suitable for wheel. Take note of any sidewall markings such as direction of rotation arrows.

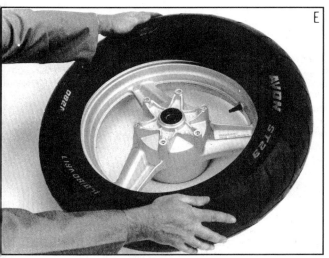

Work first bead over the rim flange.

Use a tire lever to work the second bead over rim flange.

24 Insert a brass drift into the hub and place it against the opposite bearing **(see illustration 13.9)**. Tap evenly around the inner race to drive the bearing from the hub. The bearing spacer will also come out.

25 Lay the wheel on its other side and remove the remaining bearing using the same technique.

26 Refer to Step 17 and inspect the bearings.

27 If the bearings check out okay and will be reused, wash them in solvent once again and dry them, then pack the bearings from the open side with medium weight, lithium-based multi-purpose grease.

28 Thoroughly clean the hub area of the wheel. Install the right-hand bearing into the recess in the hub, with the marked or shielded side facing out. Using a bearing driver or a socket large enough to contact the outer race of the bearing, drive it in until the snap-ring groove is visible. If you're working on a Vulcan 800 standard or Classic model, install the speedometer clutch **(see illustration 13.23b)**. Install the snap-ring.

29 Turn the wheel over and install the bearing spacer and bearing, driving the bearing into place as described in Step 28.

30 Press a little grease into the bearing in the rear wheel coupling (if you haven't just repacked it). Install the coupling to the wheel, making sure the coupling collar is located in the inside of the inner race (between the wheel and the coupling).

31 The remainder of installation is the reverse of the removal steps.

14 Tubeless tires (Vulcan 700/750 models) - general information

1 Tubeless tires are used as standard equipment on Vulcan 700/750 models. They are generally safer than tube-type tires but if problems do occur they require special repair techniques.

2 The force required to break the seal between the rim and the bead of the tire is substantial, and is usually beyond the capabilities of an individual working with normal tire irons.

3 Also, repair of the punctured tire and replacement on the wheel rim requires special tools, skills and experience that the average do-it-yourselfer lacks.

4 For these reasons, if a puncture or flat occurs with a tubeless tire, the wheel should be removed from the motorcycle and taken to a dealer service department or a motorcycle repair shop for repair or replacement of the tire.

15 Tube tires (Vulcan 800 models) – removal and installation

1 To properly remove and install tires, you will need at least two motorcycle tire irons,

some water and a tire pressure gauge.

2 Begin by removing the wheel from the motorcycle. If the tire is going to be re-used, mark it next to the valve stem, wheel balance weight or rim lock.

3 Deflate the tire by removing the valve stem core. When it is fully deflated, push the bead of the tire away from the rim on both sides. In some extreme cases, this can only be accomplished with a bead breaking tool, but most often it can be carried out with tire irons. Riding on a deflated tire to break the bead is not recommended, as damage to the rim and tire will occur.

4 Dismounting a tire is easier when the tire is warm, so an indoor tire change is recommended in cold climates. The rubber gets very stiff and is difficult to manipulate when cold.

5 Place the wheel on a thick pad or old blanket. This will help keep the wheel and tire from slipping around.

6 Once the bead is completely free of the rim, lubricate the inside edge of the rim and the tire bead with soap and water or rubber lubricant (do not use any type of petroleum-based lubricant, as it will cause the tire to deteriorate). Remove the locknut and push the tire valve through the rim.

7 Insert one of the tire irons under the bead of the tire at the valve stem and lift the bead up over the rim. This should be fairly easy. Take care not to pinch the tube as this is done. If it is difficult to pry the bead up, make sure that the rest of the bead opposite the valve stem is in the dropped center section of the rim.

8 Hold the tire iron down with the bead over the rim, then move about 1 or 2 inches to either side and insert the second tire iron. Be careful not to cut or slice the bead or the tire may split when inflated. Also, take care not to catch or pinch the inner tube as the second tire iron is levered over. For this reason, tire irons are recommended over screwdrivers or other implements.

9 With a small section of the bead up over the rim, one of the levers can be removed and reinserted 1 or 2 inches farther around the rim until about 1/4 of the tire bead is above the rim edge. Make sure that the rest of the bead is in the dropped center of the rim. At this point, the bead can usually be pulled up over the rim by hand.

10 Once all of the first bead is over the rim, the inner tube can be withdrawn from the tire and rim. Push in on the valve stem, lift up on the tire next to the stem, reach inside the tire and carefully pull out the tube. It is usually not necessary to completely remove the tire from the rim to repair the inner tube. It is sometimes recommended though, because checking for foreign objects in the tire is difficult while it is still mounted on the rim.

11 To remove the tire completely, make sure the bead is broken all the way around on the remaining edge, then stand the tire and wheel up on the tread and grab the wheel with one hand. Push the tire down

over the same edge of the rim while pulling the rim away from the tire. If the bead is correctly positioned in the dropped center of the rim, the tire should roll off and separate from the tire very easily. If tire irons are used to work this last bead over the rim, the outer edge of the rim may be marred. If a tire iron is necessary, be sure to pad the rim as described earlier.

12 Refer to Section 16 for inner tube repair procedures.

13 Mounting a tire is basically the reverse of removal. Some tires have a balance mark and/or directional arrows molded into the tire sidewall. Look for these marks so that the tire can be installed properly. The dot should be aligned with the valve stem.

14 If the tire was not removed completely to repair or replace the inner tube, the tube should be inflated just enough to make it round. Sprinkle it with talcum powder, which acts as a dry lubricant, then carefully lift up the tire edge and install the tube with the valve stem next to the hole in the rim. Once the tube is in place, push the valve stem through the rim and start the locknut on the stem.

15 Lubricate the tire bead, then push it over the rim edge and into the dropped center section opposite the inner tube valve stem. Work around each side of the rim, carefully pushing the bead over the rim. The last section may have to be levered on with tire irons. If so, take care not to pinch the inner tube as this is done.

16 Once the bead is over the rim edge, check to see that the inner tube valve stem is pointing to the center of the hub. If it's angled slightly in either direction, rotate the tire on the rim to straighten it out. Run the locknut the rest of the way onto the stem but don't tighten it completely.

17 Inflate the tube to approximately 1-1/2 times the pressure listed in the Chapter 1 Specifications and check to make sure the guidelines on the tire sidewalls are the same distance from the rim around the circumference of the tire. **Warning:** *Do not overinflate the tube or the tire may burst, causing serious injury.*

18 After the tire bead is correctly seated on the rim, allow the tire to deflate. Replace the valve core and inflate the tube to the recommended pressure, then tighten the valve stem locknut securely and tighten the cap.

16 Tubes - repair

1 Tire tube repair requires a patching kit that's usually available from motorcycle dealers, accessory stores or auto parts stores. Be sure to follow the directions supplied with the kit to ensure a safe repair. Patching should be done only when a new tube is unavailable. Replace the tube as soon as possible. Sudden deflation can cause loss of control and an accident.

2 To repair a tube, remove it from the tire,

TIRE CHANGING SEQUENCE - TUBED TIRES

 Deflate tire. After pushing tire beads away from rim flanges push tire bead into well of rim at point opposite valve. Insert tire lever next to valve and work bead over edge of rim.

Use two levers to work bead over edge of rim. Note use of rim protectors

 Remove inner tube from tire

When first bead is clear, remove tire as shown

 To install, partially inflate inner tube and insert in tire

Work first bead over rim and feed valve through hole in rim. Partially screw on retaining nut to hold valve in place.

 Check that inner tube is positioned correctly and work second bead over rim using tire levers. Start at a point opposite valve.

Work final area of bead over rim while pushing valve inwards to ensure that inner tube is not trapped.

inflate and immerse it in a sink or tub full of water to pinpoint the leak. Mark the position of the leak, then deflate the tube. Dry it off and thoroughly clean the area around the puncture.

3   Most tire patching kits have a buffer to rough up the area around the hole for proper adhesion of the patch. Roughen an area slightly larger than the patch, then apply a thin coat of the patching cement to the roughened area. Allow the cement to dry until tacky, then apply the patch.

4   It may be necessary to remove a protective covering from the top surface of the patch after it has been attached to the tube. Keep in mind that tubes made from synthetic rubber may require a special patch and adhesive if a satisfactory bond is to be achieved.

5   Before replacing the tube, check the inside of the tire to make sure the object that caused the puncture is not still inside. Also check the outside of the tire, particularly the tread area, to make sure nothing is projecting through the tire that may cause another puncture. Check the rim for sharp edges or damage. Make sure the rubber trim band is in good condition and properly installed before inserting the tube.

Chapter 8
Frame and bodywork

Contents

1 General information

The machines covered by this manual use a double cradle frame (Vulcan 700/750 models) or backbone frame (Vulcan 800 models), constructed of steel tubing. This Chapter covers the procedures necessary to remove and install the side covers and other body parts. Since many service and repair operations on these motorcycles require removal of the side covers and/or other body parts, the procedures are grouped here and referred to from other Chapters.

2 Frame - inspection and repair

Refer to illustrations 2.2a, 2.2b and 2.2c

1   The frame should not require attention unless accident damage has occurred. In most cases, frame replacement is the only satisfactory remedy for such damage. A few frame specialists have the jigs and other equipment necessary for straightening the frame to the required standard of accuracy, but even then there is no simple way of assessing to what extent the frame may have been over stressed.

2   After the machine has accumulated a lot of miles, the frame should be examined closely for signs of cracking or splitting at the welded joints **(see illustrations)**. Rust can also cause weakness at these joints. Loose engine mount bolts can cause ovaling or fracturing of the mounting tabs. Minor damage can often be repaired by welding, depending on the extent and nature of the damage.

3   Remember that a frame which is out of alignment will cause handling problems. If misalignment is suspected as the result of an accident, it will be necessary to strip the machine completely so the frame can be thoroughly checked.

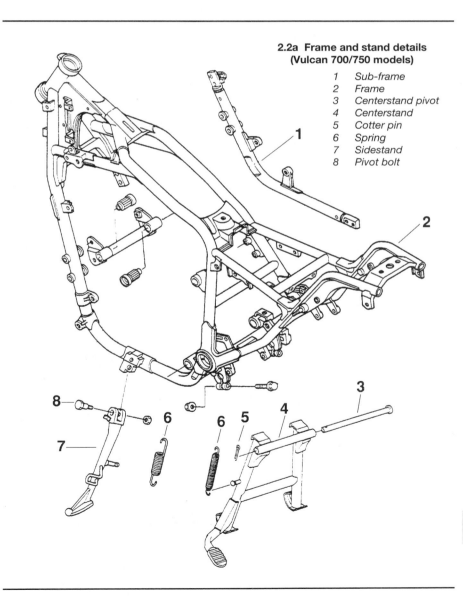

2.2a Frame and stand details (Vulcan 700/750 models)

1   Sub-frame
2   Frame
3   Centerstand pivot
4   Centerstand
5   Cotter pin
6   Spring
7   Sidestand
8   Pivot bolt

8

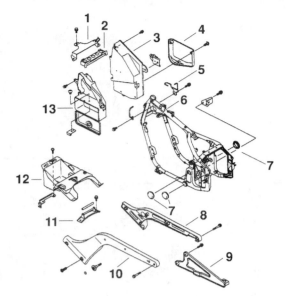

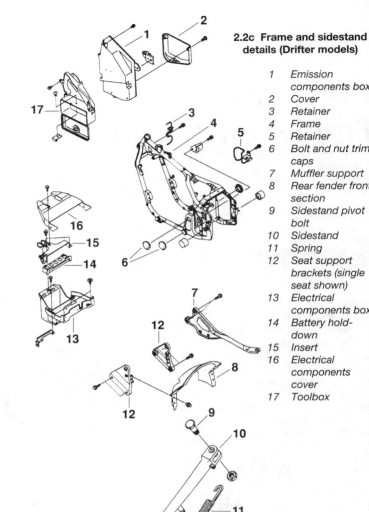

2.2b Frame and sidestand details (Vulcan 800 models)

1	Battery hold-down	8	Rear frame extension
2	Insert	9	Muffler bracket
3	Emission components box	10	Rear frame extension
4	Cover	11	Seat latch
5	Retainer	12	Electrical components box
6	Frame	13	Toolbox
7	Bolt and nut trim caps		

2.2c Frame and sidestand details (Drifter models)

1	Emission components box
2	Cover
3	Retainer
4	Frame
5	Retainer
6	Bolt and nut trim caps
7	Muffler support
8	Rear fender front section
9	Sidestand pivot bolt
10	Sidestand
11	Spring
12	Seat support brackets (single seat shown)
13	Electrical components box
14	Battery hold-down
15	Insert
16	Electrical components cover
17	Toolbox

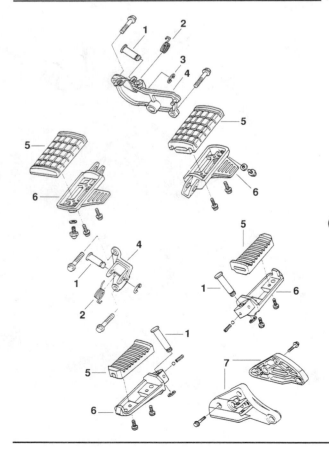

3.1a Footpeg details (Vulcan 700/750 models)

1	Pivot pin
2	Spring
3	Circlip
4	Bracket
5	Pad
6	Footpeg
7	Bracket

3 Footpegs, floorboards and brackets - removal and installation

Refer to illustrations 3.1a, 3.1b and 3.1c

1   If it's only necessary to detach the foot-peg or floorboard from the bracket, pry the C-clip off the pivot pin **(see illustrations)**, slide out the pin(s) and detach the footpeg or floorboard from the bracket. Be careful not to lose the spring. Installation is the reverse of removal, but be sure to install the spring correctly.

2   If it's necessary to remove the entire bracket from the frame, remove the bolts that secure the bracket to the frame, then detach the footpeg and bracket **(see illustrations 3.1a, 3.1b and 3.1c)**.

3   Installation is the reverse of removal.

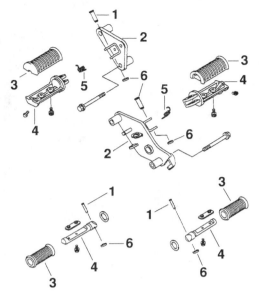
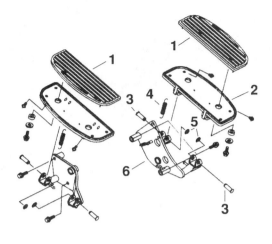

3.1b Footpeg details (Vulcan 800 standard and Classic models)

1 Pivot pin
2 Bracket
3 Pad
4 Footpeg
5 Spring
6 Circlip

3.1c Floorboard details (Drifter models)

1 Pads
2 Floorboard
3 Pivot pin
4 Spring
5 Circlips
6 Bracket

6.1 Open the toolbox on the back o the seat . . .

6.2a . . . remove the bolts (arrows) . . .

6.2b . . . lift the seat away from the support and pull it back to remove it

4 Side and centerstand - maintenance

1 The centerstand, used on Vulcan 700/750 models only, pivots on two bolts attached to the frame **(see illustration 2.1a)**. Periodically, remove the pivot bolts and grease them thoroughly to avoid excessive wear.
2 Make sure the return spring is in good condition. A broken or weak spring is an obvious safety hazard.
3 The sidestand is bolted to the frame **(see illustration 2.2a, 2.2b or 2.2c)**. An extension spring anchored to the bracket ensures that the stand is held in the retracted position.
4 Make sure the pivot bolt is tight and the extension spring is in good condition and not over stretched. An accident is almost certain to occur if the stand extends while the machine is in motion.

5 Rear view mirrors - removal and installation

1 To remove a mirror, loosen its locknut. Unscrew the mirror from the bracket on the handlebar.
2 Installation is the reverse of removal. Position the mirror.

6 Seat - removal and installation

Vulcan 700/750 models
Refer to illustrations 6.1, 6.2a, 6.2b and 6.3
1 Open the tool kit holder behind the seat **(see illustration)**.
2 Remove two mounting bolts and washers and lift the seat off **(see illustration)**.
3 Installation is the reverse of removal. Engage the hook at the front of the seat with the tab on the frame **(see illustration)**.

6.3 Slip the tab on the front of the seat into the frame bracket (arrows)

8

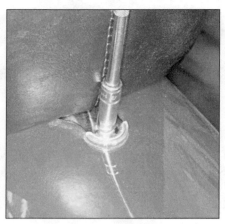

6.4 Remove the bolt at the back of the seat

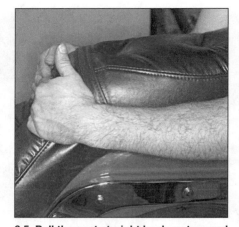

6.5 Pull the seat straight back, not up and back, to free it

6.6a Engage the center hooks (upper arrows) with their bracket (lower arrow) . . .

Vulcan 800 models (except Drifter)

Refer to illustrations 6.4, 6.5, 6.6a and 6.6b

4   Remove the bolt at the rear of the seat

6.6b . . . and slip the seat tab (right arrow) into the frame bracket (left arrow)

(see illustration).
5   Pull the seat straight back (not up and back) to unhook it at the front and center (see illustration).
6   To install the seat, engage the front tab and center hooks securely in their brackets (see illustrations), then engage the bolt at the rear.

Vulcan 800 Drifter models

Refer to illustrations 6.7 and 6.8

7   If the bike is equipped with a single seat, remove the mounting bolts at the rear (see illustration). Pull the seat back to disengage the tab at the front from the frame bracket, then lift the seat off.
8   If the bike is equipped with a dual seat, unbolt it from the seat frame (see illustration). Pull the seat back to disengage the tab at the front from the frame bracket, then lift the seat off. If necessary, unbolt the seat frame from the bike and take it off.
9   Installation is the reverse of the removal steps.

7   Side covers - removal and installation

Vulcan 700/750 models

Refer to illustrations 7.1 and 7.2

1   Remove the side cover mounting screw (see illustration).
2   Carefully pull the securing lugs out of the grommets and lift the cover off (see illustration). Caution: *Don't use force. If the cover won't come off with a light pull, make sure all fasteners have been removed.*
3   Installation is the reverse of the removal steps.

Vulcan 800 models

Refer to illustration 7.5

4   On the right side, use the ignition key to unlock the latch at the rear of the cover. Slide the cover forward to disengage the hooks at its front edge and take the cover off.
5   On the left side, remove the screw at

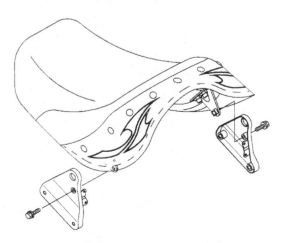

6.7 Drifter single seat and brackets

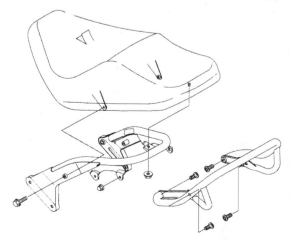

6.8 Drifter dual seat and brackets

7.1 Remove the screw (arrow) . . .

7.2 . . . and carefully disengage the posts from the grommets (arrows)

7.5 Remove the screw and disengage the front end of the cover

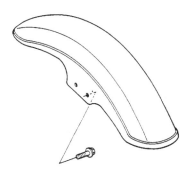

8.1a Front fender
(Vulcan 700/750 models)

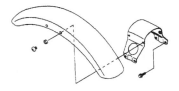

8.1b Front fender and insert (Vulcan 800 standard models; Classic similar)

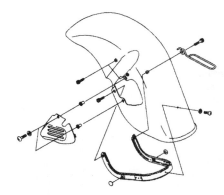

8.4 Front fender details (Vulcan 800 Drifter models)

the rear of the cover **(see illustration)**. Slide the cover forward to disengage the hooks at its front edge and take the cover off.
6   Installation is the reverse of the removal steps.

8   Front fender - removal and installation

All except Vulcan 800 Drifter models

Refer to illustration 8.1a and 8.1b
1   Unbolt the fender from the fork legs and take it off **(see illustrations)**. The wheel need not be removed.
2   Installation is the reverse of the removal steps. On Vulcan 700/750 models, be sure the longer end of the fender faces forward. On Vulcan 800 models, the arrow mark on the side of the fender faces forward.

Vulcan 800 Drifter models

Refer to illustration 8.4
3   Remove the front wheel (see Chapter 7).
4   Unbolt the fender from the fork legs and take it off **(see illustration)**.
5   Installation is the reverse of removal.

9   Rear fender - removal and installation

Vulcan 700/750 models

Refer to illustration 9.3
1   Set the bike on its centerstand.
2   Remove the seat (see Section 6).
3   Disconnect the electrical connectors for

the turn signal lights. Unbolt the seat back frame and take it off **(see illustration)**.

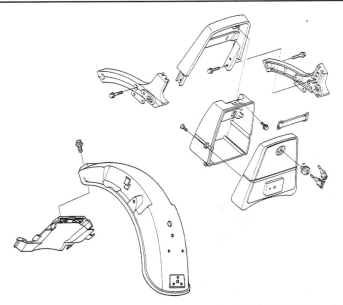

9.3 Rear fender and seat support details (Vulcan 700/750 models)

8

9.8a Unbolt the frame extensions (arrows) and detach the fender assembly from the bike

9.8b Remove the inner fender bolts (arrows)

4   Remove the mounting bolts and remove the front section of the rear fender, then unbolt and remove the rear section **(see illustration 9.3)**.

5   Installation is the reverse of the removal procedure.

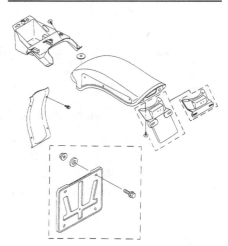

9.8c Rear fender details (Vulcan 800 standard models; Classic similar)

9.9 Position the inner fender with the UP mark upright

Vulcan 800 models (except Drifter)

Refer to illustrations 9.8a, 9.8b, 9.8c and 9.9

6   Remove the seat (see Section 6).

7   At the front edge of the rear fender, disconnect the electrical connectors for the taillights and rear turn signals.

8   Unbolt the rear subframe from each side of the motorcycle **(see illustration)**. Unbolt the fender front section and remove the rear fender from the bike **(see illustrations)**.

9   Installation is the reverse of the removal steps. If you unbolted the front section of the rear fender, be sure its UP mark faces the proper direction when the fender is installed **(see illustration)**.

Vulcan 800 Drifter models

Refer to illustration 9.15

10   Remove the seat (see Section 6).

11   Remove the cover from the electrical components under the seat.

12   Disconnect the electrical connectors at the forward edge of the fender and free the harness from the retainer.

13   Remove the exhaust system (see Chapter 4).

14   Unbolt the fender from the motorcycle and lift it rearward.

15   If necessary, disassemble the fender components **(see illustration)**.

16   Installation is the reverse of the removal steps.

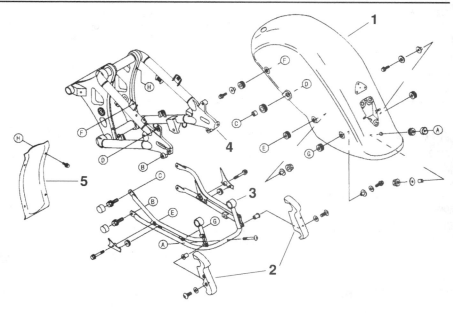

9.15 Rear fender details (Vulcan 800 Drifter models)

| 1 | Fender | 3 | Turn signal bracket | 5 | Inner fender |
| 2 | Turn signal stays | 4 | Swingarm | | |

Chapter 9
Electrical system

Contents

Specifications

Battery

Vulcan 700/750 models
Type .... 12 volt, 14Ah (amp hours), fillable
Specific gravity .... See Chapter 1
Vulcan 800 model
Type .... 12 volt, 12 Ah (amp hours), maintenance free
Open circuit voltage .... 12.6 volts minimum

Charging system

Charging system output .... 14 to 15 volts DC at 4000 rpm
Alternator output .... 50 to 80 volts AC at 4000 rpm
Stator coil resistance .... 0.3 to 0.5 ohms

Starter motor

Brush length
Standard .... 12 to 12.5 mm (15/32 to 31/64 inch)
Minimum
Vulcan 700/750 models .... 8.5 mm (11/32 inch)
Vulcan 800 models .... 5.5 mm (7/32 inch)
Commutator diameter
Standard .... 28 mm (1-7/64 inch)
Minimum .... 27 mm (1-1/16 inch)

Circuit fuse ratings

All except main fuse 10A
Main fuse 30A

Bulb wattage

Vulcan 700/750 models

Headlight	60/55 watts
Front turn signals	
1985 through 2000	
US, Canada...	23/8 watts
Australia, South Africa	23 watts
All others	21 watts
2001	23/8 watts
Speedometer, tachometer lights	3.0 watts
Indicator lights	3.4 watts
Rear turn signals	
US, Canada, Australia, South Africa	23 watts
All others	21 watts
Tail/brake lights	
1985 through 2000	
US, Canada, South Africa..	27/8 watts
All others	21/5 watts
2001	21/5 watts
License plate light	
1985 through 2000	
US, Canada, Australia, South Africa........................	8 watts
All others	5 watts
2001	5 watts

Vulcan 800 models

Headlight	60/55 watts
City light	
Standard and Classic	4 watts
Drifter	5 watts
Front turn signals	
Turn signal/running light..	23/8 watts
Turn signal only	21 watts
Speedometer lights	1.7 watts
Indicator lights	
Temperature, oil pressure	1.7 watts
Turn signal..	3.4
High beam	3.0 watts
Neutral	
Standard and Classic...	3.0 watts
Drifter	LED
Rear turn signals	
1985 through 2000	
US, Canada...	8/27 watts
All others	5/21 watts
2001	5/21 watts
Tail/brake lights	
1985 through 2000	
US, Canada, South Africa..	27/8 watts
All others	21/5 watts
2001	21/5 watts
License plate light (Drifter only)	5 watts

Torque specifications

Alternator rotor bolt	
Vulcan 700/750 models...	125 Nm (94 ft-lbs)
Vulcan 800 models...	155 Nm (115 ft-lbs)
Alternator stator screws	
Vulcan 700/750 models...	12 Nm (104 inch-lbs)
Vulcan 800 models...	13 Nm (113 inch-lbs)
Oil pressure switch	15 Nm (132 inch-lbs)
Starter mounting bolts	11 Nm (95 inch-lbs)

1   General information

The machines covered by this manual are equipped with a 12-volt electrical system. The components include a crankshaft mounted permanent magnet alternator and a solid state voltage regulator/rectifier unit.

The regulator maintains the charging system output within the specified range to prevent overcharging. The rectifier converts the AC (alternating current) output of the alternator to DC (direct current) to power the lights and other components and to charge the battery.

The alternator consists of a multi-coil stator (bolted to the left-hand crankcase cover) and a permanent magnet rotor mounted on the crankshaft.

An electric starter mounted to the engine case is standard equipment. The starting system includes the motor, the battery, the solenoid, the starter circuit relay (part of the junction box) and the various wires and switches. If the engine stop switch and the main key switch are both in the On position, the circuit relay allows the starter motor to operate only if the transmission is in Neutral (Neutral switch on) or the clutch lever is pulled to the handlebar (clutch switch on) and the sidestand is up (sidestand switch on). **Note:** *Keep in mind that electrical parts, once purchased, can't be returned. To avoid unnecessary expense, make very sure the faulty component has been positively identified before buying a replacement part.*

2   Electrical troubleshooting

A typical electrical circuit consists of an electrical component, the switches, relays, etc. related to that component and the wiring and connectors that hook the component to both the battery and the frame. To aid in locating a problem in any electrical circuit, complete wiring diagrams of each model are included at the end of this Chapter.

Before tackling any troublesome electrical circuit, first study the appropriate diagrams thoroughly to get a complete picture of what makes up that individual circuit. Trouble spots, for instance, can often be narrowed down by noting if other components related to that circuit are operating properly or not. If several components or circuits fail at one time, chances are the fault lies in the fuse or ground connection, as several circuits are often routed through the same fuse and ground connections.

Electrical problems often stem from simple causes, such as loose or corroded connections or a blown fuse. Prior to any electrical troubleshooting, always visually check the condition of the fuse, wires and connections in the problem circuit.

If testing instruments are going to be utilized, use the diagrams to plan where you will make the necessary connections in order to accurately pinpoint the trouble spot.

The basic tools needed for electrical troubleshooting include a test light or voltmeter, a continuity tester (which includes a bulb, battery and set of test leads) and a jumper wire, preferably with a circuit breaker incorporated, which can be used to bypass electrical components. Specific checks described later in this Chapter may also require an ohmmeter.

Voltage checks should be performed if a circuit is not functioning properly. Connect one lead of a test light or voltmeter to either the negative battery terminal or a known good ground (earth). Connect the other lead to a connector in the circuit being tested, preferably nearest to the battery or fuse. If the bulb lights, voltage is reaching that point, which means the part of the circuit between that connector and the battery is problem-free. Continue checking the remainder of the circuit in the same manner. When you reach a point where no voltage is present, the problem lies between there and the last good test point. Most of the time the problem is due to a loose connection. Keep in mind that some circuits only receive voltage when the ignition key is in the On position.

One method of finding short circuits is to remove the fuse and connect a test light or voltmeter in its place to the fuse terminals. There should be no load in the circuit. Move the wiring harness from side-to-side while watching the test light. If the bulb lights, there is a short to ground somewhere in that area, probably where insulation has rubbed off a wire. The same test can be performed on other components in the circuit, including the switch.

A ground check should be done to see if a component is grounded properly. Disconnect the battery and connect one lead of a self-powered test light (continuity tester) to a known good ground. Connect the other lead to the wire or ground connection being tested. If the bulb lights, the ground is good. If the bulb does not light, the ground is not good.

A continuity check is performed to see if a circuit, section of circuit or individual component is capable of passing electricity through it. Disconnect the battery and connect one lead of a self-powered test light (continuity tester) to one end of the circuit being tested and the other lead to the other end of the circuit. If the bulb lights, there is continuity, which means the circuit is passing electricity through it properly. Switches can be checked in the same way.

Remember that all electrical circuits are designed to conduct electricity from the battery, through the wires, switches, relays, etc. to the electrical component (light bulb, motor, etc.). From there it is directed to the frame (ground) where it is passed back to the battery. Electrical problems are basically an interruption in the flow of electricity from the battery or back to it.

3   Battery - inspection and maintenance

1   Most battery damage is caused by heat, vibration, and/or low electrolyte levels, so keep the battery securely mounted, check the electrolyte level frequently (on fillable batteries) and make sure the charging system is functioning properly.

2   Refer to Chapter 1 for electrolyte level and specific gravity checking procedures on fillable batteries.

3   Remove the seat (see Chapter 8). If you're working on a Drifter, remove the cover from the electrical components box. Check around the base inside of the battery for sediment, which is the result of sulfation caused by low electrolyte levels. These deposits will cause internal short circuits, which can quickly discharge the battery. Look for cracks in the case and replace the battery if either of these conditions is found.

4   Check the battery terminals and cable ends for tightness and corrosion. If corrosion is evident, remove the cables from the battery and clean the terminals and cable ends with a wire brush or knife and emery paper. Reconnect the cables and apply a thin coat of petroleum jelly to the connections to slow further corrosion.

5   The battery case should be kept clean to prevent current leakage, which can discharge the battery over a period of time (especially when it sits unused). Wash the outside of the case with a solution of baking soda and water. Do not get any baking soda solution in the battery cells. Rinse the battery thoroughly, then dry it.

6   If acid has been spilled on the frame or battery box, neutralize it with the baking soda and water solution, dry it thoroughly, then touch up any damaged paint. Make sure the battery vent tube is directed away from the frame and is not kinked or pinched.

7   If the motorcycle sits unused for long periods of time, disconnect the cables from the battery terminals. Refer to Section 4 and charge the battery approximately once every month.

4   Battery - charging

1   If the machine sits idle for extended periods or if the charging system malfunctions, the battery can be charged from an external source. Charging procedures for the fillable battery used on Vulcan 700/750 models are different from the procedures for maintenance-free batteries, which are used on Vulcan 800 models.

Fillable batteries (Vulcan 700/750 models)

2   To properly charge the battery, you will need a charger of the correct rating, a hydrometer, a clean rag and a syringe for

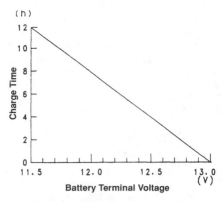

4.13 Battery charge rates and times (maintenance-free batteries)

5.1a On Vulcan 700/750 models, remove the junction box cover (labeled FUSE) . . .

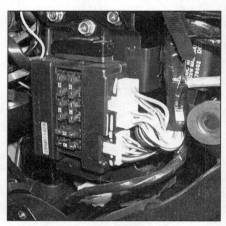

5.1b . . . for access to the fuses

5.2a Pull out the junction box (arrow) for access to the Vulcan 800 fuses . . .

adding distilled water to the battery cells.

3   The maximum charging rate for any battery is 1/10 of the rated amp/hour capacity. As an example, the maximum charging rate for a 14 amp/hour battery would be 1.4 amps. If the battery is charged at a higher rate, it could be damaged.

4   Do not allow the battery to be subjected to a so-called quick charge (high rate of charge over a short period of time) unless you are prepared to buy a new battery. The heat will warp the plates inside the battery until they touch each other, causing a short circuit.

5   When charging the battery, always remove it from the machine and be sure to check the electrolyte level before hooking up the charger. Add distilled water to any cells that are low.

6   Loosen the cell caps, hook up the battery charger leads (red to positive, black to negative), cover the top of the battery with a clean rag, then, and only then, plug in the battery charger. **Warning:** *Remember, the gas escaping from a charging battery is explosive, so keep open flames and sparks well away from the area. If the gas ignites, the entire battery can explode and spray acid. Also, the electrolyte is extremely corrosive and will damage anything it comes in contact with.*

7   Allow the battery to charge until the specific gravity is as specified (refer to Chapter 1 for specific gravity checking procedures). The charger must be unplugged and disconnected from the battery when making specific gravity checks. If the battery overheats or gases excessively, the charging rate is too high. Either disconnect the charger or lower the charging rate to prevent damage to the battery.

8   If one or more of the cells do not show an increase in specific gravity after a long slow charge, or if the battery as a whole does not seem to want to take a charge, it is time for a new battery.

9   When the battery is fully charged, unplug the charger first, then disconnect the leads from the battery. Install the cell caps and wipe any electrolyte off the outside of the battery case.

Maintenance-free batteries (Vulcan 800 models)

Refer to illustration 4.13

10   Charging the maintenance-free battery used on these models requires a digital voltmeter and a variable-voltage charger with a built-in ammeter.

11   When charging the battery, always remove it from the machine and be sure to check the electrolyte level by looking through the translucent battery case before hooking up the charger. If the electrolyte level is low, the battery must be discarded; never remove the sealing plug to add water.

12   Disconnect the battery cables (negative cable first), then connect a digital voltmeter between the battery terminals and measure the voltage.

13   If terminal voltage is 12.6 volts or higher, the battery is fully charged. If it's lower, recharge the battery. Refer to the accompanying illustration and this Chapter's Specifications for charging rate and time **(see illustration)**.

14   A quick charge can be used in an emergency, provided the maximum charge rates and times are not exceeded (exceeding the maximum rate or time may ruin the battery). A quick charge should always be followed as soon as possible by a charge at the standard rate and time.

15   Hook up the battery charger leads (positive lead to battery positive terminal and negative lead to battery negative terminal, then, and only then, plug in the battery charger. **Warning:** *The gas escaping from a charging battery is explosive, so keep open flames and sparks well away from the area. Also, the electrolyte is extremely corrosive and will damage anything it comes in contact with.*

16   Start charging at a high voltage setting (no more than 25 volts) and watch the ammeter for about 5 minutes. If the charging current doesn't increase, replace the battery with a new one.

17   When the charging current increases beyond the specified maximum, reduce the

charging voltage to reduce the charging current to the rate listed in this Chapter's Specifications. Do this periodically as the battery charges.

18   Allow the battery to charge for the specified time listed in this Chapter's Specifications. If the battery overheats or gases excessively, the charging rate is too high. Either disconnect the charger or lower the charging rate to prevent damage to the battery.

19   After the specified time, unplug the charger first, then disconnect the leads from the battery.

20   Wait 30 minutes, then measure voltage between the battery terminals. If it's 12.6 volts or higher, the battery is fully charged. If it's between 12.0 and 12.6 volts, charge the battery again (refer to this Chapter's Specifications and illustration 4.13 for charge rate and time).

5   Fuses - check and replacement

Refer to illustrations 5.1a, 5.1b, 5.2a, 5.2b and 5.4

1   On Vulcan 700/750 models, the fuses are located in the junction box on the left side of the motorcycle **(see illustrations)**.

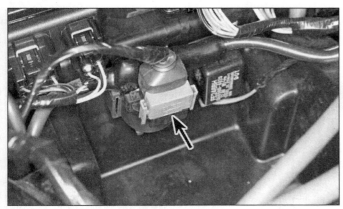

5.2b . . . except the main fuse, which is next to the starter relay (arrow)

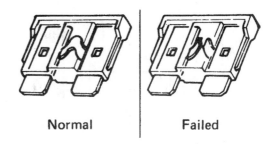

Normal   Failed

5.4 A blown "plug-in" type fuse can be identified by a broken element - be sure to replace a blown fuse with one of the same amperage rating

The fuse box contains spare fuses.

2   On Vulcan 800 models, all of the fuses except the main fuse are located under the seat, on the junction box **(see illustration)**. The main fuse is located on the starter relay **(see illustration)**. The fuses on the junction box are protected by a plastic cover, which snaps into place. This box contains fuses (and spares) which protect the fan, headlight, tail-light and accessory circuit wiring and components from damage caused by short circuits.

3   If you have a test light, the fuses can be checked without removing them. Turn the ignition to the On position, connect one end of the test light to a good ground, then probe each terminal on top of the fuse. If the fuse is good, there will be voltage available at both terminals. If the fuse is blown, there will only be voltage present at one of the terminals.

4   The "plug-in" type fuses can be pulled from position. If you can't pull the fuse out

with your fingertips, use a pair of needle-nose pliers. A blown fuse is easily identified by a break in the element **(see illustration)**.

5   If a fuse blows, be sure to check the wiring harnesses very carefully for evidence of a short circuit. Look for bare wires and chafed, melted or burned insulation. If a fuse is replaced before the cause is located, the new fuse will blow immediately.

6   Never, under any circumstances, use a higher rated fuse or bridge the fuse block terminals, as damage to the electrical system - including melted wires, ruined components, and fire - could result.

7   Occasionally a fuse will blow or cause an open circuit for no obvious reason. Corrosion of the fuse ends and fuse block terminals may occur and cause poor fuse contact. If this happens, remove the corrosion with a wire brush or emery paper, then spray the fuse end and terminals with electrical contact cleaner.

6   Junction box - check

Refer to illustrations 6.2a, 6.2b and 6.2c

1   In addition to serving as the fuse block, the junction box is used to house the starter circuit relay (not the starter relay) and the headlight relay (US and Canada only). Neither of these relays is replaceable individually. If one of them fails, the junction box must be replaced.

2   In addition to the relay checks, the fuse circuits and diode circuits should be checked also, to rule out the possibility of an open circuit condition or blown diode within the junction block as the cause of an electrical problem. Schematics of the junction box and a terminal identification chart can be found in the accompanying illustrations **(see illustrations)**.

(US and Canadian Model)   (Other than US and Canadian Model)

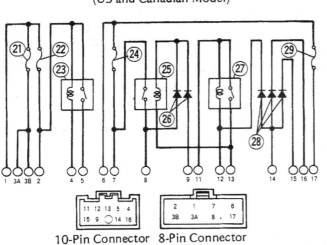

10-Pin Connector   8-Pin Connector

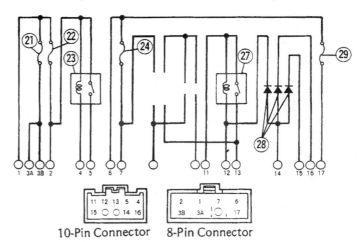

10-Pin Connector   8-Pin Connector

6.2a Junction box circuit and terminal identification (Vulcan 700/750 models)

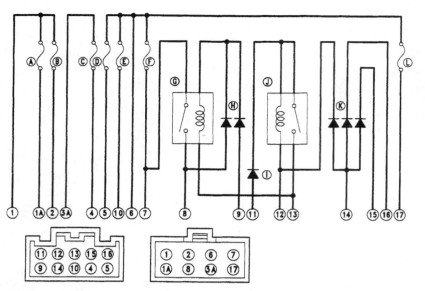

6.2b Junction box circuit and terminal identification (Vulcan 800 models, US, Canada and Australia)

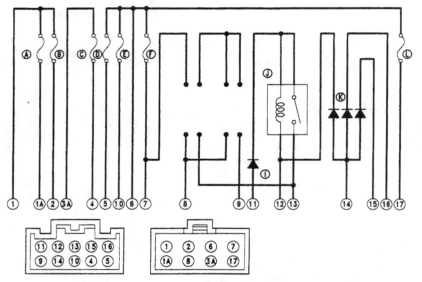

6.2c Junction box circuit and terminal identification (Vulcan 800 models except US, Canada and Australia)

Fuse circuit check

Refer to illustrations 6.4a and 6.4b

3   Remove the junction box **(see illustration 5.1a or 5.2a)**. Disconnect the electrical connectors from the box.

4   If the terminals are dirty or bent, clean and straighten them. Using the accompanying table as a guide, check the continuity across the indicated terminals with an ohmmeter - some should have no resistance and others should have infinite resistance **(see illustrations)**.

5   If the resistance values are not as specified, replace the junction box.

Diode circuit check

6   Remove the junction box **(see illustration 5.1a or 5.2a)**. Unplug the electrical connectors from the box.

7   Using an ohmmeter, check the resistance across the specified pairs of terminals, then write down the readings:

a) *Terminals 8 and 13 (US and Canada 750 models; US, Canada and Australia 800 models)*

b) *Terminals 9 and 13 (US and Canada 750 models; US, Canada and Australia 800 models)*

c) *Terminals 12 and 11 (800 models only)*

d) *Terminals 12 and 14*

e) *Terminals 14 and 15*

f) *Terminals 16 and 14*

8   Now, reverse the ohmmeter leads and

Fuse Circuit Inspection

Meter Connection		Meter Reading (Ω)
1	– 2	0
1	– 3A	0
6	– 7	0
6	– 17	0
1	– 7	∞
*3A	– 8	*∞
*8	– 17	*∞

∗ : **US and Canadian Models only**

6.4a Junction box fuse circuit test connections (Vulcan 750 models)

Fuse Circuit Inspection

Tester Connection	Tester Reading (Ω)	Tester Connection	Tester Reading (Ω)
1 - 1A	0	1A - 8	∞
1 - 2	0	2 - 8	∞
3A - 4	0	3A - 8	∞
6 - 5	0	6 - 2	∞
6 - 10	0	6 - 3A	∞
6 - 7	0	17 - 3A	∞
6 - 17	0		

6.4b Junction box fuse circuit test connections (Vulcan 800 models)

Meter Connection	Meter Reading (Ω)
2-5	∞
4-5	∞
*7-8	*∞
7-13	∞
11-13	∞
12-13	∞

* : US and Canadian Models only

6.10a Junction box relay circuit test connections (Vulcan 750 models, battery disconnected)

Meter Connection	Battery Connection +	Battery Connection −	Meter Reading (Ω)
2-5	2	4	0
*7-8	*9	13	*0
11-13	11	12	0

* : US and Canadian Models only

6.10b Junction box relay circuit test connections (Vulcan 750 models, battery connected)

	Tester Connection	Tester Reading (Ω)			Tester Connection	Tester Reading (Ω)
Headlight Relay	*7 - 8	∞		Starter Circuit Relay	9 - 11	∞
	*7 - 13	∞			12 - 13	∞
	(+) (-) 13 - 9	Not ∞ **			(+) (-) 13 - 11	∞
					(+) (-) 12 - 11	Not ∞ **

(*): U.S.A., and Canada Models only
(**): The actual reading varies with the hand tester used.

(+): Apply tester positive lead.
(−): Apply tester negative lead.

6.10c Junction box relay circuit test connections (Vulcan 800 models, battery disconnected)

check the resistances again, writing down the readings. The resistances should be low in one direction and at least ten times as high in the other direction. If the readings for any pair of terminals are low or high in both directions, a diode is defective and the junction box must be replaced.

Relay checks

Refer to illustrations 6.10a, 6.10b, 6.10c and 6.10d

9 Remove the junction box **(see illustration 5.1a or 5.2a)**. Disconnect the electrical connectors from the box.

10 Using an ohmmeter, check the continuity across the terminals indicated in the accompanying tables, with the battery disconnected and connected **(see illustrations)**.

11 If the junction box fails any of these tests, it must be replaced.

	Battery Connection (+) (−)	Tester Connection	Tester Reading (Ω)
Headlight Relay	*9 − 13	*7 − 8	0
Starter Circuit Relay	11 − 12	(+) (−) 13 − 11	Not ∞ **

(*): U.S.A., and Canada Models only
(**): The actual reading varies with the hand tester used.
(+): Apply tester positive lead.
(−): Apply tester negative lead.

6.10d Junction box relay circuit test connections (Vulcan 800 models, battery connected)

7 Lighting system - check

1 The battery provides power for operation of the headlight, taillight, brake light, license plate light and instrument cluster lights. If none of the lights operate, always check battery voltage before proceeding. Low battery voltage indicates either a faulty battery, low battery electrolyte level or a defective charging system. Refer to Chapter 1 for battery checks and Sections 28 through 32 for charging system tests. Also, check the condition of the fuses and replace any blown fuses with new ones.

Headlight

2 If the headlight is out when the engine is running (US, Canadian models) or with the lighting switch On (all other models), check the fuse first with the key On (see Section 5), then unplug the electrical connector for the headlight and use jumper wires to connect the bulb directly to the battery terminals. If the light comes on, the problem lies in the wiring or one of the switches in the circuit. Refer to Sections 19 and 20 for the switch testing procedures, and also the wiring diagrams at the end of this Chapter. On US and Canadian models also check the headlight relay in the junction box (Section 6).

3 US and Canadian Vulcan 700/750 models use an additional relay in the system, called the reserve lighting unit. On these models, the headlight doesn't come on when the ignition switch is first turned on, but comes on when the starter button is pressed and stays on until the ignition is turned off. The light will go out whenever the starter is operated after the engine has stalled (this prevents excessive strain on the battery). This component is checked by process of elimination (if all other parts and circuits in the lighting system are good, the reserve lighting device is defective). For this reason,

9

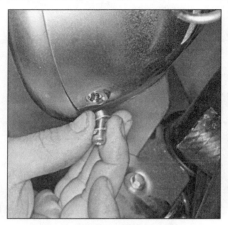

8.1a Remove the screw, washer and collar from each side . . .

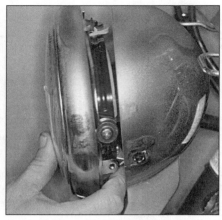

8.1b . . . and pull the headlight unit out for access to the bulb

8.2 Pull on the tabs to remove the dust cover; be sure to push the dust cover all the way on, with the TOP mark upward, after changing the bulb

it's a good idea to have a Kawasaki dealer check the lighting system before replacing the reserve lighting device. Refer to the wiring diagram at the end of this manual for details of the system.

Taillight/license plate light

4   If the taillight fails to work, check the bulbs and the bulb terminals first, then check for battery voltage at the red wire in the taillight. If voltage is present, check the ground (earth) circuit for an open or poor connection.
5   If no voltage is indicated, check the wiring between the taillight and the main (key) switch, then check the switch.

Brake light

6   See Section 14 for the brake light circuit checking procedure.

Neutral indicator light

7   If the neutral light fails to operate when the transmission is in Neutral, check the fuses and the bulb (see Section 17 for bulb removal procedures). If the bulb and fuses are in good condition, check for battery voltage at the wire attached to the neutral switch

on the left side of the engine. If battery voltage is present, refer to Section 22 for the neutral switch check and replacement procedures.
8   If no voltage is indicated, check the wires between the junction box and the bulb, the junction box and the switch and between the switch and the bulb for open circuits and poor connections.

Oil pressure warning light

9   See Section 18 for the oil pressure warning light circuit check.

Coolant temperature warning light

10   See Chapter 3, Section 5 for the coolant temperature warning light circuit check.

---

8   Headlight bulb - replacement

Refer to illustrations 8.1a, 8.1b, 8.2, 8.3, 8.4 and 8.5

1   Remove the headlight assembly securing screw, washer and collar from each side of the housing **(see illustration)**. Pull out the

assembly and disconnect the electrical connector **(see illustration)**.
2   Pull up the tab and remove the dust cover **(see illustration)**.
3   Lift up the retaining clip and swing it out of the way **(see illustration)**. **Warning:** *If the headlight has just been on, let the bulb cool before you continue. It will be hot to enough to cause burns.*
4   Remove the bulb holder **(see illustration)**.
5   When installing the new bulb, reverse the removal procedure. Be sure not to touch the bulb with your fingers - oil from your skin will cause the bulb to overheat and fail prematurely. If you do touch the bulb, wipe it off with a clean rag dampened with rubbing alcohol. Make sure the clip is securely seated **(see illustration)**.

---

9   Headlight assembly - removal and installation

Refer to illustration 9.2a, 9.2b and 9.2c

1   Remove the headlight bulb holder housing (see Section 8).

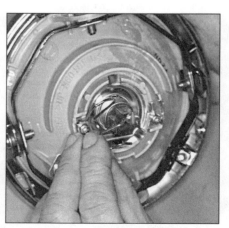

8.3 Unhook the clip and move it aside . . .

8.4 . . . then pull the bulb holder out of the socket

8.5 The clip should like this after it's installed

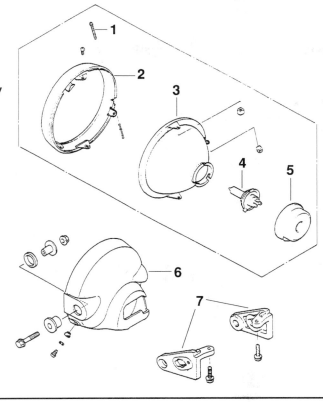

9.2a Headlight assembly details (Vulcan 700/750 models)

1 Adjusting screw
2 Headlight rim
3 Headlight housing
4 Bulb
5 Dust cover
6 Headlight assembly
7 Brackets

9.2b Remove the bolts (arrows) to separate the headlight housing from the bracket

ahead. Before adjusting the headlight, be sure to consult with local traffic laws and regulations.

2 The headlight beam can be adjusted both vertically and horizontally. Before performing the adjustment, make sure the fuel tank has at least a half tank of fuel, and have an assistant sit on the seat.

Vulcan 700/750 models

4 To adjust the horizontal position of the beam, insert a screwdriver into the hole in the headlight rim (not the headlight housing) and turn the adjuster. Turning clockwise moves the beam left; turning counterclockwise moves the beam to the right.

5 To adjust the vertical position of the beam, simply grasp the headlight bulb housing and rotate it up or down. It isn't necessary to loosen the mounting bolts.

Vulcan 800 models (except Drifter)

Refer to illustration 10.6

6 To adjust the horizontal position of the beam, insert a screwdriver into the hole in the headlight rim (not the headlight housing) and turn the adjuster **(see illustration)**.

2 Disconnect the electrical connectors inside the headlight housing and remove the headlight assembly mounting bolts and nuts **(see illustrations)**.

3 Installation is the reverse of removal. Be sure the Top mark on the lens is up. Adjust the headlight aim (see Section 10).

10 Headlight aim - check and adjustment

1 An improperly adjusted headlight may cause problems for oncoming traffic or provide poor, unsafe illumination of the road

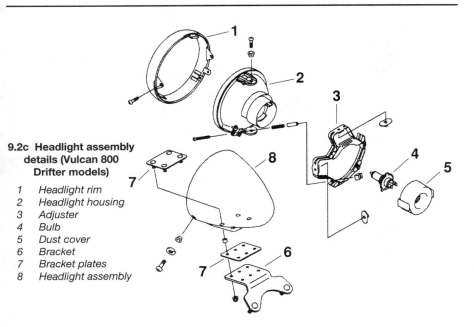

9.2c Headlight assembly details (Vulcan 800 Drifter models)

1 Headlight rim
2 Headlight housing
3 Adjuster
4 Bulb
5 Dust cover
6 Bracket
7 Bracket plates
8 Headlight assembly

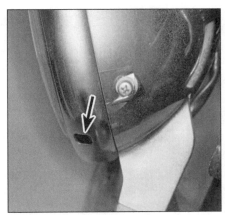

10.6 Insert a screwdriver into the hole (arrow) and turn the adjuster

11.1 Remove the lens screws (arrows) for access to the bulb (turn signal shown)

7 Insert the screwdriver into the vertical adjuster screw hole (at the upper right of the headlight rim) and turn the adjuster screw as necessary to raise or lower the beam.

Vulcan 800 Drifter models

8 To adjust the horizontal position of the beam, insert a screwdriver into the hole in the lower left side of the headlight rim (not the headlight housing) and turn the adjuster.
9 Insert the screwdriver into the vertical adjuster screw hole (at the lower right of the headlight rim) and turn the adjuster screw as necessary to raise or lower the beam.

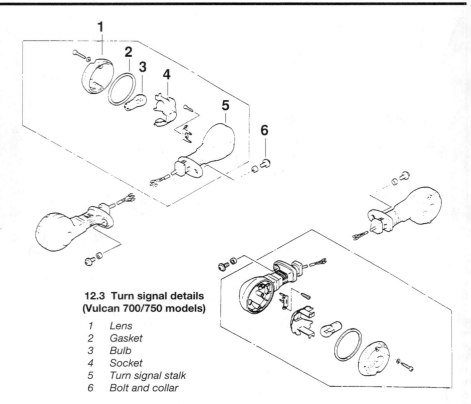

12.3 Turn signal details (Vulcan 700/750 models)

1	Lens
2	Gasket
3	Bulb
4	Socket
5	Turn signal stalk
6	Bolt and collar

12.5 Turn signal details (Vulcan 800 Drifter models)

1	Lens
2	Gasket
3	Bulb
4	Turn signal stalk
5	Mounting bracket
6	Damper
7	Collar
8	Nut
9	Cap

11 Turn signal, tail/brake light and license plate light bulbs - replacement

Refer to illustration 11.1
1 Remove the lens securing screw(s) and take off the lens **(see illustration)**.
2 Push the bulb in and turn it counter-clockwise (anti-clockwise) to remove it. Check the socket terminals for corrosion and clean them if necessary. Line up the pins on the new bulb with the slots in the socket, push in and turn the bulb clockwise until it locks in place. It is a good idea to use a paper towel or dry cloth when handling the new bulb to prevent injury if the bulb should break and to increase bulb life.
3 Position the lens on the reflector and install the screws. Be careful not to over-tighten them.

12 Turn signal assemblies - removal and installation

Refer to illustrations 12.3 and 12.5
1 The turn signal assemblies can be removed individually in the event of damage or failure.
2 To remove a turn signal assembly, first follow the wiring harness from the turn signal to its electrical connectors. Mark the wires

13.3a Here's the turn signal relay on Vulcan 700/750 models (arrow)

13.3b Here's the turn signal relay on Vulcan 800 models (arrow)

with pieces of numbered tape then unplug the electrical connectors.

3 If you're working on a Vulcan 700/750 model, remove the mounting screw and washer **(see illustration)**.

4 If you're working on a Vulcan 800 standard or Classic model, refer to the fork removal procedure in Chapter 6 to remove the front turn signal assemblies. To remove a rear assembly, unscrew the nut that secures the turn signal to the rear frame extension.

5 If you're working on a Vulcan 800 Drifter model, unscrew the nut that secures the turn signal to the mounting bracket **(see illustration)**.

6 Installation is the reverse of the removal procedure.

13 Turn signal circuit - check

Refer to illustrations 13.3a and 13.3b

1 The battery provides power for operation of the signal lights, so if they do not operate, always check the battery voltage and specific gravity first. Low battery voltage indicates either a faulty battery, low electrolyte level or a defective charging system. Refer to Chapter 1 for battery checks and Sections 28 through 32 for charging system tests. Also, check the fuses (see Section 5).

2 Most turn signal problems are the result of a burned out bulb or corroded socket. This is especially true when the turn signals function properly in one direction, but fail to flash in the other direction. Check the bulbs and the sockets (see Section 11).

3 If the bulbs and sockets check out okay, refer to the wiring diagrams at the end of this manual and check for power at the turn signal relay with the ignition On. On all models, it's under the seat **(see illustrations)**. If there's no power at the relay, check the junction box (see Section 6) and the switch (see Section 21).

4 If the junction box and switch are okay, check the wiring between the turn signal relay and the turn signal lights (see the wiring

diagrams at the end of this manual).

5 If the wiring checks out okay, replace the turn signal relay.

6 The Vulcan 700/750 A1 through A4 models have self canceling turn signals. The circuit comprises the distance sensor in the speedometer and the turn signal control unit mounted on the electrical components plate under the seat. If a fault occurs in the self canceling function, and the turn signals function normally when operated manually, check the distance sensor, control unit, and their associated wiring to the handlebar switch.

7 The distance sensor can be checked by disconnecting its wiring at the connector (which can be accessed from the headlight housing) and connecting an ohmmeter across the red and green wires on the sensor side of the connector. Disconnect the speedometer drive cable at the wheel end and have an assistant turn the inner cable slowly while you observe the meter reading. If the sensor is functioning correctly, the ohmmeter should show continuity four times per cable revolution.

8 There is no test procedure for the turn signal control unit; if the fault cannot be traced to the distance sensor, switch or wiring, the control unit should be replaced.

14 Brake light switches - check and replacement

Circuit check

1 Before checking any electrical circuit, check the fuses (see Section 5).

2 Using a test light (or voltmeter) connected to a good ground, check for voltage at the brown wire terminal in the electrical connector at the brake light switch. If there's no voltage present, check the brown wire between the switch and the junction box (see the wiring diagrams at the end of this manual).

3 If voltage is available, touch the probe

14.6 Remove the screw (arrow) and take the switch off

of the test light to the other terminal of the switch, then pull the brake lever or depress the brake pedal - if the test light doesn't light up, replace the switch.

4 If the test light does light, check the wiring between the switch and the brake lights (see the wiring diagrams at the end of this manual).

Switch replacement

Brake lever switch

Refer to illustration 14.6

5 Disconnect the electrical connectors from the switch.

6 Remove the mounting screw **(see illustration)** and detach the switch from the brake lever bracket/front master cylinder.

7 Installation is the reverse of the removal procedure. The brake lever switch isn't adjustable.

Brake pedal switch

Refer to illustration 14.10

8 Locate the switch at the brake pedal, follow its wiring harness to the electrical connector and disconnect it.

9

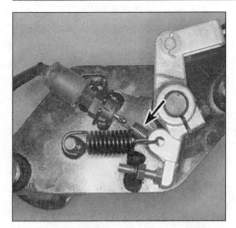

14.10 Unhook the switch spring (arrow)

9   Where necessary for access, remove the footpeg bracket from the motorcycle.
10   Unhook the switch spring **(see illustration)**. Loosen the adjuster nut, compress the retainer prongs and remove the switch from the bracket.
11   Install the switch by reversing the removal procedure.
12   Adjust the switch by following the procedure described in Chapter 1.

15   Instrument and warning light housings - removal and installation

Caution: *Keep the gauge housing in an upright position while it's off the motorcycle or the gauge(s) will be ruined.*

Vulcan 700/750 models

Refer to illustration 15.3

1   Unscrew the speedometer cable knurled nut from the speedometer and pull the speedometer cable free.
2   Remove the headlight unit from the

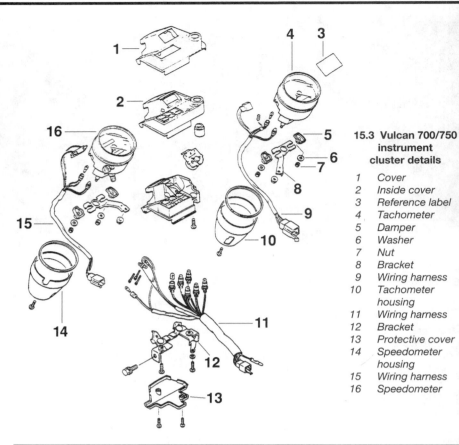

15.3 Vulcan 700/750 instrument cluster details

1   Cover
2   Inside cover
3   Reference label
4   Tachometer
5   Damper
6   Washer
7   Nut
8   Bracket
9   Wiring harness
10   Tachometer housing
11   Wiring harness
12   Bracket
13   Protective cover
14   Speedometer housing
15   Wiring harness
16   Speedometer

housing. Working inside the housing, disconnect the instrument electrical connectors.
3   Remove the gauge unit mounting bolts, one on each side of the unit, and take it off **(see illustration)**.
4   Installation is the reverse of the removal steps.

Vulcan 800 models

Refer to illustrations 15.5, 15.6 and 15.7

5   Pad the front edge of the housing with a shop towel. Remove the housing mounting bolt **(see illustration)**.
6   Push the housing forward to disengage the tab on the housing from the slot in the frame **(see illustration)**.
7   Lift the housing up. Disconnect the gauge electrical connector and unscrew the speedometer cable knurled nut **(see illustration)**. Pull the speedometer cable free of the speedometer and lift the housing off.
8   Installation is the reverse of the removal steps.

15.5 Remove the housing mounting bolt . . .

15.6 . . . pull the housing forward to disengage the tab from the slot (arrows) . . .

15.7 . . . lift the housing up, disconnect the wiring connector and unscrew the speedometer cable nut

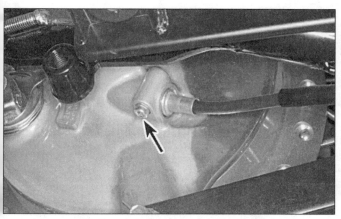

16.8 Remove the Allen bolt (arrow) . . .

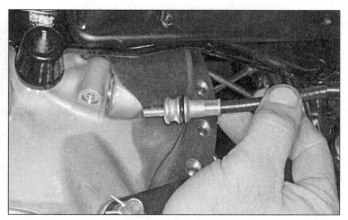

16.9 . . . and pull the cable out of the brake panel

16 Meters and gauges - check and replacement

Check

Temperature gauge (if equipped)

1   Refer to Chapter 3 for the temperature gauge checking procedure.

Speedometer and tachometer (if equipped)

2   Special instruments are required to properly check the operation of these meters. Take the instrument cluster to a Kawasaki dealer service department or other qualified repair shop for diagnosis.

Gauge replacement

3   If you're working on Vulcan 700/750 model, remove the screws that secure the protective panel to the underside of the cluster **(see illustration 15.3)**. Remove the screws that hold the white and black gauge panels together and separate the panels.
4   Remove the gauge mounting fasteners and remove the gauge from the housing.
5   Installation is the reverse of the removal steps.

Speedometer cable replacement

6   Disconnect the speedometer cable from the speedometer **(see illustration 15.7)**.

Vulcan 700/750 and Vulcan 800 Drifter models

7   Disconnect the lower end of the speedometer cable from the drive at the front wheel **(see illustration 11.3a or 11.8c in Chapter 7)**. Note carefully how the cable is routed, then remove it.

Vulcan 800 standard and Classic models

Refer to illustrations 16.8 and 16.9
8   Remove the Allen bolt that secures the

cable to the speedometer drive in the rear brake panel **(see illustration)**.
9   Pull the cable out of the drive **(see illustration)**.

All models

10   Installation is the reverse of the removal steps.

17 Instrument and warning light bulbs - replacement

1   To replace a bulb, pull the appropriate rubber socket out of the back of the instrument housing, then pull the bulb out of the socket. If the socket contacts are dirty or corroded, they should be scraped clean and sprayed with electrical contact cleaner before new bulbs are installed.
2   Carefully push the new bulb into position, then push the socket into the instrument housing.

18 Oil pressure switch - check and replacement

Refer to illustration 18.2
1   If the oil pressure warning light fails to operate properly, check the oil level and make sure it is correct.
2   If the oil level is correct, disconnect the wire from the oil pressure switch, which is located on the left side of the crankcase near the oil filter **(see illustration)**. Turn the main switch On and ground the end of the wire. If the light comes on, the oil pressure switch is defective and must be replaced with a new one (only after draining the engine oil).
3   If the light does not come on, check the oil pressure warning light bulb, the wiring between the oil pressure switch and the light, and between the light and the junction box (see the wiring diagrams at the end of this manual).
4   To replace the switch, drain the engine oil (see Chapter 1) and unscrew the switch

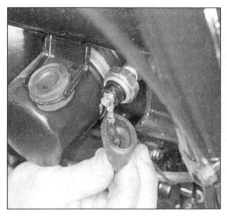

18.2 Pull back the rubber cover, loosen the screw, disconnect the wire and unscrew the switch

from the crankcase. Coat the threads of the new switch with silicone sealant, then screw the unit into its hole, tightening it to the torque listed in this Chapter's Specifications.
5   Fill the crankcase with the recommended type and amount of oil (see Chapter 1) and check for leaks.

19 Ignition main (key) switch - check and replacement

Check

1   Disconnect the ignition switch electrical connector.
2   Using an ohmmeter, check the continuity of the terminal pairs indicated in the wiring diagrams at the end of this manual. Continuity should exist between the terminals connected by a solid line when the switch is in the indicated position.
3   If the switch fails any of the tests, replace it.

Replacement

Refer to illustration 19.7
4   Remove bodywork components as nec-

9

19.7 Remove the mounting bolts (arrows) and take the switch off

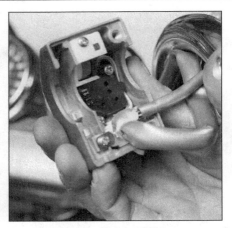

21.1 The handlebar switches are mounted inside the housings on the handlebar

21.3a There's an alignment hole for the switch housing in the handlebar (arrow) . . .

essary for access to the switch mounting screws.

5   If you haven't already done so, disconnect the switch electrical connector.

6   If you're working on a Vulcan 700/750 model, unlock the steering. Unscrew the Allen bolts from the underside of the switch. Remove the bolts and lockwashers and remove the switch.

7   If you're working on a Vulcan 800 model, free the switch wiring harness from its retainer. Unscrew the switch panel mounting bolts and take it off **(see illustration)**.

8   Installation is the reverse of the removal steps.

20   Handlebar switches - check

1   Generally speaking, the switches are reliable and trouble-free. Most troubles, when they do occur, are caused by dirty or corroded contacts, but wear and breakage of internal parts is a possibility that should not be overlooked. If breakage does occur, the entire switch and related wiring harness will

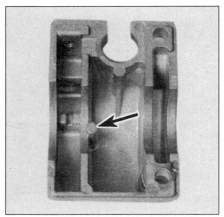

21.3b . . . be sure the tab on the switch housing (arrow) fits into the hole when the housing is installed

have to be replaced with a new one, since individual parts are not usually available.

2   The switches can be checked for continuity with an ohmmeter or a continuity test light. Always disconnect the battery ground cable, which will prevent the possibility of a short circuit, before making the checks.

3   Trace the wiring harness of the switch in question and unplug the electrical connectors.

4   Refer to the wiring diagrams at the end of this manual for switch continuity diagrams. Using the ohmmeter or test light, check for continuity between the terminals of the switch harness with the switch in the various positions. Continuity should exist between the terminals connected by a solid line when the switch is in the indicated position.

5   If the continuity check indicates a problem exists, refer to Section 21, disassemble the switch and spray the switch contacts with electrical contact cleaner. If they are accessible, the contacts can be scraped clean with a knife or polished with crocus cloth. If switch components are damaged or broken, it will be obvious when the switch is disassembled.

21   Handlebar switches - removal and installation

Refer to illustrations 21.1, 21.3a and 21.3b

1   The handlebar switches are composed of two halves that clamp around the bars. They are easily removed for cleaning or inspection by taking out the clamp screws and pulling the switch halves away from the handlebars **(see illustration)**.

2   To completely remove the switches, the mounting screws should be removed **(see illustration 21.1)** and the electrical connectors in the wiring harness should be unplugged.

3   When installing the switches, make sure the wiring harnesses are properly routed to

avoid pinching or stretching the wires. If there's an alignment tab on the switch housing, make sure it engages with the hole in the handlebar **(see illustrations)**.

22   Neutral switch - check and replacement

Refer to illustration 22.3

Check

1   The switch is at the lower rear of the engine.

2   Support the bike securely upright and remove components as necessary for access.

3   Disconnect the wire from the neutral switch **(see illustration)**. Connect one lead of an ohmmeter to a good ground (earth) and the other lead to the post on the switch.

4   When the transmission is in neutral, the ohmmeter should read 0 ohms - in any other gear, the meter should read infinite resistance.

22.3 Location of the neutral switch (arrow)

23.7a Here's a typical sidestand switch on all except Drifter models

23.7b On Drifter models, the switch fingers fit over this post (arrow)

24.1 Disconnect the horn electrical connectors (arrow) and unscrew the mounting bolt

5   If the switch doesn't check out as described, replace it. **Note:** *If the neutral light works intermittently, try removing the switch and reinstalling it temporarily without its sealing washer. If the light now works consistently, the switch plunger is worn and the switch should be replaced (don't just leave the old switch in position without the washer).*

Replacement

6   Unscrew the neutral switch from the case and remove the sealing washer.
7   Install the switch with a new sealing washer and tighten it securely.

23 Sidestand switch - check and replacement

Check

1   Support the bike securely upright.
2   Follow the wiring harness from the switch to the connector, then disconnect the connector.
3   Connect the leads of an ohmmeter to the wire terminals on the switch side of the connector.
4   With the sidestand in the up position, there should be continuity through the switch (0 ohms). With the sidestand down, there should be no continuity (infinite resistance).
5   If the switch fails either of these tests, replace it.

Replacement

Refer to illustrations 23.7a and 23.7b

6   Support the bike and raise the sidestand.
7   Remove the switch mounting screws or bolt **(see illustrations)**. Follow the wiring harness to the electrical connector, disconnect it and remove the switch.
8   Installation is the reverse of the removal procedure.

24 Horn - check, replacement and adjustment

Refer to illustration 24.1

Check

1   Disconnect the electrical connectors from the horn **(see illustration)**. Using two jumper wires, apply battery voltage directly to the terminals on the horn. If the horn sounds, check the switch (see Section 20) and the wiring between the switch and the horn (see the wiring diagrams at the end of this manual).
2   If the horn doesn't sound, replace it.

Replacement

3   Detach the electrical connectors and unbolt the horn bracket from the frame **(see illustration 24.1)**.
4   Detach the horn from the bracket and transfer the bracket to the new horn.
5   Installation is the reverse of removal.

25 Starter relay and starter circuit relay - check and replacement

Starter relay
Check

Refer to illustrations 25.2a and 25.2b

1   Remove the right side panel (Vulcan 700/750 models) and seat (Vulcan 800 models) (see Chapter 8). If you're working on a Drifter, remove the electrical components cover.
2   Disconnect the battery positive cable and the starter cable from the terminals on the starter relay **(see illustrations)**. **Caution:** *Don't let the battery positive cable make contact with anything, as it would be a direct short to ground.*
3   Connect the leads of an ohmmeter to the terminals of the starter relay.
4   Turn the ignition switch to On and the

engine stop switch to Run. Place the transmission in Neutral.
5   Press the starter button - the relay should click and the ohmmeter should indicate 0 ohms.
6   If the meter doesn't read 0 ohms or the relay doesn't click, replace it.

25.2a Starter relay (arrow) (Vulcan 700/750 models)

25.2b Starter relay (arrow) Vulcan 800 models

26.2a Pull back the cover and disconnect the starter cable

26.2b Remove the starter mounting bolts (arrows) and pull the starter out of the engine

Replacement

7   Disconnect the cable from the negative terminal of the battery.
8   Detach the battery positive cable, the starter cable and electrical connector from the relay.
9   Pull the relay holder off its mounting tabs (see illustration 25.2a or 25.2b).
10   Installation is the reverse of removal. Reconnect the negative battery cable after all the other electrical connections are made.

Starter circuit relay

11   The starter circuit relay is incorporated in the junction box; refer to the tests described in Section 6.

26   Starter motor - removal and installation

Removal

Refer to illustration 26.2a and 26.2b
1   Disconnect the cable from the negative terminal of the battery.

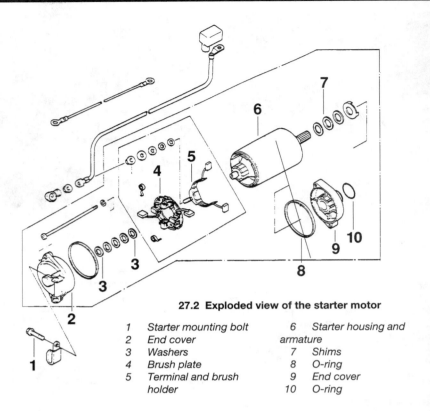

27.2 Exploded view of the starter motor

1	Starter mounting bolt	6	Starter housing and
2	End cover		armature
3	Washers	7	Shims
4	Brush plate	8	O-ring
5	Terminal and brush	9	End cover
	holder	10	O-ring

2   Remove the nut and washer retaining the starter wires to the starter, then remove the starter mounting bolts and pull the starter out of the engine (**see illustrations**).
3   Check the condition of the O-ring on the end of the starter and replace it if necessary.

Installation

4   Apply a little engine oil to the O-ring and install the starter by reversing the removal procedure.

27   Starter motor - disassembly, inspection and reassembly

1   Remove the starter motor (see Section 26).

Disassembly

Refer to illustrations 27.2, 27.4 and 27.5
2   Mark the position of the housing to each end cover. Remove the two through-bolts and detach the end cover (**see illustration**).
3   Pull the armature out of the housing (toward the reduction gear side).
4   Remove the brush plate from the housing (**see illustration**).
5   Remove the nut and push the terminal bolt through the housing. Remove the two brushes with the plastic holder from the housing (**see illustration**).

Inspection

Refer to illustrations 27.6, 27.7, 27.8a, 27.8b, 27.9 and 27.10
6   The parts of the starter motor that most likely will require attention are the brushes. Measure the length of the brushes and compare the results to the brush length listed in this Chapter's Specifications (**see illustration**). If any of the brushes are worn beyond the specified limits, replace the brush holder assembly with a new one. If the brushes are not worn excessively, cracked, chipped, or otherwise damaged, they may be reused.
7   Inspect the commutator (**see illustration**) for scoring, scratches and discol-

27.4 Remove the brush plate from the housing

27.5 Push the terminal bolt through the housing and remove the plastic brush holder

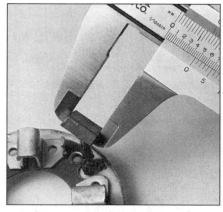

27.6 Measure the length of the brushes and compare the length of the shortest brush with the length listed in this Chapter's Specifications

27.7 Check the commutator for cracks and discoloring, then measure the diameter and compare it with the minimum diameter listed in this Chapter's Specifications

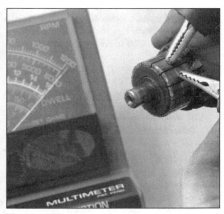

27.8a Continuity should exist between the commutator bars

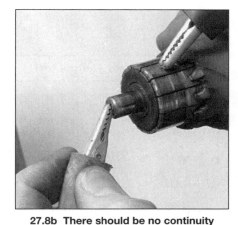

27.8b There should be no continuity between the commutator bars and the armature shaft

27.9 There should be almost no resistance (0 ohms) between the brushes and the brush plate

oration. The commutator can be cleaned and polished with crocus cloth, but do not use sandpaper or emery paper. After cleaning, wipe away any residue with a cloth soaked in an electrical system cleaner or denatured alcohol. Measure the commutator diameter and compare it to the diameter listed in this Chapter's Specifications. If it is less than the service limit, the motor must be replaced with a new one.

8   Using an ohmmeter or a continuity test light, check for continuity between the commutator bars **(see illustration)**. Continuity should exist between each bar and all of the others. Also, check for continuity between the commutator bars and the armature shaft **(see illustration)**. There should be no continuity between the commutator and the shaft. If the checks indicate otherwise, the armature is defective.

9   Check for continuity between the brush plate and the brushes **(see illustration)**. The meter should read close to 0 ohms. If it doesn't, the brush plate has an open and must be replaced.

10   Using the highest range on the ohmmeter, measure the resistance between the brush holders and the brush plate **(see illus-**

tration)**. The reading should be infinite. If there is any reading at all, replace the brush plate.

11   Check the starter pinion for worn, cracked, chipped and broken teeth. If the teeth are damaged or worn, replace the starter motor.

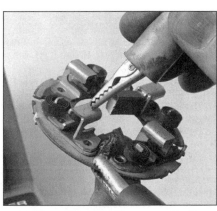

27.10 There should be no continuity between the brush plate and the brush holders (the resistance should be infinite)

Reassembly

Refer to illustrations 27.12, 27.13, 27.14a and 27.14b

12   Install the plastic brush holder into the housing. Make sure the terminal bolt and washers are assembled correctly **(see illustration)**. Tighten the terminal nut securely.

27.12 Install the washers on the starter terminal as shown

9

27.13 When installing the brush plate, make sure the brush leads fit into the notches in the plate (arrow) - also, make sure the tongue on the plate fits into the notch in the housing (arrows)

27.14a Install each brush spring on the post in this position . . .

27.14b . . . then pull the end of the spring 1/2 turn clockwise and seat the end of it in the groove in the end of the brush

13   Detach the brush springs from the brush plate (this will make armature installation much easier). Install the brush plate into the housing, routing the brush leads into the notches in the plate **(see illustration)**. Make sure the tongue on the brush plate fits into the notch in the housing.

14   Install the brushes into their holders and slide the armature into place. Install the brush springs **(see illustrations)**.

15   Install any washers that were present on the end of the armature shaft. Install the end and reduction covers, aligning the protrusions with the notches. Install the two through-bolts and tighten them securely.

28   Charging system testing - general information and precautions

1   If the performance of the charging system is suspect, the system as a whole should be checked first, followed by testing of the individual components (the alternator and the voltage regulator/rectifier). **Note:** *Before beginning the checks, make sure the battery is fully charged and that all system connections are clean and tight.*

2   Checking the output of the charging system and the performance of the various components within the charging system requires the use of special electrical test equipment. A voltmeter or a multimeter is the absolute minimum equipment required. In addition, an ohmmeter is generally required for checking the remainder of the system.

3   When making the checks, follow the procedures carefully to prevent incorrect connections or short circuits, as irreparable damage to electrical system components may result if short circuits occur. Because of the special tools and expertise required, it is recommended that the job of checking the

charging system be left to a dealer service department or a reputable motorcycle repair shop.

29   Charging system - output test

Caution: *Never disconnect the battery cables from the battery while the engine is running. If the battery is disconnected, the alternator and regulator/rectifier will be damaged.*

1   To check the charging system output, you will need a voltmeter or a multimeter with a voltmeter function.

2   The battery must be fully charged (charge it from an external source if necessary) and the engine must be at normal operating temperature to obtain an accurate reading.

3   Remove the seat (see Chapter 8). If you're working on a Drifter, remove the electrical components cover.

4   Attach the positive voltmeter lead to the battery positive terminal and the negative lead to the battery negative terminal. The voltmeter selector switch (if so equipped) must be in a DC volt range greater than 15 volts.

5   Start the engine. Run it at varying speeds up to 4,000 rpm, with headlight off and with it on (for US and Canadian models, remove the headlight fuse to turn it off with the engine running).

6   The charging system output should be within the range listed in this Chapter's Specifications. It should be at the low end of the range at low engine speeds and at the high end of the range at higher engine speeds.

7   If the output is as specified, the alternator is functioning properly. If the charging system as a whole is not performing as it should, refer to Section 32 and check the voltage regulator/rectifier.

8   Low voltage output may be the result of damaged windings in the alternator stator coils, loss of magnetism in the alternator

rotor or wiring problems. Make sure all electrical connections are clean and tight, then refer to Sections 30 and 31 for specific alternator tests.

9   High voltage output, above the specified range, may indicate a defective regulator/rectifier.

30   Alternator - output test

Refer to illustration 30.2

1   Follow the wiring harness from the alternator housing to the connector, then disconnect the connector.

2   Connect a voltmeter with a 250-volt AC scale to two of the yellow wire terminals in the alternator connector **(see illustration)** (at this point, you're measuring the alternator output before it has been rectified from alternating current to direct current, so the voltmeter must be able to measure AC).

3   Run the engine at 4,000 rpm and note the voltage reading.

30.2 Vulcan 700/750 models use three separate alternator wires; Vulcan 800 models use a three-wire connector, inside the side cover above the toolbox

32.5 The Vulcan 800 regulator/rectifier is mounted low on the left side of the bike

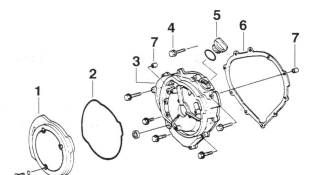

33.3 Alternator cover details (Vulcan 700/750 models)

1 Outer cover
2 O-ring
3 Inner cover
4 Top center bolt (use thread locking agent)
5 Oil filler plug and O-ring
6 Gasket
7 Dowels

4 Take three different measurements between different pairs of wires. In all cases, the voltage should be as listed in this Chapter's Specifications. **Note:** *If only one of the readings is low, one stator coil is probably defective. This will produce an occasional failure to start due to insufficient battery charge.*

a) *If the voltage reading is correct, the rectifier/regulator is probably defective. Refer to Section 32 for test procedures.*

b) *If the voltage reading is low, the alternator may be defective. Test the stator coils as described in Section 31. If the stator coils test out OK, the rotor magnets have probably lost magnetism. This can be caused by dropping or hitting the alternator, by leaving the alternator near another source of magnetism, or by age.*

31 Alternator stator coils - continuity test

1 If charging system output is low or non-existent, the alternator stator coil windings and leads should be checked for proper continuity. The test can be made with the stator in place on the machine.

2 Using an ohmmeter (preferred) or a continuity test light, check for continuity between each of the wires coming from the alternator stator (the same connector that was disconnected in Section 30 for the output test). Continuity should exist between any one wire and each of the others (Kawasaki actually specifies a resistance of 0.3 to 0.5 ohms).

3 Check for continuity between each of the wires and the engine. No continuity should exist between any of the wires and the engine.

4 If there is no continuity between any two of the wires, or if there is continuity between the wires and an engine ground, an open circuit or a short exists within the stator coils. Since repair of the stator is not feasi-

ble, it must be replaced with a new one. **Note:** *An open or shorted stator coil will cause low output or no output. Weak or damaged rotor magnets will cause low output.*

32 Voltage regulator/rectifier - check and replacement

Check

1 Testing of the voltage regulator/rectifier requires a special Kawasaki tester. Ordinary ohmmeters will produce a variety of readings which may indicate that the regulator/rectifier is defective when it is actually good.

2 If the charging system output voltage in Section 29 was too high, the regulator/rectifier may be defective. It may also be defective if the output was too low and no other cause (alternator or wiring problems) can be found.

3 If you suspect the regulator/rectifier, take it to a dealer service department or other repair shop for further checks, or substitute a known good unit and recheck the charging system output.

Replacement

Refer to illustration 32.5

4 The regulator/rectifier on Vulcan 700/750 models is mounted on the underside of the battery case. Remove the battery (see Chapter 1). Tilt the battery case onto its side for access, then remove the regulator/rectifier.

5 The regulator/rectifier on Vulcan 800 models is mounted low on the left side of the bike **(see illustration)**. Disconnect the wiring connector and remove the mounting bolts.

6 Installation is the reverse of the removal steps.

33 Alternator - removal and installation

Removal

Vulcan 700/750 models

Refer to illustration 33.3

1 Disconnect the cable from the negative

terminal of the battery.

2 The outer alternator cover can be removed with the engine in the motorcycle. Removal of the alternator rotor or stator requires removal of the engine (see Chapter 2).

3 Remove the outer cover screws **(see illustration)**. Carefully pry the outer cover off the engine and remove the O-ring.

4 If you're planning to remove the rotor or stator, remove the engine from the motorcycle (see Chapter 2).

5 Remove the alternator cover bolts **(see illustration 33.3)**. Pry the cover off the engine, using the pry points at 1 o'clock and 7 o'clock (looking at the cover from the left side of the motorcycle). Locate the cover dowels; they may have come off with the cover or stayed in the engine.

6 If you're planning to remove the rotor, remove the external oil line, oil pressure relief valve, external shift linkage cover and shift shaft washer (see Chapter 2).

Vulcan 800 models

Refer to illustrations 33.8a and 33.8b

7 Remove the cover from the engine sprocket (see Chapter 6).

8 Remove the left crankcase cover from the engine **(see illustrations)**.

33.8a Two bolts and the wiring harness grommet (arrows) are inside the engine sprocket cover

9

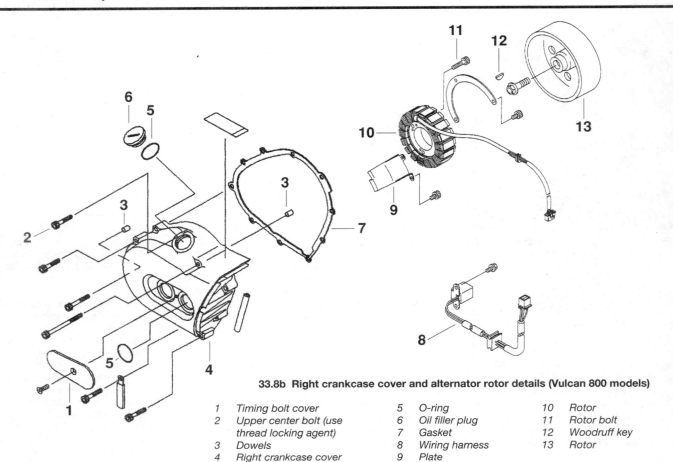

33.8b Right crankcase cover and alternator rotor details (Vulcan 800 models)

1	Timing bolt cover	5	O-ring	10	Rotor
2	Upper center bolt (use thread locking agent)	6	Oil filler plug	11	Rotor bolt
		7	Gasket	12	Woodruff key
3	Dowels	8	Wiring harness	13	Rotor
4	Right crankcase cover	9	Plate		

All models

Refer to illustrations 33.9, 33.11 and 33.12

9   Prevent the alternator rotor from turning. There are two easy ways to do this: wedge a copper penny or washer into the space between the balancer gear and alternator rotor **(see illustration)** or place the transmission in first gear and have an assistant firmly apply the rear brake.

10   Remove the rotor bolt **(see illustration**

33.9)**. Note:** *The bolt has left-hand threads (loosens in a clockwise direction).*

11   Hold the rotor from turning again, and using a rotor puller (tool no. 57001-254 or 57001-1099 or equivalent), remove the rotor from the crankshaft **(see illustration)**. **Caution:** *Don't try to remove the rotor without a puller, as it can easily be damaged. Do not pound on it or you'll weaken the rotor magnets. Pullers are readily available at dealer*

parts departments or from aftermarket tool suppliers.

12   Remove the Woodruff key from the crankshaft **(see illustration)**.

Installation

Refer to illustration 33.14

13   Clean all dirt from the crankshaft and the inside of the rotor with high flash point solvent.

33.9 Wedge the gears from below (left arrow) and turn the rotor bolt (right arrow) clockwise to loosen it

33.11 This special tool is used to remove the alternator rotor

33.12 Remove the Woodruff key from its slot

33.14 The balancer mark (left) and rotor mark (right) should rotate into alignment with each other; if this can't be done, the balancer is installed incorrectly

14   Position the rotor on the engine. Make sure the balancer and rotor marks are lined up correctly **(see illustration)**. Install the bolt, tightening it to the torque listed in this Chapter's Specifications.

15   The remainder of installation is the reverse of the removal steps. Before you install the right crankcase cover, make sure the rotor magnets haven't picked up any pieces of metal that could damage the alternator.

34 Alternator - stator coil replacement

1   Remove the alternator cover (see Section 26).

2   Remove the stator screws **(see illustration 33.8a)**, remove the wiring harness retainer and lift the stator coils out of the alternator housing.

3   Installation is the reverse of the removal steps. Tighten the stator screws to the torque listed in this Chapter's Specifications.

35 Wiring diagrams

Prior to troubleshooting a circuit, check the fuses to make sure they're in good condition. Make sure the battery is fully charged and check the cable connections.

When checking a circuit, make sure all connectors are clean, with no broken or loose terminals or wires. When disconnecting a connector, don't pull on the wires - pull only on the connector housings themselves.

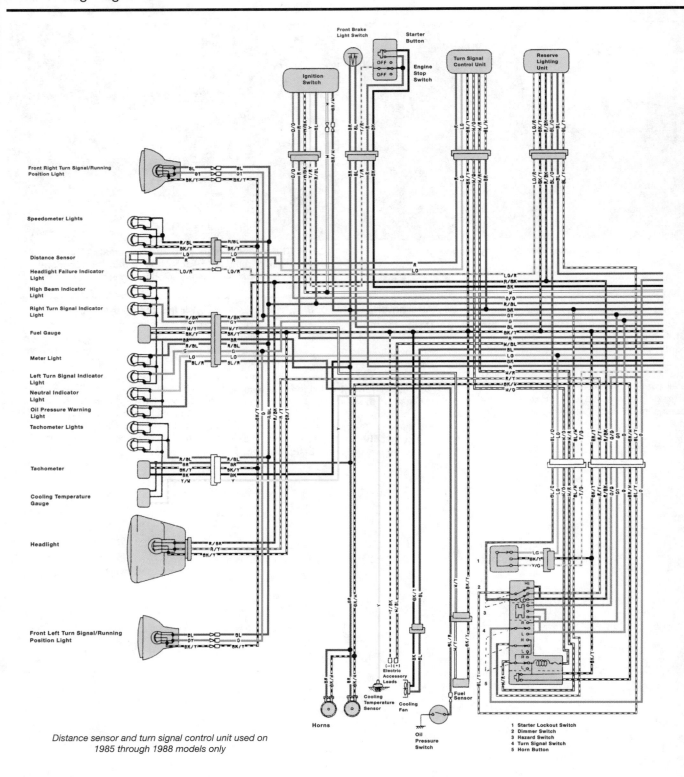

*Distance sensor and turn signal control unit used on
1985 through 1988 models only*

				LEFT HANDLEBAR SWITCH CONNECTIONS													
Horn Button			**Turn Signal Switch**							**Hazard Switch**			**Dimmer Switch**			**Starter Lockout Switch**	
Color	BK/W	BK/Y	Color	W/G	BK/Y	W/R	BL/W	G	O	GY	Color	G	O/G	GY	Color	R/Y	BL/O	BL/Y	R/BK	Released	BK/Y	Y/G	LG
Push	O—O		L		O—O—O			O—O			ON	O—O—O			HI					Released	O—O		
			R			O—O—O			O—O						LO	O	O	O	O	Pulled in	O—O		

Wiring diagram (Vulcan 750 US and Canadian models) (1 of 2)

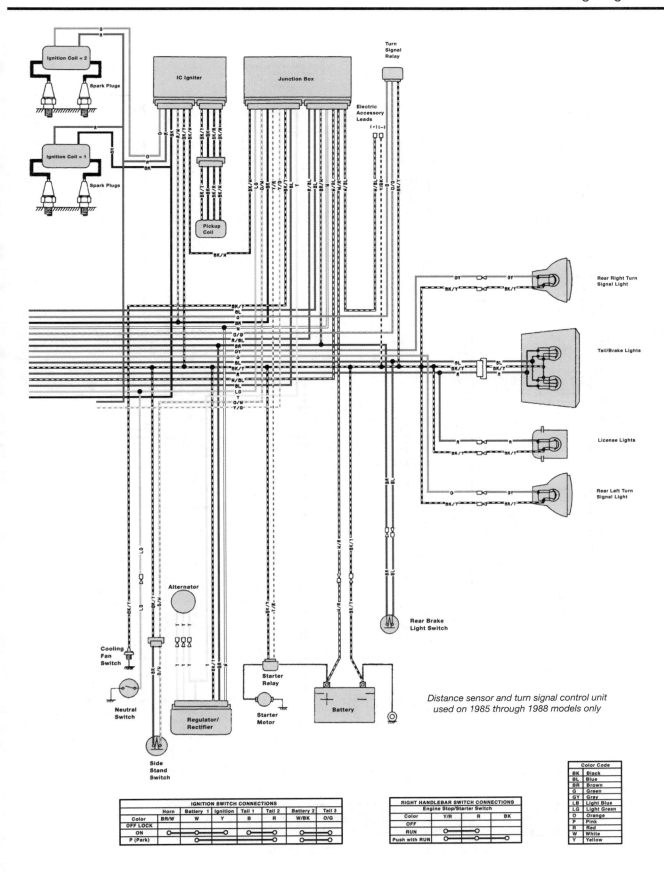

Distance sensor and turn signal control unit
used on 1985 through 1988 models only

IGNITION SWITCH CONNECTIONS							
	Horn	Battery 1	Ignition	Tail 1	Tail 2	Battery 2	Tail 3
Color	BR/W	W	Y	B	R	W/BK	O/G
OFF LOCK							
ON	○—○	○—○	○—○	○—○		○—○	
P (Park)		○—○			○—○		○—○

RIGHT HANDLEBAR SWITCH CONNECTIONS		
Engine Stop/Starter Switch		
Color	Y/R	R	BK
OFF			
RUN	○—○		
Push with RUN	○—○	○—○	

Color Code	
BK	Black
BL	Blue
BR	Brown
G	Green
GY	Gray
LB	Light Blue
LG	Light Green
O	Orange
P	Pink
R	Red
W	White
Y	Yellow

Wiring diagram (Vulcan 750 US and Canadian models) (2 of 2)

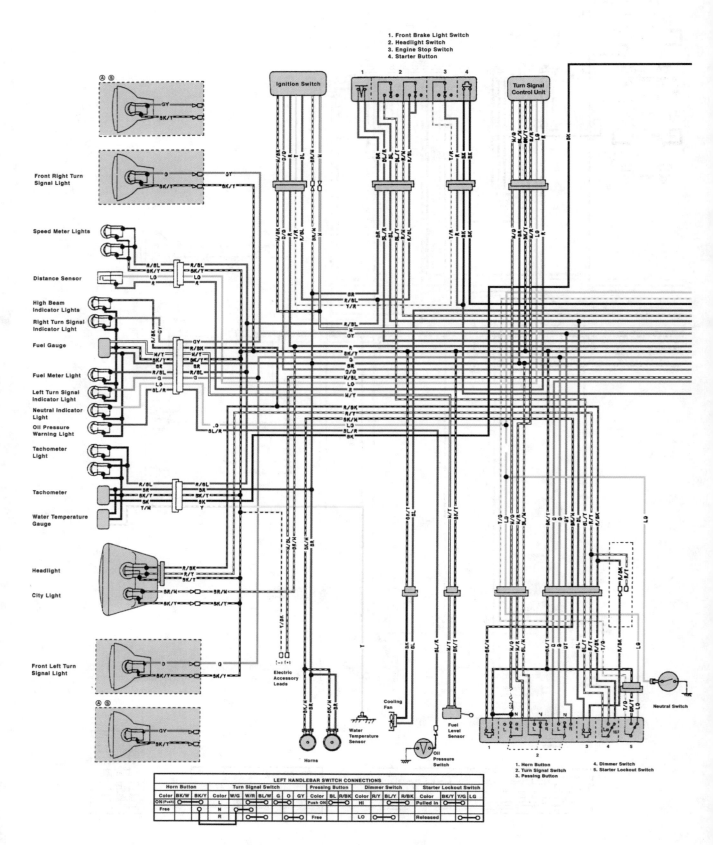

Wiring diagram (Vulcan 750 models except US and Canada) (1 of 2)

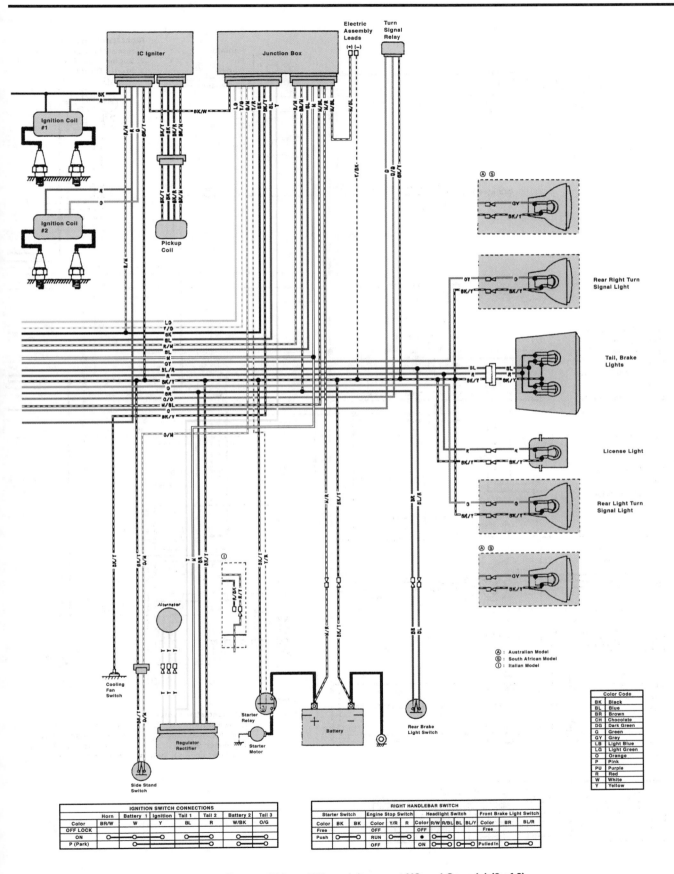

Color Code	
BK	Black
BL	Blue
BR	Brown
CH	Chocolate
DG	Dark Green
G	Green
GY	Gray
LB	Light Blue
LG	Light Green
O	Orange
P	Pink
PU	Purple
R	Red
W	White
Y	Yellow

Ⓐ : Australian Model
Ⓢ : South African Model
Ⓘ : Italian Model

IGNITION SWITCH CONNECTIONS

	Horn	Battery 1	Ignition	Tail 1	Tail 2	Battery 2	Tail 3
Color	BR/W	W	Y	BL	R	W/BK	O/G
OFF LOCK							
ON	O	O	O	O	O	O	O
P (Park)	O	O			O		O

RIGHT HANDLEBAR SWITCH

Starter Switch		Engine Stop Switch			Headlight Switch				Front Brake Light Switch		
Color	BK	BK	Color	Y/R	R	Color	R/W	R/BL	BL	BL/Y	Color	BR	BL/R
Free			OFF			OFF					Free		
Push	O—O		RUN	O—O		•	O—O				Pulled in	O—O	
			OFF			ON	O—O	O—O	O—O				

Wiring diagram (Vulcan 750 models except US and Canada) (2 of 2)

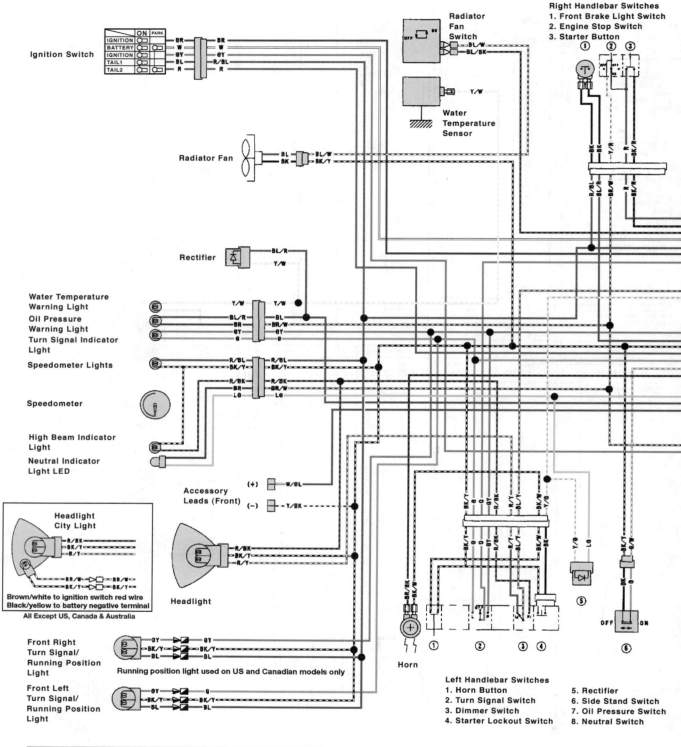

Wiring diagram (Vulcan 800 models except Drifter) (1 of 2)

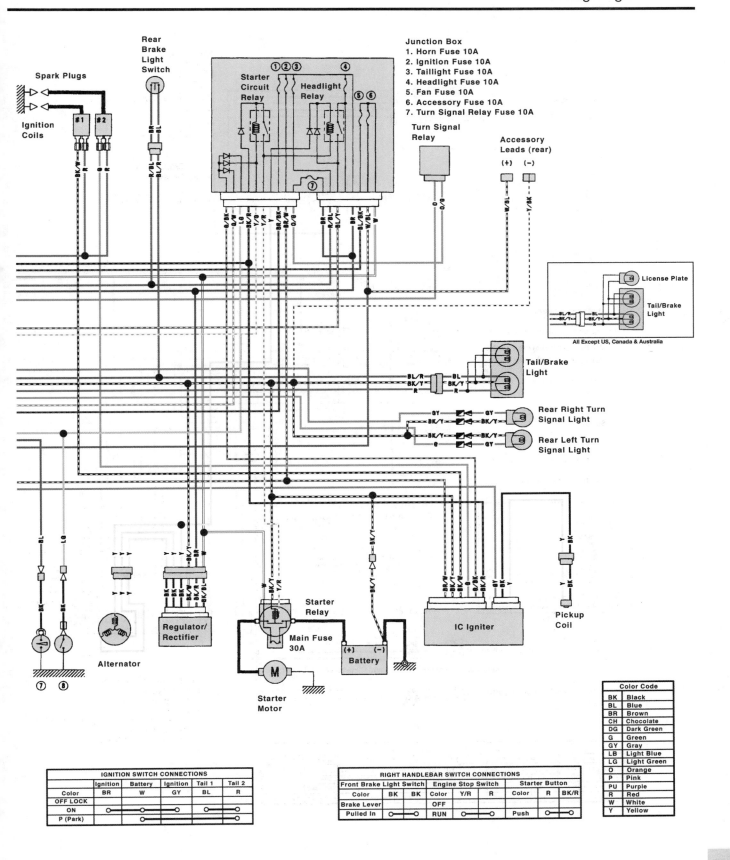

Wiring diagram (Vulcan 800 models except Drifter) (2 of 2)

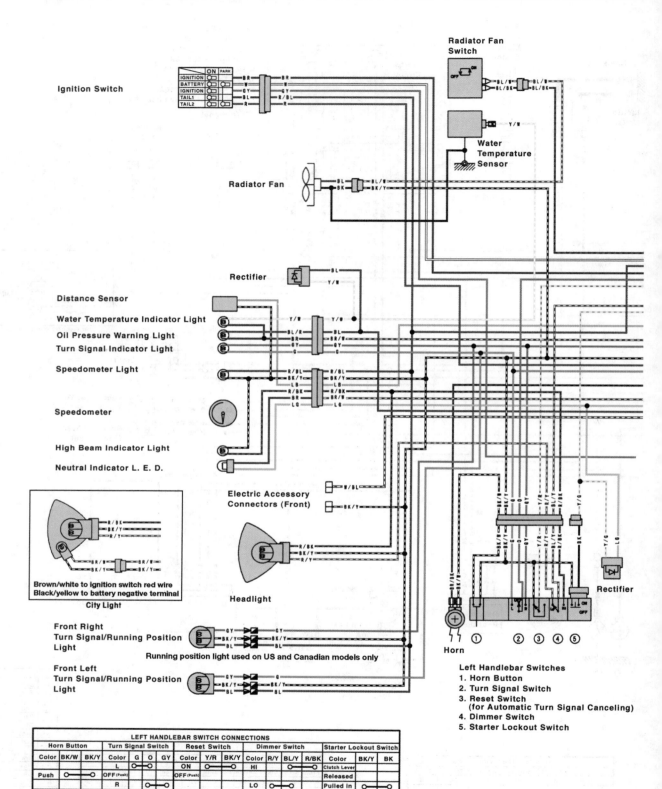

Wiring diagram (Vulcan 800 Drifter) (1 of 2)

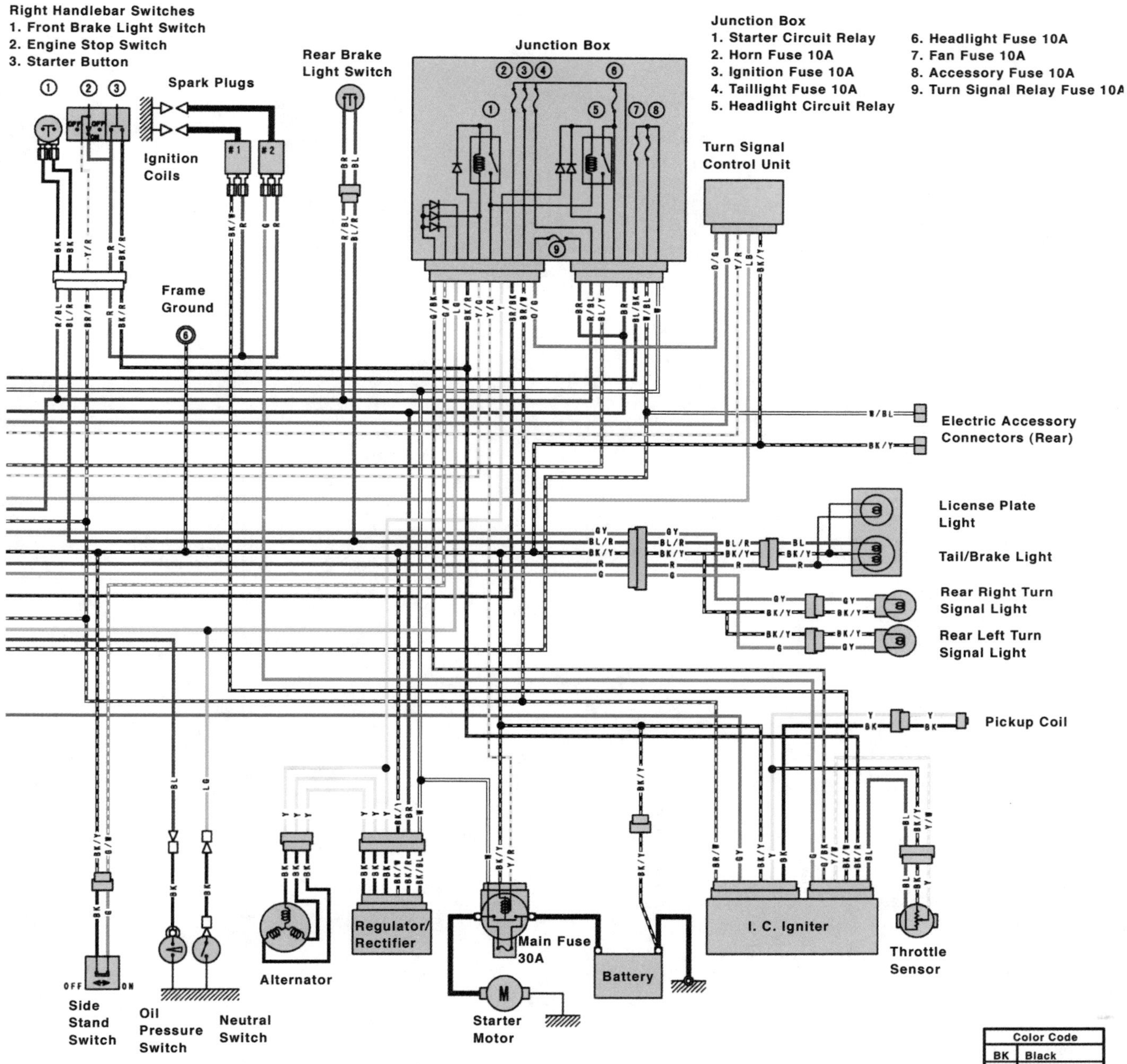

Right Handlebar Switches
1. Front Brake Light Switch
2. Engine Stop Switch
3. Starter Button

Spark Plugs

Ignition Coils

Rear Brake Light Switch

Junction Box

Junction Box
1. Starter Circuit Relay
2. Horn Fuse 10A
3. Ignition Fuse 10A
4. Taillight Fuse 10A
5. Headlight Circuit Relay
6. Headlight Fuse 10A
7. Fan Fuse 10A
8. Accessory Fuse 10A
9. Turn Signal Relay Fuse 10A

Turn Signal Control Unit

Frame Ground

Electric Accessory Connectors (Rear)

License Plate Light

Tail/Brake Light

Rear Right Turn Signal Light

Rear Left Turn Signal Light

Pickup Coil

Side Stand Switch

Oil Pressure Switch

Neutral Switch

Alternator

Regulator/ Rectifier

Starter Motor

Main Fuse 30A

Battery

I. C. Igniter

Throttle Sensor

OFF · ON

IGNITION SWITCH CONNECTIONS					
	Ignition	Battery	Ignition	Tail 1	Tail 2
Color	BR	W	GY	BL	R
OFF LOCK					
ON	o———	———o———	———o	o———	———o
P (Park)		o———			———o

RIGHT HANDLEBAR SWITCH CONNECTIONS					
Front Brake Light Switch		Engine Stop Switch		Starter Button	
Color	BK	BK	Color	Y/R	R	Color	R	BK/R
Brake Lever			OFF					
Pulled In	o———	———o	RUN	o———	———o	Push	o———	———o

Color Code	
BK	Black
BL	Blue
BR	Brown
CH	Chocolate
DG	Dark Green
G	Green
GY	Gray
LB	Light Blue
LG	Light Green
O	Orange
P	Pink
PU	Purple
R	Red
W	White
Y	Yellow

Notes

Reference

Dimensions and weights

Height

Wheelbase

Length

Wheelbase

Vulcan 700/750
    US and Canada .... 1580 mm (62.2 inches)
    All others
        1985 through 1999 .... 1585 mm (62.4 inches)
        2000 and later .... 1580 mm (62.2 inches)
Vulcan 800 standard model .... 1625 mm (63.97 inches)
Vulcan 800 Classic .... 1600 mm (62.99 inches)
Vulcan 800 Drifter .... 1615 mm (63.58 inches)

Overall length

Vulcan 700/750
    US, Canada, Australia, South Africa .... 2295 mm (90.35 inches)
    Europe
        1985 through 1999 .... 2300 mm (90.55 inches)
        2000 and later .... 2295 mm (90.35 inches)
Vulcan 800 standard model
    1995 through 1999
        US, Canada .... 2360 mm (92.91 inches)
        All others .... 2370 mm (93.31 inches)
    2000 and later .... 2360 mm (92.91 inches)
Vulcan 800 Classic
    US, Canada, Malaysia .... 2375 mm (93.50 inches)
    All others .... 2390 mm (94.09 inches)
Vulcan 800 Drifter .... 2490 mm (98.03 inches)

Overall width

Vulcan 700/750
    US and Canada .... 850 mm (33.46 inches)
    All others
        1985 through 1999 .... 860 mm (33.86 inches)
        2000 and later .... 850 mm (33.46 inches)
Vulcan 800 standard model .... 825 mm (32.48 inches)
Vulcan 800 Classic
    US, Canada, Malaysia .... 930 mm (36.61 inches)
    All others .... 940 mm (37.01 inches)
Vulcan 800 Drifter .... 1005 mm (39.57 inches)

Overall height

Vulcan 700/750
    US and Canada .... 1225 mm (48.23 inches)
    All others
        1985 through 1999 .... 1235 mm (48.62 inches)
        2000 and later .... 1225 mm (48.23 inches)
Vulcan 800 standard model .... 1170 mm (46.06 inches)
Vulcan 800 Classic
    US, Canada, Malaysia .... 1130 mm (44.49 inches)
    All others .... 1125 mm (44.29 inches)
Vulcan 800 Drifter .... 1125 mm (44.29 inches)

Minimum ground clearance
Vulcan 700/750
    US and Canada .... 150 mm (5.90 inches)
    All others
        1985 through 1999 .... 135 mm (5.31 inches)
        2000 and later .... 150 mm (5.90 inches)
Vulcan 800 standard model .... 160 mm (6.30 inches)
Vulcan 800 Classic .... 135 mm (5.31 inches)
Vulcan 800 Drifter .... 160 mm (6.30 inches)

Weight (dry)
Vulcan 700/750
    US except California, Canada .... 219 kg (481.8 lbs)
    California .... 219.5 kg (482.9 lbs)
    All others
        1985 through 1999 .... 223 kg (490.6 lb)
        2000 and later .... 219 kg (481.8 lbs)
Vulcan 800 standard model
    All except California .... 225 kg (495 lbs)
    California .... 225.5 kg (496.1 lbs)
Vulcan 800 Classic
    US except California, Canada, Malaysia .... 234 kg (514.8 lbs)
    California .... 234.5 kg (515.9 lbs)
    All others .... 235 kg (517 lbs)
Vulcan 800 Drifter
    1999 and 2000 (C model) .... 248 kg (545.6 lbs)
    2001 (E model)
        All except California .... 246 kg (541.2 lbs)
        California .... 246.5 kg (542.3 lbs)

Seat height
Vulcan 700/750
    US and Canada .... 735 mm (28.94 inches)
    All others
        1985 through 1999 .... 750 mm (29.53 inches)
        2000 and later .... 735 mm (28.94 inches)
Vulcan 800 standard model .... 710 mm (27.95 inches)
Vulcan 800 Classic .... 705 mm (27.75 inches)
Vulcan 800 Drifter .... 760 mm (29.92 inches)

Buying tools

A good set of tools is a fundamental requirement for servicing and repairing a motorcycle. Although there will be an initial expense in building up enough tools for servicing, this will soon be offset by the savings made by doing the job yourself. As experience and confidence grow, additional tools can be added to enable the repair and overhaul of the motorcycle. Many of the special tools are expensive and not often used so it may be preferable to rent them, or for a group of friends or motorcycle club to join in the purchase.

As a rule, it is better to buy more expensive, good quality tools. Cheaper tools are likely to wear out faster and need to be replaced more often, nullifying the original saving.

> ⚠️ **Warning: To avoid the risk of a poor quality tool breaking in use, causing injury or damage to the component being worked on, always aim to purchase tools which meet the relevant national safety standards.**

The following lists of tools do not represent the manufacturer's service tools, but serve as a guide to help the owner decide which tools are needed for this level of work. In addition, items such as an electric drill, hacksaw, files, soldering iron and a workbench equipped with a vise, may be needed. Although not classed as tools, a selection of bolts, screws, nuts, washers and pieces of tubing always come in useful.

For more information about tools, refer to the Haynes *Motorcycle Workshop Practice Techbook* (Bk. No. 3470).

Manufacturer's service tools

Inevitably certain tasks require the use of a service tool. Where possible an alternative tool or method of approach is recommended, but sometimes there is no option if personal injury or damage to the component is to be avoided. Where required, service tools are referred to in the relevant procedure.

Service tools can usually only be purchased from a motorcycle dealer and are identified by a part number. Some of the commonly-used tools, such as rotor pullers, are available in aftermarket form from mail-order motorcycle tool and accessory suppliers.

Maintenance and minor repair tools

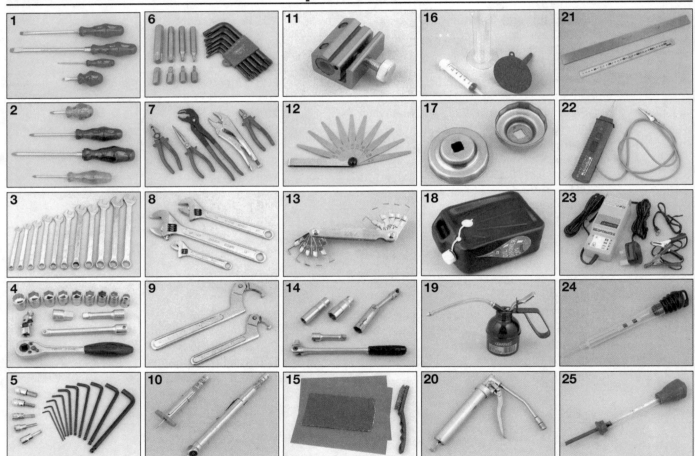

1 Set of flat-bladed screwdrivers
2 Set of Phillips head screwdrivers
3 Combination open-end and box wrenches
4 Socket set (3/8 inch or 1/2 inch drive)
5 Set of Allen keys or bits

6 Set of Torx keys or bits
7 Pliers, cutters and self-locking grips (vise grips)
8 Adjustable wrenches
9 C-spanners
10 Tread depth gauge and tire pressure gauge

11 Cable oiler clamp
12 Feeler gauges
13 Spark plug gap measuring tool
14 Spark plug wrench or deep plug sockets
15 Wire brush and emery paper

16 Calibrated syringe, measuring cup and funnel
17 Oil filter adapters
18 Oil drainer can or tray
19 Pump type oil can
20 Grease gun

21 Straight-edge and steel rule
22 Continuity tester
23 Battery charger
24 Hydrometer (for battery specific gravity check)
25 Anti-freeze tester (for liquid-cooled engines)

Repair and overhaul tools

 1
 4
 7
 10
 13

 2
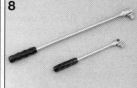 5
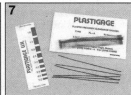 8
 11
 14

 3
 6
 9
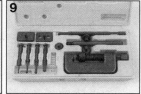 12
 15

1 Torque wrench
(small and mid-ranges)
2 Conventional, plastic or
soft-faced hammers
3 Impact driver set

4 Vernier caliper
5 Snap-ring pliers (internal
and external, or
combination)
6 Set of cold chisels
and punches

7 Selection of pullers
8 Breaker bars
9 Chain breaking/
riveting tool set
10 Wire stripper and
crimper tool

11 Multimeter (measures
amps, volts and ohms)
12 Stroboscope (for
dynamic timing checks)
13 Hose clamp
(wingnut type shown)

14 Clutch holding tool
15 One-man brake/clutch
bleeder kit

Special tools

 1
 4
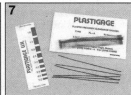 7
 10
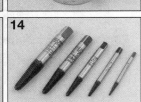 13

 2
 5
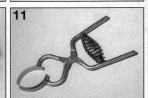 8
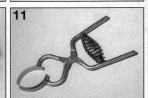 11
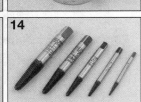 14

 3
 6
 9
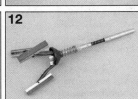 12
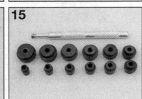 15

1 Micrometers
(external type)
2 Telescoping gauges
3 Dial gauge

4 Cylinder
compression gauge
5 Vacuum gauges (left) or
manometer (right)
6 Oil pressure gauge

7 Plastigage kit
8 Valve spring compressor
(4-stroke engines)
9 Piston pin drawbolt tool

10 Piston ring removal and
installation tool
11 Piston ring clamp
12 Cylinder bore hone
(stone type shown)

13 Stud extractor
14 Screw extractor set
15 Bearing driver set

1 Workshop equipment and facilities

The workbench

● Work is made much easier by raising the bike up on a ramp - components are much more accessible if raised to waist level. The hydraulic or pneumatic types seen in the dealer's workshop are a sound investment if you undertake a lot of repairs or overhauls **(see illustration 1.1)**.

1.1 Hydraulic motorcycle ramp

● If raised off ground level, the bike must be supported on the ramp to avoid it falling. Most ramps incorporate a front wheel locating clamp which can be adjusted to suit different diameter wheels. When tightening the clamp, take care not to mark the wheel rim or damage the tire - use wood blocks on each side to prevent this.
● Secure the bike to the ramp using tie-downs **(see illustration 1.2)**. If the bike has only a sidestand, and hence leans at a dangerous angle when raised, support the bike on an auxiliary stand.

1.2 Tie-downs are used around the passenger footrests to secure the bike

● Auxiliary (paddock) stands are widely available from mail order companies or motorcycle dealers and attach either to the wheel axle or swingarm pivot **(see illustration 1.3)**. If the motorcycle has a centerstand, you can support it under the crankcase to prevent it toppling while either wheel is removed **(see illustration 1.4)**.

1.3 This auxiliary stand attaches to the swingarm pivot

1.4 Always use a block of wood between the engine and jack head when supporting the engine in this way

Fumes and fire

● Refer to the Safety first! page at the beginning of the manual for full details. Make sure your workshop is equipped with a fire extinguisher suitable for fuel-related fires (Class B fire - flammable liquids) - it is not sufficient to have a water-filled extinguisher.
● Always ensure adequate ventilation is available. Unless an exhaust gas extraction system is available for use, ensure that the engine is run outside of the workshop.
● If working on the fuel system, make sure the workshop is ventilated to avoid a build-up of fumes. This applies equally to fume build-up when charging a battery. Do not smoke or allow anyone else to smoke in the workshop.

Fluids

● If you need to drain fuel from the tank, store it in an approved container marked as suitable for the storage of gasoline **(see illustration 1.5)**. Do not store fuel in glass jars

1.5 Use an approved can only for storing gasoline

or bottles.
● Use proprietary engine degreasers or solvents which have a high flash-point, such as kerosene, for cleaning off oil, grease and dirt - never use gasoline for cleaning. Wear rubber gloves when handling solvent and engine degreaser. The fumes from certain solvents can be dangerous - always work in a well-ventilated area.

Dust, eye and hand protection

● Protect your lungs from inhalation of dust particles by wearing a filtering mask over the nose and mouth. Many frictional materials still contain asbestos which is dangerous to your health. Protect your eyes from spouts of liquid and sprung components by wearing a pair of protective

1.6 A fire extinguisher, goggles, mask and protective gloves should be at hand in the workshop

goggles **(see illustration 1.6)**.
● Protect your hands from contact with solvents, fuel and oils by wearing rubber gloves. Alternatively apply a barrier cream to your hands before starting work. If handling hot components or fluids, wear suitable gloves to protect your hands from scalding and burns.

What to do with old fluids

● Old cleaning solvent, fuel, coolant and oils should not be poured down domestic drains or onto the ground. Package the fluid up in old oil containers, label it accordingly, and take it to a garage or disposal facility. Contact your local disposal company for location of such sites.

Note: It is illegal to dump oil down the drain. Check with your local auto parts store, disposal facility or environmental agency to see if they accept the oil for recycling.

2 Fasteners -
screws, bolts and nuts

Fastener types and applications

Bolts and screws

● Fastener head types are either of hexagonal, Torx or splined design, with internal and external versions of each type **(see illustrations 2.1 and 2.2)**; splined head fasteners are not in common use on motorcycles. The conventional slotted or Phillips head design is used for certain screws. Bolt or screw length is always measured from the underside of the head to the end of the item **(see illustration 2.11)**.

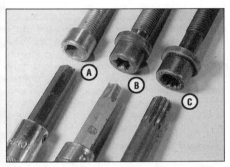

2.1 Internal hexagon/Allen (A), Torx (B) and splined (C) fasteners, with corresponding bits

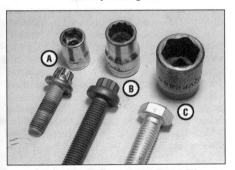

2.2 External Torx (A), splined (B) and hexagon (C) fasteners, with corresponding sockets

● Certain fasteners on the motorcycle have a tensile marking on their heads, the higher the marking the stronger the fastener. High tensile fasteners generally carry a 10 or higher marking. Never replace a high tensile fastener with one of a lower tensile strength.

Washers (see illustration 2.3)

● Plain washers are used between a fastener head and a component to prevent damage to the component or to spread the load when torque is applied. Plain washers can also be used as spacers or shims in certain assemblies. Copper or aluminum plain washers are often used as sealing washers on drain plugs.

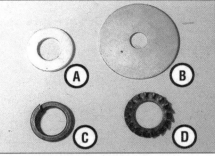

2.3 Plain washer (A), penny washer (B), spring washer (C) and serrated washer (D)

● The split-ring spring washer works by applying axial tension between the fastener head and component. If flattened, it is fatigued and must be replaced. If a plain (flat) washer is used on the fastener, position the spring washer between the fastener and the plain washer.
● Serrated star type washers dig into the fastener and component faces, preventing loosening. They are often used on electrical ground connections to the frame.
● Cone type washers (sometimes called Belleville) are conical and when tightened apply axial tension between the fastener head and component. They must be installed with the dished side against the component and often carry an OUTSIDE marking on their outer face. If flattened, they are fatigued and must be replaced.
● Tab washers are used to lock plain nuts or bolts on a shaft. A portion of the tab washer is bent up hard against one flat of the nut or bolt to prevent it loosening. Due to the tab washer being deformed in use, a new tab washer should be used every time it is removed.
● Wave washers are used to take up endfloat on a shaft. They provide light springing and prevent excessive side-to-side play of a component. Can be found on rocker arm shafts.

Nuts and cotter pins

● Conventional plain nuts are usually six-sided **(see illustration 2.4)**. They are sized by thread diameter and pitch. High tensile nuts carry a number on one end to denote their tensile strength.

2.4 Plain nut (A), shouldered locknut (B), nylon insert nut (C) and castellated nut (D)

● Self-locking nuts either have a nylon insert, or two spring metal tabs, or a shoulder which is staked into a groove in the shaft - their advantage over conventional plain nuts is a resistance to loosening due to vibration. The nylon insert type can be used a number of times, but must be replaced when the friction of the nylon insert is reduced, ie when the nut spins freely on the shaft. The spring tab type can be reused unless the tabs are damaged. The shouldered type must be replaced every time it is removed.
● Cotter pins are used to lock a castellated nut to a shaft or to prevent loosening of a plain nut. Common applications are wheel axles and brake torque arms. Because the cotter pin arms are deformed to lock around the nut a new cotter pin must always be used on installation - always use the correct size cotter pin which will fit snugly in the shaft hole. Make sure the cotter pin arms are correctly located around the nut **(see illustrations 2.5 and 2.6)**.

2.5 Bend cotter pin arms as shown (arrows) to secure a castellated nut

2.6 Bend cotter pin arms as shown to secure a plain nut

Caution: If the castellated nut slots do not align with the shaft hole after tightening to the torque setting, tighten the nut until the next slot aligns with the hole - never loosen the nut to align its slot.

● R-pins (shaped like the letter R), or slip pins as they are sometimes called, are sprung and can be reused if they are otherwise in good condition. Always install R-pins with their closed end facing forwards **(see illustration 2.7)**.

**2.7 Correct fitting of R-pin.
Arrow indicates forward direction**

Snap-rings (see illustration 2.8)

● Snap-rings (sometimes called snap-rings) are used to retain components on a shaft or in a housing and have corresponding external or internal ears to permit removal. Parallel-sided (machined) snap-rings can be installed either way round in their groove, whereas stamped snap-rings (which have a chamfered edge on one face) must be installed with the chamfer facing away from the direction of thrust load **(see illustration 2.9)**.

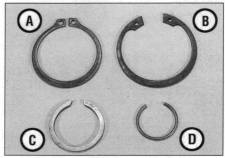

2.8 External stamped snap-ring (A), internal stamped snap-ring (B), machined snap-ring (C) and wire snap-ring (D)

● Always use snap-ring pliers to remove and install snap-rings; expand or compress them just enough to remove them. After installation, rotate the snap-ring in its groove to ensure it is securely seated. If installing a snap-ring on a splined shaft, always align its opening with a shaft channel to ensure the snap-ring ends are well supported and unlikely to catch **(see illustration 2.10)**.

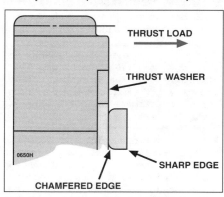

2.9 Correct fitting of a stamped snap-ring

THRUST LOAD

THRUST WASHER

SHARP EDGE

CHAMFERED EDGE

0650H

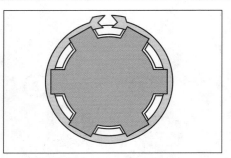

**2.10 Align snap-ring opening
with shaft channel**

● Snap-rings can wear due to the thrust of components and become loose in their grooves, with the subsequent danger of becoming dislodged in operation. For this reason, replacement is advised every time a snap-ring is disturbed.

● Wire snap-rings are commonly used as piston pin retaining clips. If a removal tang is provided, long-nosed pliers can be used to dislodge them, otherwise careful use of a small flat-bladed screwdriver is necessary. Wire snap-rings should be replaced every time they are disturbed.

Thread diameter and pitch

● Diameter of a male thread (screw, bolt or stud) is the outside diameter of the threaded portion **(see illustration 2.11)**. Most motorcycle manufacturers use the ISO (International Standards Organization) metric system expressed in millimeters. For example, M6 refers to a 6 mm diameter thread. Sizing is the same for nuts, except that the thread diameter is measured across the valleys of the nut.

● Pitch is the distance between the peaks of the thread **(see illustration 2.11)**. It is expressed in millimeters, thus a common bolt size may be expressed as 6.0 x 1.0 mm (6 mm thread diameter and 1 mm pitch). Generally pitch increases in proportion to thread diameter, although there are always exceptions.

● Thread diameter and pitch are related for conventional fastener applications and the accompanying table can be used as a guide. Additionally, the AF (Across Flats), wrench or socket size dimension of the bolt or nut **(see illustration 2.11)** is linked to thread and pitch specification. Thread pitch can be measured with a thread gauge **(see illustration 2.12)**.

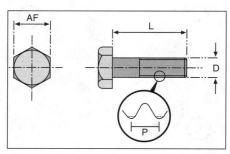

AF

L

D

P

2.11 Fastener length (L), thread diameter (D), thread pitch (P) and head size (AF)

**2.12 Using a thread gauge
to measure pitch**

AF size	Thread diameter x pitch (mm)
8 mm	M5 x 0.8
8 mm	M6 x 1.0
10 mm	M6 x 1.0
12 mm	M8 x 1.25
14 mm	M10 x 1.25
17 mm	M12 x 1.25

● The threads of most fasteners are of the right-hand type, ie they are turned clockwise to tighten and counterclockwise to loosen. The reverse situation applies to left-hand thread fasteners, which are turned counterclockwise to tighten and clockwise to loosen. Left-hand threads are used where rotation of a component might loosen a conventional right-hand thread fastener.

Seized fasteners

● Corrosion of external fasteners due to water or reaction between two dissimilar metals can occur over a period of time. It will build up sooner in wet conditions or in countries where salt is used on the roads during the winter. If a fastener is severely corroded it is likely that normal methods of removal will fail and result in its head being ruined. When you attempt removal, the fastener thread should be heard to crack free and unscrew easily - if it doesn't, stop there before damaging something.

● A smart tap on the head of the fastener will often succeed in breaking free corrosion which has occurred in the threads **(see illustration 2.13)**.

● An aerosol penetrating fluid (such as WD-40) applied the night beforehand may work its way down into the thread and ease removal. Depending on the location, you may be able to make up a modeling-clay well around the fastener head and fill it with penetrating fluid.

2.13 A sharp tap on the head of a fastener will often break free a corroded thread

● If you are working on an engine internal component, corrosion will most likely not be a problem due to the well lubricated environment. However, components can be very tight and an impact driver is a useful tool in freeing them **(see illustration 2.14)**.

2.14 Using an impact driver to free a fastener

● Where corrosion has occurred between dissimilar metals (eg steel and aluminum alloy), the application of heat to the fastener head will create a disproportionate expansion rate between the two metals and break the seizure caused by the corrosion. Whether heat can be applied depends on the location of the fastener - any surrounding components likely to be damaged must first be removed **(see illustration 2.15)**. Heat can be applied using a paint stripper heat gun or clothes iron, or by immersing the component in boiling water - wear protective gloves to prevent scalding or burns to the hands.

2.15 Using heat to free a seized fastener

● As a last resort, it is possible to use a hammer and cold chisel to work the fastener head unscrewed **(see illustration 2.16)**. This will damage the fastener, but more importantly extreme care must be taken not to damage the surrounding component.

Caution: Remember that the component being secured is generally of more value than the bolt, nut or screw - when the fastener is freed, do not unscrew it with force, instead work the fastener back and forth when resistance is felt to prevent thread damage.

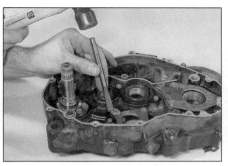

2.16 Using a hammer and chisel to free a seized fastener

Broken fasteners and damaged heads

● If the shank of a broken bolt or screw is accessible you can grip it with self-locking grips. The knurled wheel type stud extractor tool or self-gripping stud puller tool is particularly useful for removing the long studs which screw into the cylinder mouth surface of the crankcase or bolts and screws from which the head has broken off **(see illustration 2.17)**. Studs can also be removed by locking two nuts together on the threaded end of the stud and using a wrench on the lower nut **(see illustration 2.18)**.

2.17 Using a stud extractor tool to remove a broken crankcase stud

2.18 Two nuts can be locked together to unscrew a stud from a component

● A bolt or screw which has broken off below or level with the casing must be extracted using a screw extractor set. Centerpunch the fastener to centralize the drill bit, then drill a hole in the fastener **(see illustration 2.19)**. Select a drill bit which is approximately half to three-quarters the

2.19 When using a screw extractor, first drill a hole in the fastener . . .

diameter of the fastener and drill to a depth which will accommodate the extractor. Use the largest size extractor possible, but avoid leaving too small a wall thickness otherwise the extractor will merely force the fastener walls outwards wedging it in the casing thread.

● If a spiral type extractor is used, thread it counterclockwise into the fastener. As it is screwed in, it will grip the fastener and unscrew it from the casing **(see illustration 2.20)**.

2.20 . . . then thread the extractor counterclockwise into the fastener

● If a taper type extractor is used, tap it into the fastener so that it is firmly wedged in place. Unscrew the extractor (counter-clockwise) to draw the fastener out.

 Warning: Stud extractors are very hard and may break off in the fastener if care is not taken - ask a machine shop about spark erosion if this happens.

● Alternatively, the broken bolt/screw can be drilled out and the hole retapped for an oversize bolt/screw or a diamond-section thread insert. It is essential that the drilling is carried out squarely and to the correct depth, otherwise the casing may be ruined - if in doubt, entrust the work to a machine shop.

● Bolts and nuts with rounded corners cause the correct size wrench or socket to slip when force is applied. Of the types of wrench/socket available always use a six-point type rather than an eight or twelve-point type - better grip

2.21 Comparison of surface drive box wrench (left) with 12-point type (right)

is obtained. Surface drive wrenches grip the middle of the hex flats, rather than the corners, and are thus good in cases of damaged heads **(see illustration 2.21)**.

● Slotted-head or Phillips-head screws are often damaged by the use of the wrong size screwdriver. Allen-head and Torx-head screws are much less likely to sustain damage. If enough of the screw head is exposed you can use a hacksaw to cut a slot in its head and then use a conventional flat-bladed screwdriver to remove it. Alternatively use a hammer and cold chisel to tap the head of the fastener around to loosen it. Always replace damaged fasteners with new ones, preferably Torx or Allen-head type.

HAYNES
HiNT

A dab of valve grinding compound between the screw head and screwdriver tip will often give a good grip.

Thread repair

● Threads (particularly those in aluminum alloy components) can be damaged by overtightening, being assembled with dirt in the threads, or from a component working loose and vibrating. Eventually the thread will fail completely, and it will be impossible to tighten the fastener.

● If a thread is damaged or clogged with old locking compound it can be renovated with a thread repair tool (thread chaser) **(see illustrations 2.22 and 2.23)**; special thread

2.22 A thread repair tool being used to correct an internal thread

2.23 A thread repair tool being used to correct an external thread

chasers are available for spark plug hole threads. The tool will not cut a new thread, but clean and true the original thread. Make sure that you use the correct diameter and pitch tool. Similarly, external threads can be cleaned up with a die or a thread restorer file **(see illustration 2.24)**.

2.24 Using a thread restorer file

● It is possible to drill out the old thread and retap the component to the next thread size. This will work where there is enough surrounding material and a new bolt or screw can be obtained. Sometimes, however, this is not possible - such as where the bolt/screw passes through another component which must also be suitably modified, also in cases where a spark plug or oil drain plug cannot be obtained in a larger diameter thread size.

● The diamond-section thread insert (often known by its popular trade name of Heli-Coil) is a simple and effective method of replacing the thread and retaining the original size. A kit can be purchased which contains the tap, insert and installing tool **(see illustration 2.25)**. Drill out the damaged thread with the size drill specified **(see illustration 2.26)**. Carefully retap the thread **(see illustration 2.27)**. Install the

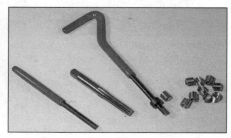

2.25 Obtain a thread insert kit to suit the thread diameter and pitch required

2.26 To install a thread insert, first drill out the original thread . . .

2.27 . . . tap a new thread . . .

2.28 . . . fit insert on the installing tool . . .

2.29 . . . and thread into the component . . .

2.30 . . . break off the tang when complete

insert on the installing tool and thread it slowly into place using a light downward pressure **(see illustrations 2.28 and 2.29)**. When positioned between a 1/4 and 1/2 turn below the surface withdraw the installing tool and use the break-off tool to press down on the tang, breaking it off **(see illustration 2.30)**.

● There are epoxy thread repair kits on the market which can rebuild stripped internal threads, although this repair should not be used on high load-bearing components.

Thread locking and sealing compounds

● Locking compounds are used in locations where the fastener is prone to loosening due to vibration or on important safety-related items which might cause loss of control of the motorcycle if they fail. It is also used where important fasteners cannot be secured by other means such as lockwashers or cotter pins.

● Before applying locking compound, make sure that the threads (internal and external) are clean and dry with all old compound removed. Select a compound to suit the component being secured - a non-permanent general locking and sealing type is suitable for most applications, but a high strength type is needed for permanent fixing of studs in castings. Apply a drop or two of the compound to the first few threads of the fastener, then thread it into place and tighten to the specified torque. Do not apply excessive thread locking compound otherwise the thread may be damaged on subsequent removal.

● Certain fasteners are impregnated with a dry film type coating of locking compound on their threads. Always replace this type of fastener if disturbed.

● Anti-seize compounds, such as copper-based greases, can be applied to protect threads from seizure due to extreme heat and corrosion. A common instance is spark plug threads and exhaust system fasteners.

3 Measuring tools and gauges

Feeler gauges

● Feeler gauges (or blades) are used for measuring small gaps and clearances **(see illustration 3.1)**. They can also be used to measure endfloat (sideplay) of a component on a shaft where access is not possible with a dial gauge.

● Feeler gauge sets should be treated with care and not bent or damaged. They are etched with their size on one face. Keep them clean and very lightly oiled to prevent corrosion build-up.

3.1 Feeler gauges are used for measuring small gaps and clearances - thickness is marked on one face of gauge

● When measuring a clearance, select a gauge which is a light sliding fit between the two components. You may need to use two gauges together to measure the clearance accurately.

Micrometers

● A micrometer is a precision tool capable of measuring to 0.01 or 0.001 of a millimeter. It should always be stored in its case and not in the general toolbox. It must be kept clean and never dropped, otherwise its frame or measuring anvils could be distorted resulting in inaccurate readings.

● External micrometers are used for measuring outside diameters of components and have many more applications than internal micrometers. Micrometers are available in different size ranges, typically 0 to 25 mm, 25 to 50 mm, and upwards in 25 mm steps; some large micrometers have interchangeable anvils to allow a range of measurements to be taken. Generally the largest precision measurement you are likely to take on a motorcycle is the piston diameter.

● Internal micrometers (or bore micrometers) are used for measuring inside diameters, such as valve guides and cylinder bores. Telescoping gauges and small hole gauges are used in conjunction with an external micrometer, whereas the more expensive internal micrometers have their own measuring device.

External micrometer

Note: *The conventional analogue type instrument is described. Although much easier to read, digital micrometers are considerably more expensive.*

● Always check the calibration of the micrometer before use. With the anvils closed (0 to 25 mm type) or set over a test gauge (for

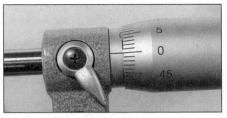

3.2 Check micrometer calibration before use

the larger types) the scale should read zero **(see illustration 3.2)**; make sure that the anvils (and test piece) are clean first. Any discrepancy can be adjusted by referring to the instructions supplied with the tool. Remember that the micrometer is a precision measuring tool - don't force the anvils closed, use the ratchet (4) on the end of the micrometer to close it. In this way, a measured force is always applied.

● To use, first make sure that the item being measured is clean. Place the anvil of the micrometer (1) against the item and use the thimble (2) to bring the spindle (3) lightly into contact with the other side of the item **(see illustration 3.3)**. Don't tighten the thimble down because this will damage the micrometer - instead use the ratchet (4) on the end of the micrometer. The ratchet mechanism applies a measured force preventing damage to the instrument.

● The micrometer is read by referring to the linear scale on the sleeve and the annular scale on the thimble. Read off the sleeve first to obtain the base measurement, then add the fine measurement from the thimble to obtain the overall reading. The linear scale on the sleeve represents the measuring range of the micrometer (eg 0 to 25 mm). The annular scale

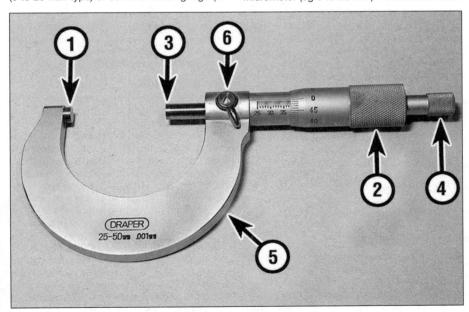

3.3 Micrometer component parts

| 1 | Anvil | 3 | Spindle | 5 | Frame |
| 2 | Thimble | 4 | Ratchet | 6 | Locking lever |

on the thimble will be in graduations of 0.01 mm (or as marked on the frame) - one full revolution of the thimble will move 0.5 mm on the linear scale. Take the reading where the datum line on the sleeve intersects the thimble's scale. Always position the eye directly above the scale otherwise an inaccurate reading will result.

In the example shown the item measures 2.95 mm **(see illustration 3.4)**:

Linear scale	2.00 mm
Linear scale	0.50 mm
Annular scale	0.45 mm
Total figure	**2.95 mm**

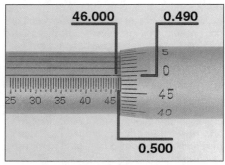

3.5 Micrometer reading of 46.99 mm on linear and annular scales . . .

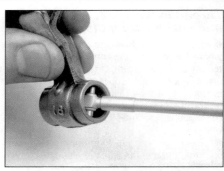

3.7 Expand the telescoping gauge in the bore, lock its position . . .

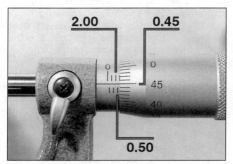

3.4 Micrometer reading of 2.95 mm

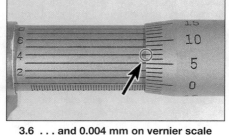

3.6 . . . and 0.004 mm on vernier scale

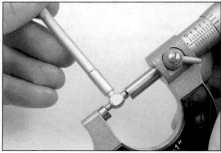

3.8 . . . then measure the gauge with a micrometer

Most micrometers have a locking lever (6) on the frame to hold the setting in place, allowing the item to be removed from the micrometer.
● Some micrometers have a vernier scale on their sleeve, providing an even finer measurement to be taken, in 0.001 increments of a millimeter. Take the sleeve and thimble measurement as described above, then check which graduation on the vernier scale aligns with that of the annular scale on the thimble **Note:** *The eye must be perpendicular to the scale when taking the vernier reading - if necessary rotate the body of the micrometer to ensure this.* Multiply the vernier scale figure by 0.001 and add it to the base and fine measurement figures.

In the example shown the item measures 46.994 mm **(see illustrations 3.5 and 3.6)**:

Linear scale (base)	46.000 mm
Linear scale (base)	00.500 mm
Annular scale (fine)	00.490 mm
Vernier scale	00.004 mm
Total figure	**46.994 mm**

Internal micrometer

● Internal micrometers are available for measuring bore diameters, but are expensive and unlikely to be available for home use. It is suggested that a set of telescoping gauges and small hole gauges, both of which must be used with an external micrometer, will suffice for taking internal measurements on a motorcycle.
● Telescoping gauges can be used to

measure internal diameters of components. Select a gauge with the correct size range, make sure its ends are clean and insert it into the bore. Expand the gauge, then lock its position and withdraw it from the bore **(see illustration 3.7)**. Measure across the gauge ends with a micrometer **(see illustration 3.8)**.
● Very small diameter bores (such as valve guides) are measured with a small hole gauge. Once adjusted to a slip-fit inside the component, its position is locked and the gauge withdrawn for measurement with a micrometer **(see illustrations 3.9 and 3.10)**.

Vernier caliper

Note: *The conventional linear and dial gauge type instruments are described. Digital types are easier to read, but are far more expensive.*
● The vernier caliper does not provide the precision of a micrometer, but is versatile in being able to measure internal and external diameters. Some types also incorporate a depth gauge. It is ideal for measuring clutch plate friction material and spring free lengths.
● To use the conventional linear scale vernier, loosen off the vernier clamp screws (1) and set its jaws over (2), or inside (3), the item to be measured **(see illustration 3.11)**. Slide the jaw into contact, using the thumbwheel (4) for fine movement of the sliding scale (5) then tighten the clamp screws (1). Read off the main scale (6) where the zero on the sliding scale (5) intersects it, taking the whole number to the left of the zero; this provides the base measurement. View along the sliding scale and select the division which

3.9 Expand the small hole gauge in the bore, lock its position . . .

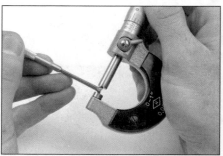

3.10 . . . then measure the gauge with a micrometer

lines up exactly with any of the divisions on the main scale, noting that the divisions usually represents 0.02 of a millimeter. Add this fine measurement to the base measurement to obtain the total reading.

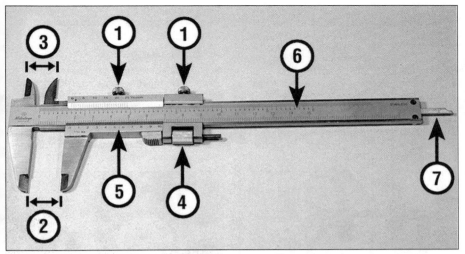

3.11 Vernier component parts (linear gauge)

1	Clamp screws	3	Internal jaws	5	Sliding scale	7	Depth gauge
2	External jaws	4	Thumbwheel	6	Main scale		

In the example shown the item measures 55.92 mm **(see illustration 3.12)**:

Base measurement	55.00 mm
Fine measurement	00.92 mm
Total figure	**55.92 mm**

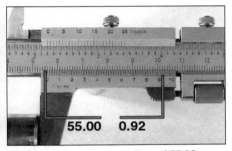

3.12 Vernier gauge reading of 55.92 mm

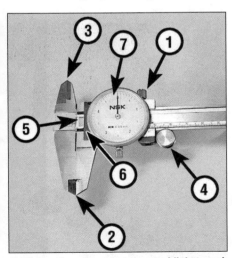

3.13 Vernier component parts (dial gauge)

1	Clamp screw	5	Main scale
2	External jaws	6	Sliding scale
3	Internal jaws	7	Dial gauge
4	Thumbwheel		

● Some vernier calipers are equipped with a dial gauge for fine measurement. Before use, check that the jaws are clean, then close them fully and check that the dial gauge reads zero. If necessary adjust the gauge ring accordingly. Slacken the vernier clamp screw (1) and set its jaws over (2), or inside (3), the item to be measured **(see illustration 3.13)**. Slide the jaws into contact, using the thumbwheel (4) for fine movement. Read off the main scale (5) where the edge of the sliding scale (6) intersects it, taking the whole number to the left of the zero; this provides the base measurement. Read off the needle position on the dial gauge (7) scale to provide the fine measurement; each division represents 0.05 of a millimeter. Add this fine measurement to the base measurement to obtain the total reading.

In the example shown the item measures 55.95 mm **(see illustration 3.14)**:

Base measurement	55.00 mm
Fine measurement	00.95 mm
Total figure	**55.95 mm**

3.14 Vernier gauge reading of 55.95 mm

Plastigage

● Plastigage is a plastic material which can be compressed between two surfaces to measure the oil clearance between them. The width of the compressed Plastigage is measured against a calibrated scale to determine the clearance.

● Common uses of Plastigage are for measuring the clearance between crankshaft journal and main bearing inserts, between crankshaft journal and big-end bearing inserts, and between camshaft and bearing surfaces. The following example describes big-end oil clearance measurement.

● Handle the Plastigage material carefully to prevent distortion. Using a sharp knife, cut a length which corresponds with the width of the bearing being measured and place it carefully across the journal so that it is parallel with the shaft **(see illustration 3.15)**. Carefully install both bearing shells and the connecting rod. Without rotating the rod on the journal tighten its bolts or nuts (as applicable) to the specified torque. The connecting rod and bearings are then disassembled and the crushed Plastigage examined.

3.15 Plastigage placed across shaft journal

● Using the scale provided in the Plastigage kit, measure the width of the material to determine the oil clearance **(see illustration 3.16)**. Always remove all traces of Plastigage after use using your fingernails.

Caution: Arriving at the correct clearance demands that the assembly is torqued correctly, according to the settings and sequence (where applicable) provided by the motorcycle manufacturer.

3.16 Measuring the width of the crushed Plastigage

Dial gauge or DTI (Dial Test Indicator)

● A dial gauge can be used to accurately measure small amounts of movement. Typical uses are measuring shaft runout or shaft endfloat (sideplay) and setting piston position for ignition timing on two-strokes. A dial gauge set usually comes with a range of different probes and adapters and mounting equipment.

● The gauge needle must point to zero when at rest. Rotate the ring around its periphery to zero the gauge.

● Check that the gauge is capable of reading the extent of movement in the work. Most gauges have a small dial set in the face which records whole millimeters of movement as well as the fine scale around the face periphery which is calibrated in 0.01 mm divisions. Read off the small dial first to obtain the base measurement, then add the measurement from the fine scale to obtain the total reading.

In the example shown the gauge reads 1.48 mm (see illustration 3.17):

Base measurement	1.00 mm
Fine measurement	0.48 mm
Total figure	**1.48 mm**

3.17 Dial gauge reading of 1.48 mm

● If measuring shaft runout, the shaft must be supported in vee-blocks and the gauge mounted on a stand perpendicular to the shaft. Rest the tip of the gauge against the center of the shaft and rotate the shaft slowly while watching the gauge reading (see illustration 3.18). Take several measurements along the length of the shaft and record the

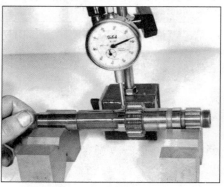

3.18 Using a dial gauge to measure shaft runout

maximum gauge reading as the amount of runout in the shaft. **Note:** *The reading obtained will be total runout at that point - some manufacturers specify that the runout figure is halved to compare with their specified runout limit.*

● Endfloat (sideplay) measurement requires that the gauge is mounted securely to the surrounding component with its probe touching the end of the shaft. Using hand pressure, push and pull on the shaft noting the maximum endfloat recorded on the gauge (see illustration 3.19).

3.19 Using a dial gauge to measure shaft endfloat

● A dial gauge with suitable adapters can be used to determine piston position BTDC on two-stroke engines for the purposes of ignition timing. The gauge, adapter and suitable length probe are installed in the place of the spark plug and the gauge zeroed at TDC. If the piston position is specified as 1.14 mm BTDC, rotate the engine back to 2.00 mm BTDC, then slowly forwards to 1.14 mm BTDC.

Cylinder compression gauges

● A compression gauge is used for measuring cylinder compression. Either the rubber-cone type or the threaded adapter type can be used. The latter is preferred to ensure a perfect seal against the cylinder head. A 0 to 300 psi (0 to 20 Bar) type gauge (for gasoline engines) will be suitable for motorcycles.

● The spark plug is removed and the gauge either held hard against the cylinder head (cone type) or the gauge adapter screwed into the cylinder head (threaded type) (see illustration 3.20). Cylinder compression is measured with the engine turning over, but not running - carry out the compression test as described in

3.20 Using a rubber-cone type cylinder compression gauge

Troubleshooting Equipment. The gauge will hold the reading until manually released.

Oil pressure gauge

● An oil pressure gauge is used for measuring engine oil pressure. Most gauges come with a set of adapters to fit the thread of the take-off point (see illustration 3.21). If the take-off point specified by the motorcycle manufacturer is an external oil pipe union, make sure that the specified replacement union is used to prevent oil starvation.

3.21 Oil pressure gauge and take-off point adapter (arrow)

● Oil pressure is measured with the engine running (at a specific rpm) and often the manufacturer will specify pressure limits for a cold and hot engine.

Straight-edge and surface plate

● If checking the gasket face of a component for warpage, place a steel rule or precision straight-edge across the gasket face and measure any gap between the straight-edge and component with feeler gauges (see illustration 3.22). Check diagonally across the component and between mounting holes (see illustration 3.23).

3.22 Use a straight-edge and feeler gauges to check for warpage

3.23 Check for warpage in these directions

● Checking individual components for warpage, such as clutch plain (metal) plates, requires a perfectly flat plate or piece of plate glass and feeler gauges.

4 Torque and leverage

What is torque?

● Torque describes the twisting force around a shaft. The amount of torque applied is determined by the distance from the center of the shaft to the end of the lever and the amount of force being applied to the end of the lever; distance multiplied by force equals torque.

● The manufacturer applies a measured torque to a bolt or nut to ensure that it will not loosen in use and to hold two components securely together without movement in the joint. The actual torque setting depends on the thread size, bolt or nut material and the composition of the components being held.

● Too little torque may cause the fastener to loosen due to vibration, whereas too much torque will distort the joint faces of the component or cause the fastener to shear off. Always stick to the specified torque setting.

Using a torque wrench

● Check the calibration of the torque wrench and make sure it has a suitable range for the job. Torque wrenches are available in Nm (Newton-meters), kgf m (kilograms-force meter), lbf ft (pounds-feet), lbf in (inch-pounds). Do not confuse lbf ft with lbf in.

● Adjust the tool to the desired torque on the scale **(see illustration 4.1)**. If your torque wrench is not calibrated in the units specified, carefully convert the figure (see *Conversion Factors*). A manufacturer sometimes gives a torque setting as a range (8 to 10 Nm) rather than a single figure - in this case set the tool midway between the two settings. The same torque may be expressed as 9 Nm ± 1 Nm. Some torque wrenches have a method of locking the setting so that it isn't inadvertently altered during use.

4.1 Set the torque wrench index mark to the setting required, in this case 12 Nm

● Install the bolts/nuts in their correct location and secure them lightly. Their threads must be clean and free of any old locking compound. Unless specified the threads and flange should be dry - oiled threads are necessary in certain circumstances and the manufacturer will take this into account in the specified torque figure. Similarly, the manufacturer may also specify the application of thread-locking compound.

● Tighten the fasteners in the specified sequence until the torque wrench clicks, indicating that the torque setting has been reached. Apply the torque again to double-check the setting. Where different thread diameter fasteners secure the component, as a rule tighten the larger diameter ones first.

● When the torque wrench has been finished with, release the lock (where applicable) and fully back off its setting to zero - do not leave the torque wrench tensioned. Also, do not use a torque wrench for loosening a fastener.

Angle-tightening

● Manufacturers often specify a figure in degrees for final tightening of a fastener. This usually follows tightening to a specific torque setting.

● A degree disc can be set and attached to the socket **(see illustration 4.2)** or a protractor can be used to mark the angle of movement on the bolt/nut head and the surrounding casting **(see illustration 4.3)**.

4.2 Angle tightening can be accomplished with a torque-angle gauge . . .

4.3 . . . or by marking the angle on the surrounding component

Loosening sequences

● Where more than one bolt/nut secures a component, loosen each fastener evenly a little at a time. In this way, not all the stress of the joint is held by one fastener and the components are not likely to distort.

● If a tightening sequence is provided, work in the REVERSE of this, but if not, work from the outside in, in a criss-cross sequence **(see illustration 4.4)**.

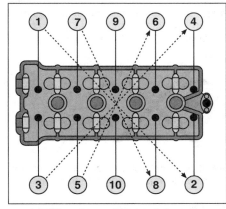

4.4 When loosening, work from the outside inwards

Tightening sequences

● If a component is held by more than one fastener it is important that the retaining bolts/nuts are tightened evenly to prevent uneven stress build-up and distortion of sealing faces. This is especially important on high-compression joints such as the cylinder head.

● A sequence is usually provided by the manufacturer, either in a diagram or actually marked in the casting. If not, always start in the center and work outwards in a criss-cross pattern **(see illustration 4.5)**. Start off by securing all bolts/nuts finger-tight, then set the torque wrench and tighten each fastener by a small amount in sequence until the final torque is reached. By following this practice,

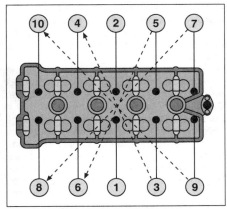

4.5 When tightening, work from the inside outwards

the joint will be held evenly and will not be distorted. Important joints, such as the cylinder head and big-end fasteners often have two- or three-stage torque settings.

Applying leverage

● Use tools at the correct angle. Position a socket or wrench on the bolt/nut so that you pull it towards you when loosening. If this can't be done, push the wrench without curling your fingers around it **(see illustration 4.6)** - the wrench may slip or the fastener loosen suddenly, resulting in your fingers being crushed against a component.

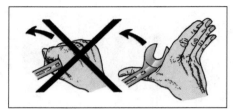

4.6 If you can't pull on the wrench to loosen a fastener, push with your hand open

● Additional leverage is gained by extending the length of the lever. The best way to do this is to use a breaker bar instead of the regular length tool, or to slip a length of tubing over the end of the wrench or socket.
● If additional leverage will not work, the fastener head is either damaged or firmly corroded in place (see *Fasteners*).

5 Bearings

Bearing removal and installation

Drivers and sockets

● Before removing a bearing, always inspect the casing to see which way it must be driven out - some casings will have retaining plates or a cast step. Also check for any identifying markings on the bearing and, if installed to a certain depth, measure this at this stage. Some roller bearings are sealed on one side - take note of the original installed position.
● Bearings can be driven out of a casing using a bearing driver tool (with the correct size head) or a socket of the correct diameter. Select the driver head or socket so that it contacts the outer race of the bearing, not the balls/rollers or inner race. Always support the casing around the bearing housing with wood blocks, otherwise there is a risk of fracture. The bearing is driven out with a few blows on the driver or socket from a heavy mallet. Unless access is severely restricted (as with wheel bearings), a pin-punch is not recommended unless it is moved around the bearing to keep it square in its housing.

● The same equipment can be used to install bearings. Make sure the bearing housing is supported on wood blocks and line up the bearing in its housing. Install the bearing as noted on removal - generally they are installed with their marked side facing outwards. Tap the bearing squarely into its housing using a driver or socket which bears only on the bearing's outer race - contact with the bearing balls/rollers or inner race will destroy it **(see illustrations 5.1 and 5.2)**.
● Check that the bearing inner race and balls/rollers rotate freely.

5.1 Using a bearing driver against the bearing's outer race

5.2 Using a large socket against the bearing's outer race

Pullers and slide-hammers

● Where a bearing is pressed on a shaft a puller will be required to extract it **(see illustration 5.3)**. Make sure that the puller clamp or legs fit securely behind the bearing and are unlikely to slip out. If pulling a bearing

5.3 This bearing puller clamps behind the bearing and pressure is applied to the shaft end to draw the bearing off

off a gear shaft for example, you may have to locate the puller behind a gear pinion if there is no access to the race and draw the gear pinion off the shaft as well **(see illustration 5.4)**.

> *Caution: Ensure that the puller's center bolt locates securely against the end of the shaft and will not slip when pressure is applied. Also ensure that puller does not damage the shaft end.*

5.4 Where no access is available to the rear of the bearing, it is sometimes possible to draw off the adjacent component

● Operate the puller so that its center bolt exerts pressure on the shaft end and draws the bearing off the shaft.
● When installing the bearing on the shaft, tap only on the bearing's inner race - contact with the balls/rollers or outer race will destroy the bearing. Use a socket or length of tubing as a drift which fits over the shaft end **(see illustration 5.5)**.

5.5 When installing a bearing on a shaft use a piece of tubing which bears only on the bearing's inner race

● Where a bearing locates in a blind hole in a casing, it cannot be driven or pulled out as described above. A slide-hammer with knife-edged bearing puller attachment will be required. The puller attachment passes through the bearing and when tightened expands to fit firmly behind the bearing **(see illustration 5.6)**. By operating the slide-hammer part of the tool the bearing is jarred out of its housing **(see illustration 5.7)**.
● It is possible, if the bearing is of reasonable weight, for it to drop out of its housing if the casing is heated as described opposite. If this

5.6 Expand the bearing puller so that it locks behind the bearing . . .

5.7 . . . attach the slide hammer to the bearing puller

method is attempted, first prepare a work surface which will enable the casing to be tapped face down to help dislodge the bearing - a wood surface is ideal since it will not damage the casing's gasket surface. Wearing protective gloves, tap the heated casing several times against the work surface to dislodge the bearing under its own weight **(see illustration 5.8)**.

5.8 Tapping a casing face down on wood blocks can often dislodge a bearing

● Bearings can be installed in blind holes using the driver or socket method described above.

Drawbolts

● Where a bearing or bushing is set in the eye of a component, such as a suspension linkage arm or connecting rod small-end, removal by drift may damage the component. Furthermore, a rubber bushing in a shock absorber eye cannot successfully be driven out of position. If access is available to a hydraulic press, the task is straightforward. If not, a drawbolt can be fabricated to extract the bearing or bushing.

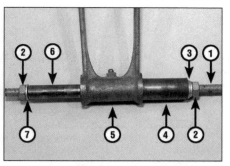

5.9 Drawbolt component parts assembled on a suspension arm

1 Bolt or length of threaded bar
2 Nuts
3 Washer (external diameter greater than tubing internal diameter)
4 Tubing (internal diameter sufficient to accommodate bearing)
5 Suspension arm with bearing
6 Tubing (external diameter slightly smaller than bearing)
7 Washer (external diameter slightly smaller than bearing)

5.10 Drawing the bearing out of the suspension arm

● To extract the bearing/bushing you will need a long bolt with nut (or piece of threaded bar with two nuts), a piece of tubing which has an internal diameter larger than the bearing/bushing, another piece of tubing which has an external diameter slightly smaller than the bearing/bushing, and a selection of washers **(see illustrations 5.9 and 5.10)**. Note that the pieces of tubing must be of the same length, or longer, than the bearing/bushing.

● The same kit (without the pieces of tubing) can be used to draw the new bearing/bushing back into place **(see illustration 5.11)**.

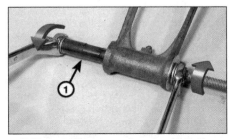

5.11 Installing a new bearing (1) in the suspension arm

Temperature change

● If the bearing's outer race is a tight fit in the casing, the aluminum casing can be heated to release its grip on the bearing. Aluminum will expand at a greater rate than the steel bearing outer race. There are several ways to do this, but avoid any localized extreme heat (such as a blow torch) - aluminum alloy has a low melting point.

● Approved methods of heating a casing are using a domestic oven (heated to 100°C/200°F) or immersing the casing in boiling water **(see illustration 5.12)**. Low temperature range localized heat sources such as a paint stripper heat gun or clothes iron can also be used **(see illustration 5.13)**. Alternatively, soak a rag in boiling water, wring it out and wrap it around the bearing housing.

> ⚠ **Warning: All of these methods require care in use to prevent scalding and burns to the hands. Wear protective gloves when handling hot components.**

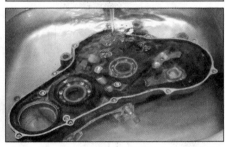

5.12 A casing can be immersed in a sink of boiling water to aid bearing removal

5.13 Using a localized heat source to aid bearing removal

● If heating the whole casing note that plastic components, such as the neutral switch, may suffer - remove them beforehand.

● After heating, remove the bearing as described above. You may find that the expansion is sufficient for the bearing to fall out of the casing under its own weight or with a light tap on the driver or socket.

● If necessary, the casing can be heated to aid bearing installation, and this is sometimes the recommended procedure if the motorcycle manufacturer has designed the housing and bearing fit with this intention.

● Installation of bearings can be eased by placing them in a freezer the night before installation. The steel bearing will contract slightly, allowing easy insertion in its housing. This is often useful when installing steering head outer races in the frame.

Bearing types and markings

● Plain shell bearings, ball bearings, needle roller bearings and tapered roller bearings will all be found on motorcycles (**see illustrations 5.14 and 5.15**). The ball and roller types are usually caged between an inner and outer race, but uncaged variations may be found.

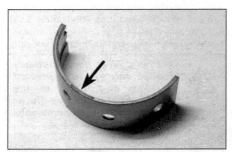

5.14 Shell bearings are either plain or grooved. They are usually identified by color code (arrow)

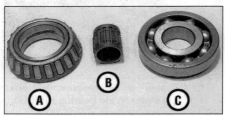

5.15 Tapered roller bearing (A), needle roller bearing (B) and ball journal bearing (C)

● Shell bearings (often called inserts) are usually found at the crankshaft main and connecting rod big-end where they are good at coping with high loads. They are made of a phosphor-bronze material and are impregnated with self-lubricating properties.
● Ball bearings and needle roller bearings consist of a steel inner and outer race with the balls or rollers between the races. They require constant lubrication by oil or grease and are good at coping with axial loads. Taper roller bearings consist of rollers set in a tapered cage set on the inner race; the outer race is separate. They are good at coping with axial loads and prevent movement along the shaft - a typical application is in the steering head.
● Bearing manufacturers produce bearings to ISO size standards and stamp one face of the bearing to indicate its internal and external diameter, load capacity and type (**see illustration 5.16**).
● Metal bushings are usually of phosphor-bronze material. Rubber bushings are used in suspension mounting eyes. Fiber bushings have also been used in suspension pivots.

5.16 Typical bearing marking

Bearing troubleshooting

● If a bearing outer race has spun in its housing, the housing material will be damaged. You can use a bearing locking compound to bond the outer race in place if damage is not too severe.
● Shell bearings will fail due to damage of their working surface, as a result of lack of lubrication, corrosion or abrasive particles in the oil (**see illustration 5.17**). Small particles of dirt in the oil may embed in the bearing material whereas larger particles will score the bearing and shaft journal. If a number of short journeys are made, insufficient heat will be generated to drive off condensation which has built up on the bearings.

5.17 Typical bearing failures

● Ball and roller bearings will fail due to lack of lubrication or damage to the balls or rollers. Tapered-roller bearings can be damaged by overloading them. Unless the bearing is sealed on both sides, wash it in kerosene to remove all old grease then allow it to dry. Make a visual inspection looking to dented balls or rollers, damaged cages and worn or pitted races (**see illustration 5.18**).
● A ball bearing can be checked for wear by listening to it when spun. Apply a film of light oil to the bearing and hold it close to the ear - hold the outer race with one hand and spin the inner

5.18 Example of ball journal bearing with damaged balls and cages

5.19 Hold outer race and listen to inner race when spun

race with the other hand (**see illustration 5.19**). The bearing should be almost silent when spun; if it grates or rattles it is worn.

6 Oil seals

Oil seal removal and installation

● Oil seals should be replaced every time a component is dismantled. This is because the seal lips will become set to the sealing surface and will not necessarily reseal.
● Oil seals can be pried out of position using a large flat-bladed screwdriver (**see illustration 6.1**). In the case of crankcase seals, check first that the seal is not lipped on the inside, preventing its removal with the crankcases joined.

6.1 Pry out oil seals with a large flat-bladed screwdriver

● New seals are usually installed with their marked face (containing the seal reference code) outwards and the spring side towards the fluid being retained. In certain cases, such as a two-stroke engine crankshaft seal, a double lipped seal may be used due to there being fluid or gas on each side of the joint.

● Use a bearing driver or socket which bears only on the outer hard edge of the seal to install it in the casing - tapping on the inner edge will damage the sealing lip.

Oil seal types and markings

● Oil seals are usually of the single-lipped type. Double-lipped seals are found where a liquid or gas is on both sides of the joint.
● Oil seals can harden and lose their sealing ability if the motorcycle has been in storage for a long period - replacement is the only solution.
● Oil seal manufacturers also conform to the ISO markings for seal size - these are molded into the outer face of the seal (see illustration 6.2).

6.2 These oil seal markings indicate inside diameter, outside diameter and seal thickness

7 Gaskets and sealants

Types of gasket and sealant

● Gaskets are used to seal the mating surfaces between components and keep lubricants, fluids, vacuum or pressure contained within the assembly. Aluminum gaskets are sometimes found at the cylinder joints, but most gaskets are paper-based. If the mating surfaces of the components being joined are undamaged the gasket can be installed dry, although a dab of sealant or grease will be useful to hold it in place during assembly.
● RTV (Room Temperature Vulcanizing) silicone rubber sealants cure when exposed to moisture in the atmosphere. These sealants are good at filling pits or irregular gasket faces, but will tend to be forced out of the joint under very high torque. They can be used to replace a paper gasket, but first make sure that the width of the paper gasket is not essential to the shimming of internal components. RTV sealants should not be used on components containing gasoline.
● Non-hardening, semi-hardening and hard setting liquid gasket compounds can be used with a gasket or between a metal-to-metal joint. Select the sealant to suit the application: universal non-hardening sealant can be used on virtually all joints; semi-hardening on joint faces which are rough or damaged; hard setting sealant on joints which require a permanent bond and are subjected to high temperature and pressure. **Note:** *Check first if the paper gasket has a bead of sealant*

impregnated in its surface before applying additional sealant.
● When choosing a sealant, make sure it is suitable for the application, particularly if being applied in a high-temperature area or in the vicinity of fuel. Certain manufacturers produce sealants in either clear, silver or black colors to match the finish of the engine. This has a particular application on motorcycles where much of the engine is exposed.
● Do not over-apply sealant. That which is squeezed out on the outside of the joint can be wiped off, whereas an excess of sealant on the inside can break off and clog oilways.

Breaking a sealed joint

● Age, heat, pressure and the use of hard setting sealant can cause two components to stick together so tightly that they are difficult to separate using finger pressure alone. Do not resort to using levers unless there is a pry point provided for this purpose (see illustration 7.1) or else the gasket surfaces will be damaged.
● Use a soft-faced hammer (see illustration 7.2) or a wood block and conventional hammer to strike the component near the mating surface. Avoid hammering against cast extremities since they may break off. If this method fails, try using a wood wedge between the two components.

Caution: If the joint will not separate, double-check that you have removed all the fasteners.

7.1 If a pry point is provided, apply gentle pressure with a flat-bladed screwdriver

7.2 Tap around the joint with a soft-faced mallet if necessary - don't strike cooling fins

Removal of old gasket and sealant

● Paper gaskets will most likely come away complete, leaving only a few traces stuck on

Most components have one or two hollow locating dowels between the two gasket faces. If a dowel cannot be removed, do not resort to gripping it with pliers - it will almost certainly be distorted. Install a close-fitting socket or Phillips screwdriver into the dowel and then grip the outer edge of the dowel to free it.

the sealing faces of the components. It is imperative that all traces are removed to ensure correct sealing of the new gasket.
● Very carefully scrape all traces of gasket away making sure that the sealing surfaces are not gouged or scored by the scraper (see illustrations 7.3, 7.4 and 7.5). Stubborn deposits can be removed by spraying with an aerosol gasket remover. Final preparation of

7.3 Paper gaskets can be scraped off with a gasket scraper tool . . .

7.4 . . . a knife blade . . .

7.5 . . . or a household scraper

7.6 Fine abrasive paper is wrapped around a flat file to clean up the gasket face

7.7 A kitchen scourer can be used on stubborn deposits

the gasket surface can be made with very fine abrasive paper or a plastic kitchen scourer **(see illustrations 7.6 and 7.7)**.

● Old sealant can be scraped or peeled off components, depending on the type originally used. Note that gasket removal compounds are available to avoid scraping the components clean; make sure the gasket remover suits the type of sealant used.

8 Chains

Breaking and joining final drive chains

● Drive chains for all but small bikes are continuous and do not have a clip-type connecting link. The chain must be broken using a chain breaker tool and the new chain securely riveted together using a new soft rivet-type link. Never use a clip-type connecting link instead of a rivet-type link, except in an emergency. Various chain breaking and riveting tools are available, either as separate tools or combined as illustrated in the accompanying photographs - read the instructions supplied with the tool carefully.

> ⚠ **Warning: The need to rivet the new link pins correctly cannot be overstressed - loss of control of the motorcycle is very likely to result if the chain breaks in use.**

● Rotate the chain and look for the soft link. The soft link pins look like they have been

8.1 Tighten the chain breaker to push the pin out of the link . . .

8.2 . . . withdraw the pin, remove the tool . . .

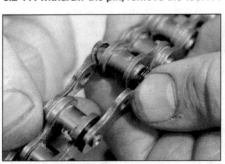

8.3 . . . and separate the chain link

deeply center-punched instead of peened over like all the other pins **(see illustration 8.9)** and its sideplate may be a different color. Position the soft link midway between the sprockets and assemble the chain breaker tool over one of the soft link pins **(see illustration 8.1)**. Operate the tool to push the pin out through the chain **(see illustration 8.2)**. On an O-ring chain, remove the O-rings **(see illustration 8.3)**. Carry out the same procedure on the other soft link pin.

> **Caution: Certain soft link pins (particularly on the larger chains) may require their ends to be filed or ground off before they can be pressed out using the tool.**

● Check that you have the correct size and strength (standard or heavy duty) new soft link - do not reuse the old link. Look for the size marking on the chain sideplates **(see illustration 8.10)**.

● Position the chain ends so that they are engaged over the rear sprocket. On an O-ring

8.4 Insert the new soft link, with O-rings, through the chain ends . . .

8.5 . . . install the O-rings over the pin ends . . .

8.6 . . . followed by the sideplate

chain, install a new O-ring over each pin of the link and insert the link through the two chain ends **(see illustration 8.4)**. Install a new O-ring over the end of each pin, followed by the sideplate (with the chain manufacturer's marking facing outwards) **(see illustrations 8.5 and 8.6)**. On an unsealed chain, insert the link through the two chain ends, then install the sideplate with the chain manufacturer's marking facing outwards.

● Note that it may not be possible to install the sideplate using finger pressure alone. If using a joining tool, assemble it so that the plates of the tool clamp the link and press the sideplate over the pins **(see illustration 8.7)**. Otherwise, use two small sockets placed over

8.7 Push the sideplate into position using a clamp

8.8 Assemble the chain riveting tool over one pin at a time and tighten it fully

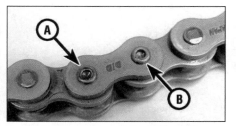

8.9 Pin end correctly riveted (A), pin end unriveted (B)

the rivet ends and two pieces of the wood between a C-clamp. Operate the clamp to press the sideplate over the pins.

● Assemble the joining tool over one pin (following the manufacturer's instructions) and tighten the tool down to spread the pin end securely **(see illustrations 8.8 and 8.9)**. Do the same on the other pin.

> **Warning: Check that the pin ends are secure and that there is no danger of the sideplate coming loose. If the pin ends are cracked the soft link must be replaced.**

Final drive chain sizing

● Chains are sized using a three digit number, followed by a suffix to denote the chain type **(see illustration 8.10)**. Chain type is either standard or heavy duty (thicker sideplates), and also unsealed or O-ring/X-ring type.

● The first digit of the number relates to the pitch of the chain, ie the distance from the center of one pin to the center of the next pin **(see illustration 8.11)**. Pitch is expressed in eighths of an inch, as follows:

8.10 Typical chain size and type marking

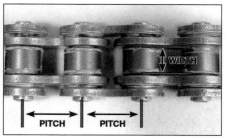

8.11 Chain dimensions

Sizes commencing with a 4 (for example 428) have a pitch of 1/2 inch (12.7 mm)

Sizes commencing with a 5 (for example 520) have a pitch of 5/8 inch (15.9 mm)

Sizes commencing with a 6 (for example 630) have a pitch of 3/4 inch (19.1 mm)

● The second and third digits of the chain size relate to the width of the rollers, for example the 525 shown has 5/16 inch (7.94 mm) rollers **(see illustration 8.11)**.

9 Hoses

Clamping to prevent flow

● Small-bore flexible hoses can be clamped to prevent fluid flow while a component is worked on. Whichever method is used, ensure that the hose material is not permanently distorted or damaged by the clamp.

a) A brake hose clamp available from auto parts stores **(see illustration 9.1)**.
b) A wingnut type hose clamp **(see illustration 9.2)**.

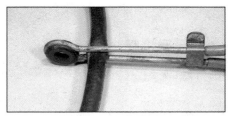

9.1 Hoses can be clamped with an automotive brake hose clamp . . .

9.2 . . . a wingnut type hose clamp . . .

c) Two sockets placed on each side of the hose and held with straight-jawed self-locking pliers **(see illustration 9.3)**.
d) Thick card stock on each side of the hose held between straight-jawed self-locking pliers **(see illustration 9.4)**.

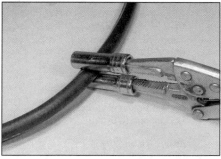

9.3 . . . two sockets and a pair of self-locking grips . . .

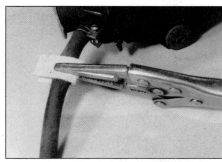

9.4 . . . or thick card and self-locking grips

Freeing and fitting hoses

● Always make sure the hose clamp is moved well clear of the hose end. Grip the hose with your hand and rotate it while pulling it off the union. If the hose has hardened due to age and will not move, slit it with a sharp knife and peel its ends off the union **(see illustration 9.5)**.

● Resist the temptation to use grease or soap on the unions to aid installation; although it helps the hose slip over the union it will equally aid the escape of fluid from the joint. It is preferable to soften the hose ends in hot water and wet the inside surface of the hose with water or a fluid which will evaporate.

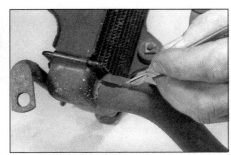

9.5 Cutting a coolant hose free with a sharp knife

Conversion Factors

Length (distance)

Inches (in)	X	25.4	= Millimeters (mm)	X 0.0394	= Inches (in)
Feet (ft)	X	0.305	= Meters (m)	X 3.281	= Feet (ft)
Miles	X	1.609	= Kilometers (km)	X 0.621	= Miles

Volume (capacity)

Cubic inches (cu in; in^3)	X	16.387	= Cubic centimeters (cc; cm^3)	X 0.061	= Cubic inches (cu in; in^3)
Imperial pints (Imp pt)	X	0.568	= Liters (l)	X 1.76	= Imperial pints (Imp pt)
Imperial quarts (Imp qt)	X	1.137	= Liters (l)	X 0.88	= Imperial quarts (Imp qt)
Imperial quarts (Imp qt)	X	1.201	= US quarts (US qt)	X 0.833	= Imperial quarts (Imp qt)
US quarts (US qt)	X	0.946	= Liters (l)	X 1.057	= US quarts (US qt)
Imperial gallons (Imp gal)	X	4.546	= Liters (l)	X 0.22	= Imperial gallons (Imp gal)
Imperial gallons (Imp gal)	X	1.201	= US gallons (US gal)	X 0.833	= Imperial gallons (Imp gal)
US gallons (US gal)	X	3.785	= Liters (l)	X 0.264	= US gallons (US gal)

Mass (weight)

Ounces (oz)	X	28.35	= Grams (g)	X 0.035	= Ounces (oz)
Pounds (lb)	X	0.454	= Kilograms (kg)	X 2.205	= Pounds (lb)

Force

Ounces-force (ozf; oz)	X	0.278	= Newtons (N)	X 3.6	= Ounces-force (ozf; oz)
Pounds-force (lbf; lb)	X	4.448	= Newtons (N)	X 0.225	= Pounds-force (lbf; lb)
Newtons (N)	X	0.1	= Kilograms-force (kgf; kg)	X 9.81	= Newtons (N)

Pressure

Pounds-force per square inch (psi; lbf/in^2; lb/in^2)	X	0.070	= Kilograms-force per square centimeter (kgf/cm^2; kg/cm^2)	X 14.223	= Pounds-force per square inch (psi; lbf/in^2; lb/in^2)
Pounds-force per square inch (psi; lbf/in^2; lb/in^2)	X	0.068	= Atmospheres (atm)	X 14.696	= Pounds-force per square inch (psi; lbf/in^2; lb/in^2)
Pounds-force per square inch (psi; lbf/in^2; lb/in^2)	X	0.069	= Bars	X 14.5	= Pounds-force per square inch (psi; lbf/in^2; lb/in^2)
Pounds-force per square inch (psi; lbf/in^2; lb/in^2)	X	6.895	= Kilopascals (kPa)	X 0.145	= Pounds-force per square inch (psi; lbf/in^2; lb/in^2)
Kilopascals (kPa)	X	0.01	= Kilograms-force per square centimeter (kgf/cm^2; kg/cm^2)	X 98.1	= Kilopascals (kPa)

Torque (moment of force)

Pounds-force inches (lbf in; lb in)	X	1.152	= Kilograms-force centimeter (kgf cm; kg cm)	X 0.868	= Pounds-force inches (lbf in; lb in)
Pounds-force inches (lbf in; lb in)	X	0.113	= Newton meters (Nm)	X 8.85	= Pounds-force inches (lbf in; lb in)
Pounds-force inches (lbf in; lb in)	X	0.083	= Pounds-force feet (lbf ft; lb ft)	X 12	= Pounds-force inches (lbf in; lb in)
Pounds-force feet (lbf ft; lb ft)	X	0.138	= Kilograms-force meters (kgf m; kg m)	X 7.233	= Pounds-force feet (lbf ft; lb ft)
Pounds-force feet (lbf ft; lb ft)	X	1.356	= Newton meters (Nm)	X 0.738	= Pounds-force feet (lbf ft; lb ft)
Newton meters (Nm)	X	0.102	= Kilograms-force meters (kgf m; kg m)	X 9.804	= Newton meters (Nm)

Vacuum

Inches mercury (in. Hg)	X	3.377	= Kilopascals (kPa)	X 0.2961	= Inches mercury
Inches mercury (in. Hg)	X	25.4	= Millimeters mercury (mm Hg)	X 0.0394	= Inches mercury

Power

Horsepower (hp)	X	745.7	= Watts (W)	X 0.0013	= Horsepower (hp)

Velocity (speed)

Miles per hour (miles/hr; mph)	X	1.609	= Kilometers per hour (km/hr; kph)	X 0.621	= Miles per hour (miles/hr; mph)

Fuel consumption*

Miles per gallon, Imperial (mpg)	X	0.354	= Kilometers per liter (km/l)	X 2.825	= Miles per gallon, Imperial (mpg)
Miles per gallon, US (mpg)	X	0.425	= Kilometers per liter (km/l)	X 2.352	= Miles per gallon, US (mpg)

Temperature

Degrees Fahrenheit = (°C x 1.8) + 32

Degrees Celsius (Degrees Centigrade; °C) = (°F - 32) x 0.56

*It is common practice to convert from miles per gallon (mpg) to liters/100 kilometers (l/100km), where mpg (Imperial) x l/100 km = 282 and mpg (US) x l/100 km = 235

A number of chemicals and lubricants are available for use in motorcycle maintenance and repair. They include a wide variety of products ranging from cleaning solvents and degreasers to lubricants and protective sprays for rubber, plastic and vinyl.

• **Contact point/spark plug cleaner** is a solvent used to clean oily film and dirt from points, grim from electrical connectors and oil deposits from spark plugs. It is oil free and leaves no residue. It can also be used to remove gum and varnish from carburetor jets and other orifices.

• **Carburetor cleaner** is similar to contact point/spark plug cleaner but it usually has a stronger solvent and may leave a slight oily residue. It is not recommended for cleaning electrical components or connections.

• **Brake system cleaner** is used to remove grease or brake fluid from brake system components (where clean surfaces are absolutely necessary and petroleum-based solvents cannot be used); it also leaves no residue.

• **Silicone-based lubricants** are used to protect rubber parts such as hoses and grommets, and are used as lubricants for hinges and locks.

• **Multi-purpose grease** is an all purpose lubricant used wherever grease is more practical than a liquid lubricant such as oil. Some multi-purpose grease is colored white and specially formulated to be more resistant to water than ordinary grease.

• **Gear oil** (sometimes called gear lube) is a specially designed oil used in transmissions and final drive units, as well as other areas where high friction, high temperature lubrication is required. It is available in a number of viscosities (weights) for various applications.

• **Motor oil**, of course, is the lubricant specially formulated for use in the engine.

It normally contains a wide variety of additives to prevent corrosion and reduce foaming and wear. Motor oil comes in various weights (viscosity ratings) of from 5 to 80. The recommended weight of the oil depends on the seasonal temperature and the demands on the engine. Light oil is used in cold climates and under light load conditions; heavy oil is used in hot climates where high loads are encountered. Multi-viscosity oils are designed to have characteristics of both light and heavy oils and are available in a number of weights from 5W-20 to 20W-50.

• **Gasoline additives** perform several functions, depending on their chemical makeup. They usually contain solvents that help dissolve gum and varnish that build up on carburetor and inlet parts. They also serve to break down carbon deposits that form on the inside surfaces of the combustion chambers. Some additives contain upper cylinder lubricants for valves and piston rings.

• **Brake and clutch fluid** is a specially formulated hydraulic fluid that can withstand the heat and pressure encountered in break/clutch systems. Care must be taken that this fluid does not come in contact with painted surfaces or plastics. An opened container should always be resealed to prevent contamination by water or dirt.

• **Chain lubricants** are formulated especially for use on motorcycle final drive chains. A good chain lube should adhere well and have good penetrating qualities to be effective as a lubricant inside the chain and on the side plates, pins and rollers. Most chain lubes are either the foaming type or quick drying type and are usually marketed as sprays. Take care to use a lubricant marked as being suitable for O-ring chains.

• **Degreasers** are heavy duty solvents used to remove grease and grime that may accumulate on the engine and frame components. They can be sprayed or

brushed on and, depending on the type, are rinsed with either water or solvent.

• **Solvents** are used alone or in combination with degreasers to clean parts and assemblies during repair and overhaul. The home mechanic should use only solvents that are non-flammable and that do not produce irritating fumes.

• **Gasket sealing compounds** may be used in conjunction with gaskets, to improve their sealing capabilities, or alone, to seal metal-to-metal joints. Many gasket sealers can withstand extreme heat, some are impervious to gasoline and lubricants, while others are capable of filling and sealing large cavities. Depending on the intended use, gasket sealers either dry hard or stay relatively soft and pliable. They are usually applied by hand, with a brush or are sprayed on the gasket sealing surfaces.

• **Thread locking compound** is an adhesive locking compound that prevents threaded fasteners from loosening because of vibration. It is available in a variety of types for different applications.

• **Moisture dispersants** are usually sprays that can be used to dry out electrical components such as the fuse block and wiring connectors. Some types an also be used as treatment for rubber and as a lubricant for hinges, cables and locks.

• **Waxes and polishes** are used to help protect painted and plated surfaces from the weather. Different types of pain may require the use of different types of wax polish. Some polishes utilize a chemical or abrasive cleaner to help remove the top layer of oxidized (dull) paint on older vehicles. In recent years, many non-wax polishes (that contain a wide variety of chemicals such as polymers and silicones) have been introduced. These non-wax polishes are usually easier to apply and last longer than conventional waxes and polishes.

Preparing for storage

Before you start

If repairs or an overhaul is needed, see that this is carried out now rather than left until you want to ride the bike again.

Give the bike a good wash and scrub all dirt from its underside. Make sure the bike dries completely before preparing for storage.

Engine

● Remove the spark plug(s) and lubricate the cylinder bores with approximately a teaspoon of motor oil using a spout-type oil can (see illustration 1). Reinstall the spark plug(s). Crank the engine over a couple of times to coat the piston rings and bores with oil. If the bike has a kickstart, use this to turn the engine over. If not, flick the kill switch to the OFF position and crank the engine over on the starter (see illustration 2). If the nature of the ignition system prevents the starter operating with the kill switch in the OFF position, remove the spark plugs and fit them back in their caps; ensure that the plugs are grounded against the cylinder head when the starter is operated (see illustration 3).

> ⚠️ **Warning: It is important that the plugs are grounded away from the spark plug holes otherwise there is a risk of atomized fuel from the cylinders igniting.**

> **HAYNES HINT** *On a single cylinder four-stroke engine, you can seal the combustion chamber completely by positioning the piston at TDC on the compression stroke.*

● Drain the carburetor(s) otherwise there is a risk of jets becoming blocked by gum deposits from the fuel (see illustration 4).

● If the bike is going into long-term storage, consider adding a fuel stabilizer to the fuel in the tank. If the tank is drained completely, corrosion of its internal surfaces may occur if left unprotected for a long period. The tank can be treated with a rust preventative especially for this purpose. Alternatively, remove the tank and pour half a liter of motor oil into it, install the filler cap and shake the tank to coat its internals with oil before draining off the excess. The same effect can also be achieved by spraying WD40 or a similar water-dispersant around the inside of the tank via its flexible nozzle.

● Make sure the cooling system contains the correct mix of antifreeze. Antifreeze also contains important corrosion inhibitors.

● The air intakes and exhaust can be sealed off by covering or plugging the openings. Ensure that you do not seal in any condensation; run the engine until it is hot, then switch off and allow to cool. Tape a piece

Squirt a drop of motor oil into each cylinder

Flick the kill switch to OFF . . .

. . . and ensure that the metal bodies of the plugs (arrows) are grounded against the cylinder head

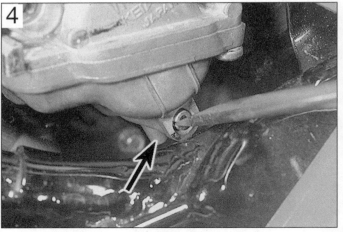

Connect a hose to the carburetor float chamber drain stub (arrow) and unscrew the drain screw

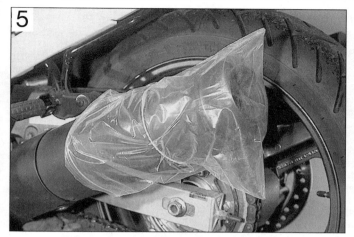

Exhausts can be sealed off with a plastic bag

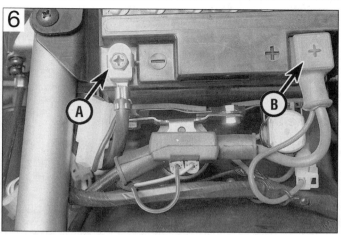

Disconnect the negative lead (A) first, followed by the positive lead (B)

of thick plastic over the silencer end(s) **(see illustration 5)**. Note that some advocate pouring a tablespoon of motor oil into the silencer(s) before sealing them off.

Battery

● Remove it from the bike - in extreme cases of cold the battery may freeze and crack its case **(see illustration 6)**.
● Check the electrolyte level and top up if necessary (conventional refillable batteries). Clean the terminals.
● Store the battery off the motorcycle and away from any sources of fire. Position a wooden block under the battery if it is to sit on the ground.
● Give the battery a trickle charge for a few hours every month **(see illustration 7)**.

Tires

● Place the bike on its centerstand or an auxiliary stand which will support the motorcycle in an upright position. Position wood blocks under the tires to keep them off the ground and to provide insulation from damp. If the bike is being put into long-term storage, ideally both tires should be off the

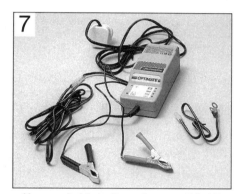

Use a suitable battery charger - this kit also assesses battery condition

ground; not only will this protect the tires, but will also ensure that no load is placed on the steering head or wheel bearings.
● Deflate each tire by 5 to 10 psi, no more or the beads may unseat from the rim, making subsequent inflation difficult on tubeless tires.

Pivots and controls

● Lubricate all lever, pedal, stand and

footrest pivot points. If grease nipples are fitted to the rear suspension components, apply lubricant to the pivots.
● Lubricate all control cables.

Cycle components

● Apply a wax protectant to all painted and plastic components. Wipe off any excess, but don't polish to a shine. Where fitted, clean the screen with soap and water.
● Coat metal parts with Vaseline (petroleum jelly). When applying this to the fork tubes, do not compress the forks otherwise the seals will rot from contact with the Vaseline.
● Apply a vinyl cleaner to the seat.

Storage conditions

● Aim to store the bike in a shed or garage which does not leak and is free from damp.
● Drape an old blanket or bedspread over the bike to protect it from dust and direct contact with sunlight (which will fade paint). Beware of tight-fitting plastic covers which may allow condensation to form and settle on the bike.

Getting back on the road

Engine and transmission

● Change the oil and replace the oil filter. If this was done prior to storage, check that the oil hasn't emulsified - a thick whitish substance which occurs through condensation.
● Remove the spark plugs. Using a spout-type oil can, squirt a few drops of oil into the cylinder(s). This will provide initial lubrication as the piston rings and bores comes back into contact. Service the spark plugs, or buy new ones, and install them in the engine.

● Check that the clutch isn't stuck on. The plates can stick together if left standing for some time, preventing clutch operation. Engage a gear and try rocking the bike back and forth with the clutch lever held against the handlebar. If this doesn't work on cable-operated clutches, hold the clutch lever back against the handlebar with a strong rubber band or cable tie for a couple of hours **(see illustration 8)**.
● If the air intakes or silencer end(s) were blocked off, remove the plug or cover used.
● If the fuel tank was coated with a rust

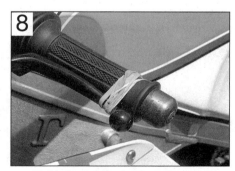

Hold clutch lever back against the handlebar with rubber bands or a cable tie

preventative, oil or a stabilizer added to the fuel, drain and flush the tank and dispose of the fuel sensibly. If no action was taken with the fuel tank prior to storage, it is advised that the old fuel is disposed of since it will go bad over a period of time. Refill the fuel tank with fresh fuel.

Frame and running gear

● Oil all pivot points and cables.

● Check the tire pressures. They will definitely need inflating if pressures were reduced for storage.

● Lubricate the final drive chain (where applicable).

● Remove any protective coating applied to the fork tubes (stanchions) since this may well destroy the fork seals. If the fork tubes weren't protected and have picked up rust spots, remove them with very fine abrasive paper and refinish with metal polish.

● Check that both brakes operate correctly. Apply each brake hard and check that it's not possible to move the motorcycle forwards, then check that the brake frees off again once released. Brake caliper pistons can stick due to corrosion around the piston head, or on the sliding caliper types, due to corrosion of the slider pins. If the brake doesn't free after repeated operation, take the caliper off for examination. Similarly drum brakes can stick due to a seized operating cam, cable or rod linkage.

● If the motorcycle has been in long-term storage, replace the brake fluid and clutch fluid (where applicable).

● Depending on where the bike has been stored, the wiring, cables and hoses may have been nibbled by rodents. Make a visual check and investigate disturbed wiring loom tape.

Battery

● If the battery has been previously removed and given top up charges it can simply be reconnected. Remember to connect the positive cable first and the negative cable last.

● On conventional refillable batteries, if the battery has not received any attention, remove it from the motorcycle and check its electrolyte level. Top up if necessary then charge the battery. If the battery fails to hold a charge and a visual check show heavy white sulfation of the plates, the battery is probably defective and must be replaced. This is particularly likely if the battery is old. Confirm battery condition with a specific gravity check.

● On sealed (MF) batteries, if the battery has not received any attention, remove it from the motorcycle and charge it according to the information on the battery case - if the battery fails to hold a charge it must be replaced.

Starting procedure

● If a kickstart is fitted, turn the engine over a couple of times with the ignition OFF to distribute oil around the engine. If no kickstart is fitted, flick the engine kill switch OFF and the ignition ON and crank the engine over a couple of times to work oil around the upper cylinder components. If the nature of the ignition system is such that the starter won't work with the kill switch OFF, remove the spark plugs, fit them back into their caps and ground their bodies on the cylinder head. Reinstall the spark plugs afterwards.

● Switch the kill switch to RUN, operate the choke and start the engine. If the engine won't start don't continue cranking the engine - not only will this flatten the battery, but the starter motor will overheat. Switch the ignition off and try again later. If the engine refuses to start, go through the troubleshooting procedures in this manual. **Note:** *If the bike has been in storage for a long time, old fuel or a carburetor blockage may be the problem. Gum deposits in carburetors can block jets - if a carburetor cleaner doesn't prove successful the carburetors must be dismantled for cleaning.*

● Once the engine has started, check that the lights, turn signals and horn work properly.

● Treat the bike gently for the first ride and check all fluid levels on completion. Settle the bike back into the maintenance schedule.

This Section provides an easy reference-guide to the more common faults that are likely to afflict your machine. Obviously, the opportunities are almost limitless for faults to occur as a result of obscure failures, and to try and cover all eventualities would require a book. Indeed, a number have been written on the subject.

Successful troubleshooting is not a mysterious 'black art' but the application of a bit of knowledge combined with a systematic and logical approach to the problem. Approach any troubleshooting by first accurately identifying the symptom and then checking through the list of possible causes, starting with the simplest or most obvious and progressing in stages to the most complex. Take nothing for granted, but above all apply liberal quantities of common sense.

The main symptom of a fault is given in the text as a major heading below which are listed the various systems or areas which may contain the fault. Details of each possible cause for a fault and the remedial action to be taken are given. Further information should be sought in the relevant Chapter.

1 Engine doesn't start or is difficult to start
- ☐ Starter motor doesn't rotate
- ☐ Starter motor rotates but engine does not turn over
- ☐ Starter works but engine won't turn over (seized)
- ☐ No fuel flow
- ☐ Engine flooded
- ☐ No spark or weak spark
- ☐ Compression low
- ☐ Stalls after starting
- ☐ Rough idle

2 Poor running at low speed
- ☐ Spark weak
- ☐ Fuel/air mixture incorrect
- ☐ Compression low
- ☐ Poor acceleration

3 Poor running or no power at high speed
- ☐ Firing incorrect
- ☐ Fuel/air mixture incorrect
- ☐ Compression low
- ☐ Knocking or pinging
- ☐ Miscellaneous causes

4 Overheating
- ☐ Engine overheats
- ☐ Firing incorrect
- ☐ Fuel/air mixture incorrect
- ☐ Compression too high
- ☐ Engine load excessive
- ☐ Lubrication inadequate
- ☐ Miscellaneous causes

5 Clutch problems
- ☐ Clutch slipping
- ☐ Clutch not disengaging completely

6 Gearchanging problems
- ☐ Doesn't go into gear, or lever doesn't return
- ☐ Jumps out of gear
- ☐ Overselects

7 Abnormal engine noise
- ☐ Knocking or pinging
- ☐ Piston slap or rattling
- ☐ Valve noise
- ☐ Other noise

8 Abnormal driveline noise
- ☐ Clutch noise
- ☐ Transmission noise
- ☐ Final drive noise

9 Abnormal frame and suspension noise
- ☐ Front end noise
- ☐ Shock absorber noise
- ☐ Brake noise

10 Oil pressure warning light comes on
- ☐ Engine lubrication system
- ☐ Electrical system

11 Excessive exhaust smoke
- ☐ White smoke
- ☐ Black smoke

12 Poor handling or stability
- ☐ Handlebar hard to turn
- ☐ Handlebar shakes or vibrates excessively
- ☐ Handlebar pulls to one side
- ☐ Poor shock absorbing qualities

13 Braking problems
- ☐ Brakes are spongy, don't hold
- ☐ Brake lever or pedal pulsates
- ☐ Brakes drag

14 Electrical problems
- ☐ Battery dead or weak
- ☐ Battery overcharged

1 Engine doesn't start or is difficult to start

Starter motor doesn't rotate

☐ Engine kill switch OFF.
☐ Fuse blown. Check main fuse and starter circuit fuse (Chapter 9).
☐ Battery voltage low. Check and recharge battery (Chapter 9).
☐ Starter motor defective. Make sure the wiring to the starter is secure. Make sure the starter relay clicks when the start button is pushed. If the relay clicks, then the fault is in the wiring or motor.
☐ Starter relay faulty. Check it according to the procedure in Chapter 9.
☐ Starter switch not contacting. The contacts could be wet, corroded or dirty. Disassemble and clean the switch (Chapter 9).
☐ Wiring open or shorted. Check all wiring connections and harnesses to make sure that they are dry, tight and not corroded. Also check for broken or frayed wires that can cause a short to ground (see wiring diagram, Chapter 9).
☐ Ignition (main) switch defective. Check the switch according to the procedure in Chapter 9. Replace the switch with a new one if it is defective.
☐ Engine kill switch defective. Check for wet, dirty or corroded contacts. Clean or replace the switch as necessary (Chapter 9).
☐ Faulty neutral, side stand or clutch switch. Check the wiring to each switch and the switch itself according to the procedures in Chapter 9.

Starter motor rotates but engine does not turn over

☐ Starter motor clutch defective. Inspect and repair or replace (Chapter 2).
☐ Damaged idler or starter gears. Inspect and replace the damaged parts (Chapter 2).

Starter works but engine won't turn over (seized)

☐ Seized engine caused by one or more internally damaged components. Failure due to wear, abuse or lack of lubrication. Damage can include seized valves, followers/rocker arms, camshafts, pistons, crankshaft, connecting rod bearings, or transmission gears or bearings. Refer to Chapter 2 for engine disassembly.

No fuel flow

☐ No fuel in tank.
☐ Fuel tank breather hose obstructed.
☐ Fuel filter is blocked (see Chapter 1).

Engine flooded

☐ Starting technique incorrect. Under normal circumstances the machine should start with little or no throttle. When the engine is cold, the choke should be operated and the engine started without opening the throttle. When the engine is at operating temperature, only a very slight amount of throttle should be necessary.

No spark or weak spark

☐ Ignition switch OFF.
☐ Engine kill switch turned to the OFF position.
☐ Battery voltage low. Check and recharge the battery as necessary (Chapter 9).
☐ Spark plugs dirty, defective or worn out. Locate reason for fouled plugs using spark plug condition chart and follow the plug maintenance procedures (Chapter 1).
☐ Spark plug caps or secondary (HT) wiring faulty. Check condition. Replace either or both components if cracks or deterioration are evident (Chapter 5).

☐ Spark plug caps not making good contact. Make sure that the plug caps fit snugly over the plug ends.
☐ Ignition HT coils defective. Check the coils, referring to Chapter 5.
☐ IC igniter unit defective. Refer to Chapter 5 for details.
☐ Pick-up coil defective. Check the unit, referring to Chapter 5 for details.
☐ Ignition or kill switch shorted. This is usually caused by water, corrosion, damage or excessive wear. The switches can be disassembled and cleaned with electrical contact cleaner. If cleaning does not help, replace the switches (Chapter 9).
☐ Wiring shorted or broken between:

a) Ignition (main) switch and engine kill switch (or blown fuse)
b) IC igniter unit and engine kill switch
c) IC igniter unit and ignition HT coils
d) Ignition HT coils and spark plugs
e) IC igniter unit and ignition pick-up coil.

☐ Make sure that all wiring connections are clean, dry and tight. Look for chafed and broken wires (Chapters 5 and 9).

Compression low

☐ Spark plugs loose. Remove the plugs and inspect their threads. Reinstall and tighten to the specified torque (Chapter 1).
☐ Cylinder head not sufficiently tightened down. If the cylinder head is suspected of being loose, then there's a chance that the gasket or head is damaged if the problem has persisted for any length of time. The head bolts should be tightened to the proper torque in the correct sequence (Chapter 2).
☐ Improper valve clearance. This means that the valve is not closing completely and compression pressure is leaking past the valve. Check and adjust the valve clearances (Chapter 1).
☐ Cylinder and/or piston worn. Excessive wear will cause compression pressure to leak past the rings. This is usually accompanied by worn rings as well. A top-end overhaul is necessary (Chapter 2).
☐ Piston rings worn, weak, broken, or sticking. Broken or sticking piston rings usually indicate a lubrication or fuelling problem that causes excess carbon deposits or seizures to form on the pistons and rings. Top-end overhaul is necessary (Chapter 2).
☐ Piston ring-to-groove clearance excessive. This is caused by excessive wear of the piston ring lands. Piston replacement is necessary (Chapter 2).
☐ Cylinder head gasket damaged. If a head is allowed to become loose, or if excessive carbon build-up on the piston crown and combustion chamber causes extremely high compression, the head gasket may leak. Retorquing the head is not always sufficient to restore the seal, so gasket replacement is necessary (Chapter 2).
☐ Cylinder head warped. This is caused by overheating or improperly tightened head bolts. Machine shop resurfacing or head replacement is necessary (Chapter 2).
☐ Valve spring broken or weak. Caused by component failure or wear; the springs must be replaced (Chapter 2).
☐ Valve not seating properly. This is caused by a bent valve (from over-revving or improper valve adjustment), burned valve or seat (improper fuelling) or an accumulation of carbon deposits on the seat (from fuelling or lubrication problems). The valves must be cleaned and/or replaced and the seats serviced if possible (Chapter 2).

1 Engine doesn't start or is difficult to start (continued)

Stalls after starting

☐ Improper choke action. Make sure the choke linkage shaft is getting a full stroke and staying in the out position (Chapter 4).
☐ Ignition malfunction. See Chapter 5.
☐ Carburetor malfunction. See Chapter 4.
☐ Fuel contaminated. The fuel can be contaminated with either dirt or water, or can change chemically if the machine is allowed to sit for several months or more. Drain the tank (Chapter 4).
☐ Intake air leak. Check for loose carburetor intake rubber retaining clips and damaged/disconnected vacuum hoses (Chapter 4).
☐ Engine idle speed incorrect. Turn idle adjusting screw until the engine idles at the specified rpm (Chapter 1).

Rough idle

☐ Ignition malfunction. See Chapter 5.
☐ Idle speed incorrect. See Chapter 1.
☐ Carburetors not synchronized (Vulcan 700/750 models). Adjust them with vacuum gauge or manometer set as described in Chapter 4.
☐ Carburetor malfunction. See Chapter 4.
☐ Fuel contaminated. The fuel can be contaminated with either dirt or water, or can change chemically if the machine is allowed to sit for several months or more. Drain the tank (Chapter 4).
☐ Intake air leak. Check for loose carburetor intake rubber retaining clips and damaged/disconnected vacuum hoses. Replace the intake ducts if they are split or deteriorated (Chapter 4).
☐ Air filter clogged. Replace the air filter element (Chapter 1).

2 Poor running at low speeds

Spark weak

☐ Battery voltage low. Check and recharge battery (Chapter 9).
☐ Spark plugs fouled, defective or worn out. Refer to Chapter 1 for spark plug maintenance.
☐ Spark plug cap or HT wiring defective. Refer to Chapters 1 and 5 for details on the ignition system.
☐ Spark plug caps not making contact.
☐ Incorrect spark plugs. Wrong type, heat range or cap configuration. Check and install correct plugs listed in Chapter 1.
☐ IC igniter unit faulty. See Chapter 4.
☐ Pick-up coil defective. See Chapter 4.
☐ Ignition coils defective. See Chapter 5.

Fuel/air mixture incorrect

☐ Pilot screws incorrectly set (Chapter 4).
☐ Pilot jet or air passage blocked. Remove and overhaul the carburetors (Chapter 4).
☐ Air filter clogged, poorly sealed or missing (Chapter 1).
☐ Air filter housing poorly sealed. Look for cracks, holes or loose clamps and replace or repair defective parts.
☐ Fuel tank breather hose obstructed.
☐ Intake air leak. Check for loose carburetor intake duct retaining clips and damaged/disconnected vacuum hoses. Replace the intake ducts if they are split or deteriorated (Chapter 4).

Compression low

☐ Spark plugs loose. Remove the plugs and inspect their threads. Reinstall and tighten to the specified torque (Chapter 1).
☐ Cylinder head not sufficiently tightened down. If the cylinder head is suspected of being loose, then there's a chance that the gasket and head are damaged if the problem has persisted for any length of time. The head bolts should be tightened to the proper torque in the correct sequence (Chapter 2).
☐ Improper valve clearance. This means that the valve is not closing completely and compression pressure is leaking past the valve. Check and adjust the valve clearances (Vulcan 800 models) (Chapter 1).

☐ Cylinder and/or piston worn. Excessive wear will cause compression pressure to leak past the rings. This is usually accompanied by worn rings as well. A top-end overhaul is necessary (Chapter 2).
☐ Piston rings worn, weak, broken, or sticking. Broken or sticking piston rings usually indicate a lubrication or fuelling problem that causes excess carbon deposits or seizures to form on the pistons and rings. Top-end overhaul is necessary (Chapter 2).
☐ Piston ring-to-groove clearance excessive. This is caused by excessive wear of the piston ring lands. Piston replacement is necessary (Chapter 2).
☐ Cylinder head gasket damaged. If a head is allowed to become loose, or if excessive carbon build-up on the piston crown and combustion chamber causes extremely high compression, the head gasket may leak. Retorquing the head is not always sufficient to restore the seal, so gasket replacement is necessary (Chapter 2).
☐ Cylinder head warped. This is caused by overheating or improperly tightened head bolts. Machine shop resurfacing or head replacement is necessary (Chapter 2).
☐ Valve spring broken or weak. Caused by component failure or wear; the springs must be replaced (Chapter 2).
☐ Valve not seating properly. This is caused by a bent valve (from over-revving or improper valve adjustment), burned valve or seat (improper fuelling) or an accumulation of carbon deposits on the seat (from fuelling, lubrication problems). The valves must be cleaned and/or replaced and the seats serviced if possible (Chapter 2).

Poor acceleration

☐ Carburetor fault. Remove and overhaul the carburetors (Chapter 4).
☐ Engine oil viscosity too high. Using a heavier oil than that recommended in Chapter 1 can damage the oil pump or lubrication system and cause drag on the engine.
☐ Brakes dragging. Usually caused by debris which has entered the brake piston seals, or from a warped disc or drum or bent axle. Repair as necessary (Chapter 7).

3 Poor running or no power at high speed

Firing incorrect

☐ Air filter restricted. Clean or replace filter (Chapter 1).
☐ Spark plugs fouled, defective or worn out. See Chapter 1 for spark plug maintenance.
☐ Spark plug caps or HT wiring defective. See Chapters 1 and 5 for details of the ignition system.
☐ Spark plug caps not in good contact. See Chapter 5.
☐ Incorrect spark plugs. Wrong type, heat range or cap configuration. Check and install correct plugs listed in Chapter 1.
☐ IC igniter unit defective. See Chapter 5.
☐ Pick-up coil defective. See Chapter 5.
☐ Ignition coils defective. See Chapter 5.

Fuel/air mixture incorrect

☐ Carburetor fault. Remove and overhaul the carburetors (Chapter 4).
☐ Air filter clogged, poorly sealed, or missing (Chapter 1).
☐ Air filter housing poorly sealed. Look for cracks, holes or loose clamps, and replace or repair defective parts.
☐ Fuel tank breather hose obstructed.
☐ Intake air leak. Check for loose carburetor intake duct retaining clips and damaged/disconnected vacuum hoses. Replace the intake ducts if they are split or deteriorated (Chapter 4).

Compression low

☐ Spark plugs loose. Remove the plugs and inspect their threads. Reinstall and tighten to the specified torque (Chapter 1).
☐ Cylinder head not sufficiently tightened down. If the cylinder head is suspected of being loose, then there's a chance that the gasket and head are damaged if the problem has persisted for any length of time. The head bolts should be tightened to the proper torque in the correct sequence (Chapter 2).
☐ Improper valve clearance. This means that the valve is not closing completely and compression pressure is leaking past the valve. Check and adjust the valve clearances (Vulcan 800 models) (Chapter 1).
☐ Cylinder and/or piston worn. Excessive wear will cause compression pressure to leak past the rings. This is usually accompanied by worn rings as well. A top-end overhaul is necessary (Chapter 2).
☐ Piston rings worn, weak, broken, or sticking. Broken or sticking piston rings usually indicate a lubrication or fuelling problem that causes excess carbon deposits or seizures to form on the pistons and rings. Top-end overhaul is necessary (Chapter 2).
☐ Piston ring-to-groove clearance excessive. This is caused by excessive wear of the piston ring lands. Piston replacement is necessary (Chapter 2).

☐ Cylinder head gasket damaged. If a head is allowed to become loose, or if excessive carbon build-up on the piston crown and combustion chamber causes extremely high compression, the head gasket may leak. Retorquing the head is not always sufficient to restore the seal, so gasket replacement is necessary (Chapter 2).
☐ Cylinder head warped. This is caused by overheating or improperly tightened head bolts. Machine shop resurfacing or head replacement is necessary (Chapter 2).
☐ Valve spring broken or weak. Caused by component failure or wear; the springs must be replaced (Chapter 2).
☐ Valve not seating properly. This is caused by a bent valve (from over-revving or improper valve adjustment), burned valve or seat (improper fuelling) or an accumulation of carbon deposits on the seat (from fuelling or lubrication problems). The valves must be cleaned and/or replaced and the seats serviced if possible (Chapter 2).

Knocking or pinging

☐ Carbon build-up in combustion chamber. Use of a fuel additive that will dissolve the adhesive bonding the carbon particles to the crown and chamber is the easiest way to remove the build-up. Otherwise, the cylinder head will have to be removed and decarbonized (Chapter 2).
☐ Incorrect or poor quality fuel. Old or improper grades of fuel can cause detonation. This causes the piston to rattle, thus the knocking or pinging sound. Drain old fuel and always use the recommended fuel grade.
☐ Spark plug heat range incorrect. Uncontrolled detonation indicates the plug heat range is too hot. The plug in effect becomes a glow plug, raising cylinder temperatures. Install the proper heat range plug (Chapter 1).
☐ Improper air/fuel mixture. This will cause the cylinders to run hot, which leads to detonation. An intake air leak can cause this imbalance. See Chapter 4.

Miscellaneous causes

☐ Throttle valve doesn't open fully. Adjust the throttle grip freeplay (Chapter 1).
☐ Clutch slipping. May be caused by loose or worn clutch components. Refer to Chapter 2 for clutch overhaul procedures.
☐ Engine oil viscosity too high. Using a heavier oil than the one recommended in Chapter 1 can damage the oil pump or lubrication system and cause drag on the engine.
☐ Brakes dragging. Usually caused by debris which has entered the brake piston seals, or from a warped disc or bent axle. Repair as necessary.

4 Overheating

Engine overheats

- [ ] Coolant level low. Check and add coolant (Chapter 1).
- [ ] Leak in cooling system. Check cooling system hoses and radiator for leaks and other damage. Repair or replace parts as necessary (Chapter 3).
- [ ] Thermostat sticking open or closed. Check and replace as described in Chapter 3.
- [ ] Faulty pressure cap. Remove the cap and have it pressure tested (Chapter 3).
- [ ] Coolant passages clogged. Have the entire system drained and flushed, then refill with fresh coolant.
- [ ] Water pump defective. Remove the pump and check the components (Chapter 3).
- [ ] Clogged radiator fins. Clean them by blowing compressed air through the fins from the backside.
- [ ] Cooling fan or fan switch fault (Chapter 3).

Firing incorrect

- [ ] Spark plugs fouled, defective or worn out. See Chapter 1 for spark plug maintenance.
- [ ] Incorrect spark plugs.
- [ ] IC igniter unit defective. See Chapter 5.
- [ ] Pick-up coil faulty. See Chapter 5.
- [ ] Faulty ignition coils. See Chapter 5.

Fuel/air mixture incorrect

- [ ] Carburetor fault. Remove and overhaul the carburetors (Chapter 4).
- [ ] Air filter clogged, poorly sealed, or missing (Chapter 1).
- [ ] Air filter housing poorly sealed. Look for cracks, holes or loose clamps, and replace or repair defective parts.
- [ ] Fuel tank breather hose obstructed.
- [ ] Intake air leak. Check for loose carburetor intake duct retaining clips and damaged/disconnected vacuum hoses. Replace the intake ducts if they are split or deteriorated (Chapter 4).

Compression too high

- [ ] Carbon build-up in combustion chamber. Use of a fuel additive that will dissolve the adhesive bonding the carbon particles to the piston crown and chamber is the easiest way to remove the build-up. Otherwise, the cylinder head will have to be removed and decarbonized (Chapter 2).
- [ ] Improperly machined head surface or installation of incorrect gasket during engine assembly.

Engine load excessive

- [ ] Clutch slipping. Can be caused by damaged, loose or worn clutch components. Refer to Chapter 2 for overhaul procedures.
- [ ] Engine oil level too high. The addition of too much oil will cause pressurization of the crankcase and inefficient engine operation. Check Specifications and drain to proper level (Chapter 1).
- [ ] Engine oil viscosity too high. Using a heavier oil than the one recommended in Chapter 1 can damage the oil pump or lubrication system as well as cause drag on the engine.
- [ ] Brakes dragging. Usually caused by debris which has entered the brake piston seals, or from a warped disc or drum or bent axle. Repair as necessary.

Lubrication inadequate

- [ ] Engine oil level too low. Friction caused by intermittent lack of lubrication or from oil that is overworked can cause overheating. The oil provides a definite cooling function in the engine. Check the oil level (Chapter 1).
- [ ] Poor quality engine oil or incorrect viscosity or type. Oil is rated not only according to viscosity but also according to type. Some oils are not rated high enough for use in this engine. Check the Specifications section and change to the correct oil (Chapter 1).

Miscellaneous causes

- [ ] Modification to exhaust system. Most aftermarket exhaust systems cause the engine to run leaner, which makes it run hotter.

5 Clutch problems

Clutch slipping

- [ ] Clutch cable freeplay incorrectly adjusted (Chapter 1).
- [ ] Friction plates worn or warped. Overhaul the clutch assembly (Chapter 2).
- [ ] Plain plates warped (Chapter 2).
- [ ] Clutch springs broken or weak. Old or heat-damaged (from slipping clutch) springs should be replaced with new ones (Chapter 2).
- [ ] Clutch pushrod bent. Check and, if necessary, replace (Chapter 2).
- [ ] Clutch center or housing unevenly worn. This causes improper engagement of the plates. Replace the damaged or worn parts (Chapter 2).

Clutch not disengaging completely

- [ ] Clutch cable freeplay incorrectly adjusted (Chapter 1).
- [ ] Clutch plates warped or damaged. This will cause clutch drag, which in turn will cause the machine to creep. Overhaul the clutch assembly (Chapter 2).
- [ ] Clutch spring tension uneven. Usually caused by a sagged or broken spring. Check and replace the springs as a set (Chapter 2).
- [ ] Engine oil deteriorated. Old, thin, worn out oil will not provide proper lubrication for the plates, causing the clutch to drag. Replace the oil and filter (Chapter 1).
- [ ] Engine oil viscosity too high. Using a heavier oil than recommended in Chapter 1 can cause the plates to stick together, putting a drag on the engine. Change to the correct weight oil (Chapter 1).
- [ ] Clutch housing bearing seized. Lack of lubrication, severe wear or damage can cause the bearing to seize on the input shaft. Overhaul of the clutch, and perhaps transmission, may be necessary to repair the damage (Chapter 2).
- [ ] Loose clutch center nut. Causes housing and center misalignment putting a drag on the engine. Engagement adjustment continually varies. Overhaul the clutch assembly (Chapter 2).

6 Gearchanging problems

Doesn't go into gear or lever doesn't return

- [ ] Clutch not disengaging. See above.
- [ ] Shift fork(s) bent or seized. Often caused by dropping the machine or from lack of lubrication. Overhaul the transmission (Chapter 2).
- [ ] Gear(s) stuck on shaft. Most often caused by a lack of lubrication or excessive wear in transmission bearings and bushings. Overhaul the transmission (Chapter 2).
- [ ] Gear shift drum binding. Caused by lubrication failure or excessive wear. Replace the drum and bearing (Chapter 2).
- [ ] Gear shift lever pawl spring weak or broken (Chapter 2).
- [ ] Gear shift lever broken. Splines stripped out of lever or shaft, caused by allowing the lever to get loose or from dropping the machine. Replace necessary parts (Chapter 2).
- [ ] Gear shift mechanism stopper arm broken or worn. Full engagement and rotary movement of shift drum results. Replace the arm (Chapter 2).
- [ ] Stopper arm spring broken. Allows arm to float, causing sporadic shift operation. Replace spring (Chapter 2).

Jumps out of gear

- [ ] Shift fork(s) worn. Overhaul the transmission (Chapter 2).
- [ ] Gear groove(s) worn. Overhaul the transmission (Chapter 2).
- [ ] Gear dogs or dog slots worn or damaged. The gears should be inspected and replaced. No attempt should be made to service the worn parts.

Overselects

- [ ] Stopper arm spring weak or broken (Chapter 2).
- [ ] Return spring post broken or distorted (Chapter 2).

7 Abnormal engine noise

Knocking or pinging

- [ ] Carbon build-up in combustion chamber. Use of a fuel additive that will dissolve the adhesive bonding the carbon particles to the piston crown and chamber is the easiest way to remove the build-up. Otherwise, the cylinder head will have to be removed and decarbonized (Chapter 2).
- [ ] Incorrect or poor quality fuel. Old or improper fuel can cause detonation. This causes the pistons to rattle, thus the knocking or pinging sound. Drain the old fuel and always use the recommended grade fuel (Chapter 4).
- [ ] Spark plug heat range incorrect. Uncontrolled detonation indicates that the plug heat range is too hot. The plug in effect becomes a glow plug, raising cylinder temperatures. Install the proper heat range plug (Chapter 1).
- [ ] Improper air/fuel mixture. This will cause the cylinders to run hot and lead to detonation. Blocked carburetor jets or an air leak can cause this imbalance. See Chapter 4.

Piston slap or rattling

- [ ] Cylinder-to-piston clearance excessive. Caused by improper assembly. Inspect and overhaul top-end parts (Chapter 2).
- [ ] Connecting rod bent. Caused by over-revving, trying to start a badly flooded engine or from ingesting a foreign object into the combustion chamber. Replace the damaged parts (Chapter 2).
- [ ] Piston pin or piston pin bore worn or seized from wear or lack of lubrication. Replace damaged parts (Chapter 2).
- [ ] Piston ring(s) worn, broken or sticking. Overhaul the top-end (Chapter 2).
- [ ] Piston seizure damage. Usually from lack of lubrication or overheating. Replace the pistons and cylinders, as necessary (Chapter 2).
- [ ] Connecting rod bearing clearance excessive. Caused by excessive wear or lack of lubrication. Replace worn parts.

Valve noise

- [ ] Incorrect valve clearances. Adjust the clearances by referring to Chapter 1.
- [ ] Valve spring broken or weak. Check and replace weak valve springs (Chapter 2).
- [ ] Camshaft or cylinder head worn or damaged. Lack of lubrication at high rpm is usually the cause of damage. Insufficient oil or failure to change the oil at the recommended intervals are the chief causes. Since there are no replaceable bearings in the head, the head itself will have to be replaced if there is excessive wear or damage (Chapter 2).

Other noise

- [ ] Cylinder head gasket leaking.
- [ ] Exhaust pipe leaking at cylinder head connection. Caused by improper fit of pipe(s) or loose exhaust nuts. All exhaust fasteners should be tightened evenly and carefully. Failure to do this will lead to a leak.
- [ ] Crankshaft runout excessive. Caused by a bent crankshaft (from over-revving) or damage from an upper cylinder component failure. Can also be attributed to dropping the machine on either of the crankshaft ends.
- [ ] Engine mounting bolts loose. Tighten all engine mount bolts (Chapter 2).
- [ ] Crankshaft bearings worn (Chapter 2).
- [ ] Camchain, tensioner or guides worn. Replace according to the procedure in Chapter 2.

8 Abnormal driveline noise

Clutch noise

- ☐ Clutch outer drum/friction plate clearance excessive (Chapter 2).
- ☐ Loose or damaged clutch pressure plate and/or bolts (Chapter 2).

Transmission noise

- ☐ Bearings worn. Also includes the possibility that the shafts are worn. Overhaul the transmission (Chapter 2).
- ☐ Gears worn or chipped (Chapter 2).
- ☐ Metal chips jammed in gear teeth. Probably pieces from a broken clutch, gear or shift mechanism that were picked up by the gears. This will cause early bearing failure (Chapter 2).

- ☐ Engine oil level too low. Causes a howl from transmission. Also affects engine power and clutch operation (Chapter 1).

Final drive noise

- ☐ Chain not adjusted properly (Vulcan 800 models) (Chapter 1).
- ☐ Front or rear sprocket loose. Tighten fasteners (Chapter 6).
- ☐ Sprockets worn. Replace sprockets (Chapter 6).
- ☐ Rear sprocket warped. Replace sprockets (Chapter 6).
- ☐ Differential oil level low (Vulcan 700/750 models). Top up with the correct oil (Chapter 1).
- ☐ Differential worn or damaged. Have it repaired or replace it (Chapter 7).

9 Abnormal frame and suspension noise

Front end noise

- ☐ Low fluid level or improper viscosity oil in forks. This can sound like spurting and is usually accompanied by irregular fork action (Chapter 6).
- ☐ Spring weak or broken. Makes a clicking or scraping sound. Fork oil, when drained, will have a lot of metal particles in it (Chapter 6).
- ☐ Steering head bearings loose or damaged. Clicks when braking. Check and adjust or replace as necessary (Chapters 1 and 6).
- ☐ Triple clamps loose. Make sure all clamp bolts are tightened to the specified torque (Chapter 6).
- ☐ Fork tube bent. Good possibility if machine has been dropped. Replace tube with a new one (Chapter 6).
- ☐ Front axle bolt or axle pinch bolts loose. Tighten them to the specified torque (Chapter 7).
- ☐ Loose or worn wheel bearings. Check and replace as needed (Chapter 7).

Shock absorber noise

- ☐ Fluid level incorrect. Indicates a leak caused by defective seal. Shock will be covered with oil. Replace shock or seek advice on repair from a Kawasaki dealer (Chapter 6).
- ☐ Defective shock absorber with internal damage. This is in the body of the shock and can't be remedied. The shock must be replaced

with a new one (Chapter 6).
- ☐ Bent or damaged shock body. Replace the shock with a new one (Chapter 6).
- ☐ Loose or worn suspension linkage components (Vulcan 800 models). Check and replace as necessary (Chapter 6).

Brake noise

- ☐ Squeal caused by dust on brake pads. Usually found in combination with glazed pads. Clean using brake cleaning solvent (Chapter 7).
- ☐ Contamination of brake pads. Oil, brake fluid or dirt causing brake to chatter or squeal. Clean or replace pads (Chapter 7).
- ☐ Pads glazed. Caused by excessive heat from prolonged use or from contamination. Do not use sandpaper/emery cloth or any other abrasive to roughen the pad surfaces as abrasives will stay in the pad material and damage the disc. A very fine flat file can be used, but pad replacement is suggested as a cure (Chapter 7).
- ☐ Disc warped. Can cause a chattering, clicking or intermittent squeal. Usually accompanied by a pulsating lever and uneven braking. Replace the disc (Chapter 7).
- ☐ Loose or worn wheel bearings. Check and replace as needed (Chapter 7).

10 Oil pressure warning light comes on

Engine lubrication system

- ☐ Engine oil pump defective, blocked oil strainer screen or failed relief valve. Carry out oil pressure check (Chapter 1).
- ☐ Engine oil level low. Inspect for leak or other problem causing low oil level and add recommended oil (Chapter 1).
- ☐ Engine oil viscosity too low. Very old, thin oil or an improper weight of oil used in the engine. Change to correct oil (Chapter 1).
- ☐ Camshaft or journals worn. Excessive wear causing drop in oil pressure. Replace cam and/or cylinder head. Abnormal wear could be caused by oil starvation at high rpm from low oil level or improper weight or type of oil (Chapter 1).

- ☐ Crankshaft and/or bearings worn. Same problems as above. Check and replace crankshaft and/or bearings (Chapter 2).

Electrical system

- ☐ Oil pressure switch defective. Check the switch according to the procedure in Chapter 9. Replace it if it is defective.
- ☐ Oil pressure indicator light circuit defective. Check for pinched, shorted, disconnected or damaged wiring (Chapter 9).

11 Excessive exhaust smoke

White smoke

- ☐ Piston oil ring worn. The ring may be broken or damaged, causing oil from the crankcase to be pulled past the piston into the combustion chamber. Replace the rings with new ones (Chapter 2).
- ☐ Cylinders worn, cracked, or scored. Caused by overheating or oil starvation. Install a new cylinder block (Chapter 2).
- ☐ Valve oil seal damaged or worn. Replace oil seals with new ones (Chapter 2).
- ☐ Valve guide worn. Perform a complete valve job (Chapter 2).
- ☐ Engine oil level too high, which causes the oil to be forced past the rings. Drain oil to the proper level (Chapter 1).
- ☐ Head gasket broken between oil return and cylinder. Causes oil to be pulled into the combustion chamber. Replace the head gasket and check the head for warpage (Chapter 2).
- ☐ Abnormal crankcase pressurization, which forces oil past the rings. Clogged breather is usually the cause.

Black smoke

- ☐ Air filter clogged. Clean or replace the element (Chapter 1).
- ☐ Carburetor flooding. Remove and overhaul the carburetor(s) (Chapter 4).
- ☐ Main jet too large. Remove and overhaul the carburetor(s) (Chapter 4).
- ☐ Choke cable stuck (Chapter 4).
- ☐ Fuel level too high. Check the fuel level (Chapter 4).

12 Poor handling or stability

Handlebar hard to turn

- ☐ Steering head bearing adjuster nut too tight. Check adjustment as described in Chapter 1.
- ☐ Bearings damaged. Roughness can be felt as the bars are turned from side-to-side. Replace bearings and races (Chapter 6).
- ☐ Races dented or worn. Denting results from wear in only one position (e.g., straight ahead), from a collision or hitting a pothole or from dropping the machine. Replace races and bearings (Chapter 6).
- ☐ Steering stem lubrication inadequate. Causes are grease getting hard from age or being washed out by high pressure car washes. Disassemble steering head and repack bearings (Chapter 6).
- ☐ Steering stem bent. Caused by a collision, hitting a pothole or by dropping the machine. Replace damaged part. Don't try to straighten the steering stem (Chapter 6).
- ☐ Front tire air pressure too low (Chapter 1).

Handlebar shakes or vibrates excessively

- ☐ Tires worn or out of balance (Chapter 7).
- ☐ Swingarm bearings worn. Replace worn bearings (Chapter 6).
- ☐ Wheel rim(s) warped or damaged. Inspect wheels for runout (Chapter 7).
- ☐ Wheel bearings worn. Worn front or rear wheel bearings can cause poor tracking. Worn front bearings will cause wobble (Chapter 7).
- ☐ Handlebar clamp bolts loose (Chapter 6).
- ☐ Fork yoke bolts loose. Tighten them to the specified torque (Chapter 6).
- ☐ Engine mounting bolts loose. Will cause excessive vibration with increased engine rpm (Chapter 2).

Handlebar pulls to one side

- ☐ Frame bent. Definitely suspect this if the machine has been dropped. May or may not be accompanied by cracking near the bend. Replace the frame (Chapter 8).
- ☐ Wheels out of alignment. Caused by improper location of axle spacers or from bent steering stem or frame (Chapters 6 and 8).
- ☐ Swingarm bent or twisted. Caused by age (metal fatigue) or impact damage. Replace the arm (Chapter 6).
- ☐ Steering stem bent. Caused by impact damage or by dropping the motorcycle. Replace the steering stem (Chapter 6).
- ☐ Fork tube bent. Disassemble the forks and replace the damaged parts (Chapter 6).
- ☐ Fork oil level uneven. Check and add or drain as necessary (Chapter 1).

Poor shock absorbing qualities

Too hard:
- a) Fork oil level excessive (Chapter 1).
- b) Fork oil viscosity too high. Use a lighter oil (see the Specifications in Chapter 1).
- c) Fork tube bent. Causes a harsh, sticking feeling (Chapter 6).
- d) Shock shaft or body bent or damaged (Chapter 6).
- e) Fork internal damage (Chapter 6).
- f) Shock internal damage.
- g) Tire pressure too high (Chapter 1).

Too soft:
- a) Fork or shock oil insufficient and/or leaking (Chapter 1).
- b) Fork oil level too low (Chapter 6).
- c) Fork oil viscosity too light (Chapter 6).
- d) Fork springs weak or broken (Chapter 6).
- e) Shock internal damage or leakage (Chapter 6).

13 Braking problems

Brakes are spongy, don't hold

☐ Air in brake line. Caused by inattention to master cylinder fluid level or by leakage. Locate problem and bleed brakes (Chapter 7).
☐ Pad or disc worn (Chapters 1 and 7).
☐ Brake fluid leak. See paragraph 1.
☐ Contaminated pads. Caused by contamination with oil, grease, brake fluid, etc. Clean or replace pads. Clean disc thoroughly with brake cleaner (Chapter 7).
☐ Brake fluid deteriorated. Fluid is old or contaminated. Drain system, replenish with new fluid and bleed the system (Chapter 7).
☐ Master cylinder internal parts worn or damaged causing fluid to bypass (Chapter 7).
☐ Master cylinder bore scratched by foreign material or broken spring. Repair or replace master cylinder (Chapter 7).
☐ Disc warped. Replace disc (Chapter 7).

Brake lever or pedal pulsates

☐ Disc warped. Replace disc (Chapter 7).

☐ Axle bent. Replace axle (Chapter 7).
☐ Brake caliper bolts loose (Chapter 7).
☐ Wheel warped or otherwise damaged (Chapter 7).
☐ Wheel bearings damaged or worn (Chapter 7).
☐ Brake drum out of round. Replace brake drum.

Brakes drag

☐ Master cylinder piston seized. Caused by wear or damage to piston or cylinder bore (Chapter 7).
☐ Lever binding. Check pivot and lubricate (Chapter 7).
☐ Brake caliper piston seized in bore. Caused by wear or ingestion of dirt past deteriorated seal (Chapter 7).
☐ Brake caliper mounting bracket pins corroded. Clean off corrosion and lubricate (Chapter 7).
☐ Brake pad or shoe damaged. Material separated from backing plate. Usually caused by faulty manufacturing process or from contact with chemicals. Replace pads or shoes (Chapter 7).
☐ Pads improperly installed (Chapter 7).
☐ Drum brake springs weak. Replace springs

14 Electrical problems

Battery dead or weak

☐ Battery faulty. Caused by sulfated plates which are shorted through sedimentation. Also, broken battery terminal making only occasional contact (Chapter 9).
☐ Battery cables making poor contact (Chapter 9).
☐ Load excessive. Caused by addition of high wattage lights or other electrical accessories.
☐ Ignition (main) switch defective. Switch either grounds internally or fails to shut off system. Replace the switch (Chapter 9).
☐ Regulator/rectifier defective (Chapter 9).
☐ Alternator stator coil open or shorted (Chapter 9).
☐ Wiring faulty. Wiring grounded or connections loose in ignition, charging or lighting circuits (Chapter 9).

Battery overcharged

☐ Regulator/rectifier defective. Overcharging is noticed when battery gets excessively warm (Chapter 9).
☐ Battery defective. Replace battery with a new one (Chapter 9).
☐ Battery amperage too low, wrong type or size. Install manufacturer's specified amp-hour battery to handle charging load (Chapter 9).

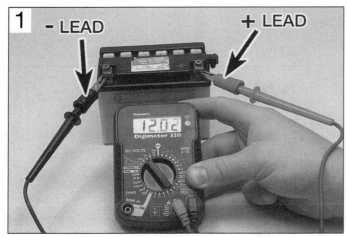

Measuring open-circuit battery voltage

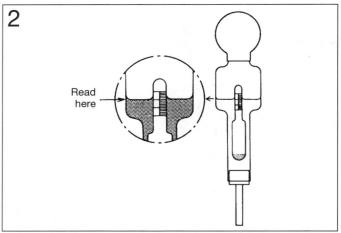

Float-type hydrometer for measuring battery specific gravity

Checking engine compression

● Low compression will result in exhaust smoke, heavy oil consumption, poor starting and poor performance. A compression test will provide useful information about an engine's condition and if performed regularly, can give warning of trouble before any other symptoms become apparent.
● A compression gauge will be required, along with an adapter to suit the spark plug hole thread size. Note that the screw-in type gauge/adapter set up is preferable to the rubber cone type.
● Before carrying out the test, first check the valve clearances as described in Chapter 1 (Vulcan 800 models).
● Compression testing procedures for the motorcycles covered in this manual are described in Chapter 2).

Checking battery open-circuit voltage

⚠️ *Warning: The gases produced by the battery are explosive - never smoke or create any sparks in the vicinity of the battery. Never allow the electrolyte to contact your skin or clothing - if it does, wash it off and seek immediate medical attention.*

● Before any electrical fault is investigated the battery should be checked.
● You'll need a dc voltmeter or multimeter to check battery voltage. Check that the leads are inserted in the correct terminals on the meter, red lead to positive (+), black lead to

negative (-). Incorrect connections can damage the meter.
● A sound, fully-charged 12 volt battery should produce between 12.3 and 12.6 volts across its terminals (12.8 volts for a maintenance-free battery). On machines with a 6 volt battery, voltage should be between 6.1 and 6.3 volts.
1 Set a multimeter to the 0 to 20 volts dc range and connect its probes across the battery terminals. Connect the meter's positive (+) probe, usually red, to the battery positive (+) terminal, followed by the meter's negative (-) probe, usually black, to the battery negative terminal (-) **(see illustration 1)**.
2 If battery voltage is low (below 10 volts on a 12 volt battery or below 4 volts on a six volt battery), charge the battery and test the voltage again. If the battery repeatedly goes flat, investigate the motorcycle's charging system.

Checking battery specific gravity (SG)

⚠️ *Warning: The gases produced by the battery are explosive - never smoke or create any sparks in the vicinity of the battery. Never allow the electrolyte to contact your skin or clothing - if it does, wash it off and seek immediate medical attention.*

● The specific gravity check gives an indication of a battery's state of charge.
● A hydrometer is used for measuring specific gravity. Make sure you purchase one which has a small enough hose to insert in the aperture of a motorcycle battery.
● Specific gravity is simply a measure of the electrolyte's density compared with that of water. Water has an SG of 1.000 and fully-

charged battery electrolyte is about 26% heavier, at 1.260.
● Specific gravity checks are not possible on maintenance-free batteries. Testing the open-circuit voltage is the only means of determining their state of charge.
1 To measure SG, remove the battery from the motorcycle and remove the first cell cap. Draw some electrolyte into the hydrometer and note the reading **(see illustration 2)**. Return the electrolyte to the cell and install the cap.
2 The reading should be in the region of 1.260 to 1.280. If SG is below 1.200 the battery needs charging. Note that SG will vary with temperature; it should be measured at 20°C (68°F). Add 0.007 to the reading for every 10°C above 20°C, and subtract 0.007 from the reading for every 10°C below 20°C. Add 0.004 to the reading for every 10°F above 68°F, and subtract 0.004 from the reading for every 10°F below 68°F.
3 When the check is complete, rinse the hydrometer thoroughly with clean water.

Checking for continuity

● The term continuity describes the uninterrupted flow of electricity through an electrical circuit. A continuity check will determine whether an **open-circuit** situation exists.
● Continuity can be checked with an ohmmeter, multimeter, continuity tester or battery and bulb test circuit **(see illustrations 3, 4 and 5)**.
● All of these instruments are self-powered by a battery, therefore the checks are made with the ignition OFF.
● As a safety precaution, always disconnect the battery negative (-) lead before making checks, particularly if ignition switch checks are being made.
● If using a meter, select the appropriate

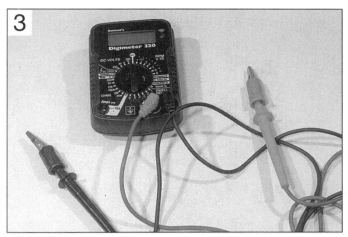

Digital multimeter can be used for all electrical tests

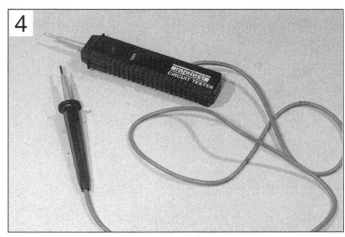

Battery-powered continuity tester

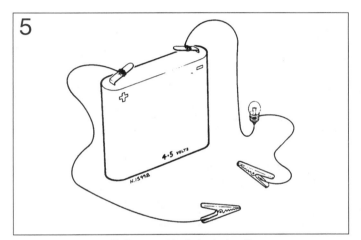

Battery and bulb test circuit

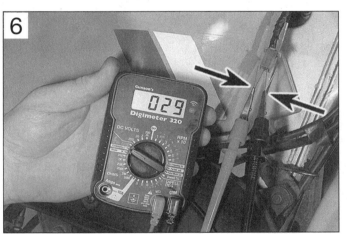

Continuity check of front brake light switch using a meter - note cotter pins used to access connector terminals

ohms scale and check that the meter reads infinity (∞). Touch the meter probes together and check that meter reads zero; where necessary adjust the meter so that it reads zero.

● After using a meter, always switch it OFF to conserve its battery.

Switch checks

1 If a switch is at fault, trace its wiring up to the wiring connectors. Separate the wire connectors and inspect them for security and condition. A build-up of dirt or corrosion here will most likely be the cause of the problem - clean up and apply a water dispersant such as WD40.

2 If using a test meter, set the meter to the ohms x 10 scale and connect its probes across the wires from the switch **(see illustration 6)**. Simple ON/OFF type switches, such as brake light switches, only have two wires whereas combination switches, like the ignition switch, have many internal links.

Study the wiring diagram to ensure that you are connecting across the correct pair of wires. Continuity (low or no measurable resistance - 0 ohms) should be indicated with the switch ON and no continuity (high resistance) with it OFF.

3 Note that the polarity of the test probes doesn't matter for continuity checks, although care should be taken to follow specific test procedures if a diode or solid-state component is being checked.

4 A continuity tester or battery and bulb circuit can be used in the same way. Connect its probes as described above **(see illustration 7)**. The light should come on to indicate continuity in the ON switch position, but should extinguish in the OFF position.

Wiring checks

● Many electrical faults are caused by damaged wiring, often due to incorrect routing or chaffing on frame components.

● Loose, wet or corroded wire connectors

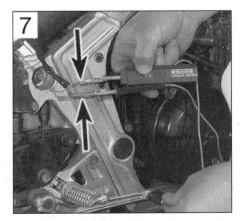

Continuity check of rear brake light switch using a continuity tester

can also be the cause of electrical problems, especially in exposed locations.

Continuity check of front brake light switch sub-harness

A simple test light can be used for voltage checks

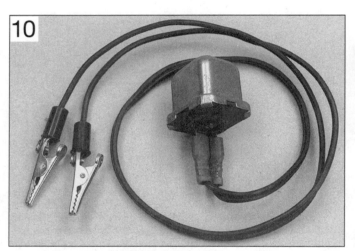

A buzzer is useful for voltage checks

Checking for voltage at the rear brake light power supply wire using a meter . . .

1 A continuity check can be made on a single length of wire by disconnecting it at each end and connecting a meter or continuity tester across both ends of the wire **(see illustration 8)**.

2 Continuity (low or no resistance - 0 ohms) should be indicated if the wire is good. If no continuity (high resistance) is shown, suspect a broken wire.

Checking for voltage

● A voltage check can determine whether current is reaching a component.

● Voltage can be checked with a dc voltmeter, multimeter set on the dc volts scale, test light or buzzer **(see illustrations 9 and 10)**. A meter has the advantage of being able to measure actual voltage.

● When using a meter, check that its leads are inserted in the correct terminals on the meter, red to positive (+), black to negative (-). Incorrect connections can damage the meter.

● A voltmeter (or multimeter set to the dc volts scale) should always be connected in parallel (across the load). Connecting it in series will destroy the meter.

● Voltage checks are made with the ignition ON.

1 First identify the relevant wiring circuit by referring to the wiring diagram at the end of this manual. If other electrical components share the same power supply (ie are fed from the same fuse), take note whether they are working correctly - this is useful information in deciding where to start checking the circuit.

2 If using a meter, check first that the meter leads are plugged into the correct terminals on the meter (see above). Set the meter to the dc volts function, at a range suitable for the battery voltage. Connect the meter red probe (+) to the power supply wire and the black probe to a good metal ground on the motor-

cycle's frame or directly to the battery negative (-) terminal **(see illustration 11)**. Battery voltage should be shown on the meter with the ignition switched ON.

3 If using a test light or buzzer, connect its positive (+) probe to the power supply terminal and its negative (-) probe to a good ground on the motorcycle's frame or directly to the battery negative (-) terminal **(see illustration 12)**. With the ignition ON, the test light should illuminate or the buzzer sound.

4 If no voltage is indicated, work back towards the fuse continuing to check for voltage. When you reach a point where there is voltage, you know the problem lies between that point and your last check point.

Checking the ground

● Ground connections are made either

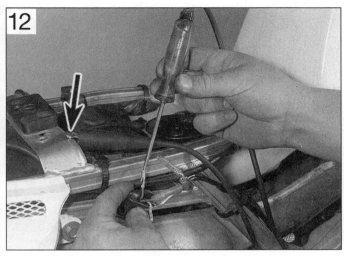

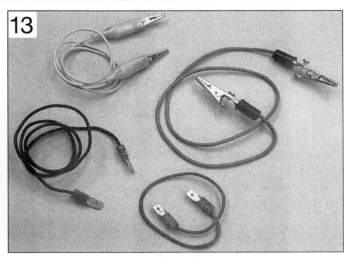

. . . or a test light - note the ground connection to the frame (arrow)

A selection of jumper wires for making ground checks

directly to the engine or frame (such as sensors, neutral switch etc. which only have a positive feed) or by a separate wire into the ground circuit of the wiring harness. Alternatively a short ground wire is sometimes run directly from the component to the motorcycle's frame.

● Corrosion is often the cause of a poor ground connection.

● If total failure is experienced, check the security of the main ground lead from the negative (-) terminal of the battery and also the main ground point on the wiring harness. If corroded, dismantle the connection and clean all surfaces back to bare metal.

1 To check the ground on a component, use an insulated jumper wire to temporarily bypass its ground connection **(see illustration 13)**. Connect one end of the jumper wire between the ground terminal or metal body of the component and the other end to the motorcycle's frame.

2 If the circuit works with the jumper wire installed, the original ground circuit is faulty. Check the wiring for open-circuits or poor connections. Clean up direct ground connections, removing all traces of corrosion and remake the joint. Apply petroleum jelly to the joint to prevent future corrosion.

Tracing a short-circuit

● A short-circuit occurs where current shorts to ground bypassing the circuit components. This usually results in a blown fuse.

● A short-circuit is most likely to occur where the insulation has worn through due to wiring chafing on a component, allowing a direct path to ground on the frame.

1 Remove any body panels necessary to access the circuit wiring.

2 Check that all electrical switches in the circuit are OFF, then remove the circuit fuse and connect a test light, buzzer or voltmeter (set to the dc scale) across the fuse terminals. No voltage should be shown.

3 Move the wiring from side to side while observing the test light or meter. When the test light comes on, buzzer sounds or meter shows voltage, you have found the cause of the short. It will usually shown up as damaged or burned insulation.

4 Note that the same test can be performed on each component in the circuit, even the switch.

Notes

A

ABS (Anti-lock braking system) A system, usually electronically controlled, that senses incipient wheel lockup during braking and relieves hydraulic pressure at wheel which is about to skid.

Aftermarket Components suitable for the motorcycle, but not produced by the motorcycle manufacturer.

Allen key A hexagonal wrench which fits into a recessed hexagonal hole.

Alternating current (ac) Current produced by an alternator. Requires converting to direct current by a rectifier for charging purposes.

Alternator Converts mechanical energy from the engine into electrical energy to charge the battery and power the electrical system.

Ampere (amp) A unit of measurement for the flow of electrical current. Current = Volts ÷ Ohms.

Ampere-hour (Ah) Measure of battery capacity.

Angle-tightening A torque expressed in degrees. Often follows a conventional tightening torque for cylinder head or main bearing fasteners **(see illustration)**.

Angle-tightening cylinder head bolts

Antifreeze A substance (usually ethylene glycol) mixed with water, and added to the cooling system, to prevent freezing of the coolant in winter. Antifreeze also contains chemicals to inhibit corrosion and the formation of rust and other deposits that would tend to clog the radiator and coolant passages and reduce cooling efficiency.

Anti-dive System attached to the fork lower leg (slider) to prevent fork dive when braking hard.

Anti-seize compound A coating that reduces the risk of seizing on fasteners that are subjected to high temperatures, such as exhaust clamp bolts and nuts.

API American Petroleum Institute. A quality standard for 4-stroke motor oils.

Asbestos A natural fibrous mineral with great heat resistance, commonly used in the composition of brake friction materials. Asbestos is a health hazard and the dust created by brake systems should never be inhaled or ingested.

ATF Automatic Transmission Fluid. Often used in front forks.

ATU Automatic Timing Unit. Mechanical device for advancing the ignition timing on early engines.

ATV All Terrain Vehicle. Often called a Quad.

Axial play Side-to-side movement.

Axle A shaft on which a wheel revolves. Also known as a spindle.

B

Backlash The amount of movement between meshed components when one component is held still. Usually applies to gear teeth.

Ball bearing A bearing consisting of a hardened inner and outer race with hardened steel balls between the two races.

Bearings Used between two working surfaces to prevent wear of the components and a build-up of heat. Four types of bearing are commonly used on motorcycles: plain shell bearings, ball bearings, tapered roller bearings and needle roller bearings.

Bevel gears Used to turn the drive through 90°. Typical applications are shaft final drive and camshaft drive **(see illustration)**.

BHP Brake Horsepower. The British measure-ment for engine power output. Power output is now usually expressed in kilowatts (kW).

Bevel gears are used to turn the drive through 90°

Bias-belted tire Similar construction to radial tire, but with outer belt running at an angle to the wheel rim.

Big-end bearing The bearing in the end of the connecting rod that's attached to the crankshaft.

Bleeding The process of removing air from a hydraulic system via a bleed nipple or bleed screw.

Bottom-end A description of an engine's crankcase components and all components contained therein.

BTDC Before Top Dead Center in terms of piston position. Ignition timing is often expressed in terms of degrees or millimeters BTDC.

Bush A cylindrical metal or rubber component used between two moving parts.

Burr Rough edge left on a component after machining or as a result of excessive wear.

C

Cam chain The chain which takes drive from the crankshaft to the camshaft(s).

Canister The main component in an evap-orative emission control system (California market only); contains activated charcoal granules to trap vapors from the fuel system rather than allowing them to vent to the atmosphere.

Castellated Resembling the parapets along the top of a castle wall. For example, a castellated wheel axle or spindle nut.

Catalytic converter A device in the exhaust system of some machines which

Cush drive rubber segments dampen out transmission shocks

converts certain pollutants in the exhaust gases into less harmful substances.

Charging system Description of the components which charge the battery, ie the alternator, rectifer and regulator.

Clearance The amount of space between two parts. For example, between a piston and a cylinder, between a bearing and a journal, etc.

Coil spring A spiral of elastic steel found in various sizes throughout a vehicle, for example as a springing medium in the suspension and in the valve train.

Compression Reduction in volume, and increase in pressure and temperature, of a gas, caused by squeezing it into a smaller space.

Compression damping Controls the speed the suspension compresses when hitting a bump.

Compression ratio The relationship between cylinder volume when the piston is at top dead center and cylinder volume when the piston is at bottom dead center.

Continuity The uninterrupted path in the flow of electricity. Little or no measurable resistance.

Continuity tester Self-powered bleeper or test light which indicates continuity.

Cp Candlepower. Bulb rating commonly found on US motorcycles.

Crossply tire Tire plies arranged in a criss-cross pattern. Usually four or six plies used, hence 4PR or 6PR in tire size codes.

Cush drive Rubber damper segments fitted between the rear wheel and final drive sprocket to absorb transmission shocks **(see illustration)**.

D

Degree disc Calibrated disc for measuring piston position. Expressed in degrees.

Dial gauge Clock-type gauge with adapters for measuring runout and piston position. Expressed in mm or inches.

Diaphragm The rubber membrane in a master cylinder or carburetor which seals the upper chamber.

Diaphragm spring A single sprung plate often used in clutches.

Direct current (dc) Current produced by a dc generator.

Decarbonization The process of removing carbon deposits - typically from the combustion chamber, valves and exhaust port/system.

Detonation Destructive and damaging explosion of fuel/air mixture in combustion chamber instead of controlled burning.

Diode An electrical valve which only allows current to flow in one direction. Commonly used in rectifiers and starter interlock systems.

Disc valve (or rotary valve) An induction system used on some two-stroke engines.

Double-overhead camshaft (DOHC) An engine that uses two overhead camshafts, one for the intake valves and one for the exhaust valves.

Drivebelt A toothed belt used to transmit drive to the rear wheel on some motorcycles. A drivebelt has also been used to drive the camshafts. Drivebelts are usually made of Kevlar.

Driveshaft Any shaft used to transmit motion. Commonly used when referring to the final driveshaft on shaft drive motorcycles.

E

ECU (Electronic Control Unit) A computer which controls (for instance) an ignition system, or an anti-lock braking system.

EGO Exhaust Gas Oxygen sensor. Some-times called a Lambda sensor.

Electrolyte The fluid in a lead-acid battery.

EMS (Engine Management System) A computer controlled system which manages the fuel injection and the ignition systems in an integrated fashion.

Endfloat The amount of lengthways movement between two parts. As applied to a crankshaft, the distance that the crankshaft can move side-to-side in the crankcase.

Endless chain A chain having no joining link. Common use for cam chains and final drive chains.

EP (Extreme Pressure) Oil type used in locations where high loads are applied, such as between gear teeth.

Evaporative emission control system Describes a charcoal filled canister which stores fuel vapors from the tank rather than allowing them to vent to the atmosphere. Usually only fitted to California models and referred to as an EVAP system.

Expansion chamber Section of two-stroke engine exhaust system so designed to improve engine efficiency and boost power.

F

Feeler blade or gauge A thin strip or blade of hardened steel, ground to an exact thickness, used to check or measure clearances between parts.

Final drive Description of the drive from the transmission to the rear wheel. Usually by chain or shaft, but sometimes by belt.

Firing order The order in which the engine cylinders fire, or deliver their power strokes, beginning with the number one cylinder.

Flooding Term used to describe a high fuel level in the carburetor float chambers, leading to fuel overflow. Also refers to excess fuel in the combustion chamber due to incorrect starting technique.

Free length The no-load state of a component when measured. Clutch, valve and fork spring lengths are measured at rest, without any preload.

Freeplay The amount of travel before any action takes place. The looseness in a linkage, or an assembly of parts, between the initial application of force and actual movement. For example, the distance the rear brake pedal moves before the rear brake is actuated.

Fuel injection The fuel/air mixture is metered electronically and directed into the engine intake ports (indirect injection) or into the cylinders (direct injection). Sensors supply information on engine speed and conditions.

Fuel/air mixture The charge of fuel and air going into the engine. See Stoichiometric ratio.

Fuse An electrical device which protects a circuit against accidental overload. The typical fuse contains a soft piece of metal which is calibrated to melt at a predetermined current flow (expressed as amps) and break the circuit.

G

Gap The distance the spark must travel in jumping from the center electrode to the side electrode in a spark plug. Also refers to the distance between the ignition rotor and the pickup coil in an electronic ignition system.

Gasket Any thin, soft material - usually cork, cardboard, asbestos or soft metal - installed between two metal surfaces to ensure a good seal. For instance, the cylinder head gasket seals the joint between the block and the cylinder head.

Gauge An instrument panel display used to monitor engine conditions. A gauge with a movable pointer on a dial or a fixed scale is an analog gauge. A gauge with a numerical readout is called a digital gauge.

Gear ratios The drive ratio of a pair of gears in a gearbox, calculated on their number of teeth.

Glaze-busting see **Honing**

Grinding Process for renovating the valve face and valve seat contact area in the cylinder head.

Ground return The return path of an electrical circuit, utilizing the motorcycle's frame.

Gudgeon pin The shaft which connects the connecting rod small-end with the piston. Often called a piston pin or wrist pin.

H

Helical gears Gear teeth are slightly curved and produce less gear noise that straight-cut gears. Often used for primary drives.

Helicoil A thread insert repair system. Commonly used as a repair for stripped spark plug threads **(see illustration)**.

Installing a Helicoil thread insert in a cylinder head

Honing A process used to break down the glaze on a cylinder bore (also called glaze-busting). Can also be carried out to roughen a rebored cylinder to aid ring bedding-in.

HT (High Tension) Description of the electrical circuit from the secondary winding of the ignition coil to the spark plug.

Hydraulic A liquid filled system used to transmit pressure from one component to another. Common uses on motorcycles are brakes and clutches.

Hydrometer An instrument for measuring the specific gravity of a lead-acid battery.

Hygroscopic Water absorbing. In motorcycle applications, braking efficiency will be reduced if DOT 3 or 4 hydraulic fluid absorbs water from the air - care must be taken to keep new brake fluid in tightly sealed containers.

I

lbf ft Pounds-force feet. An imperial unit of torque. Sometimes written as ft-lbs.

lbf in Pound-force inch. An imperial unit of torque, applied to components where a very low torque is required. Sometimes written as inch-lbs.

IC Abbreviation for Integrated Circuit.

Ignition advance Means of increasing the timing of the spark at higher engine speeds. Done by mechanical means (ATU) on early engines or electronically by the ignition control unit on later engines.

Ignition timing The moment at which the spark plug fires, expressed in the number of crankshaft degrees before the piston reaches the top of its stroke, or in the number of millimeters before the piston reaches the top of its stroke.

Infinity (∞) Description of an open-circuit electrical state, where no continuity exists.

Inverted forks (upside down forks) The sliders or lower legs are held in the yokes and the fork tubes or stanchions are connected to the wheel axle (spindle). Less unsprung weight and stiffer construction than conventional forks.

J

JASO **Japan Automobile Standards Organ-ization.** JASO MA is a standard for motorcycle oil equivalent to API SJ, but designed to prevent problems with wet-type motorcycle clutches.

Joule The unit of electrical energy.

Journal The bearing surface of a shaft.

K

Kickstart Mechanical means of turning the engine over for starting purposes.

Only usually fitted to mopeds, small capacity motorcycles and off-road motorcycles.

Kill switch Handebar-mounted switch for emergency ignition cut-out. Cuts the ignition circuit on all models, and additionally prevent starter motor operation on others.

km Symbol for kilometer.

kmh Abbreviation for kilometers per hour.

L

Lambda sensor A sensor fitted in the exhaust system to measure the exhaust gas oxygen content (excess air factor). Also called oxygen sensor.

Lapping see **Grinding**.

LCD Abbreviation for Liquid Crystal Display.

LED Abbreviation for Light Emitting Diode.

Liner A steel cylinder liner inserted in an aluminum alloy cylinder block.

Locknut A nut used to lock an adjustment nut, or other threaded component, in place.

Lockstops The lugs on the lower triple clamp (yoke) which abut those on the frame, preventing handlebar-to-fuel tank contact.

Lockwasher A form of washer designed to prevent an attaching nut from working loose.

LT Low Tension Description of the electrical circuit from the power supply to the primary winding of the ignition coil.

M

Main bearings The bearings between the crankshaft and crankcase.

Maintenance-free (MF) battery A sealed battery which cannot be topped up.

Manometer Mercury-filled calibrated tubes used to measure intake tract vacuum. Used to synchronize carburetors on multi-cylinder engines.

Tappet shims are measured with a micrometer

Micrometer A precision measuring instru-ment that measures component outside diameters **(see illustration)**.

MON (Motor Octane Number) A measure of a fuel's resistance to knock.

Monograde oil An oil with a single viscosity, eg SAE80W.

Monoshock A single suspension unit linking the swingarm or suspension linkage to the frame.

mph Abbreviation for miles per hour.

Multigrade oil Having a wide viscosity range (eg 10W40). The W stands for Winter, thus the viscosity ranges from SAE10 when cold to SAE40 when hot.

Multimeter An electrical test instrument with the capability to measure voltage, current and resistance. Some meters also incorporate a continuity tester and buzzer.

N

Needle roller bearing Inner race of caged needle rollers and hardened outer race. Examples of uncaged needle rollers can be found on some engines. Commonly used in rear suspension applications and in two-stroke engines.

Nm Newton meters.

NOx Oxides of Nitrogen. A common toxic pollutant emitted by gasoline engines at higher temperatures.

O

Octane The measure of a fuel's resistance to knock.

OE (Original Equipment) Relates to components fitted to a motorcycle as standard or replacement parts supplied by the motorcycle manufacturer.

Ohm The unit of electrical resistance. Ohms = Volts 4 Current.

Ohmmeter An instrument for measuring electrical resistance.

Oil cooler System for diverting engine oil outside of the engine to a radiator for cooling purposes.

Oil injection A system of two-stroke engine lubrication where oil is pump-fed to the engine in accordance with throttle position.

Open-circuit An electrical condition where there is a break in the flow of electricity - no continuity (high resistance).

O-ring A type of sealing ring made of a special rubber-like material; in use, the O-ring is compressed into a groove to provide the sealing action.

Oversize (OS) Term used for piston and ring size options fitted to a rebored cylinder.

Overhead cam (sohc) engine An engine with single camshaft located on top of the cylinder head.

Overhead valve (ohv) engine An engine with the valves located in the cylinder head, but with the camshaft located in the engine block or crankcase.

Oxygen sensor A device installed in the exhaust system which senses the oxygen content in the exhaust and converts this information into an electric current. Also called a Lambda sensor.

P

Plastigage A thin strip of plastic thread, available in different sizes, used for measuring clearances. For example, a strip of Plastigage is laid across a bearing journal. The parts are assembled and dismantled; the width of the crushed strip indicates the clearance between journal and bearing.

Polarity Either negative or positive ground, determined by which battery lead is connected to the frame (ground return). Modern motorcycles are usually negative ground.

Pre-ignition A situation where the fuel/air mixture ignites before the spark plug fires. Often due to a hot spot in the combustion chamber caused by carbon build-up. Engine has a tendency to 'run-on'.

Pre-load (suspension) The amount a spring is compressed when in the unloaded state. Preload can be applied by gas, spacer or mechanical adjuster.

Premix The method of engine lubrication on some gasoline two-stroke engines. Engine oil is mixed with the gasoline in the fuel tank in a specific ratio. The fuel/oil mix is sometimes referred to as "petrol".

Primary drive Description of the drive from the crankshaft to the clutch. Usually by gear or chain.

PS Pferdestärke - a German interpretation of BHP.

PSI Pounds-force per square inch. Imperial measurement of tire pressure and cylinder pressure measurement.

PTFE Polytetrafluroethylene. A low friction substance.

Pulse secondary air injection system A process of promoting the burning of excess fuel present in the exhaust gases by routing fresh air into the exhaust ports.

Q

Quartz halogen bulb Tungsten filament surrounded by a halogen gas. Typically used for the headlight **(see illustration)**.

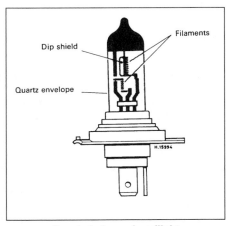

Quartz halogen headlight bulb construction

R

Rack-and-pinion A pinion gear on the end of a shaft that mates with a rack (think of a geared wheel opened up and laid flat). Sometimes used in clutch operating systems.

Radial play Up and down movement about a shaft.

Radial ply tires Tire plies run across the tire (from bead to bead) and around the circumference of the tire. Less resistant to tread distortion than other tire types.

Radiator A liquid-to-air heat transfer device designed to reduce the temperature of the coolant in a liquid cooled engine.

Rake A feature of steering geometry - the angle of the steering head in relation to the vertical **(see illustration)**.

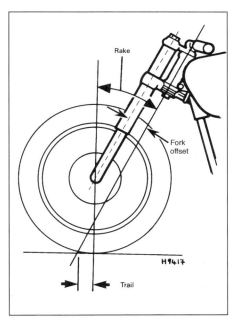

Steering geometry

Rebore Providing a new working surface to the cylinder bore by boring out the old surface. Necessitates the use of oversize piston and rings.

Rebound damping A means of controlling the oscillation of a suspension unit spring after it has been compressed. Resists the spring's natural tendency to bounce back after being compressed.

Rectifier Device for converting the ac output of an alternator into dc for battery charging.

Reed valve An induction system commonly used on two-stroke engines.

Regulator Device for maintaining the charging voltage from the generator or alternator within a specified range.

Relay A electrical device used to switch heavy current on and off by using a low current auxiliary circuit.

Resistance Measured in ohms. An electrical component's ability to pass electrical current.

RON (Research Octane Number) A measure of a fuel's resistance to knock.

rpm revolutions per minute.

Runout The amount of wobble (in-and-out movement) of a wheel or shaft as it's rotated. The amount a shaft rotates 'out-of-true'. The out-of-round condition of a rotating part.

S

SAE (Society of Automotive Engineers) A standard for the viscosity of a fluid.

Sealant A liquid or paste used to prevent leakage at a joint. Sometimes used in conjunction with a gasket.

Service limit Term for the point where a component is no longer useable and must be replaced.

Shaft drive A method of transmitting drive from the transmission to the rear wheel.

Shell bearings Plain bearings consisting of two shell halves. Most often used as big-end and main bearings in a four-stroke engine. Often called bearing inserts.

Shim Thin spacer, commonly used to adjust the clearance or relative positions between two parts. For example, shims inserted into or under tappets or followers to control valve clearances. Clearance is adjusted by changing the thickness of the shim.

Short-circuit An electrical condition where current shorts to ground bypassing the circuit components.

Skimming Process to correct warpage or repair a damaged surface, eg on brake discs or drums.

Slide-hammer A special puller that screws into or hooks onto a component such as a shaft or bearing; a heavy sliding handle on the shaft bottoms against the end of the shaft to knock the component free.

Small-end bearing The bearing in the upper end of the connecting rod at its joint with the gudgeon pin.

Snap-ring A ring-shaped clip used to prevent endwise movement of cylindrical parts and shafts. An internal snap-ring is installed in a groove in a housing; an external snap-ring fits into a groove on the outside of a cylindrical piece such as a shaft. Also known as a snap-ring.

Spalling Damage to camshaft lobes or bearing journals shown as pitting of the working surface.

Specific gravity (SG) The state of charge of the electrolyte in a lead-acid battery. A measure of the electrolyte's density compared with water.

Straight-cut gears Common type gear used on gearbox shafts and for oil pump and water pump drives.

Stanchion The inner sliding part of the front forks, held by the yokes. Often called a fork tube.

Stoichiometric ratio The optimum chemical air/fuel ratio for a gasoline engine, said to be 14.7 parts of air to 1 part of fuel.

Sulphuric acid The liquid (electrolyte) used in a lead-acid battery. Poisonous and extremely corrosive.

Surface grinding (lapping) Process to correct a warped gasket face, commonly used on cylinder heads.

T

Tapered-roller bearing Tapered inner race of caged needle rollers and separate tapered outer race. Examples of taper roller bearings can be found on steering heads.

Tappet A cylindrical component which transmits motion from the cam to the valve stem, either directly or via a pushrod and rocker arm. Also called a cam follower.

TCS Traction Control System. An electron-ically-controlled system which senses wheel spin and reduces engine speed accordingly.

TDC Top Dead Center denotes that the piston is at its highest point in the cylinder.

Thread-locking compound Solution applied to fastener threads to prevent loosening. Select type to suit application.

Thrust washer A washer positioned between two moving components on a shaft. For example, between gear pinions on gearshaft.

Timing chain See **Cam Chain**.

Timing light Stroboscopic lamp for carrying out ignition timing checks with the engine running.

Top-end A description of an engine's cylinder block, head and valve gear components.

Torque Turning or twisting force about a shaft.

Torque setting A prescribed tightness specified by the motorcycle manufacturer to ensure that the bolt or nut is secured correctly. Undertightening can result in the bolt or nut coming loose or a surface not being sealed. Overtightening can result in stripped threads, distortion or damage to the component being retained.

Torx key A six-point wrench.

Tracer A stripe of a second color applied to a wire insulator to distinguish that wire from another one with the same color insulator. For example, Br/W is often used to denote a brown insulator with a white tracer.

Trail A feature of steering geometry. Distance from the steering head axis to the tire's central contact point.

Triple clamps The cast components which extend from the steering head and support the fork stanchions or tubes. Often called fork yokes.

Turbocharger A centrifugal device, driven by exhaust gases, that pressurizes the intake air. Normally used to increase the power output from a given engine displacement.

TWI Abbreviation for Tire Wear Indicator. Indicates the location of the tread depth indicator bars on tires.

U

Universal joint or U-joint (UJ) A double-pivoted connection for transmitting power from a driving to a driven shaft through an angle. Typically found in shaft drive assemblies.

Unsprung weight Anything not supported by the bike's suspension (ie the wheel, tires, brakes, final drive and bottom (moving) part of the suspension).

V

Vacuum gauges Clock-type gauges for measuring intake tract vacuum. Used for carburetor synchronization on multi-cylinder engines.

Valve A device through which the flow of liquid, gas or vacuum may be stopped, started or regulated by a moveable part that opens, shuts or partially obstructs one or more ports or passageways. The intake and exhaust valves in the cylinder head are of the poppet type.

Valve clearance The clearance between the valve tip (the end of the valve stem) and the rocker arm or tappet/follower. The valve clearance is measured when the valve is closed. The correct clearance is important - if too small the valve won't close fully and will burn out, whereas if too large noisy operation will result.

Valve lift The amount a valve is lifted off its seat by the camshaft lobe.

Valve timing The exact setting for the opening and closing of the valves in relation to piston position.

Vernier caliper A precision measuring instrument that measures inside and outside dimensions. Not quite as accurate as a micrometer, but more convenient.

VIN Vehicle Identification Number. Term for the bike's engine and frame numbers.

Viscosity The thickness of a liquid or its resistance to flow.

Volt A unit for expressing electrical "pressure" in a circuit. Volts = current x ohms.

W

Water pump A mechanically-driven device for moving coolant around the engine.

Watt A unit for expressing electrical power. Watts = volts x current.

Wet liner arrangement

Wear limit see **Service limit**

Wet liner A liquid-cooled engine design where the pistons run in liners which are directly surrounded by coolant **(see illustration)**.

Wheelbase Distance from the center of the front wheel to the center of the rear wheel.

Wiring harness or loom Describes the electrical wires running the length of the motorcycle and enclosed in tape or plastic sheathing. Wiring coming off the main harness is usually referred to as a sub harness.

Woodruff key A key of semi-circular or square section used to locate a gear to a shaft. Often used to locate the alternator rotor on the crankshaft.

Wrist pin Another name for gudgeon or piston pin.

Notes

Note: *References throughout this index are in the form – "Chapter number"•"Page number"*